O9-BTO-708

I Never Knew
C I Had a
hoice SECOND EDITION

BY GERALD COREY:

Theory and Practice of Counseling and Psychotherapy (Second Edition)
Manual for Theory and Practice of Counseling and Psychotherapy
(Second Edition)
Case Approach to Counseling and Psychotherapy
Theory and Practice of Group Counseling
Manual for Theory and Practice of Group Counseling

BY GERALD COREY AND MARIANNE SCHNEIDER COREY:

Groups: Process and Practice (Second Edition)
Professional and Ethical Issues in Counseling and Psychotherapy
(with Patrick Callanan)
Group Techniques (with Patrick Callanan and J. Michael Russell)

I Never Knew
I Had a
Choice SECOND EDITION

Gerald Corey

California State University, Fullerton
Diplomate in Counseling Psychology,
American Board of Professional Psychology

in collaboration with

Marianne Schneider Corey

BROOKS/COLE PUBLISHING COMPANY
Monterey, California

Brooks/Cole Publishing Company
A Division of Wadsworth, Inc.

© 1983, 1978 by Wadsworth, Inc., Belmont, California 94002. All rights reserved.
No part of this book may be reproduced, stored in a retrieval system, or transcribed,
in any form or by any means—electronic, mechanical, photocopying, recording,
or otherwise—without the prior written permission of the publisher,
Brooks/Cole Publishing Company, Monterey, California 93940, a division of
Wadsworth, Inc.

Printed in the United States of America

10   9   8   7   6   5   4   3   2

Library of Congress Cataloging in Publication Data

Corey, Gerald F.
    I never knew I had a choice.

    Includes bibliographies and index.
    1. Self-perception.   2. Choice (Psychology)
3. Emotions.   4. Success.   I. Corey, Marianne
Schneider, 1942–   . II. Title.
BF697.C67   1982   158   82-4300
ISBN 0-534-01201-9   AACR2

Subject Editor: *Claire Verduin*   Manuscript Editor: *Bill Waller*
Production Editor: *John Bergez*   Interior and Cover Design: *Katherine Minerva*
Cover Art: *Terril Neely*   Illustrations: *Ron Grauer*
Typesetting: *Graphic Typesetting Service, Los Angeles*

Photo Credits *Page 11:* courtesy of Bob Fitch, Black Star. *Page 31*, © Richard Kalvar,
Magnum Photos, Inc., New York. *Page 61:* courtesy of David Baker, Stock, Boston, Inc.
Page 79: courtesy of Susan W. Dryfoos, Monkmeyer Press Photo Service, New York.
Pages 90, 233 (girl and Dad), and 337: courtesy of David S. Strickler, Monkmeyer. *Page
107:* photo by Elliott Erwitt, © Magnum Photos, Inc., New York. *Page xiv and 129
(morning exercise):* courtesy of George Belierose, Stock, Boston. *Page xii and 129 (field
hockey):* photo by Roger Mallock, © Magnum Photos, Inc., New York. *Page 129 (father
and son):* © by Nancy J. Pierce, Photo Researchers, Inc., New York. *Pages 166 (boy with
father), xi and 215 (family at beach), and 350:* courtesy of Paul Conklin, Monkmeyer. *Page
166 (woman in hard hat):* courtesy of Dan McCoy, Black Star. *Page 186:* courtesy of
Barbara Alper, Stock, Boston. *Page 215 (men hugging):* courtesy of Rene Burri, Magnum.
Page 215 (couple hugging): courtesy of Stock, Boston. *Page xiii and 215 (boys):* courtesy of
Hiroji Kubota, Magnum. *Page 233 (man and woman):* courtesy of Mimi Forsyth,
Monkmeyer. *Page 290 (mother shopping):* courtesy of Irene Baker, Monkmeyer. *Page 290
(camerawoman):* courtesy of Martin Adler Levick, Black Star. *Page 290 (man in shop):*
courtesy of Peter Vandermark, Stock, Boston. *Page 312:* courtesy of Jim Morrison, Stock,
Boston. *Page 379:* courtesy of Doug Wilson, Black Star. *Page 402:* courtesy of Freda
Leinwand, New York.

In memory of my friend Jim Morelock,
a searcher who lived and died with dignity
and self-respect,
who struggled and questioned,
who made the choice to live his days fully
until time ran out on him at age 25.

Preface

I Never Knew I Had a Choice is designed as a resource for college students of any age and for all others who wish to expand their self-awareness and explore the choices available to them in significant areas of their lives. The topics discussed include choosing a personal style of learning; approaches to personal growth; stages in personality development and the struggle for autonomy; the body; the roles that sexuality, love, intimacy, work, and solitude play in our lives; the meaning of loneliness, death, and loss; and the ways in which we choose our values and philosophies of life.

This is a personal book, because I encourage readers to examine carefully the choices they have made and how these choices affect their present level of satisfaction. It is also a personal book inasmuch as I describe my own concerns, struggles, decisions, and values in regard to many of the issues raised.

The experiences of those who have read and used the first edition of *I Never Knew I Had a Choice* reveal that the themes explored have application to a diversity of ages and backgrounds. Readers who have taken the time to write us about their reactions say that the book encouraged them to take an honest look at their lives and challenge themselves to make certain changes. Although the book was written primarily for a college market, some readers have shared it with friends and relatives.

I wrote this book for use in college courses dealing with the psychology of adjustment, personality development, applied psychology, educational psychology, personal growth, and self-awareness. It has also been adopted in courses ranging from the training of teachers and counselors to introductory psychology. My experience has been that active, open, and personal participation in these courses can lead to expanded self-awareness and greater autonomy in living. Some of the unique problems and challenges associated with teaching this kind of course are discussed in the *Instructor's Manual* that accompanies the text.

The book itself is designed to be a personal workbook as well as a classroom text. Each chapter begins with a "Self-Inventory" that gives readers the chance to focus on their own present beliefs and attitudes. Within the chapters, sections called "Time Out for Personal Reflection" provide an opportunity to pause and reflect on the issues raised. Additional "Activities and Exercises" are given at the end of each chapter for classroom participation or activity outside the class. Each chapter also contains a "Suggested Readings" list; most of the books listed are available in paperback. The final chapter provides a consumer's guide to professional resources for those who wish to continue their personal learning through some form of counseling or group experience.

What are the changes from the original to this second edition? The introductory chapter now includes material on personal learning, with the emphasis on how students can get the most benefit from the book and the course. Chapter 2 ("Approaches to Personal Growth") is a new chapter that gives an overview of six contemporary psychological approaches to personality and personal growth. Practical methods and techniques flowing from each of these approaches are applied to the task of dealing constructively with barriers that obstruct psychological growth. Chapter 3 is an overview of personality growth from the life-span point of view; it presents an expanded description of crises associated with each stage of life. Chapter 4 ("Your Body"), a new chapter, challenges readers to examine their attitudes and feelings about their bodies and their physical well-being, as well as the pervasive impact their view of their bodies has on all areas of their psychological development.

All the other chapters have been updated as appropriate, with some new material and case illustrations. Chapter 8 ("Work") has been redone to increase its relevance for student readers. Chapter 12 ("A Consumer's Guide to Resources for Continued Personal Growth") has been shortened considerably through the deletion of technical material on the various approaches to counseling and psychotherapy. It now focuses on what readers can do if they wish to act on any new insights they have acquired about themselves through the course.

Although my own approach can be broadly characterized as humanistic and existential, my aim has been to challenge readers to recognize and assess their own choices, beliefs, and values, rather than to convert them to a particular point of view. My basic premise is that a commitment of self-exploration can create new potentials for a choice. Many of my clients are relatively well-functioning people who desire more from life and who want to recognize and remove blocks to their personal creativity and freedom. It is for people like these that I've written *I Never Knew I Had a Choice*.

Acknowledgments

I want to acknowledge the contributions of a number of people to this book. Most significant is my wife, Marianne Schneider Corey, who has collaborated with me on this project. While I did most of the actual writing, Marianne and I discussed at length each of the issues explored, and many of the ideas and illustrative examples in these pages are hers. Some of our friends have commented that I have provided the body and Marianne has given the book its soul!

I want to express my deep appreciation for the insightful suggestions given to me by friends, associates, reviewers, readers, and students. The following people provided helpful reviews for this revision: Bruce E. Bailey, Stephen F. Austin State University (Texas); John R. Blair, Eastern Michigan University; Betty C. Chandler, Oscar Rose Junior College (Oklahoma); Kathy Carpenter, Kearney State College (Nebraska); Kenneth E. Coffield, University of Alabama, Huntsville; Jeffrey A. Kottler; C. K. Patel, Triton College (Illinois); Ronald E. Ponsford, Northwest Nazarene College (Indiana); and William Buryl West, Middle Tennessee State University. Student reviewers included Sandy Jacobs, Donna L. Robbins, Mary Singleton, Frank Smaldino, and Diana J. Vasquez. Dr. Allan Abbott and his wife, Katherine, provided much help in connection with Chapter 4.

The reviewers of the first edition played a significant role in shaping this book. They include: John Brennecke, Mt. San Antonio College (California); Patrick Callanan; Lani Carney; Alan Dahms, Metropolitan College (Denver); Logan Fox, El Camino College (California); Todd Gaffaney, Cerritos College (California); M. Michael Klaber, University of

Hartford (Connecticut); Chuck Lee, Orange Coast Community College (California); George McWilliams, Ventura College (California); Dru Spiro, Lincoln Land Community College (Illinois); and Velma Walker, Tarrant County Community College (Texas). Friends and former students who provided many valuable ideas include Merri Chalenor, Randy Corliss, Jim Morelock, Karen Palmer, and Linda Weber. I am indebted to my friend and colleague J. Michael Russell, California State University, Fullerton, for many provocative discussions concerning the issues raised in this book.

Finally, I would like to acknowledge the contributions and support of the Brooks/Cole staff, especially Claire Verduin, John Bergez, Katherine Minerva, and Bill Waller.

Gerald Corey

Contents

Chapter Three   Personality Development: Stages in the Struggle for Autonomy   71

Chapter Four   Your Body   113

Chapter One

Introduction: Personal Learning

About This Book

A client of mine who had been in individual therapy for close to a year said one day: "One thing that I can see now that I did not see before is that I *have a choice*—that things do not have to stay the way they are and that I can change my life if I want to. *I never knew I had a choice!*" This remark captures the central message of this book: we are *not* passive victims of life, we *do* make choices, and we *do* have the power to change major aspects of our lives as we struggle toward a more authentic existence.

Some of the choices that will be examined in this book are these:

- We can become independent persons with our own unique identities, or we can remain dependent on others to mold us.
- We can remain children, emotionally speaking, or we can work toward becoming psychological adults.
- We can become aware of early decisions that we made about ourselves and about life, or we can remain blind to the many ways in which we continue to be influenced and limited by our past.
- We can make new decisions that will change the course of our lives, or we can cling to old decisions without ever reexamining their validity.
- We can take control of our bodies, or we can let our bodies control us.
- We can make sexuality an enriching part of our experience, or we can choose to deny our sexuality or to experience only mechanical sex in which we and others become objects instead of persons.
- We can allow society to dictate what it means to be a woman or a man, or we can decide for ourselves on a sex-role identity.
- We can recognize our need for love, even though we might experience fears in opening ourselves to loving; or we can choose not to risk trusting ourselves in loving relationships.
- We can create meaningful, committed relationships, or we can avoid intimacy and commitment.
- We can become slaves to our work, or we can find meaning through work.
- We can choose to learn about ourselves from our lonely experiences, or we can avoid fully experiencing the lonely periods in our lives.
- We can recreate ourselves by finding time alone in which to discover new facets within, or we can flee from time alone for fear of feeling empty and lonely when we have only ourselves.
- We can take our mortality as a challenge to live each day as fully as possible, or we can deny the reality of death and its meaning for us.

- We can actively search for a purpose in living and thus give meaning to our work and our play, or we can avoid asking ourselves what the point of our lives really is.
- We can carve out our own meanings and values, or we can let others tell us what we should value.

As we recognize that we are not merely passive victims of our circumstances, we can consciously become the architects of our lives. Even though others may have drawn the initial blueprints, we can recognize the plan, take a stand, and change the design. This book is intended to stimulate your thinking about changes *you* want to make and encourage you to carry them out.

In developing the various chapters, I talked with both students and instructors in courses such as Psychology of Personal Growth at many community colleges. A frequent theme was that students selected such a course because of their interest in discovering more about themselves and their relationships with others. Most of them were looking for a *practical* course, one that dealt with real issues in everyday living and that would provide an impetus for their own personal growth. Accordingly, I have focused on helping you to recognize blocks to your creative and productive energies, to find ways of removing these obstructions, and to make conscious choices to modify your attitudes and behavior.

Another dimension of this book is the disclosures I've made about my own life. It seemed fitting to write in a personal style and to openly share with you how I arrived at some of the beliefs and values I write about. I hope that knowing my assumptions, biases, and struggles helps you evaluate your own position with more clarity. I'm not suggesting that you adopt my philosophy of life but rather that you ask how the issues I raise concern *you*. What are *your* answers? What are the choices *you've* made for yourself? What choices do you want to make now?

Basically, then, *I Never Knew I Had a Choice* is designed for anyone who seriously wants to examine his or her life and who wants to live by choice rather than by past conditioning. You might say "Well, surely this includes everyone, for who isn't interested in growing, learning more about himself, or being the master of her fate rather than being directed and shaped by others?" Yet there is a degree of uncomfortableness, and even fear, associated with discovering ourselves. Many people may prefer to remain unaware, to allow others to choose for them, and to be content with the status quo. Consequently, I ask you to think about the price involved in expanding your awareness and choosing for yourself.

Are you comfortable with yourself now? Do you see any risks in making a personal commitment to explore various aspects of your life? Are you reluctant to recognize problem areas, for fear that you'll feel overwhelmed if you begin to question your life? These are important questions, and, since personal awareness and growth cannot be forced on us, it is vital that you decide whether you genuinely want to do all that is involved in self-exploration.

My Philosophy

Anyone who writes about human concerns and values has a basic viewpoint, or philosophy, that determines his or her approach, even if that philosophy is not stated explicitly. Since this is a book about personal choices, it's especially appropriate that I tell you my basic assumptions and philosophical orientation.

Fundamentally, my approach in *I Never Knew I Had a Choice* is humanistic and personal; that is, I emphasize the healthy and effective personality and the common struggles that most of us experience in becoming autonomous. I especially emphasize accepting personal responsibility for the choices we make and consciously deciding whether and how we want to change our lives. This emphasis is in keeping with the existential viewpoint in psychology, whose proponents assume that we have a strong drive toward health and psychological wholeness and that we are motivated to become all that we are able to become. Both my own thinking and the theoretical approach I take in my professional work have been greatly influenced by people who have contributed to this tradition, including Carl Rogers, Abraham Maslow, Fritz Perls, Sidney Jourard, Clark Moustakas, Viktor Frankl, and Rollo May.

Throughout this book I draw upon my personal experience and professional work with students and with clients in counseling. In addition, I include the observations my wife, Marianne, makes through her counseling practice, as well as her comments on our own marriage and family life. I have used these experiences to develop the theme that freedom of choice is not something given to us but something we must actively achieve for ourselves. As Harry Browne (1973) argues in his book, *How I Found Freedom in an Unfree World*, it is a great mistake to assume that we cannot change or become free until others give us permission to. Instead, Browne insists, we must retain final "permission rights" for ourselves. In doing so, however, we should not expect that others will necessarily change also. We don't have the power to change others, unless they themselves want to change. Moreover, we can easily get hung up by focusing on all the ways we wish others in our lives would change, instead of working on changing ourselves. If we wait for others to become different, or if we blame others for the fact that we're not as happy as we'd like, we diminish our power to take full control of our own lives.

Although this book deals with questions in what is often called "the psychology of adjustment," I have an uneasy feeling about this common phrase. My thinking is geared to personal *growth, awareness, and choice* and to the courage we must have if we are honestly to face our struggles as we try to take charge of our lives. In contrast, the term *adjustment* is frequently taken to mean that there is an ideal norm that people should be measured by. This notion raises many problems; for example, you may ask: What is the desired norm of adjustment? Who determines the standards of "good" adjustment? Is it possible that the same person could be considered well adjusted in our culture and poorly adjusted in some other culture?

A further bias I have against the "adjustment" concept of human behavior is that often those who claim to be well-adjusted are the ones who have settled for a complacent and dead existence, one that has neither challenge nor excitement. My hope is that we can create our own definitions of ourselves as persons, rather than being primarily ruled by other people's norms or expectations. Although I believe that it is unwise to merely "do your own thing" in an irresponsible manner, I also believe that we can consider the good of others and still retain our integrity by making our own choices in life.

Instead of talking about *adjustment*, then, I prefer to talk about *growth*. A psychology of growth rests on the assumption that growth is a lifelong adventure, not some fixed point at which we arrive. Personal growth is best viewed as a *process* rather than as a goal or an end. A growth-oriented perspective assumes that we will face numerous crises at the various stages of our development. These crises can be challenges to give our lives new meaning. In order to continue to grow, we have to be willing to let go of some of our old ways of thinking and being in order to make room for new behavior. During your reading and studying, you might try to become alert to ways in which you've stopped growing, to your fears of doing what is necessary to grow, and, most important, to the degree of personal growth you're willing to invest in.

Suggestions for Using This Book

I hope you'll treat this book, and the course, in a personal way. Rather than merely reading *I Never Knew I Had a Choice* as a textbook or thinking about how the issues I raise apply to others, you may profit most by attempting to apply this material to yourself. With this in mind, I'd like to make some suggestions.

1. At the beginning of each of the subsequent chapters is a self-inventory. These inventories are designed to involve yourself personally with each topic. You may want to bring your responses to class and discuss your views or compare them with those of others. If you're reading this book alone, you may wish to have a close friend or your spouse answer some of the questions, and then share the results. You may also find it useful to retake the inventories after you finish studying each chapter.

...TELL HIM TO HAVE A SEAT, I'VE ONE THING TO FINISH UP.

2. In many of the chapters, examples are drawn from everyday life. How does each example apply to you?

3. Rather than reading simply to learn facts, take your own position on the issues I raise. As much as possible, put yourself into what you read.

4. Questions and exercises are inserted into the main part of the chapters. Since these exercises are designed to help you focus on specific topics, it will be most valuable if you take the time to do these exercises as you read. Actually writing down your responses in the text will help you begin to think about how each topic applies to you.

5. At the end of each chapter are additional activities and exercises suggested for both in-class and out-of-class practice. Select a few that are most meaningful for you.

6. One activity I suggest throughout the book is keeping a journal. You might purchase a separate notebook in which to write your reactions to each topic or to do more extensive writing on some of the exercises. Many students have claimed that the time they took to write in their journals was most productive, because it gave them a written account that they could read at various times. Later, you can look for patterns in your journal; doing so can help you identify some of your critical choices and areas of conflict. Frequently, I give concrete suggestions concerning things you might include in your journal, but the important thing is for you to decide what to put in and how to use it. In your journal, consider writing about some of the following topics:

- what I learned about others and myself through today's class session
- the topics that were of most interest to me (and why)
- the topics that held the least interest for me (and why)
- the topics I wanted to talk about
- the topics I avoided talking about
- particular sections (or issues) in the chapter that had the greatest impact on me (and why)
- some of the things I am learning about myself in reading the book
- some specific things I am doing in everyday life as a result of this class
- some concrete changes in my attitudes, values, and behavior that I find myself most wanting to make
- what I am willing to do to make these changes
- some barriers I encounter in making the changes I want to make

It is best to write what first comes to your consciousness. Spontaneous reactions tend to tell you more about yourself than well-thought-out comments.

7. Many students who examine the personal topics discussed in this book develop an interest in going into some of them in greater depth. For this reason, I give a list of selected books for each chapter. The lists

are annotated to give you an idea of the potential usefulness of each book for you.

8. As you work with the ideas in this book, I hope that you'll keep in mind that growth and change entail risk and a willingness to experience some anxiety. Mistakes can be significant learning experiences, and I doubt that we can gain very much if we're unwilling to explore for fear of making them. Making mistakes usually isn't fatal, and it can be an essential part of growing.

An Introduction to Personal Learning

Perhaps you have always equated making mistakes with failing. I just mentioned that the willingness to risk mistakes is essential if we are to change in a positive direction. The remainder of this chapter encourages you to take a critical look at the attitudes you've developed about learning and to consider the advantages of making learning a personal venture. Guidelines are given to help you assume an active and involved stance toward your learning in this course.

For me, school during childhood and adolescence was a meaningless and sometimes painful experience. In addition, my educational experiences from grammar school through graduate school in many ways taught me to be a passive learner. The *traditional education* that I was exposed to is one of two extreme types of teaching.

This traditional schooling taught me that pleasing the teacher was more important than pleasing myself; that accepting the opinions of an authority was more valuable than becoming a questioner; that learning facts and information was more valuable than learning about myself; that learning was motivated by external factors; that there was a right answer to every problem; that school life and everyday life were separate; that the sharing of personal feelings and concerns had no place in the classroom; and that the purpose of school was mainly to cultivate the intellect and acquire basic skills, not to encourage me to understand myself more fully and make choices based on this self-awareness. The focus of this approach is on mastery of reading, writing, and arithmetic. From time to time this form of education is in vogue, especially when critics point out the poor quality of students that schools turn out.

At the other extreme is *progressive,* or *open, education.* Under the guise of being "humanistic," some teachers provide very little structure, make few demands, ignore factual material, and underplay the importance of learning fundamental skills. They may respond to the authoritarianism of traditionalists by becoming permissive and catering to the passing whims of students. For me, this is not genuine humanistic education, for it does not truly challenge learners both personally and intellectually.

I am not, therefore, making a case for an educational program that deals exclusively with what the learners want. I do think that it is essential to learn basic skills, but I also think that academic learning of content is most fruitful when it is combined with the personal concerns of the learners.

In the courses I teach on the university level, I have certain standards and expectations. In fact, I have the reputation of being very demanding, and many students avoid taking my classes because they think that I have unrealistically high expectations and demand too much reading and written work. It's true that I expect my students to do quite a bit of writing, mostly in the form of reaction or position papers in which they can express their own feelings, thoughts, and values. I do encourage them to read many books that deal with the issues related to the course. However, my major goal in most of my courses is to encourage students to examine personal issues, and I find that it is possible to combine cognitive, or intellectual, learning with the more personal kind of learning that involves feelings, values, belief systems, and the personal experiences of the students.

You can get the most out of this course if you develop an active style of learning in which you raise questions and search for answers within yourself. Since this kind of personal learning might be different from most of your past experiences in school, it's appropriate at this point for you to review your own experiences as a learner and to think about the effects your education has had on you.

Reviewing Your Experiences as a Learner

Whatever your own school experiences have been like, it's important to think about them, because school is a powerful shaper of our attitudes and personalities. Understanding the effects our schooling has had on us in the past and continues to have on us as adults puts us in a better position to consciously modify those effects.

I hope that you'll try to determine how some of your present values and beliefs are related to these experiences. If you like the kind of learner you now are, or if you have had mostly positive experiences with school, then you can build on this positive framework as you approach this course. You can continue to find ways of involving yourself with the

material you will read, study, and discuss. If you feel cheated by a negative educational experience, you can begin to change it. *You* can make this class different by applying some of the ideas provided in this chapter. Once you become aware of those aspects of your education that you don't like, *you* can decide to change your style of learning.

Time Out for Personal Reflection

The following questions are designed to help you focus on your past and present experiences as a learner and on the effects these experiences have had on you. In taking this inventory, respond quickly by giving your initial reaction. Indicate your response by circling the corresponding letter. You may choose more than one response for each item, or, if none of the responses fits you, you can write your own response on the blank line provided.

1. How would you evaluate your elementary school experience?
   a. It was a pleasant time for me.
   b. I dreaded going to school.
   c. I feel that it taught me a lot about life.
   d. Although I learned facts and information, I learned little about myself.

   e. _____

2. How would you evaluate your high school experience?
   a. I have mostly favorable memories of this time.
   b. I got more from the social aspects of high school than I did in terms of learning.
   c. I remember it as a lonely time.
   d. I was very involved in my classes.

   e. _____

3. How do you evaluate your present college experience?
   a. I like what I'm getting from my college education.
   b. I see college as an extension of my earlier schooling experiences.
   c. I'm learning more about myself as a result of attending college.
   d. I'm here mainly to get a degree; learning is secondary.

   e. _____

4. To what degree do you see yourself as a "teacher pleaser"?
   a. In the past, I worked very hard to gain the approval of my teachers.

    b. I'm now more concerned with pleasing myself than I am with pleasing my teachers.

    c. It's very important to me to please those who are in authority.

    d. Good grades are more important than what I learn.

    e. _____

5. To what degree have you been a questioner?

    a. I generally haven't questioned authority.

    b. I've been an active learner, and I've raised many questions.

    c. Basically, I see myself as a passive learner.

    d. I didn't raise questions earlier in my schooling, but now I'm willing to question the meaning of what I do in school.

    e. _____

6. Have you been motivated externally or internally?

    a. I've been motivated primarily by competition and other forms of external motivation.

    b. I've learned things mainly because of the satisfaction I get from learning.

    c. I see myself as having a lot of curiosity and a need to explore.

    d. I've generally learned what I think will be on a test or what will help me get a job.

    e. _____

7. To what degree are you a confident learner?

    a. I'm afraid of making mistakes and looking foolish.

    b. I often look for the "correct way" or the "one right answer."

    c. I trust my own judgment, and I live by my values.

    d. I think there can be many right answers to a problem.

    e. _____

8. To what degree has your learning been real and meaningful?

    a. School has been a place where I learn things that are personally meaningful.

    b. School has been a place where I mostly perform meaningless tasks and pursue meaningless goals.

    c. I've learned how to apply what I learn in school to my life outside of school.

    d. I've tended to see school learning and real life as separate.

    e. _____

9. To what degree have feelings been a part of your schooling?

    a. School has dealt with issues that relate to my personal concerns.

    b. *I've believed that what I feel has no place in school.*
    c. *The emphasis has been on the intellect, not on feelings.*
    d. *I've learned to distrust my feelings.*

    e. _____

10. *How much freedom have you experienced in your schooling?*
    a. *Schooling has taught me how to handle freedom in my own learning.*
    b. *I've found it difficult to accept freedom in school.*
    c. *I've experienced schools as places that restrict my freedom and do not encourage me to make my own choices.*
    d. *I've experienced schools as sources of encouragement to make and accept my own choices.*

    e. _____

Some suggestions for using this inventory:

Now that you've taken this inventory, I have some suggestions for applying the results to yourself. Look over your responses and then decide which of the following questions might be meaningful follow-up activities for you.

1. *How would you describe yourself as a learner during your elementary school years? During your high school years? As a college student?*
2. *What effects do you think your schooling has had on you as a person?*
3. *If you don't like the kind of learner you've been up until now, what can you do about it? What changes would you like to make?*
4. *What important things (both positive and negative) did you learn about yourself as a result of your schooling?*

When you've completed your review of your school experience, you might consider (a) bringing your responses to class and sharing them, and/or (b) using your journal to write down memories of school experiences that have had an impact on you and to keep an ongoing account of significant events in your present learning.

Choosing a New Learning Style

In the preceding section, I encouraged you to take a critical look at your past learning patterns and at the ways in which you might now be continuing those patterns. If you've become aware of a failure to exercise your power as a learner, you can decide on being a more active learner now.

What is most important is that you take responsibility for your own learning. Students who fail to see their own role in the learning process could easily blame the system to support a stance of helplessness. I have little sympathy with those who maintain an apathetic attitude toward their own learning while doing nothing but complaining about their boring teachers and their irrelevant classes. If you're dissatisfied with your education, I hope you'll look at yourself and see how much you're willing to invest in order to make it more vital. Are you just waiting for others to make your learning meaningful? How much are you willing to do to change the things you don't like? Are you accepting your share of responsibility for putting something into the learning process?

Many students who complain among themselves seem unwilling to risk approaching their instructors and talking about their feelings. Consequently, I encourage students to refrain from making excuses why they "can't" approach their instructors and to have the courage to express their views directly. I encourage you to do the same.

I'm sure that you can think of other ways to assume responsibility for changing those aspects of your education that you want to change. Regardless of the format or structure of a course, you can actively search for ways of becoming personally involved in the issues it deals with. For example, this book discusses personal topics that have a direct bearing on your life. Whatever the limits set by your instructor, you will have many opportunities to decide how involved to become in these issues. Whether the class is conducted primarily as a lecture, a lecture/discussion, an experiential group with some structure, or an open-ended group, you can decide to be only marginally involved or to actively apply these topics to yourself. During a lecture, you can raise many of your own unanswered questions and think about your daily behavior. The central issue is not the structure of the classroom situation but the decisions you make concerning your commitment to take an honest look at your own life.

Making your learning personal doesn't mean that you should divulge your secrets or become an open book for others to look at; nor does it mean that you must turn your class into a therapy or encounter group. It *does* mean coming to a new understanding of yourself, and that involves questioning your assumptions about how you live.

One way to begin is to think about your reasons for taking this course and your expectations concerning what you will learn. The following "Time Out" may help you focus on these issues.

Time Out for Personal Reflection

1. What are your main reasons for taking this course?

   _____

   _____

   _____

2. What do you expect this course to be like? Check all the comments that fit you.

   _____   I expect to talk openly about issues that matter to me.
   _____   I expect to get answers to certain problems in my life.
   _____   I hope that I will become a more fulfilled person.
   _____   I hope that I will have less fear of expressing my feelings and ideas.
   _____   I expect to be challenged on why I am the way I am.
   _____   I expect to learn more about how other people function.
   _____   I expect that I will understand myself more fully by the end of the course than I do now.

   List other specific expectations:

   _____

   _____

   _____

3. What do you *most* want to accomplish in this course?

   _____

   _____

4. What are you willing to invest in order to become actively involved in your learning? Check the appropriate comments.

   _____   I'm willing to participate in class discussions.
   _____   I will read the material and think about how it applies to me.
   _____   I'm willing to question my assumptions and look at my values.
   _____   I'm willing to spend some time most days reflecting on the issues raised in this course.
   _____   I'm willing to keep a journal and to record my reactions to what I read and experience.

Mention any other things you're willing to do in order to be actively involved:

_____

_____

_____

Getting the Most from Your Course: Guidelines for Personal Learning

To a large degree, what you get from this course will depend on what you're willing to invest of yourself; so it's important that you clarify your goals and the steps you can take to reach them. The following guidelines may help you become active and involved as you read the book and participate in your class.

1. *Preparation.* Reading and writing, of course, are excellent devices for getting the most from this class. Many students have been conditioned to view reading as an unpleasant assignment, and they tolerate textbooks as something to plow through for an examination. You can selectively read this book—and the books that interest you in the "Suggested Readings"—in a personal way that will stimulate you intellectually and emotionally. Read this book for your personal benefit, and make use of the "Time Outs" and exercises to help you apply the material to your own life.

Writing can also give you a focus. In addition to completing the "Time Outs," you can take personal notes, keep a log or journal, and write brief reactions about the personal impact of the topics. This can be done in the margins as you read and as you feel touched personally. It is helpful to simply write in a free-flowing and unedited style, rather than attempting to analyze what you write. Don't allow yourself to get "frozen" by being critical of your writing. The major idea is to keep some record of personally significant issues. In this way, you can begin to see relationships between what you are experiencing in class and what you are doing with this learning outside of class.

2. *Dealing with fears.* Personal learning entails experiencing some common fears. Some of these fears are the fear of discovering terrible things about yourself; the fear of the unknown; the fear of looking foolish in front of others; the fear of being criticized or ridiculed; the fear of speaking out in front of others; and the fear of taking an honest look at yourself.

Besides these fears, you might experience fears concerning others as you approach this course. For example, you might feel intimidated by the authority of the instructor. If you elevate your instructor to an unrealistically high position, he or she is likely to become somewhat threatening to you. You might fear what the other students will think of you if you participate in class. You might wonder whether you have anything valuable or interesting to contribute or whether you'll be accepted if you express certain values.

It's natural to experience some fear about participating personally and actively in the class, especially since this kind of participation may involve taking risks you don't usually take in your courses. What is critical is how you deal with any fears you experience. You have the choice of remaining a passive observer or recognizing your fears and dealing with them openly, even though you might experience some degree of discomfort. Facing your fears takes both courage and a genuine desire to increase your awareness of yourself, but by doing so you take a first big step toward expanding the range of your choices.

3. *Deciding what you want for yourself.* If you do make the decision to invest yourself in the course, then I cannot overemphasize the importance of deciding on your own concrete goals. If you come to class with only vague ideas of what you want, the chances are that you'll be disappointed. You can increase your chances of having a profitable experience by taking the time and effort to think about what problems and personal concerns you're willing to explore.

4. *Risks.* If you make the choice to invest yourself fully in the course, you should be prepared for the possibility of some disruption in your life. You may find yourself changing. It can be a shock to discover that those who are close to you do not appreciate your changes. They may prefer that you remain as you are. Thus, instead of receiving their support, you may encounter their resistance.

5. *Establishing trust.* You can choose to take the initiative in establishing the trust necessary for you to participate in this course in a meaningful way, or you can wait for others to create a climate of trust. Often students have feelings of mistrust or other negative feelings toward an instructor yet avoid doing anything. One way to establish trust is to seek out your instructor and discuss any feelings you have that might prevent you from participating fully in the course. The same applies to any feelings of mistrust you have toward other class members. By expressing your feelings, you can actively help establish a higher level of trust.

6. *Self-disclosure* Disclosing yourself to others is one way to come to know yourself more fully. Sometimes participants in self-awareness courses or experiential groups fear that they must relinquish their privacy in order to be active participants. However, you can be open and at the same time retain your need for privacy by deciding how much you will disclose and when it is appropriate to do so. Of course, you have the options of not revealing yourself or revealing only safe aspects.

7. *Expressing your feelings and thoughts.* Too often people assume that others know them intuitively. The fact is that others don't know what we think and feel unless we tell them directly. In your class there may be times when you experience boredom, anger, joy, closeness, or disappointment. You can decide whether it's appropriate to keep these feelings to yourself or to share them with others in your class. For example, if you do some work in small groups and you find that you are persistently bored, your expression of your boredom could help your group assess the meaningfulness of their interaction.

8. *Being direct.* You can adopt a style of being direct in your communication. You'll be more direct if you make "I" statements than if you say "you" when you really mean "I." For example, instead of saying "You can't trust people with what you feel, because they will let you down if you make yourself vulnerable," substitute "I" for "you." In this way, you take responsibility for your own statement. Similarly, it will help your communication if you make eye contact and speak directly *to* a person, rather than speak *at* or *about* the person.

9. *Questioning.* If you want to get the most from your interactions in class, avoid adopting a style of asking questions of others. Continually asking questions can lead to a never-ending chain of "whys" and "becauses." Moreover, questioning can be a way of avoiding personal involvement. I have seen people in a class or group push others to be personal by asking them many personal questions, even though they were not willing to become personally involved themselves. Questions keep the questioner safe and unknown; it's more honest and more productive to make personal *statements*.

10. *Listening.* You can work on developing the skill of really listening to what others are saying without thinking of what you will say in reply. The first step in understanding what others say about you is to listen carefully, neither accepting what they say wholesale nor rejecting it outright. *Active listening* (really hearing the full message another is sending) requires remaining open and carefully considering what others say, instead of rushing to give reasons and explanations.

11. *Thinking for yourself.* Only you can make the choice whether to do your own thinking or to let others do your thinking and deciding for you. Many people seek counseling because they have lost the ability to find their own way and have become dependent on others to direct their lives and take responsibility for their decisions. If you value thinking and deciding for yourself, it is important for you to realize that neither your fellow students nor your instructor can give you answers.

12. *Self-fulfilling prophecies.* You can avoid limiting your ability to change by letting go of ways in which you've categorized yourself or been categorized by others. If *you* start off with the assumption that you're stupid, helpless, or boring, you'll probably convince others as well. For example, if you see yourself as boring, you'll probably present yourself in such a way that others will respond to you as a boring person. If you like the idea of changing some of the ways in which you see yourself and present yourself to others, you can experiment with going beyond some of your self-limiting labels. Allowing yourself to believe that a particular change is possible is a large part of experiencing that change. And, once you experience *yourself* differently, others might experience you differently too.

13. *Practicing outside of class.* One important way of getting the maximum benefit from a class dealing with personal learning is to think about ways of applying what you learn in class to your everyday life. As I mentioned at the beginning of this list, you can do this by keeping a journal and by writing personal reactions to your experiences in and out of class. You can make specific contracts with yourself (or with others) detailing what you're willing to do to experiment with new behavior and work toward the changes you want to make. By practicing new behavior, you can make the experience of this class a catalyst for you to put your new insights into action.

At this point, it would be worthwhile to pause and assess your readiness for taking an honest look at yourself. Right now you may or may not feel motivated to examine the issues explored in the following chapters. You may feel that you don't need to explore these topics, or you may see yourself as being not quite ready. If you do feel some hesitation, I hope that you'll leave the door open and give yourself and the course a chance. I've had many students who entered a self-development and experiential course mainly for the units, only to leave feeling very excited and committed to go further. If you open yourself to change and try the techniques I've suggested, you may well experience a similar sense of excitement and promise.

CHANGE THE WAY YOU SEE YOURSELF.

Chapter Summary

This chapter has presented an overview of the choices that will be examined in this book. Suggestions were made on how to use the book and how to get the most from this course. The chapter also described my basic assumptions and philosophy so that you can evaluate what I say in terms of my perspective on the role of choice in everyday life.

I've also encouraged you to review your school experiences and to make an inventory of the ways in which your present attitudes toward learning have been influenced. I've stressed that becoming aware of the effects schooling has had on you gives you the power to choose a new learning style.

A major purpose of this chapter has been to challenge you to examine your own responsibility for making your learning meaningful. It's easy to lash out at impersonal institutions if you feel apathetic about your learning. It's more difficult and more honest to look at *yourself* and ask such questions as: When I find myself in an exciting class, do I get fully involved and take advantage of the opportunity for learning? Do I expect instructors to entertain and *teach* me, while I sit back passively? If I'm bored, what am I doing about it?

Even if your earlier educational experiences have taught you to be a passive learner and to fear taking risks in your classes, once you become aware of this influence, you acquire the power to change your learning style. In this chapter, I've asked you to decide how personal you want your learning to be in the course you're about to experience, and I've suggested several guidelines to help you personalize your own learning.

List some of the major ideas in this chapter that had the greatest impact on you. You might write down statements that captured your own experience and also some that you disagreed with.

_____

_____

_____

_____

_____

_____

Activities and Exercises

1. Recall the one teacher in your life who had the most significant impact on you—either positive or negative. Briefly describe the effect this teacher had on you.

2. Make a list of the fears or anxieties you experience in regard to school. For example, do you fear expressing your opinions because you wonder what others will think? Do you fear authority and seek to please? Do you worry about maintaining passing grades? After you've listed your fears, write down some specific things you can do to deal with them.

3. In your journal, keep a record of specific situations that you feel you handle in a nonassertive manner—particularly those that occur in class. Keeping such a record will increase your awareness of *how* and *when* you behave in nonassertive ways. You should also write down how you'd like to handle these situations more assertively. When you

do behave assertively, record these instances too. Finally, be sure to include how you feel when you behave assertively and nonassertively.

4. The following are exercises that you can do at home. They are intended to help you focus on specific ways in which you behave assertively or nonassertively. I've drawn the examples from typical fears and concerns often expressed by college students. Study the situations by putting yourself in each one and deciding how you might typically respond. Then keep an account in your journal of actual instances you encounter in your classes.

   a. *Situation.* You'd like to ask a question in class, but you're afraid that your question will sound dumb and that others will laugh.

   Issues. Will you simply refrain from asking questions? If so, is this a pattern you're willing to continue? Are you willing to practice asking questions, even though you might experience some anxiety? What do you imagine will happen if you ask questions? What would you like to have happen?

   b. *Situation.* You feel that you have a hang-up concerning authority figures. You feel intimidated, afraid to venture your opinions, and even more afraid to register a point of view opposed to your instructor's.

   Issues. Does this description fit you? If it does, do you want to change? Do you ever examine where you picked up your attitudes toward yourself in relation to authority? Do you think they're still appropriate for you?

   c. *Situation.* You and most of the other students think that your instructor is very boring. He goes strictly by the book and lectures from your textbook. However, it isn't worth it to you to change to another instructor, because the change would mess up your schedule.

   Issues. What options do you have if you stay in the class? Are you condemned to tolerating boredom for a semester? Are you content to tell yourself that there's really nothing you can do, since all the power belongs to the instructor? Are you willing to go to your instructor during office hours and tell him how you experience the class? Do you have any ideas or suggestions for making the class more lively?

   d. *Situation.* In your psychology class, there are a few students who dominate the discussion time. They go on with long-winded stories, they continually make their own points, and they are irritating you and most of the class. The instructor doesn't deal with the situation.

Issues. Have you experienced this kind of situation? What alternatives do you see yourself as having? Might you openly tell these persons in class that you would appreciate it if others had a chance to express themselves? Would you confront them privately?

e. *Situation.* There is a great deal of hostility in your class; the class members show little respect for one another. You feel somewhat overwhelmed by this hostility.

Issues. Would you tend to withdraw, or would you deal openly with your feelings about this hostility? What can you do when you're aware that somebody treats another class member with disrespect? What fears do you have about confronting the tensions you sense in the room? What steps might you take to confront them?

f. *Situation.* Your instructor seems genuinely interested in the students and the course, and she has extended herself by inviting you to come to her office if you have any problems with the course. You're having real difficulty grasping the material, and you're falling behind and doing poorly on the tests and assignments. Nevertheless, you keep putting off going to see the instructor to talk about your problems in the class.

Issues. Have you been in this situation before? If so, what kept you from talking with your instructor? If you find yourself in this kind of situation, are you willing to seek help before it's too late?

5. In your journal, write down other situations that relate to being assertive or nonassertive in your classes. For each situation, describe how you see yourself responding. List all the options you can think of. If you decide that you're willing to take definite steps toward becoming more assertive, begin with the class in which you feel the most safety. In your journal, keep an account of what you do and of the results. You shouldn't expect to change your learning style immediately; be patient with yourself, but do practice, and do make an effort to try new behavior even if you feel some discomfort.

Suggested Readings

At the end of each chapter, I list several books that are relevant to the topic of that chapter. The following are some books that deal with many of the general themes discussed in *I Never Knew I Had a Choice.* You might want to select several of them for supplementary reading.

Arkoff, A. (Ed.). *Psychology and Human Growth*. Boston: Allyn & Bacon, 1975. A book of readings on topics such as problems in identity, body image, sex-role image, achievement, aggression, sex, anxiety, defense, growth, death, love, marriage, family life, and work.

Bach, R. *Jonathan Livingston Seagull*. New York: Macmillan, 1970. A moving story about a seagull in search of freedom and autonomy. He continued to do things that others said he could never do.

Brennecke, J., & Amick, R. *The Struggle for Significance* (3rd ed.). Encino, Calif.: Glencoe, 1980. A book that deals with most of the topics covered in this book, written in a thought-provoking style.

Brown, G. *Human Teaching for Human Learning: An Introduction to Confluent Education*. New York: Viking, 1971. This excellent book provides an introduction to "confluent education." Brown describes a variety of effective techniques that can be used to bring together the intellectual and emotional aspects of learning. He gives examples of how humanistic education has worked for elementary and secondary teachers.

Browne, Harry. *How I Found Freedom in an Unfree World*. New York: Avon, 1973. The author points out many ways in which we aren't free and, at the same time, makes a case for how we can achieve freedom in an unfree world. The central message is that we shouldn't wait for someone else to give us permission to change; we can achieve freedom if we focus on changing ourselves and avoid changing others.

Daniels, V., & Horowitz, L. *Being and Caring*. Palo Alto, Calif.: Mayfield, 1976. A very well-written self-development book that deals with the themes that we are responsible for finding our own way and that with awareness we can create our own world. The authors discuss issues of awareness, acceptance, self-honesty, living with feeling, being and sharing, and centeredness.

Greenwald, J. *Be the Person You Were Meant to Be*. New York: Dell, 1973. The core of this book deals with behavior and relationships that are either "nourishing" or "toxic." It is an invitation to look at your life-style to decide on ways in which you might want to change.

Kangas, J., & Solomon, G. *The Psychology of Strength*. Englewood Cliffs, N.J.: Prentice-Hall, 1975. This is a guide to the fulfillment of your human potential. It describes the process of being strong in relation to yourself and to others as you meet the challenges and crises of life.

Lair, J. *I Ain't Much, Baby—But I'm All I've Got*. New York: Doubleday, 1972. A very personal account of one man's struggle to find meaning in his world. Lair emphasizes that we have choices that lead to either constructive or destructive living. His choice to drastically change his life was made in a hospital bed while he was recovering from a heart attack. He writes about self-acceptance, trust, love, sexuality, death, and spirituality.

Lair, J. *I Ain't Well—But I Sure Am Better*. Greenwich, Conn.: Fawcett, 1975. A continuation of his earlier book, this book reveals the author's methods for continuing the search for personal and spiritual growth. He emphasizes the importance of genuine and deep friendships in his "mutual-need therapy."

Lyon, W. *Let Me Live!* North Quincy, Mass.: Christopher Press, 1975. This is a book that will probably capture your interest and make you think. Its theme is that we get from life what we deserve. Topics include a view of the world and life, "you make me sick, so let's get married," love, sex, meaning, "therapy-therapy," autonomy, femininity, masculinity, and becoming your own parent.

May, R. *The Courage to Create.* New York: Bantam, 1975. This book is a collection of lectures by Rollo May on the theme of the courage to choose and create— a potential that May believes is in all of us.

Pirsig, R. *Zen and the Art of Motorcycle Maintenance.* New York: Bantam, 1974. This is both a story of a father and son on a journey of self-discovery and a philosophical treatment of many issues relating to the quality and meaning of life.

Rogers, C. *Freedom to Learn: A View of What Education Might Become.* Columbus, Ohio: Charles E. Merrill, 1969. Rogers calls for freedom instead of stifling, authoritarian approaches to education. Methods for creating a climate of freedom are discussed.

Stevens, J. *Awareness: Exploring, Experimenting, Experiencing.* Moab, Utah: Real People Press, 1971. The theme is how we can explore and expand our self-awareness. The bulk of the book consists of experiments that can be done by yourself.

Approaches to Personal Growth

Prechapter Self-Inventory

This chapter's inventory is designed to help you focus on the ideas associated with several approaches to personality and personal growth. It also gives you a chance to reflect on some of the facets of your own personality.

I recommend that you take these "Prechapter Self-Inventories" rapidly by giving your initial reaction to each statement. There are no correct or incorrect answers, since each inventory is an aid in identifying *your* beliefs. You might want to take the inventory again after you've read and studied the chapter (or later on in the course) to determine whether you've changed your thinking on any items. Use the inventory to clarify your own viewpoints on issues.

For each statement, indicate the response that most closely identifies your beliefs and attitudes. Use this code: 5 = I *strongly agree* with this statement; 4 = I *agree* in most respects; 3 = I am *undecided*; 2 = I *disagree* in most respects; 1 = I *strongly disagree*.

1. Our personalities are largely determined by the events during the first five years of life.
2. As children, most of us make decisions about ourselves and then continue to act on these assumptions during our adult years.
3. Most people I know tend to follow the values of their parents.
4. Many people adopt the life-style of their parents well into adulthood as a way of keeping their parents alive within them.
5. In order to be an autonomous person, it is necessary to deal with the "unfinished business" of childhood.
6. Events in my life do not cause personality problems; rather, it is my interpretation of and beliefs about these events that cause difficulties.
7. Feelings such as anxiety, depression, anger, and so forth are the result of our thought patterns and what we tell ourselves.
8. There are a lot of "shoulds," "oughts," and "musts" that are a part of my everyday behavior.
9. Immature people tend to live in the here and now, while living for the future is a sign of a mature person.
10. I typically avoid unpleasant feelings or situations rather than recognizing and dealing with them.
11. Dreams can tell me a good deal about my conflicts, and I can learn about myself if I pay attention to my dreams.
12. I sometimes avoid taking risks that are necessary for living fully in

the present because of my fears that terrible things will occur if I take these risks.

——————— 13. I strive to live up to my potential.

——————— 14. I sometimes hang on to the past in order to justify my unwillingness to take responsibility for my present actions.

——————— 15. Most of the time I have difficulty in living in the present, for I am often ruminating about the past or thinking about some future event.

——————— 16. Basically, I accept myself the way I am.

——————— 17. I sometimes see myself as a victim of circumstances beyond my control.

——————— 18. I have difficulty in expressing anger. I sometimes let others take advantage of me and feel that I don't have the right to express my feelings and thoughts.

——————— 19. I frequently say "yes" when I really want to say "no."

——————— 20. If I were personally competent, I wouldn't have conflicts and problems.

Introduction

This chapter describes several theories of personality, as well as techniques for personal growth that are associated with these theoretical perspectives. My approach is admittedly selective, focusing on those concepts and techniques that I find especially valuable in my work with personal-growth groups. My emphasis is on how each theory can help us become autonomous, self-directed people who are open to making choices.

We typically encounter barriers in three major areas of psychological development: *feeling, thinking,* and *behaving.* Do you have trouble recognizing certain of your *feelings,* such as anger, jealousy, depression, anxiety, guilt, or rejection? Even if you are aware of what you might refer to as "negative feelings," do you have difficulty expressing them? Perhaps you learned that it is unacceptable to get angry, or that you shouldn't feel jealousy ("it's a sign of insecurity"), or that you should cheer yourself up if you feel sad or depressed. Yet keeping feelings locked within us typically has undesirable consequences. Somehow the feelings that we try to deny will find expression, either in other feelings or through bodily symptoms (such as hypertension, migraine headaches, or digestive problems). This chapter presents some ways to challenge assumptions that result in the damming up of our emotions.

You may also experience barriers in the *thinking* area. The cognitive behavioral psychologists—who stress the influence of thinking and other cognitive factors on behavior—have contributed to our understanding of personality disorders by their emphasis on the "self-talk" that we all engage in. They have pointed out that we incorporate many unfounded beliefs and attitudes that we grasp as truths. Are you aware of irrational beliefs that you cling to yet somehow don't know how to resolve? Perhaps you are living by childhood decisions that are no longer useful to you. The process of becoming an autonomous person involves *thinking critically* about your early decisions and deciding how you want to modify them.

Finally, you are likely to have some difficulty in the *behavioral* area of your life. How many times have you been clearly aware of your feelings and thoughts and yet found that changing your behavior was difficult indeed? For example, you may either drink or smoke marijuana excessively and realize full well how this affects you physically, emotionally, and socially. In spite of some of your best intentions, however, there may be many times when you do not change these behavioral patterns.

Each theory presented in this chapter offers some key ways of examining your feeling, thinking, and behaving. Each approach challenges you to look at what you are doing and to consider the range of options open to you in making specific modifications in these three areas of development. The six pathways to personal growth we will now examine are psychoanalysis, Transactional Analysis, rational-emotive therapy, Gestalt therapy, behavioral therapy, and self-actualization psychology.

Psychoanalysis: Emphasis on Early Development

Sigmund Freud's contributions to an understanding of how and why we behave as we do are not fully appreciated. Some writers see his ideas as interesting from the vantage point of history but not directly related to personality and personal growth. Actually, the Freudian psychoanalytic theory of personality tells us much about how childhood experiences influence our later development.

Personality Development

One of the most significant contributions of the psychoanalytic approach is the idea that all of us pass through stages of psychological and psychosexual development. According to this viewpoint, our personal, sexual, and social development is largely based on our experiences during

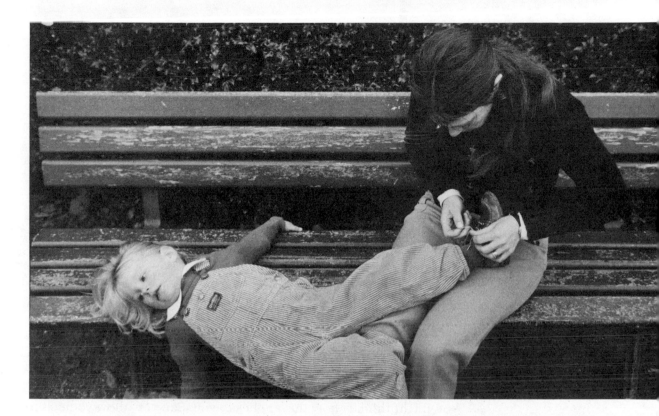

the first five years of life. During this time, we go through three stages (which Freud termed *oral*, *anal*, and *phallic*), and our later personality development hinges on how well we have resolved the demands and conflicts of each stage. I have found evidence to support this assumption in my counseling practice, in the sense that most of the problems that people wrestle with in adulthood seem to have some relationship to unresolved conflicts dating from their early childhood years. In the next chapter, I'll discuss the three Freudian stages in more detail; here I want to give a general overview of the psychoanalytic approach.

According to psychoanalytic theorists, we experience a number of critical conflicts before we begin school, and we are presented with several developmental tasks. One task is to develop a sense of trust in the world, which requires that we feel loved and accepted. If love is absent, we will suffer during later years from an inability to trust ourselves and others, a fear of loving and becoming intimate, and low self-esteem. Many adults want to change such tendencies. They may fear rejection, they may think that they have little to offer, or they may come to believe that they must continually meet others' expectations if they are to be loved. It is very difficult to experience intimate relationships if we have not felt loved and wanted during the first years of life. Let me hasten to add that I don't take a fatalistic view that we're doomed if we didn't get our quota of love. Many people reexperience their childhood feelings of hurt and rejection through some form of counseling; in this way, they come to understand that the fact that they didn't feel loved by their parents doesn't mean that they are unlovable or that others find them unlovable now. With awareness, we can open ourselves up and begin to trust.

A second task of early childhood is learning how to recognize and deal with negative feelings, such as hostility, anger, rage, and aggression. Perhaps you can think of a time in your own childhood when you were extremely angry with your parents, or perhaps you've seen a small child exclaim: "I hate you, and I wish you were dead! You're mean and I don't ever want to see you again!" A parent might respond: "Don't you *ever* talk to me like that. You should be ashamed of yourself!" If children consistently receive messages that *they* are bad for having such *feelings*, they may repress "bad" feelings out of fear of being abandoned by their parents. In this way, they learn to dissociate themselves from feelings such as anger, for they learn that *they* are unacceptable when they have these feelings.

You might think of how this applies to you. Can you allow yourself to feel and directly express your anger? Many students and clients I've worked with have learned to erect a false front to hide their negative feelings. In fact, many of them have real difficulty even experiencing their negative feelings, let alone *expressing* them.

A third significant developmental task is forming a sex-role identity. Before children enter school, they begin to decide how they feel about themselves in their roles as boys and girls. Children exhibit a natural curiosity about sexual matters, and very early in life they form attitudes toward their sexuality and sexual feelings, their bodies, and what they think is right and wrong. Many adults suffer from deep feelings of guilt concerning sexual pleasure or feelings. Some have learned that their sexual organs are disgusting; others have traumatic memories associated with sexual intercourse. Much sexual dysfunctioning in adulthood has its roots in early conditioning and experiences.

Again, I want to emphasize that, although I believe that the events of the first five years of our lives have a significant influence on our later behavior, I don't accept the notion that we are determined by these events. If I did not believe in the possibility of overcoming our early conditioning, I could not in good faith be a psychotherapist. Many people learn new values, come to accept new feelings and attitudes, and overcome much of their past negative conditioning.

In contrast, many people steadfastly hang on to the past as an excuse for not taking any action to change in the present. We can't change in a positive direction unless we stop blaming others for the way we are now. Statements that begin "If it hadn't been for. . . ," are too often used to justify an immobile position. For example: "If it hadn't been for the fact that I was adopted and had several foster parents, I'd be able to feel loved now, and I wouldn't be stuck with feelings of abandonment." "If only my parents had done more for me, I could feel a sense of security and trust." "If only my parents had done less for me, I could have grown up independent." "If only my parents had given me a healthy outlook on sex, I wouldn't feel so guilty now about my sexual feelings."

I remember one client who used to blame his mother for everything. Because she had dominated his father, he felt that he could not trust any woman now. If he couldn't trust his own mother, he reasoned, then whom could he trust? At 25, he saw himself as fearing independence, and he blamed his mother for his fear. He refused to date, and he tried to convince himself that he did so because his mother had "messed up my life by making me afraid." He continually wanted to use his therapy sessions to dwell on the past and blame his present problems on what his parents had and hadn't done. Through counseling, he became aware that his dwelling on his past and his focusing on others were ways he avoided assuming responsibility for his own life. After actively questioning some of his beliefs about women and about himself, he decided that not all women were like his mother, that he didn't have to respond to women in the way his father had, and that he could change his life now if he was willing to accept the responsibility for doing so.

It may often be important to go through a stage of experiencing feelings of anger and hurt for having been cheated in the past, but I think it is imperative that we eventually claim for ourselves the power we have been giving to the people who were once significant in our lives. Unless we recognize and exercise the power we now have to take care of ourselves, we close the door to new choices and new growth.

The Unconscious and Choice

One of Freud's greatest contributions was the concept of the *unconscious*. From his clinical experiences with numerous patients, he concluded that problems of personality and behavior could be traced to the functioning of unconscious processes. This idea—that our behavior is strongly influenced by internal dramas taking place entirely outside of our awareness—has had a revolutionary impact on our understanding of ourselves.

According to Freud, conscious experience is but a thin slice of human behavior. Below the surface, an unconscious store of painful memories, forbidden desires, and other material too threatening to accept remains hidden from our conscious view. Even though we are unaware of this repressed material, it does motivate our behavior and influence our actions.

I don't accept the deterministic position that we are condemned to being blindly driven by forces beyond our control. There are ways to expand our consciousness by uncovering unconscious motives and thus assuming the power to exercise choice.

One way of making the unconscious accessible is to learn to understand the meaning of our dreams. In psychoanalytic practice, dream analysis is an important procedure for uncovering unconscious material and gaining insight into unresolved problems. Indeed, Freud himself called dreams "the royal road to the unconscious." During sleep, our defenses are lowered, and repressed feelings surface. Unconscious wishes, needs, and fears are expressed—some of them so unacceptable to the dreamer that they are expressed in disguised or symbolic form rather than openly and directly.

Dreams have two levels of content: the *latent content* and the *manifest content*. The *latent content* consists of the disguised, hidden, symbolic, and unconscious meanings. Because they are so painful and threatening, the unconscious impulses that make up the latent content are transformed into the more acceptable *manifest content*, which is the dream as it appears to the dreamer. In psychoanalytic dream analysis, the therapist assists the client to understand the disguised meaning of dream symbols, largely through a process known as *interpretation*.

Although I value Freud's insights into the nature of dreams, my approach in working with my clients' dreams is rather different from a psychoanalyst's. Instead of interpreting dreams for my clients, I prefer to have them become all the parts of a dream and then give their own meaning to the dream.

Emotional Defenses and Anxiety

Another dimension of the psychoanalytic view is its description of the way we develop defenses to protect ourselves from threatening thoughts and feelings. According to this view, anxiety results when unconscious material cannot be held in check. For example, I counseled a woman who experienced panic when she began to allow herself to feel her sexuality. She had been very controlled and had claimed that she couldn't "let herself go" with her husband. As she began to understand the "father" inside of her who was constantly urging her to be proper and to act "like a lady," she loosened up and gave up some of her control. Then she was struck with guilt, and she began to feel evil and nasty. She could hear her father's warnings: "Watch out for men; they only want to see how far they can go with you" and "I know that you'll *never* do anything to make me feel disappointed in you!" Her control, then, was her defense against feeling guilty. As she experimented with relinquishing this control, she felt overwhelming anxiety. She needed to learn how to function without having to exercise excessive self-control in order to avoid feelings of guilt.

Most of us use a variety of defenses to ward off anxiety and potential threats to our self-esteem. When I didn't get a position that I'd applied for at a university, I convinced myself that my failure had nothing to do with my qualifications but was due to university politics. When that argument failed to soothe my wounded pride, I tried to tell myself that I really didn't want the job anyway, because it would have entailed a lot of administrative busywork.

The main thing that most defenses have in common, when they function as defense mechanisms, is that they generally operate on an unconscious level and tend to deny or distort reality. Nevertheless, defenses can be appropriate means of coping, and to some degree we all need them. For instance, one young man I worked with recalled bitter and frightening battles between his mother and father. He recalled that he had been too young to leave and that he had feared that his father might kill his mother during one of his rages. He had defended himself by becoming numb and shutting off his feelings. Had he not reacted in this way, he might have experienced great stress, to the point of emotional breakdown. The problem when he came to see me was that he had continued to numb himself and to feel very little. Since this defense was no longer necessary, he could reexamine the appropriateness of shutting off his feelings in order to survive.

Many people wear emotional suits of armor to defend themselves, even though there is no enemy and nothing to defend against. My work has shown me time and time again that people can choose to drop pretenses and to make themselves vulnerable by revealing themselves to selected people. I'm not advocating being totally open and defenseless with everyone and in all situations, but I do believe that too many of us conceal ourselves when we don't need to. If we so choose, we can begin to let those people we care about know more of us, and we can minimize our distortion and denial of reality. I've come to believe that excessive defenses are incompatible with personal growth. If we have a basic sense of security, we can be less defensive and more open to seeing reality as it is, instead of as we wish it would be.

Transactional Analysis: Toward Personal Autonomy

Transactional Analysis (TA) offers another useful framework for understanding how our present behavior is influenced by what happened to us as children. Unlike psychoanalysis, TA does not focus on the role of the unconscious. Rather, it emphasizes how our early decisions affect our behavior, and it provides concepts and tools for examining these decisions. A few basic concepts of TA will be discussed as they relate to the lifelong struggle to become an independent person.

Recognizing Early Learnings and Decisions

During our early years, we receive many direct and indirect "messages" concerning who we are and what we are expected to become. I find concepts from Transactional Analysis to be useful in gaining a more precise picture of how we incorporate these messages and how they affect the decisions that constitute the design of our lives. Developed by Eric Berne and extended by Claude Steiner, TA assumes that we can learn to think and decide for ourselves once we understand the nature and impact of these early messages.

Life scripts.   The concept of *life scripts* is an important contribution of TA. Life scripts are made up of both parental teachings and the early decisions we make as children. Often, we continue to follow these scripts as adults.

Scripting begins in infancy with subtle, nonverbal messages from our parents. During our earliest years, we learn much about our worth as persons and our place in life. Later, scripting occurs in both subtle and direct ways. Some of the messages we might "hear" include: "Always listen to authority." "Don't act like a child." "We know that you can perform well, and we expect the best from you, so be sure you don't let us down." "Never trust people; rely on yourself." "You're really stupid, and we're convinced that you'll never amount to much." Often these messages are sent in disguised ways. For example, our parents may never have told us directly that sexual feelings are bad or that touching is inappropriate. However, their behavior with each other and with us might have taught us to think in this way. Moreover, what parents *don't* say or do is just as important as what they say directly. If no mention is ever made of sexuality, for instance, that very fact communicates significant attitudes.

According to TA theory, our life scripts form the core of our personal identities. Our experiences may lead us to such conclusions as: "I really don't have any right to exist." "I can only be loved if I'm productive and successful." "I'd better not trust my feelings, because they'll only get me in trouble." These basic themes running through our lives tend to determine our behavior, and very often they are difficult to unlearn. In many subtle ways, these early decisions about ourselves can come back to haunt us in later life.

A couple of examples may help to clarify how early messages and the decisions we make about them influence us in day-to-day living. In my own case, even though I now experience myself as successful, for many years of my life I felt unsuccessful and unworthy. I haven't erased old tapes completely, and I still experience self-doubts and sometimes question my worth. I don't think that I can change such long-lasting feelings by simply telling myself "Okay, now that I'm meeting with some success, I'm a successful person." It may be necessary to deal again and again with feelings of being insecure and unworthy. In fact, even striving for and attaining success can be a compulsive way of denying basic feelings of inadequacy. In short, although I believe that I can change some of my basic attitudes about myself, I don't think I can ever get rid of all vestiges of my early learnings. In general, although we need not be determined by old decisions, it's wise to be continually aware of manifestations of our old ways that interfere with our attempts to develop new ways of thinking and being.

A second illustration of how we can be affected by early decisions concerns a woman I'll call Pamela. Pamela is 38 years old, and she has been divorced three times. She finds it very difficult to take anything for herself or to experience needing anything from anyone. Instead, she has continually sought ways of being a "giver." She has told herself that she must be strong, that she mustn't allow herself to depend on others, and that she mustn't cry or experience grief. Yet Pamela isn't satisfied to continue living in this way, for she has felt lonely and resentful much of the time. She has typically picked men whom she views as weak—men who can give her nothing but whom she can take care of, thereby satisfying her "giving" needs. She sees the dishonesty in believing that she has been unselfish; she is aware that she has been motivated more by her own need *to be needed* than by her concerns for others. Gradually, she has also become aware that her parents used to "tell" her such things as: "Always be strong. Don't let yourself need anything from anyone, and in that way you'll never get let down." "Keep your feelings to yourself; if you feel like crying, don't do it in front of others." "Remember that the way to win approval and affection is to do things for others. Always put others before yourself." Pamela's behavior was determined by these values until she realized that she could change her early decisions if she so chose.

Injunctions.   Let's look more closely at the nature of the early messages (often called *injunctions*) that we incorporate into our life-styles. First of all, I want to stress that these injunctions aren't just planted in our heads while we sit by passively. By making decisions in response to real or imagined injunctions, we assume some of the responsibility for indoctrinating ourselves. Thus, if we hope to free ourselves, we must become aware of what these "oughts" and "shoulds" are and of how we allow them to operate in our lives.

Robert and Mary Goulding, the directors of the Western Institute for Group and Family Therapy in Watsonville, California, are among the leaders in the field of Transactional Analysis. The following list, based on the Gouldings' works (1978, 1979), includes common injunctions and some possible decisions that could be made in response to them.

1. *Don't:* Children who hear and accept this message will believe that they cannot do anything right, and they will look to others to make their decisions for them.
    Possible decisions: "I'm scared of making the wrong decision, so I simply won't decide." "Because I made a dumb choice, I won't decide on anything important again!"
2. *Don't be:* This lethal message is often given nonverbally by the way parents hold (or don't hold) the child. The basic message is "I wish you hadn't been born."
    Possible decisions: "I'll keep trying until I get you to love me." "If things get terrible, I'll kill myself."
3. *Don't be close:* Related to this injunction are the messages *Don't trust* and *Don't love.*

Possible decisions: "I let myself love once, and it backfired. Never again!" "Because it's scary to get close, I'll keep myself distant."

4. *Don't be important:* If you are constantly discounted when you speak, it is not surprising that you will get the message that *you* are unimportant.

Possible decisions: "If, by chance, I ever do become important, I'll never let anyone know it." "I'll keep a low profile."

5. *Don't be a child:* This message says: "Always act adult!" "Don't be childish and make a fool of yourself." "Keep control of yourself."

Possible decisions: "I'll take care of others and won't ask for much myself." "I won't let myself have fun."

6. *Don't grow:* This message is given by the frightened parent who discourages the child from growing up in many ways.

Possible decisions: "I'll stay a child, and that way I'll get my parents to approve of me." "I won't be sexual, and that way my father won't push me away."

7. *Don't succeed:* If children are positively reinforced for failing, they may accept the message not to seek success.

Possible decisions: "I'll never do anything perfect enough, so why try." "I'll succeed, even if it kills me."

8. *Don't be you:* This involves suggesting to children that they are the wrong sex.

Possible decisions: "They'd love me only if I were a boy (girl), so it's impossible to get their love." "I'll pretend I'm a boy (girl)."

9. *Don't be sane* and *don't be well:* Some children get attention only when they are physically sick or acting crazy.

Possible decisions: "I'll get sick, and then I'll be included." "I am crazy."

10. *Don't belong:* This injunction may indicate that the family feels that it does not belong anywhere.

Possible decisions: "I'll be a loner forever." "I'll never belong anywhere."

At this point, think about some of the childhood conclusions that you made about yourself and about life. For example, you might have made any one of the following early decisions:

· "I will be loved only when I live up to what others expect of me."
· "I'd better listen to authorities outside of myself, because I can't trust myself to make decent decisions."
· "I won't let myself trust people, and that way they won't ever let me down again."

Themes like these run through your life to determine not only your self-image but also your behavior. It is a difficult matter to unlearn some of these self-defeating assumptions and learn new and constructive ones in their place. This is one reason for learning how to critically evaluate questions such as:

· What messages have I listened to and "bought"?
· How valid are the sources of these messages?
· In what ways do I now continue to tell myself self-defeating sentences?
· How can I challenge some of the decisions I made about myself and make new ones that will lead to a positive orientation?

While some of our early decisions may have been made to ensure physical and psychological survival—and thus have been appropriate at the time—many of them are both archaic and inappropriate as they are carried into our adult life. Through the process of increased self-awareness, we are able to critically examine early decisions to determine if we will continue to live by them.

Learning to Challenge Our Inner Parents

I'd like to expand a bit on the general concepts of TA and discuss some related ideas about challenging early messages and working toward autonomy. I use the term *inner parent* to refer to the attitudes and beliefs we have about ourselves and others that are a direct result of things we've learned from our parents or parental substitutes. I see the willingness to challenge this inner parent—or "inner custodian," as Sheehy (1976) refers to it—as a mark of autonomy. Since being autonomous means that we are in control of the direction of our lives, it implies that we have discovered an identity that is separate and distinct from the identities of our parents and of others. We haven't really achieved autonomy if our actions are dictated by an unquestioned inner parent.

Many of us, however, are reluctant to give up our inner parents, and we keep them alive and functioning in many ways. By doing so, we become incapable of directing ourselves. Some of the ways in which we can cling to our parents and other significant figures are:

· Choosing to live at home because it's more secure than having to leave and establish our own way of life.
· Making decisions that are primarily motivated by a need to please our parents rather than by a need to please ourselves.
· Attaching ourselves to a substitute parent, such as some hero, guru, or model.

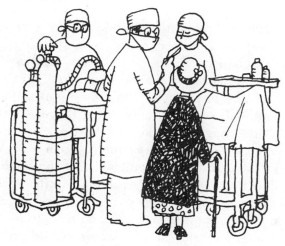

PLEASE, MOTHER!

- Marrying a person who is an extension of our father or mother in the hope that he or she will take care of our unmet needs.
- Striving to become perfect parents, thus making up for all that we never had as children.
- Clinging to the irrational notion that we haven't exhausted all the possible ways of pleasing our parents, and continuing to search and search in the hope that someday we will find a way to make them proud of us.

Although becoming autonomous involves challenging our inner parents, it doesn't necessarily involve rejecting all or most of our parents' values. Some of our early decisions may have stimulated growth, and many of the values we incorporated from our parents may be healthy standards for guiding our behavior. No doubt our past has contributed in many respects to the good qualities we possess, and many of the things that we like about ourselves may be largely due to the influence of the people who were important to us in our early years. What is essential is that we look for the subtle ways in which we have psychologically incorporated our parents' values in our lives without a deliberate choice.

How do we learn to recognize the influence that our parents continue to have on us? One way to begin is by talking back and engaging in dialogue with our inner parents. In other words, we can begin to notice some of the things we do and some of the things we avoid doing, and then ask ourselves why. For instance, suppose you avoided enrolling in a college course because you'd long ago branded yourself "stupid." You might tell yourself that you'd never be able to pass that class, so why even try? In this case, an early decision that you'd made about your intellectual capabilities would prevent you from branching out to new endeavors. However, rather than stopping at this first obstacle, you could challenge yourself by asking: "Who says that I'm too stupid? Even if my father or my teachers have told me that I'm slow, is this really true? Why have I bought this view of myself uncritically? Let me check it out and see for myself whether it's really true."

In carrying out this kind of dialogue, we can talk to the different selves we have within us. For example, you may be struggling to open yourself to people and trust them, while at the same time you hear the inner injunction "Never trust anybody." In this case you can carry on a two-way discussion between your trusting side and your suspicious side. The important point is that we don't have to passively accept as truth the messages we learned when we were children. As adults, we can now put these messages to the test.

Becoming Our Own Parents

Achieving emotional maturity involves divorcing ourselves from our inner parents and becoming our own "parents." But maturity is not some fixed destination at which we finally arrive; it is rather a direction in which we can choose to travel. What are some of the characteristics of the person who is moving toward becoming his or her own parent? There is no authoritative list of the qualities of an autonomous person, but the following characteristics may stimulate you to come up with your own view of what kind of parent you want to be for yourself and what criteria make sense to you in evaluating your own degree of psychological maturity. For each of these characteristics, ask yourself whether it applies to you and whether you agree that it is a mark of one who is becoming independent. I encourage you to add to or modify this list as you see fit.

1. People moving in the direction of autonomy recognize the ways in which their inner parents control them. They see how they are controlled by guilt or by the promise of love and how they have cooperated in giving parents and parent substitutes undue power in their lives.
2. People moving in the direction of autonomy have a desire to become free and responsible, standing on their own two feet and doing for themselves what they are capable of doing.
3. People moving in the direction of autonomy have a sense of identity and uniqueness. Rather than looking outside of themselves, they find

answers within. Instead of asking "What do you expect of me? What will it take for me to win your approval? What should I be and do?" they ask "What can I do that will make me pleased with myself? Who is it that I want to become? What seems right for me? What do I expect of myself?"

4. People moving in the direction of autonomy have a sense of commitment and responsibility. They are committed to some ideals and personal goals that make sense to them. Their sense of commitment includes the willingness to accept responsibility for their actions rather than blaming circumstances or other people for the way their lives are going.

5. The discovery of a meaning or purpose in life is an important mark of independent people. Although this meaning can be derived from many sources, their lives are characterized by purpose and direction.

In order to become our own parents, Gould (1978) says, it is essential that we deal with the unfinished business from childhood that periodically intrudes in our adult relationships. Referring to this unfinished business as the "angry demons of childhood consciousness," he asserts that our central developmental task consists of striving for a fuller and more independent *adult consciousness*. We accomplish this transformation from childhood to adult consciousness by reformulating our definition of self, which is a risky and continuing process. Thus, developing a mature personality involves eliminating the distortions of childhood demons and the protective devices we've developed to cope with these demons. Gould captures the essence of this struggle toward autonomy when he says: "As our life experience builds, ideally we abandon unwarranted expectations, rigid rules and inflexible roles. We come to be the owners of our own selves, with a fuller, more independent adult consciousness" (pp. 37–38).

Time Out for Personal Reflection

The following self-inventory is designed to increase your awareness of the injunctions that you have incorporated as a part of your self-system and to help you challenge the validity of messages that you may not have critically examined.

1. Place a check (√) in the space provided for each of the following injunctions that you think applies to you.

Some Common "Don't" Injunctions

_____ *Don't be (or don't exist).*

_____ *Don't be you.*

_____ *Don't think.*

_____ *Don't feel.*

_____ *Don't be close.*

_____ *Don't trust.*

_____ *Don't be sexy.*

_____ *Don't fail.*

_____ *Don't make it.*

_____ *Don't be foolish.*

_____ *Don't be important.*

_____ *Don't brag.*

_____ *Don't let us down.*

_____ *Don't grow or change.*

_____ *Don't be rude.*

List any other "don't" messages you heard frequently:

_____

_____

Check the following ways that you sometime badger yourself with self-demands:

Some "Ought," "Should," "Must," and "Do" Messages:

Be perfect.

_____ *You ought to say only kind things.*

_____ *You should be more than you are.*

_____ *You must be obedient.*

_____ *You should work up to your potential.*

_____ *You ought to be practical at all times.*

_____ *You should listen to authority figures.*

_____ *You should always put your best foot forward.*

_____ *You ought to put others before yourself.*

_____ *You ought to be seen but not heard.*

List any other injunctions that you can think of that apply to you:

_____

_____

_____

2. *What are some messages you've received concerning the following:*

    Your self-worth? _____

    Your potential to succeed? _____

    Your sex role? _____

    Your intelligence? _____

    Your trust in yourself? _____

    Trusting others? _____

    Making yourself vulnerable? _____

    Your security? _____

    Your aliveness as a person? _____

    Your creativity? _____

    Your ability to be loved? _____

    Your capacity to give love? _____

3. *Complete the following sentences by giving the first response that comes to mind.*

    a. *To me, being an independent person means* _____

    _____

    b. *The things that I received from my parents that I most value are*

    _____

    _____

    c. *The things that I received from my parents that I least like and most want to change are* _____

    _____

    d. *If I could change one thing about my past, it would be* _____

    _____

    e. *My fears of being independent are these:* _____

    _____

    f. *One thing I most want for my children is* _____

    _____

g. I find it difficult to be my own person when _____

_____

h. I feel the freest when _____

_____

Rational-Emotive Therapy: Disputing Irrational Beliefs

Related to the notion of uncritically accepting parental injunctions and basing life decisions on them is the assumption that we actually cause our personal difficulties by clinging to irrational beliefs and indoctrinating ourselves with these self-defeating thoughts. Rational-emotive therapy (RET) contends that as humans we will make mistakes, so it is important to accept ourselves as being fallible and not to be excessively demanding of ourselves.

RET maintains that feelings of anxiety, depression, rejection, anger, and alienation are initiated and perpetuated by a self-defeating belief system based on irrational ideas that were uncritically embraced at an early age. These self-defeating beliefs are supported and maintained by negative, absolutistic, and illogical statements that we make to ourselves over and over again: "If I don't win universal love and approval, then I'll never be happy"; "If I make a mistake, that would be horrible"; and so forth.

Albert Ellis (1979), the developer of RET, has devised an A-B-C theory of personality that explains how people develop negative evaluations of themselves. According to Ellis, it is our faulty thinking, not actual events that happen in our lives, that creates emotional upsets.

An example will clarify this A-B-C concept. Assume that Sally's parents abandoned her when she was a child ("A," the activating event). Sally's emotional reaction may be feelings of depression, worthlessness, rejection, and unlovability ("C," the emotional consequence). However, Ellis asserts, it is not "A" (her parents' abandonment of her) that caused her feelings of rejection and unlovability; rather it is at point "B" (her belief system) that the cause of her low self-esteem lies. Sally made her mistake when she told herself that there must have been something terrible about herself for her parents not to want her. Sally's irrational beliefs are involved in the sentences she continues to tell herself: "I am to blame for what my parents did." "If I were more lovable, they would have wanted to keep me."

According to Ellis (1979), most of our irrational ideas can be reduced to three main forms of what he refers to as *must*urbation: (1) "I *must* be competent, and I *must* win the approval of all the significant people in my life"; (2) "Others *must* treat me fairly and considerately"; and (3) "My life *must* be easy and pleasant. I need and *must* have the things I want."

RET is designed to teach people how to *dispute* irrational beliefs such as those listed above. Let's apply RET to Sally's example. She does not need to continue believing that she is basically unlovable. Instead of clinging to the belief that something must have been wrong with *her* for her parents to have rejected her, she can begin to dispute this self-defeating statement and think along different lines: "It hurts that my parents didn't want me, but perhaps *they* had certain problems that kept them from being good parents." "Maybe my parents didn't love me, yet it is a large world and I'd be foolish to assume that nobody could love me." "While it is unfortunate that I didn't have parents in growing up, it is not devastating, and I no longer have to be a little girl waiting for their protection."

Ellis stresses that we feel about ourselves the way we think. Thus, if you hope to change a negative self-image, it is essential to learn how to dispute the illogical sentences you now continue to feed yourself and to challenge irrational premises that you have accepted uncritically. Further, you also need to work and practice at replacing these self-sabotaging beliefs with constructive ones. If you wish to study common ways of combating this self-indoctrination process, I refer you to Ellis and Harper (1975), *A New Guide to Rational Living*.

Gestalt Therapy: Living in the Here and Now

Developed by Fritz Perls (1969), Gestalt therapy is based on the premise that people must find their own way in life and accept personal responsibility. It focuses on moment-to-moment awareness of our experiencing, together with the almost immediate awareness of our blocks to such experiencing. According to the Gestalt approach, the way to become an autonomous person is to identify and deal with unfinished business from the past that interferes with current functioning.

Key Concepts

Several key concepts of the Gestalt approach have applicability for anyone who wants to develop a self-help program leading to personal growth.

1. *The here and now.* One of Perls's most significant contributions is his emphasis on learning how to appreciate and fully experience the present moment. According to Perls (1969), most of us miss living in the present, for we are either preoccupied with past events or are too focused on the future. For Perls, power is in the present. As we direct our energies toward what might have been or to what might be, our capacity to seize the power of the moment diminishes dramatically.

2. *Awareness and responsibility.* Perls contends that most of us go through life like zombies, never fully aware and thus never fully alive. Awareness is the continuing process of recognizing what we are thinking about and what we are feeling, sensing, and doing. Gestalt therapy techniques focus on *what* people are doing and *how* they are doing it. Some key questions are:

· What are you feeling as you speak?
· How do you experience your body right now?
· Can you direct your attention to your gestures?

The Gestalt approach aims at helping people use their senses fully and become aware of how they block what is going on in the present. The assumption is that through awareness we can become whole again by recognizing, accepting, and integrating denied parts of ourselves.

3. *Unfinished business.* Our ability to live fully in the present is hindered by unfinished business from our past. This excess baggage typically involves unexpressed feelings such as resentment, anger, grief, pain, anxiety, guilt, sadness, and discouragement. All of these feelings are associated with past events that clamor for completion. This unfinished business gets in the way of effective contact with ourself and others until it is recognized, expressed, and dealt with in the present.

4. *Avoidance.* Related to unfinished business is avoidance. It refers to the defensive methods people use to keep from experiencing the uncomfortable emotions associated with unfinished situations.

We have a tendency to avoid confronting and fully experiencing our anxiety, anger, guilt, and grief. Yet all of these unexpressed feelings become a nagging undercurrent that keeps us from being fully alive. Perls (1969) speaks of the catastrophic fears that prevent growth: "If I really allowed myself to cry over all the pain in my life, I'm afraid I'd never stop crying"; "If I felt my grief over my losses, I'm fearful of getting so depressed that I'll become paralyzed"; "If I got angry, I'm afraid that people wouldn't want anything to do with me."

If we are interested in growing, we will have to take the risks involved in facing that which we are working so hard to avoid. It is through experiencing the parts of us that we are trying to deny or disown that the process of integration will occur, allowing us to get beyond the place where we are stuck.

Techniques for Personal Growth

Gestalt therapy techniques are lively, encourage action, often lead to an intensification of feeling, and can increase awareness of what we are experiencing at a given moment. In Gestalt therapy there is a minimum of *talking about* feelings, events, conflicts, and experiences. Instead, people are asked to "become a conflict" or "be what they are feeling," activities that will become clear in the discussion of techniques that follows.

1. *Assuming responsibility.* The Gestalt approach emphasizes assuming full responsibility for ourselves. This implies that we are aware of our thoughts, feelings, and actions and that we avoid placing the blame on others for what we are experiencing. Statements that reflect a lack of willingness to accept personal responsibility include: "You are *making* me bored"; "you are *making* me angry"; "you are *getting* me jealous"; "you *make* me feel inadequate and inferior." Statements implying that others are responsible for what we are feeling actually give other people power over us. If we feel frightened, angry, jealous, bored, or inadequate, and we say "*You* are making me feel this way," we delegate control to others and refuse to take charge of our own lives.

In Gestalt therapy, clients are encouraged to try changing these "you" statements to "I" statements. Thus, a client may be encouraged to say "I am aware of feeling bored, and I take responsibility for my boredom" or "I feel angry, and I take responsibility for this feeling." Working to accept responsibility for feelings is a step toward becoming able to change them.

2. *Dialogues.* The dialogue technique often helps people accept the disowned and denied part of themselves. For example, Leroy says that he is having a difficult time in dealing with his father. Leroy would like to get closer to him, yet he is not sure that he wants to take the chance of his father's rejection. The dialogue technique would work like this: Leroy sits in a red chair and says what he'd most like to say to his father, whom he imagines is sitting in a black chair facing him. Then Leroy trades chairs, this time "becoming his father." He responds as he expects

THE TROUBLE WITH YOU IS...

his father would (or as he would like him to respond, or the way he fears he will respond). This process of changing chairs and continuing a dialogue in the present tense can help Leroy experience more intensely what he is feeling, clarify some of the things he might want to actually tell his father, and get a sense of what it might be like to be his father.

3. *Making the rounds.* In group situations I frequently ask people to say something that they have not been expressing that seems to be getting in the way of their being who they would like to be. For example, Lynn says "I really would like to trust people in this group, but I'm finding myself very reserved and unwilling to open up for fear I'll be judged." If Lynn would like to change the feeling of fearing judgment, and if she is willing to take part in an exercise, I am likely to say: "Lynn, would you be willing to stand up and go to each person in the group and complete this sentence: 'I am afraid to open up to you, because if I do, then you will....'" After Lynn has "made the rounds," she is asked what it was like for her to complete these sentences, and if she still feels as fearful of being judged. We can then pursue in more detail the issues of trust, the risks of disclosure, feeling judgment from others, and whatever else she is feeling. By doing this, Lynn has confronted her fears and taken an active step toward creating trust for her in this group.

4. *Reversal.* This technique consists of giving expression to a side of yourself that is rarely displayed, simply because you don't want to see or accept a part of yourself. The theory underlying this technique is that integration is possible when we allow ourselves to plunge into the very thing that we have been avoiding. For example, a soft-spoken person

may be encouraged to speak loudly; a tough guy, to let himself be gentle; a person who comes across apologetically, to brag for a few minutes; and a person who claims to be very accepting of everyone, to be as judgmental as possible for a few minutes.

5. *Exaggeration.* This exercise involves becoming more aware of signals we send through body language. The opposite of the reversal technique just described, this method asks us to repeatedly exaggerate a movement, posture, gesture, or vocal quality. The idea is to help us experience more intensely the feelings associated with the behavior, which should, in turn, help us understand its meaning. In group situations various participants are asked to continue talking as they exaggerate a habitual smile, to be as highly judgmental as possible, or to be as apologetic as possible. Paying attention to what we are experiencing as we work at exaggerating a trait we would like to get rid of usually brings a good many emotions to the surface.

6. *Dream work.* The Gestalt approach assumes that dreams contain an existential message to us, telling us about who we are and what our life situation is like. The dreamer works with his or her own dream, giving it meaning. Dreams typically represent a part of the personality that has been disowned. By taking on the personality of each part in the dream, the dreamer moves toward an internal integration.

A suggested exercise: Take one of your dreams, and write down as much as you can remember about it. Remember each person, object, event, and mood. Then, allow yourself to "become" each part of your dream, giving it voice and personality. Be that person or object, and tell your story. You can let yourself have a dialogue with the various parts of the dream. As you act out each of these parts as fully as possible, you will probably become increasingly aware of the conflicts and polarities within you and of a range of feelings. Pay attention to what you are doing in the dream. How are you feeling? It is important that you work in the present tense, for doing so brings your dream to life. You might want to keep a record of your dreams in your journal and try this Gestalt approach to working with them.

A Commentary on Gestalt Techniques

I imagine that some of you may well be thinking that the techniques I've described are a bit strange, to say the least. Some of you may fear what others will think if they catch you talking to an empty chair!

I do hope that you push past any resistances you may have about looking foolish and doing dumb things. If you are willing to adopt an experimental attitude, you are likely to increase your present-centered awareness of what you are feeling, thinking, and doing. You can then decide on how you may want to modify your behavior.

Time Out for Personal Reflection

A. Albert Ellis (1977) has developed a list of irrational beliefs, which he calls *"musturbatory ideologies."* This self-inventory is a modification of some of these key irrational beliefs, along with major sub-ideas. Respond to each statement with T (true) if it applies to you more than it does not, and F (false) if the statement does not apply to you.

_____ 1. I prefer to avoid facing life's difficulties rather than develop the self-discipline to face reality.

_____ 2. Unless things go the way I want them to, quickly and easily, I get very upset.

_____ 3. Unless I find the ideal solution to a problem, the results are catastrophic.

_____ 4. Unless I win the approval of just about everyone, I consider myself a worthless person.

_____ 5. Life will be unbearable unless I am thoroughly competent in everything that I attempt.

_____ 6. It is wrong for me to question those in authority, and I must have their approval.

_____ 7. In order to survive, I *must* have the love from those who are significant in my life.

_____ 8. I should always be perfect, and I fully deserve to feel guilty if I make any mistakes.

_____ 9. *It is best to avoid contact with others, because if they rejected me, I'd be devastated.*

_____ 10. *I must continually rate myself and be a severe self-critic; if I don't, I'll never really accomplish a thing.*

A few suggestions for making use of this inventory:

1. List any other musts that govern your life. What is one central irrational belief that seems to get in the way of your living as effectively as you'd like?

_____

_____

_____

_____

2. Think about the statements you see as applying to you. Ask yourself where and how you incorporated each assumption. What do you get from clinging to this belief? How do you imagine that your life would be different if you were to successfully dispute this belief.

3. For about a week, keep a record of situations in which you tell yourself that you must or should do something in order to avoid dire consequences. Look for patterns in the ways you might drive yourself out of fear of suffering catastrophic outcomes.

B. The following self-inventory is based upon some key concepts associated with the Gestalt approach to personal growth. Respond to each statement with T (true) if it applies to you more than it does not, and F (false) if the statement does not apply to you.

_____ 1. *I often find myself preoccupied with past events or with the future, to the point that I miss living in the present.*

_____ 2. *I am typically aware of messages my body is sending me.*

_____ 3. *I am aware of "unfinished business" such as feelings of anger, grief, guilt, and sadness that does, at times, interfere with my living the way I'd like.*

_____ 4. *I have many fears that keep me from facing the unfinished business in my life.*

_____ 5. *I tend to place the responsibility on others for "making" me feel bored, inadequate, and angry.*

_____ 6. *I believe that my dreams are a useful resource for finding out what my concerns are.*

_____   7. *I often find that I rehearse what I want to say, almost to the point of attempting to put on a performance aimed at gaining others' approval.*

_____   8. *I am aware of many conflicting sides within myself, or divergent parts of me (love/hate; wanting closeness/wanting distance; wanting to be taken care of/wanting to be self-sufficient).*

_____   9. *Gestalt therapy seems to have some promising elements that I can apply to everyday living.*

List one Gestalt concept or exercise that you are willing to consider experimenting with.

_____

_____

Behavior Therapy: Techniques for Personal Change

There is a trend toward "giving psychology away." This means that psychologists are sharing their knowledge so that the "consumers" can increasingly lead self-managed and self-directed lives rather than depend on experts to deal with their problems. Psychologists who share this orientation are concerned with teaching people the skills they will need to manage their own lives effectively.

Behavior therapy is a practical approach that emphasizes both the thoughts that lead to specific troublesome behaviors and the importance of taking action to change those behaviors. This approach is useful in helping us eliminate problematic behavior and acquire new skills. Although some people view behavior therapy as a means of controlling the client, contemporary behavioral approaches emphasize the necessity of the client's taking action, which implies that the client must be an active participant in the therapeutic process. Thus, behavior therapy provides many tools for modifying behavior patterns, learning how to cope with stress, eliminating habits perceived as undesirable, challenging fears, and developing a variety of self-management programs.

In self-management programs people make decisions about specific behaviors they want to control or change. Some examples include excessive eating, drinking, or smoking. People often realize that a major reason for their not achieving their goals is a lack of the necessary skills. It is in such areas that a self-directed approach can provide a plan that will lead to change.[1]

A Model for Self-Directed Change

The following is an adaptation and modification of the systematic model for self-directed change presented by Watson and Tharp (1981).[2] I use this model in my counseling practice with both individuals and groups.

1. *Select your goals.* (In counseling applications, the client, not the counselor, selects the goals.) What do *you* want for yourself? How do you want to be different?

2. *Translate your goals into target behaviors*—that is, the behaviors you need to change or acquire in order to reach your goal. What specific behaviors would you like to increase? What behaviors do you want to decrease? How might you reach your goal?

3. *Observe your behavior* by focusing your awareness on what you're doing. Keep a record of your behavior. You might carry in your pocket a small notebook to keep track of behaviors (and feelings associated with them) you want to change.

4. *Develop a contract.* After you've increased your awareness of a particular behavior pattern, you can devise a plan for change. This involves, first, negotiating a working contract, with yourself, your counselor, or another person, and, second, actually doing things to change. These two steps make up the action phase of the program.

5. *Arrange to get information and feedback.* If you want to know how effective your new behavior is, it's essential to get reaction from others and think about it. Is your changed behavior working for you?

6. *Revise your plan of action as needed.* The more you learn about yourself and the impact you have on others, the more you can refine your plans to change.

---

[1]Two books that I find especially helpful in teaching people how to take increasing charge of their own lives are *Self-Directed Behavior: Self-Modification for Personal Adjustment*, by Watson and Tharp (1981), and *Toward a Self-Managed Life-Style*, by Williams and Long (1979).

[2]Adapted from *Self-Directed Behavior: Self-Modification for Personal Adjustment*, 3rd edition, by D. L. Watson and R. G. Tharp. Copyright © 1977, 1981 by Wadsworth Publishing Company, Inc. Used by permission of the publisher, Brooks/Cole Publishing Company, Monterey, California.

A Case Illustration

The following illustration will help make the above outline more concrete. I used that model with a client whom I'll call Roger. Initially, Roger had a great deal of difficulty focusing on *what* he wanted to change. He had sought counseling because he felt inferior and frightened, and because he didn't like himself. One of his goals that we worked on for a long while was to reduce his self-deprecating remarks. He would continually put himself down, calling himself stupid and berating himself for being such a "clod."

Another of Roger's goals was to return to college. He had dropped out after his first year, because he had been convinced that he was too stupid to learn. Eventually, he did reapply to the same community college he had left five years before. After being accepted, he began by carrying a light load. Since he wanted to feel better about himself, I thought that it was crucial that he take some definite steps to increase his self-respect. At the same time, taking a full load might have set him up for failure, which would have given him additional ammunition to bombard himself with; so we both decided that it would be more realistic to start with a couple of classes the first semester. Roger selected two courses that particularly interested him: the psychology of personal adjustment and U.S. government.

I suggested to Roger that he keep a small spiral notebook in his pocket and that he observe certain behaviors that we were working on changing. For example, he had real fears about going to class. He feared being called on and not knowing the answer, and he feared looking like a fool in front of his peers. He would tell himself that he was too dumb to go to college. I asked him to write down a few of the sentences he tended to repeat to himself, such as: "I'm really dumb." "It would be terrible if I made a mistake." "Everybody is looking at me, and I'm sure they think I'm a jerk." I asked him to record each time that he told himself one of these self-defeating sentences. In this way, he became increasingly aware of how often, and in what situations, he put himself down. During our sessions, we discussed the observations he'd made of himself during the previous week.

As Roger began to get a clearer picture of his self-defeating behaviors, we formulated a plan for change. Roger did several things. He learned self-relaxation, which he practiced for about 20 minutes each day. He then began to use relaxation exercises before he entered threatening situations, such as taking a test, approaching an instructor, or being involved in other interpersonal situations. He also attended a one-day assertion-training workshop, because he wanted to learn how to express directly both positive and negative feelings. We then worked with many of the situations that he practiced in his assertion workshop. For instance, he needed to confront the mechanic who had charged him a hefty fee to "repair" his car engine, which still didn't work. I became the mechanic who tried to give him the brush-off, and Roger acted out the way he intended to deal with him. I gave him feedback, pointing out areas of strength and things he could do to be more direct and to avoid backing down from his legitimate demands.

Roger had a great deal of difficulty in relating effectively with people. Although he definitely wanted to feel more comfortable and confident in social situations, he would typically shy away and keep to himself. I suggested that he attend one of my weekend personal-growth groups, where he could begin to apply what he was learning in his individual counseling sessions to interactions with others in a relatively safe, supportive, and structured group situation. At the outset of the group session, he made a contract to initiate contacts with others in the group. During the breaks he did go up to others and begin talking to them. This was new behavior for him; his old style would have been to sit alone in a corner and not bother anyone. Then we worked in the group with how he felt when he walked up to people and began a conversation. He was given a lot of positive feedback by the members for his willingness to get involved and do things that were difficult for him. He was also assured that people liked him and saw good qualities in him. They were not bored when he spoke, and his worst fears about how others might respond to him never materialized.

In the group, Roger also learned new behavior by *modeling*—that is, by imitating certain behaviors of another male member whom he respected. Another behavioristic technique that we employed was that of *rehearsal*. Roger wanted to approach his boss and ask him for a change of schedule at work so that he could begin to take a full load of courses. Before attending the group session, Roger had felt that he didn't want to risk making his boss unhappy and that he didn't want to put anyone out. During the workshop, Roger focused more on his legitimate needs, and he came to the conclusion that he deserved this consideration. He began by playing the role of his boss (saying how the change in schedule would be most inconvenient), while another group member played Roger's role. Then they switched roles, and Roger firmly and clearly stated his position. He thus had a chance to rehearse the application of his new learnings to this difficult situation. He had the opportunity to get feedback and to improve his effectiveness. Then he actually went out and applied his new style in real life.

Assertiveness Training

One of the behavioral techniques that proved valuable to Roger was assertiveness training. The popularity of this approach indicates that there are many of us who could get more from life if we learned how to clearly express what we need and want. Many people restrict their choices because of their fears of asking directly for what they want or expressing any negative feelings. Assertiveness training is directed to these problems.

The titles of popular books on assertiveness training give us a sense of what it is. Alberti and Emmons (1975) urge us to *Stand Up, Speak Out, Talk Back*, while Fensterheim and Baer (1975) tell us *Don't Say Yes When You Want to Say No*. Similarly, Smith (1975) voices the common complaint *When I Say No, I Feel Guilty*. The theme of all these books is basically the same: You can come to understand your rights and express them, you can break away from a self-limiting way of life, and you can learn how to express both your negative and positive feelings.

Assertiveness trainers distinguish between being assertive and being aggressive. Being *assertive* means recognizing your right to have your own feelings, thoughts, and opinions and learning how to express them in a way that isn't designed to alienate others. Being *aggressive* means attacking others, blaming them for your problems, putting them down, and threatening them. The goal of assertiveness training is to teach us how to be assertive in asking for what we want and in sticking to our realistic demands without being aggressive.

Assertiveness training uses role-playing techniques. For example, suppose that you feel put down whenever you participate in a particular class. Your teacher makes sarcastic remarks, and you're left feeling that what you said is unimportant or foolish. You could decide not to participate anymore, or you might just sit back and feel hostile and never say anything about the matter. On the other hand, you might decide to talk directly with this instructor in private and express how you feel about his or her remarks. If you were in an assertiveness-training group, the trainer (leader) or another member might play the role of your instructor. You could then say to this person the things you want to say to your instructor. If you had trouble behaving assertively, the trainer or another member could model an assertive style, and you could then practice again. You could also switch roles, first playing the instructor and then playing the student. You'd then get feedback on how you come across. If you were presenting yourself in a harsh manner, for example, this could be pointed out to you. With the help of this feedback, you could then change the ways in which you express yourself.

Assertive behavior is practiced first in the role-playing situation, then in real-life situations. If applying assertive behavior in real life is too threatening, you can create an imaginary situation and practice it there first. For example, suppose that you'd like to speak out more in class. However, week after week goes by, and you still find yourself sitting quietly, wanting to say what you think but feeling paralyzed. You might think to yourself: "What I've got to say isn't important," or "Others can say it better than I can," or "Who am I to have a conviction?" You might fear that you'd sound stupid or that the instructor would criticize you. To change this nonassertive behavior, you could begin by relaxing. Then you could imagine yourself in the classroom situation and go through all the motions of participating. Next, you might begin in small ways to apply your new behavior in your classes. For example, you could make a contract to ask at least two questions during each class session. Or, if you fear talking with your instructor, you could decide to approach him or her after class, even if only for a minute. Gradually, you could take on more demanding tasks as you build confidence in your ability to express yourself.

Since most of us can benefit from assertiveness training, I recommend that you select one of the popular books listed in the "Suggested Readings" for this chapter and that you begin to apply these principles to your participation in this class. You can also apply the concepts I've discussed to other areas of your life, particularly at work and in close personal relationships.

Self-Actualization: A Model for Personal Growth

The focus of this chapter has been on pathways to personal growth. *I Never Knew I Had a Choice* is based on a humanistic view of people. A central concept of this approach to personal growth is that of *self-actualization*. It is best to consider self-actualization as a continual process, not a fixed state at which we can say that we've "arrived." Thus, it is more accurate to speak of a *self-actualizing* person rather than a *self-actualized* one.

Striving for self-actualization means working toward becoming all that we are capable of becoming. While humanistic psychology is based on the premise that we have such a "growth urge," you should not think that this is an automatic process. Since we realize that growth can be painful, we experience a constant struggle between our desire for security or dependence and our desire to experience the delights and pains of growth.

Self-actualization was a central theme in the work of Abraham Maslow (1968, 1970, 1971). Maslow used the phrase "the psychopathology of the average" to highlight his contention that merely "normal" people may never extend themselves to become what they are capable of becoming. Further, he criticized the Freudian orientation for its preoccupation with the sick and crippled side of human nature; if we base our findings on a sick population, Maslow reasoned, we will have a sick psychology. Thus, he believed that too much research is conducted into anxiety, hostility, and neuroses and too little into what we might become and to joy, creativity, and self-fulfillment.

In his quest to create a humanistic psychology that would focus on our potential as human beings, Maslow studied what he believed were self-actualizing people and found that they differed in important ways from so-called "normals." Some of the characteristics that Maslow found in these people were a capacity to tolerate and even welcome uncertainty in their lives, an acceptance of themselves and others, spontaneity and creativity, a need for privacy and solitude, autonomy, a capacity for deep and intense interpersonal relationships, a genuine caring for others, a sense of humor, an inner-directedness (as opposed to the tendency to live by others' expectations), and the absence of artificial dichotomies within themselves (such as work/play, love/hate, weak/strong).

Carl Rogers (1961, 1980), a major figure in the development of humanistic psychology, has built his entire theory and practice of psychotherapy on the concept of the "fully functioning person," which is much like Maslow's notion of the "self-actualizing" person. According to Rogers, most people ask basic questions such as: Who am I? How can I discover my real self? How can I become what I deeply wish to become? How can I get behind my facades and become myself? Rogers found that, when people give up their facades and accept themselves, they move in the direction of being open to experience (that is, they begin to see reality without distorting it), they trust themselves and look to themselves for the answers to their problems, and they no longer attempt to become

fixed entities or products, realizing instead that growth is a continual process. Such people, Rogers writes, are in a fluid process of challenging and revising their perceptions and beliefs as they open themselves to new experiences.

In contrast to those students of human behavior who assume that we are by nature irrational and destructive of ourselves and others unless we are socialized, Rogers exhibits a deep faith in human beings. He sees people as naturally social and forward-moving, as striving to become fully functioning, and as having at their deepest core a positive goodness. In short, people are to be trusted; and, as they are basically cooperative and constructive, there is no need to control their aggressive impulses.

We can summarize some of the basic ideas of the humanistic approach by means of Maslow's model of the self-actualizing person. Maslow describes self-actualization in his book *Motivation and Personality* (1970), and he also treats the concept in his other books (1968, 1971). The following section summarizes Maslow's view of the characteristics of self-actualizing people.

Overview of Maslow's Theory

Self-awareness.   Self-actualizing people are more aware of themselves, of others, and of reality than are nonactualizing people. Specifically, they demonstrate the following behavior and traits:

1. *Efficient perception of reality:*
   Self-actualizing people see reality as it is.
   They have an ability to detect phoniness.
   They avoid seeing things in preconceived categories.
2. *Ethical awareness:*
   Self-actualizing people display a knowledge of what is right and wrong for them.
   They have a sense of inner direction.
   They avoid being pressured by others and living by others' standards.
3. *Freshness of appreciation:*
   Like children, self-actualizing people have an ability to perceive life in a fresh way.
4. *Peak moments:*
   Self-actualizing people experience times of being one with the universe; they experience moments of joy.
   They have the ability to be changed by such moments.

Freedom.   Self-actualizing people are willing to make choices for themselves, and they are free to be and to express their potentials. This freedom entails a sense of detachment and a need for privacy, a creativity and spontaneity, and an ability to accept responsibility for choices.

1. *Detachment:*
   For self-actualizing people, the need for privacy is crucial.
   They have a need for solitude, to put things in perspective.
   They have an ability to be objective—to accept life as it is.
2. *Creativity:*
   Creativity is a universal characteristic of self-actualizing people.
   Creativity may be in any area of life; it shows itself as inventiveness.
3. *Spontaneity:*
   Self-actualizing people don't need to show off.

They display a naturalness and lack of pretentiousness.
They act with ease and grace.

Basic honesty and caring. Self-actualizing people show a deep caring and honesty with themselves and with others. These qualities are reflected in their interest in humankind and in their interpersonal relationships.

1. *Sense of social interest:*
   Self-actualizing people have a concern for the welfare of others.
   They have a sense of communality with all other people.
   They have an interest in bettering the world.
2. *Interpersonal relationships:*
   Self-actualizing people have a capacity for real love and fusion with another.
   They are able to love and respect themselves.
   They are able to go outside themselves in a mature love.
   They are motivated by the urge to grow in their relationships.
3. *Sense of humor:*
   Self-actualizing people can laugh at themselves.
   They can laugh at the human condition.
   Their humor is not hostile.

Trust and autonomy. Self-actualizing people exhibit faith in themselves and others; they are independent; they accept themselves as valuable persons; and their lives have meaning.

1. *Search for purpose and meaning:*
   Self-actualizing people have a sense of mission, of a calling in which their potential can be fulfilled.
   They are engaged in a search for identity, often through work that is a deeply significant part of their lives.
2. *Autonomy and independence:*
   Self-actualizing people have the ability to be independent.
   They resist blind conformity.
   They are not tradition-bound in making decisions.
3. *Acceptance of self and others:*
   Self-actualizing people avoid fighting reality.
   They accept nature as it is.
   They are comfortable with the world.[3]

[3] Adapted from *Motivation and Personality*, by A. H. Maslow. Copyright © 1970 by Harper & Row, Publishers, Inc. Used by permission.

How do we achieve self-actualization? There is no set of techniques for achieving this goal, but in a sense the rest of this book, including the activities and Time Out sections, is about ways of beginning this lifelong quest. As you read about the struggles we face in trying to become all we are capable of becoming, I hope you will begin to see some options for living a fuller life.

Time Out for Personal Reflection

To what degree do you have a healthy and positive view of yourself? Are you able to appreciate yourself, or do you discount your own worth? Take this self-inventory by rating yourself with the following code: 1 = this statement is true of me most *of the time; 2 = this statement is true of me* some *of the time; 3 = this statement is true of me* very rarely.

_____ 1. *I generally think and choose for myself.*

_____ 2. *I usually like the person that I am.*

_____ 3. *I know what I want.*

_____ 4. *I am able to ask for what I want.*

_____ 5. *I feel a sense of personal power.*

_____ 6. *I am open to change.*

_____ 7. *I feel equal to others.*

_____ 8. *I am sensitive to the needs of others.*

_____ 9. *I care about others.*

_____ 10. *I can act in accordance with my own judgment without feeling guilty if others disapprove of me.*

_____ 11. *I do not expect others to make me feel alive.*

_____ 12. *I can accept responsibility for my own actions.*

_____ 13. *I am able to accept compliments.*

_____ 14. *I can give affection.*

_____ 15. *I can receive affection.*

_____ 16. *I do not live by a long list of "shoulds," "oughts," and "musts."*

_____ 17. *I am not so security-bound that I will not explore new things.*

_____ 18. *I am generally accepted by others.*

_____ 19. *I can give myself credit for what I do well.*

_____ 20. *I am able to enjoy my own company.*

_____ 21. *I am capable of forming intimate and meaningful relationships.*

_____ 22. *I live in the here and now and do not get stuck in dwelling on the past or the future.*

_____ 23. *I feel a sense of significance.*

_____ *24. I am not diminished when I am with those I respect.*
_____ *25. I believe in my ability to succeed in projects that are meaningful to me.*

Now go back over this inventory and identify not more than five areas that keep you from being as self-accepting as you might be. What can you do to increase your awareness of situations in which you do not fully accept yourself? For example, if you have trouble giving yourself credit for things you do well, how can you become aware of times when you discount yourself? When you do become conscious of situations in which you put yourself down, think of alternatives.

Chapter Summary

My central purpose in this chapter has been to highlight some of the psychological approaches to personality and to describe some of the techniques for personal growth based on these theories. I have not attempted a systematic treatment of the differing views. Rather, I've stressed those concepts and techniques that I find most useful in my practice as a counseling psychologist.

This chapter discussed some of the major tasks that are to be accomplished in the struggle to become an autonomous and self-actualizing person. The focus was on barriers that typically obstruct our psychological growth and on practical methods of removing these barriers.

Activities and Exercises

1. In your journal, write an account of the first five years of your life. Although you may think that you can't remember much about this time, the following guidelines should help in your recall.
   a. Write down a few key questions that you would like answered about your early years.
   b. Seek out your relatives, and ask them some of these questions.
   c. Collect any reminders of your early years, particularly pictures.
   d. If possible, visit the place or places where you lived and went to school.
2. Rewrite your past the way you *wish* it had been. Think of the things you wanted (and allow yourself to have them in fantasy), and remember situations that you wish had been different. After you reconstruct

your past the way you'd like it to have been, write a brief account of how you think your life would be different today if you had experienced *that* past instead of your real one.

3. Choose from among the many exercises in this chapter any that you'd be willing to integrate into a self-help program during your time in this course. What things are you willing to do to bring about some of the changes you want in your life?

4. Summarize the main injunctions you received as a child. Bring your list to class, and in a small group explore the injunctions that have had the *greatest* impact on you. What are the circumstances surrounding these injunctions? In what ways have you helped to keep these injunctions alive through a self-indoctrination process? How do you think they have negatively influenced your self-concept? Elect a recorder in your group to summarize the most commonly mentioned injunctions and their effects.

5. Pictures often say more about you than words. What do your pictures tell about you? Look through any pictures of yourself as a child and as an adolescent, and see if there are any themes. What do most of your pictures reveal about the way you felt about yourself? Bring some of these pictures to class. Have other members look at them and tell you what they think you were like then. Pictures can also be used to tap forgotten memories.

6. Look over the common irrational beliefs as outlined by Albert Ellis. In a small group, discuss some of your own irrational beliefs. For example, do you tell yourself that you need to be approved of by everyone, and that it will be terrible if someone disapproves of you? Do you have an unrealistic standard of being perfect? When you fail at something or make a mistake, do you feel like a failure as a person? Bring a few of these beliefs to class and discuss how they affect you in your everyday life.

7. Again in small groups, each member can be given an opportunity to review events that happened, beliefs attached to these events, and feelings associated with the events. Use Ellis's A-B-C model of personality. For example, assume that a friend breaks off a relationship with you. As a result, you *feel* hurt and rejected, and you begin to think that something is wrong with you. What are some of the self-statements that you make? How does your interpretation of this event contribute to your feelings of rejection? What are some new sentences that you can say to yourself?

8. Review the section on behavioral technique in which I describe a model for self-directed changes. Think of a specific behavior you would like to change and apply these steps to yourself. Be sure to keep observational records in your journal. After looking over a week's records, decide on a plan for action, and then keep track of your progress.

Suggested Readings

Alberti, R. E., & Emmons, M. L. *Stand Up, Speak Out, Talk Back.* New York: Pocket Books, 1975. A popularized version of guidelines for assertion training, with many examples of assertive and nonassertive behavior as applied to daily life.

Alberti, R. E., & Emmons, M. L. *Your Perfect Right: A Guide to Assertive Behavior* (3rd ed.). San Luis Obispo, Calif.: Impact, 1978. This is my recommendation for those who want a single book on the principles and techniques of assertion training.

Berne, E. *What Do You Say After You Say Hello?* New York: Bantam, 1975. Based on Transactional Analysis, this book demonstrates how we learn certain scripts that determine our present behavior and how we can change them.

Corey, G. *Theory and Practice of Group Counseling.* Monterey, Calif.: Brooks/Cole, 1981. This text gives an overview of 11 contemporary therapeutic approaches and focuses on the application of key concepts to the practice of group counseling and therapy.

Corey, G. *Theory and Practice of Counseling and Psychotherapy* (2nd ed.). Monterey, Calif.: Brooks/Cole, 1982. An overview of counseling theories and techniques. The book has chapters on the psychoanalytic, existential, rational-emotive, Gestalt, Transactional Analysis, and behavioral approaches.

Ellis, A. *Humanistic Psychotherapy: The Rational-Emotive Approach.* New York: McGraw-Hill, 1973. This book presents in a clear, straightforward manner the basic concepts of RET that can be applied to personal growth.

Ellis, A., & Grieger, R. *Handbook of Rational-Emotive Therapy.* New York: Springer, 1977. This is one of the better books on RET that discusses its theoretical and applied aspects.

Ellis, A., & Harper, R. A. *A New Guide to Rational Living.* Englewood Cliffs, N.J.: Prentice-Hall, 1975. An easy-to-read self-help book that presents a clear approach to RET, based on homework assignments and self-questioning.

Ellis, A., & Whiteley, J. M. (Eds.). *Theoretical and Empirical Foundations of Rational-Emotive Therapy.* Monterey, Calif.: Brooks/Cole, 1979. This is a comprehensive and technical treatment of the theoretical and practical aspects of RET.

Fensterheim, H., & Baer, J. *Don't Say Yes When You Want to Say No.* New York: Dell, 1975. A practical guide to learning to assert your rights in work, marriage, sexual relationships, social relationships, and family life.

Gould, R. L. *Transformations: Growth and Change in Adult Life.* New York: Simon & Schuster (Touchstone Book), 1978. Covering the entire life span, this book discusses the major tasks in achieving autonomy.

Goulding, M., & Goulding, R. *Changing Lives through Redecision Therapy.* New York: Brunner/Mazel, 1979. An excellent presentation of the major concepts of TA, this text deals in depth with concepts such as injunctions, early decisions, and redecisions.

Goulding, R., & Goulding, M. *The Power Is in the Patient.* San Francisco: TA Press, 1978. A collection of essays on personal growth from a TA perspective.

Hall, C. *A Primer of Freudian Psychology.* New York: New American Library (Mentor), 1973. This is a very useful, concise, and clear overview of the major concepts of the Freudian psychoanalytic theory of personality.

James, M., & Jongeward, D. *Born to Win: Transactional Analysis with Gestalt Experiments.* Reading, Mass.: Addison-Wesley, 1971. This is a readable guide to combining Gestalt exercises with TA concepts for the goal of personal growth. Topics include scripts, games, early decisions, injunctions, and autonomy.

Maslow, A. *Toward a Psychology of Being* (2nd ed.). New York: Van Nostrand Reinhold, 1968. A classic in humanistic psychology, this book deals with values, growth and motivation, creativity, and the self-actualizing person.

Maslow, A. *Motivation and Personality* (2nd ed.). New York: Harper & Row, 1970. Maslow describes his findings as they relate to the characteristics of self-actualizing people.

Maslow, A. *The Farther Reaches of Human Nature.* New York: Viking, 1971. This is a good overview of Maslow's ideas on self-actualization, values, society, creativity, education, and psychology.

Nye, R. D. *Three Psychologies: Perspectives from Freud, Skinner, and Rogers* (2nd ed.). Monterey, Calif.: Brooks/Cole, 1981. An excellent and concise overview of major systems in psychological thought, with the focus on comparisons and contrasts among psychoanalysis, behaviorism, and humanism.

Perls, F. *Gestalt Therapy Verbatim.* Moab, Utah: Real People Press, 1969. This is a useful book to get a flavor of Gestalt concepts and a first-hand account of the style in which Perls worked.

Rainwater, J. *You're in Charge: A Guide to Becoming Your Own Therapist.* Los Angeles: Guild of Tutors Press, 1979. This is an excellent self-help book based on principles and techniques of Gestalt therapy. The author suggests exercises to increase self-awareness. She has useful ideas for keeping a journal, the uses of autobiography, working with dreams, the constructive use of fantasy, and the art of living in the here and now.

Rogers, C. *On Becoming a Person*. Boston: Houghton Mifflin, 1961. Rogers applies his ideas to the process of psychotherapy, to family life, and to living a full life.

Rogers, C. *A Way of Being*. Palo Alto, Calif.: Houghton Mifflin, 1980. A collection of the author's articles that deal with a range of topics.

Schultz, D. *Growth Psychology: Models of the Healthy Personality*. New York: D. Van Nostrand, 1977. This is a useful source for readers who are interested in a fuller discussion of Rogers' model of the fully functioning person and Maslow's model of the self-actualizing person. In addition, the book deals with the characteristics of the healthy personality from the theoretical perspectives of Gordon Allport, Erich Fromm, Carl Jung, Viktor Frankl, and Fritz Perls.

Schultz, D. *Theories of Personality* (2nd ed.). Monterey, Calif.: Brooks/Cole, 1981. Schultz gives a clear presentation of the key concepts of a range of contemporary theories of personality.

Sheehy, G. *Passages: Predictable Crises of Adult Life*. New York: Dutton, 1976. From a life-span perspective, this is an interesting account of the crises at each stage of development.

Smith, M. *When I Say No, I Feel Guilty*. New York: Bantam, 1975. An easy-to-read, practical guide that can be applied in a personal way to situations requiring assertive skills.

Steiner, C. *Scripts People Live: Transactional Analysis of Life Scripts*. New York: Bantam, 1975. One of the best accounts of life scripts is given in this interesting and useful book.

Watson, D. L., & Tharp, R. G. *Self-Directed Behavior: Self-Modification for Personal Adjustment* (3rd ed.). Monterey, Calif.: Brooks/Cole, 1981. Based on behavioral principles, this book is aimed at assisting readers to achieve more self-determination and control over their lives.

Williams, R., & Long, J. *Toward a Self-Managed Life Style* (2nd ed.). Boston: Houghton Mifflin, 1979. A useful and easy-to-read book that presents a model for self-control methods in such diverse areas as weight control, smoking and drinking control, study skills, career planning, personal problems, and interpersonal relationships. It applies behavioral principles to changing everyday behavior.

Chapter Three

Personality Development: Stages in the Struggle for Autonomy

Prechapter Self-Inventory

For each statement, indicate the response that most closely identifies your beliefs and attitudes. Use this code: 5 = I *strongly agree* with this statement; 4 = I *agree* in most respects; 3 = I am *undecided;* 2 = I *disagree* in most respects; 1 = I *strongly disagree.*

_____ 1. I hold most of the same values, attitudes, and beliefs that my parents hold.

_____ 2. I'm capable of looking at my past decisions and then making new decisions that will significantly change the course of my life.

_____ 3. "Shoulds" and "oughts" often get in the way of my living my life the way I want.

_____ 4. I'm an independent person more than I'm a dependent one.

_____ 5. To a large degree, I've been shaped by the events of my childhood and adolescent years.

_____ 6. Struggles and crises are necessary for personal growth.

_____ 7. When I think of my early childhood years, I remember feeling secure, accepted, and loved.

_____ 8. I have trouble recognizing and expressing "negative" feelings, such as rage, anger, hatred, jealousy, and aggression.

_____ 9. I had desirable models to pattern my behavior after when I was a child and an adolescent.

_____ 10. In looking back at my early school-age years, I think that I had a positive self-concept and that I experienced more successes than failures.

_____ 11. I went through a stage of rebellion during my adolescent years.

_____ 12. My adolescent years were lonely ones.

_____ 13. For the most part, the life choices we make during our early adult years are irrevocable.

_____ 14. I remember being significantly influenced by peer-group pressure during my adolescent and early adult years.

_____ 15. Most people experience a crisis as they approach middle age.

_____ 16. The older we get, the more restricted our choices become.

_____ 17. I have fears of aging.

_____ 18. Most old people don't have much to live for.

_____ 19. If I've successfully mastered life's basic problems through middle age, I'll feel productive during the later years of my life.

_____ 20. I expect to experience a meaningful and rich life when I reach old age.

Here are a few suggestions for using this self-inventory:

· Retake the inventory after reading the chapter and again at the end of the course, and compare your answers.
· Have someone who knows you well take the inventory for you, giving the responses he or she thinks actually describe you. Then you can discuss any discrepancies between your sets of responses.
· In your class, compare your responses with those of the other class members, and discuss the similarities and differences between your attitudes and theirs.

Introduction

This chapter lays the groundwork for much of the rest of the book by focusing on our lifelong struggle to achieve psychological emancipation and autonomy. The achievement of personal autonomy is a continuing process, not something we arrive at once and for all. Indeed, the central message throughout this book is that you must continually make choices concerning the kind of person you want to be and that the choices you make, or fail to make, determine the course and meaning of your life.

Our attitudes toward our bodies, sex, love, intimacy, work, loneliness, death and dying, and values—the themes I'll be discussing in the chapters to come—are largely shaped by our experiences and decisions during our early years. However, each period of life has its own challenges and meanings, and we continue to develop and change as we encounter new stages of life. Before going on to discuss these specific themes, therefore, I want to look at the developmental stages that make up a complete human life, from infancy through old age.

Stages of Personality Development: Introduction

In the previous chapter, I discussed the importance of gaining an awareness of early messages and decisions in developing a more independent personality. In this chapter, I describe the highlights and developmental tasks of the major stages of life. I encourage you to apply this discussion to your own life. As you read, it might be useful to construct a chart of the major events that have occurred in each of the stages of life you've experienced so far. Further suggestions for personal applications are given whenever appropriate.

My discussion of the stages of personality development incorporates elements from Erik Erikson's view, as well as from Freudian theory and humanistic psychology. Although he was intellectually indebted to Freud, Erikson suggested that we should view human development in a more positive light, emphasizing health and growth. In *Childhood and Society*, Erikson (1964) extended Freud's notion of psychosexual stages of development by defining some of the social "tasks" of each stage. According to this theory, *psychosexual* and *psychosocial* growth occur in parallel fashion; in each stage of life, we face the task of establishing a new equilibrium between ourselves and our social world.

Erikson described human development over the entire life span in terms of eight stages, each marked by a particular crisis to be resolved. When you think of the word *crisis,* you may think of a gigantic problem or catastrophic happening, and then it might seem that Erikson's view has little to do with you. But for Erikson, *crisis* means a *turning point* in life, a moment of transition characterized by the potential to either go forward or go backward in development. At these critical points along our developmental path, we either achieve growth through successful resolution of our conflicts or fail to resolve our conflicts, with the result that we encounter difficulties in later stages. In large part, our futures are shaped by the decisions we make at each of these turning points in life.

In *Passages,* Gail Sheehy (1976) describes some predictable crises of adult life. For Sheehy, these crises are *passages* to new stages of life. She assumes that, to become autonomous and authentic persons, we must be willing to face squarely the struggles posed during life; otherwise, we allow others to define who we are.

In addition to the writers I've mentioned, I've also borrowed some ideas from Berne (1975), Steiner (1975), Gould (1978), and Havighurst (1972). And I've blended many of their concepts with the humanistic view by focusing on the choices open to us in each stage of life. Using Erikson's eight stages as a framework for my discussion, I'll focus on the issue of choice and provide examples that illustrate this theme. According to Erikson, the stages of development and the central issues we face in each stage are:

1. infancy: trust versus mistrust
2. early childhood: autonomy versus shame and doubt
3. preschool age: initiative versus guilt

ERIKSON'S 8 CRITICAL STAGES OF LIFELONG DEVELOPMENT.

4. school age: industry versus inferiority
5. adolescence: identity versus identity diffusion
6. young adulthood: intimacy versus isolation
7. middle age: generativity versus self-absorption or stagnation
8. later life: integrity versus despair

Infancy: Trust versus Mistrust

From birth to age 2, a child's basic task is to develop a sense of trust in self, others, and the environment. Infants need to count on others; they need to sense that they are cared for and loved and that the world is a secure place. They learn this sense of trust by being held, caressed, and taken care of.

Erikson contends that infants form a basic conception of the social world. If the significant other persons in an infant's life provide the needed warmth, cuddling, and attention, the child develops a sense of trust. When these conditions are *not* present, the child becomes suspicious about interacting with others and acquires a general sense of mistrust toward human relationships. Although neither orientation is fixed to one's personality for life, it is clear that well-nurtured infants are in a more favorable position with respect to future personal growth than are their more neglected peers.

A sense of being loved is also the best safeguard against fear, insecurity, and inadequacy. Children who receive love from parents or parental substitutes generally have little difficulty accepting themselves, while children who feel unloved and unwanted may find it very hard to accept themselves. In addition, rejected children learn to mistrust the world and to view it primarily in terms of its ability to do them harm. Some of the effects of rejection in infancy include tendencies in later childhood to be fearful, insecure, jealous, aggressive, hostile, and isolated.

According to the Freudian view, the events of the first year of life are extremely important for later development and adjustment. Infants who do not get the basic nurturing needs met during this time (known as the *oral stage*) may develop greediness and acquisitiveness in later life. Material things thus become substitutes for what the children really want—love and attention from parents. For instance, a person whose oral needs are unmet may become a compulsive eater, in which case food becomes a symbol for love. Other personality problems that might stem from this period include a mistrustful and suspicious view of the world, a tendency to reject affection from others, an inability to form intimate relationships, a fear of loving and trusting, and feelings of isolation.

The case of 9-year-old Joey, the "mechanical boy" described by Bettelheim (1967) in *The Empty Fortress*, is a dramatic illustration of how the pain of extreme rejection during infancy can affect us later on. When Joey first went to Bettelheim's school, he seemed devoid of any feeling. He thought of himself as functioning by remote control, with the help of an elaborate system of machines. He had to have his "carburetor" to breathe, "exhaust pipes" to exhale from, and a complex system of wires and motors in order to move. His delusion was so convincing that the staff members at the school sometimes found themselves taking care to be sure that Joey was plugged in properly and that they didn't step on any of his wires.

Neither Joey's father nor his mother had been prepared for his birth, and they had related to him as a thing, not a person. His mother simply ignored him; she reported that she had no feeling of dislike toward Joey but that "I simply did not want to take care of him." He was a difficult baby who cried most of the time, and he was kept on a rigid schedule. He wasn't touched unless necessary, and he wasn't cuddled or played with. Joey developed more and more unusual symptoms, such as head banging, rocking, and a morbid fascination with machines. Evidently, Joey discovered that machines were better than people; they didn't hurt you, and they could be shut off. During years of intense treatment with Bettelheim, Joey gradually learned how to trust, and he also learned that feelings are real and that it can be worth it to feel.

Another case that illustrates the possible effects of severe deprivation during the early developmental years is that of Sally, who is now in her early forties. Sally was given up by her natural parents and spent the first decade of her life in orphanages and foster homes. She recalls pleading with one set of foster parents who had kept her for over a year and then said that they had to send her away. As a child, Sally came to the conclusion that she was at fault; if her own parents didn't want her, who could? She spent years trying to figure out what she had done wrong and why so many people always "sent her away."

As an adult, Sally still yearns for what she missed during infancy and childhood. Thus, she has never really attained maturity; socially and emotionally, she is much like a child. Sally has never allowed herself to get close to anyone, for she fears that they will leave if she does. As a child, she learned to isolate herself emotionally in order to survive; now, even though she is 42, she still operates on the assumptions that she had as a child. Because of her fear of being deserted, she won't allow herself to venture out and take even minimal risks.

Sally is not unusual. I have worked with a number of women and men who suffer from the effects of early psychological deprivation, and I have observed that, in most cases, such deprivation has lingering adverse effects on a person's ability to form meaningful relationships later in life. Many people I encounter—of all ages—struggle with the issue of trusting others in a loving relationship. They are unable to trust that another can or will love them, they fear being rejected, and they fear even more the possibility of closeness and being accepted and loved. Many of these people don't trust themselves or others sufficiently to make themselves vulnerable enough to experience love.

At this point, you might pause to ask yourself these questions:

· Am I able to trust others? Myself?
· Am I willing to open myself—to make myself known to a few selected people in my life?

· Do I basically accept myself as being OK, or do I seek confirmation outside of myself? Am I hungry for approval from others? How far will I go in my attempt to be liked? Do I need to be liked and approved of by everyone? Do I dare make enemies, or must I be "nice" to everyone?

Early Childhood: Autonomy versus Shame and Doubt

Freud called ages 2 and 3 the *anal stage*. The tasks children must master at this time include learning independence, accepting personal power, and learning skills to cope with negative feelings such as rage and aggression. Their most critical task is to begin the journey toward autonomy by progressing from being taken care of by others to being able to care for their own physical needs.

In this second stage, children take their first steps toward becoming self-supporting. They assume a more active role in taking care of their own needs, and they begin to communicate what they want from others. During this time, children also face continual parental demands. For instance, they are restricted from physically exploring their environment, they begin to be disciplined, and they have toilet training imposed on them. According to the Freudian view, parental feelings and attitudes associated with toilet training are highly significant for their children's later personality development. Thus, problems in adulthood such as compulsive orderliness or messiness may be due to parental attitudes during this time. For instance, a father who insists that his son be unrealistically clean may find that the son develops into a sloppy person as a reaction against overly strict training—or that he becomes even more compulsively clean.

Erikson identifies this period as the time for developing a sense of autonomy. Children who fail to master the task of establishing some control over themselves and coping with the world around them develop a sense of shame and feelings of doubt about their capabilities. Erikson emphasizes that during this time children become aware of their emerging skills and have a drive to try them out. Parents who do too much for their children hamper their proper development. They are saying, however indirectly, "Let us do this for you, because you're too clumsy, too slow, or too incapable of doing things for yourself." Young children need to experiment; they need to be allowed to make mistakes and still feel that they are basically worthwhile. If parents insist on keeping their children dependent on them, the children will begin to doubt the value of their own abilities. If parents don't appreciate their children's efforts, the children may feel ashamed of themselves.

Young children also must learn to accept their "negative" feelings. They will surely experience rage, hatred, hostility, destructiveness, and ambivalence, and they need to feel that such feelings are permissible and that they aren't evil for having them. Of course, they also need to learn how to express their feelings in constructive ways.

In many ways, then, early childhood is a time when we struggle between a sense of self-reliance and a sense of self-doubt. Many people I work with in counseling seek professional help precisely because they have a low level of autonomy. They doubt their ability to stand alone, so they depend on others to do for them things they could do for themselves. This applies particularly to some marriages; some people marry so that they will have a mother figure or a father figure to protect them and take care of their needs. Similarly, many of us have grave difficulty in recognizing our negative feelings, even when they are fully justified. We swallow our anger and rationalize away other feelings, because we learned when we were 2 or 3 years old that we were unacceptable when we had such feelings. As children, we might have shouted at our parents: "I hate you! I never want to see you again!" Then we may have heard an equally enraged parent reply: "How dare you say such a thing—after all I've done for you! I don't ever want to hear that from you again!" We soon take these messages to mean: "Don't be angry! Never hate those you love! Keep control of yourself!" And we do just that—keeping many of our feelings to ourselves, stuffing them in the pits of our stomachs and pretending we didn't experience them. Is it any wonder that so many of us suffer from migraine headaches, peptic ulcers, hypertension, or heart disease?

Again, take time out to reflect in a personal way on some of your current struggles in the area of autonomy and self-worth. You might ask yourself:

· Am I able to recognize my own feelings, particularly if they are "unacceptable" to others? How do I express my anger to those I love? Can I tolerate the ambivalence of feeling love and hate toward the same person?

· Do I take care of myself, or do I lean on others to support me? Do I keep myself a psychological cripple by encouraging others to do for me what I can do for myself?

· How assertive am I? Do I let others know what I want, without becoming aggressive? Or do I let myself be manipulated and pushed by others?

Preschool Age: *Initiative versus Guilt*

The preschool years (ages 4 to 6) are characterized by play and by anticipation of roles. During this time, children seek to find out how much they can do. They imitate others; they begin to develop a sense of right and wrong; they widen their circle of significant other persons; they take more initiative; they learn to give and receive love and affection; they identify with their own sex; they begin to learn more complex social skills; they learn basic attitudes regarding sexuality; and they increase their capacity to understand and use language.

According to Erikson, the basic task of the preschool years is to establish a sense of *competence* and *initiative*. Preschool children begin to initiate many of their own activities as they become physically and psychologically ready to engage in pursuits of their own choosing. If they are allowed realistic freedom to choose their own activities and to make some of their own decisions, they tend to develop a positive orientation characterized by confidence in their ability to initiate and follow through. On the other hand, if they are unduly restricted, or if their choices are ridiculed, they tend to experience a sense of guilt and ultimately to withdraw from taking an active and initiating stance.

In Freudian theory, this is the *phallic stage*, during which children become increasingly interested in sexual matters and begin to acquire a clearer sense of sex-role identity. Preschool children begin to pay attention to their genitals and experience pleasure from genital stimulation. They typically engage in both masturbatory and sex-play activities. They begin to show considerable curiosity about the differences between the sexes and the differences between adults and children. This is the time for questions such as "Where do babies come from?" and "Why are boys and girls different?" Parental attitudes toward these questions, which can be communicated nonverbally as well as verbally, are critical in helping children form a positive attitude toward their own sexuality. Since this is a time of conscience formation, one danger is that parents may instill rigid and unrealistic moral standards, which can lead to an overdeveloped conscience. Children who learn that their bodies and their impulses are evil soon begin to feel guilty about their natural impulses and feelings. Carried into adult life, these attitudes can prevent people from appreciating and enjoying sexual intimacy. Another danger is that strict parental indoctrination, which can be accomplished in subtle, nonverbal ways, will lead to an infantile conscience. Children may thus develop a fear of questioning and thinking for themselves, instead blindly accepting the dictates of their parents. Other effects of such indoctrination include rigidity, severe conflicts, guilt, remorse, and self-condemnation.

To accept their sexual feelings as natural and to develop a healthy concept of their bodies and their sex-role identities, children need adequate models. In addition to forming attitudes toward their bodies and sexuality, they begin to formulate their conceptions of what it means to be feminine or masculine. By simply being with their parents, they are getting some perspective on the way men and women relate with one another, and they are acquiring basic attitudes toward such relationships. They are also deciding how they feel about themselves in their roles as boys and girls.

Our learnings and decisions during the phallic stage pave the way for our ability to accept ourselves as men or women in adulthood. Many people seek counseling because of problems they experience in regard to their sexual identities. Some men are very confused about what it means to be a man in this society. Some are stuck in a stereotype of the masculine role, which for them means never being tender or passionate, never feeling intensely (*thinking* their way through life instead), never crying, and, above all, *always* being "strong." Because they fear that they might not be manly enough, these men often have a desperate drive to succeed financially or to prove their "manhood," or else they measure themselves against some yardstick of what they think constitutes the normal male. On the other side, there are some biological men who have tried to convince themselves and others that there are simply no differences between themselves and women. Some of these men resist doing anything that might be labeled "masculine," and they hold up as ideal the concept of unisex. And there are men who look to consciousness-raising groups to tell them how they should behave as men.

Of course, such problems are not limited to men. Many women seek some form of therapy because of a sex-role identity crisis. There are women who have submerged their identities totally in the roles of mother and housewife, because they feel they have no other choice. Others, who want to be wives and mothers, have become aware that they also want something more. Unfortunately, some women have identified themselves completely with some type of women's movement, to the point of losing any independent, unique sense of what it means to be a woman. I don't mean to suggest that consciousness-raising groups for both women and men cannot be useful, but I do believe that some people can use a "movement" to find answers outside of themselves, instead of struggling and deciding on their own direction.

Again, pause and reflect on some of your own current struggles with these issues.

- Do you have a clear picture of who you are as a woman (man)? What are your standards of femininity (masculinity)? Where did you get them?
- Are you comfortable with your own sexuality? With your body? With giving and receiving sensual and sexual pleasure? Are there any unresolved conflicts from your childhood that get in the way of your enjoyment? Do your present behavior and current conflicts indicate areas of unfinished business?

Summary of the First Six Years of Life

In describing the events of the first six years of life, I have relied rather heavily on the psychoanalytic view of psychosexual and psychosocial development, as originally formulated by Freud and later extended and modified by Erikson. This approach emphasizes the critical nature of the early developmental years in the formation of our personalities. In my work with clients in individual counseling and with relatively well-functioning people in therapeutic groups, I have come to see these early years as a strong influence on our levels of integration and functioning as adults.

When I think of the most typical problems and conflicts I encounter in my counseling work and in my college classes, the following areas come to mind: inability to trust oneself and others; inability to freely accept and give love; difficulty in recognizing and expressing negative feelings; guilt over feelings of anger or hatred toward those one loves; inability or unwillingness to control one's own life; difficulties in fully accepting one's sexuality or in finding meaning in sexual intimacy; difficulty in accepting oneself as a woman or a man; and problems concerning a lack of meaning or purpose in life or a clear sense of personal identity and aspirations. Notice that most of these adult problems are directly related to the turning points and tasks of the early developmental years. I don't think the effects of early learning are irreversible in most cases, but these experiences, whether favorable or unfavorable, clearly influence how we relate to future critical periods in our lives.

If you still wonder about the extent to which normal children really experience the crises I've described, I suggest reading Dorothy Baruch's very moving book, *One Little Boy* (1964). Baruch vividly describes the evolution of a boy named Ken through play therapy, and she makes a strong case that his feelings are typical of most children. In her work with Ken, she drew on a psychoanalytic perspective and had him relive many of the unresolved conflicts of his early childhood. Almost immediately he crawled onto her lap and allowed himself to be loved and cared for. During the early stages of play therapy, Baruch created a climate in which he could freely give vent to all his feelings. As he felt increasingly safe, he began to express pent-up feelings of hostility and rage directed toward both his brother and his father. He built things of clay, and then he destroyed them. He took delight in making bombs and then "destroying" his father. Before his therapy, he had hardly been able to breathe because of severe asthma attacks. As he let go of many of the bottled-up feelings that he had been afraid to experience, he was able to breathe more freely, and many other crippling psychosomatic symptoms decreased.

Ken had developed many fears surrounding sexual matters, and during his play therapy he expressed in symbolic ways his guilt over masturbation, his castration anxiety, and his preoccupation with sex differences. Through the medium of play therapy, he was able to work through much of the unfinished business that presented so many problems in his later childhood. He grew to trust more; he became able to accept love and to express negative feelings without being destructive or feeling guilty; and he began to accept his sexual feelings as natural. He learned the difference between having feelings and acting out all of them. My students have gained a much deeper knowledge of the events of early childhood by reading *One Little Boy*, and almost all of them report that the book provided a rich and moving experience.

Another book that I highly recommend is Virginia Axline's *Dibs: In Search of Self* (1976). Most of my students say they are moved to tears as they read how Dibs struggles and finds himself in his play therapy. Although Axline used a client-centered approach in her play therapy (as opposed to Baruch's psychoanalytic approach), we see similar results as Dibs learns to trust and as he expresses his fears. I like the way Axline puts it:

> Dibs experienced profoundly the complex process of growing up, of reaching out for the precious gifts of life, of drenching himself in the sunshine of his hopes and in the rain of his sorrows. Slowly, tentatively, he discovered that the security of his world was not wholly outside of himself, but that the stabilizing center he searched for with such intensity was deep down inside that self [p. ix].

School Age: Industry versus Inferiority

During middle childhood (from age 6 to age 12), children face the following key developmental tasks: to engage in social tasks; to expand their knowledge and understanding of the physical and social worlds; to continue to learn and expand their concepts of an appropriate feminine or masculine role; to develop a sense of values; to learn new communication skills; to learn how to read, write, and calculate; to learn to give and take; to learn how to accept people who are culturally different; to learn to tolerate ambiguity; and to learn physical skills.

For Freudians, this period is the *latency stage*, characterized by a relative decline in sexual interests and the emergence of new interests, activities, and attitudes. With the events of the hectic phallic period behind them, children take a long breathing spell and consolidate their positions. Their attention turns to new fields, such as school, playmates, books, and other features of the real world. Their hostile reactions tend to diminish, and they begin to reach out for friendly relationships with others in the environment.

Erikson, however, disagrees with the Freudian view of this period as a time of latency and neutrality. He argues that the middle-childhood years present unique psychosocial demands that children must meet successfully if their development is to proceed. According to Erikson, the central task of this period is to achieve a sense of *industry;* failure to do so results in a sense of *inadequacy* and *inferiority*. The development of a sense of industry includes focusing on creating and producing and on attaining goals. Of course, starting school is a critical event of this time. Children who encounter failure during the early grades may experience severe handicaps later on. A child with early learning problems may begin to feel worthless as a person. Such a feeling may, in turn, drastically affect his or her relationships with peers, which are also vital at this time.

Helen's case illustrates some of the common conflicts of the elementary school years. When Helen started kindergarten—a bit too early—she was smaller than most of the other children. Although she had looked forward to beginning school and tried to succeed, for the most part she felt overwhelmed. She began to fail at many of the tasks her peers were enjoying and mastering. School-age children are in the process of developing their self-concepts, whether positive or negative, and Helen's view of her capacity to succeed was growing dimmer. Gradually, she began to avoid even simple tasks and to find many excuses to rationalize away her failures. She wanted to hide the fact that she was not keeping up with the other children. She was fearful of learning and trying new things, so she clung to secure, familiar ways. She grew increasingly afraid of making mistakes, for she believed that everything she did had to be perfect. If she did some art work, for instance, she would soon become frustrated and rip up the piece of paper because her picture wasn't coming out exactly as she wanted it to. Basically, Helen was afraid of putting her potential to the test, and she would generally freeze up when she had to be accountable for anything she produced. Her teachers' consistent evaluation of her was, "Helen is a sensitive child who needs a lot of encouragement and direction. She could do much more than she does, but she quits too soon, because she feels that what she does isn't good enough."

Helen grew to resent the fact that some of her teachers were not demanding much of her because they didn't want to push her. She then felt even more different from her peers, completing the vicious circle. Despite her will to try and her desire to succeed, she was prevented from venturing out by her fears of gambling and making mistakes. When she was in the third grade, she was at least a grade level behind in reading, despite the fact that she had repeated kindergarten. As she began to feel stupid and embarrassed because she couldn't read as well as the other children, she shied away from reading aloud. Eventually, she received instruction in remedial reading in a clinic, and this attention seemed to help. She was also given an intelligence test at the clinic, and the results were "low average." The reading staff and those who tested Helen were surprised, for they saw her as creative, insightful, and much brighter than the results showed. Again, Helen froze up when she felt that she had to perform on a test.

Helen's case indicates that the first few years of school can have a powerful impact on a child's life and future adjustment to school. Her school experiences colored her view of her self-worth and affected her relationships with other children. However, although her initial experiences were difficult ones, Helen was not doomed to a life of functioning below her real potential. With the concern of her teachers and parents, much was done to help her break out of this negative cycle.

Development of the Self-Concept

Your self-concept is essentially how you see yourself and how you feel about that self-perception. This picture of yourself includes your view of your worth, value, and possibilities. It includes the way you see yourself in relation to others, the way you'd ideally like to be, and the degree to which you accept yourself as you are. From age 6 to age 12, the view you have of yourself is influenced greatly by the quality of your school experiences, by contact with your peer group and with teachers, and by your interactions with your family.

To a large extent your self-concept is formed by what others tell you about yourself, especially during the formative years of childhood. Whether you develop a basically positive or negative outlook on yourself has a good deal to do with what significant people have expected of you.

This view of yourself has a significant impact on how you present yourself to others and how you act and feel when you are with others. For example, you may feel inadequate around authority figures. Perhaps you tell yourself that you have nothing to say or that whatever you might say would be stupid. Since you have this view of yourself, you behave in ways that persuade people to adopt your view of yourself. More often than not, others will see and respond to you in the way you "tell" them that you are. It is difficult for those who are close to you to treat you in a positive way when you consistently discount yourself. Why should others treat you better than you treat yourself? On the other hand, people with positive self-concepts are likely to behave confidently, which causes others to react to them positively.

Since this self-presentation is so vital, it is essential that you increase your awareness of how realistic your self-concept is. Becoming aware of *how* you've formed your view of yourself is basic to any efforts to change.

One way to acquire this awareness is to spend time reviewing some of the significant experiences of your childhood and adolescence. In particular, you can reflect on how these experiences have affected the way you feel about your competence and worth.

It is helpful to recall specific instances in which you have made certain decisions. For example, as a child you might have decided that you were "stupid" and therefore engaged in withdrawal behavior. Now, as an adult, you might still act in many ways like that scared child. As you come to realize that you accepted an inaccurate view of yourself, you can begin to challenge that early decision and start to behave in new, more rewarding ways.

Time Out for Personal Reflection

Reflect on your childhood years, and then take the following self-inventory. Respond quickly, marking "T" if you believe the statement is more true than false for you as a child, and "F" if it tends not to fit your childhood experiences.

1. *As a child, I felt loved and accepted.*
2. *I basically trusted the world.*
3. *I felt that I was an acceptable and valuable person.*
4. *I didn't need to work for others' approval.*
5. *I felt I was liked by my peers.*
6. *I made the transition from home to school well.*
7. *I didn't experience a great deal of shame and self-doubt as a child.*
8. *Elementary school was a positive experience for me.*
9. *I had adequate models as I was growing up.*
10. *I felt that it was OK for me to express negative feelings.*
11. *My parents trusted my ability to do things for myself.*
12. *I believe that I developed a natural and healthy concept of my body and my sex-role identity.*
13. *I assumed a degree of initiative during my early school years.*
14. *I had friends as a child.*
15. *I felt that I could talk to my parents about my problems.*

Look over your responses. What do they tell you about the person you now are? If you could live your childhood over again, how would you like it to be? Record some of your impressions in your journal.

Because your view of yourself has a great influence on the quality of your interpersonal relationships, I invite you to look carefully at some of the views you have of yourself and also to consider how you arrived at these views. To do this, reflect on these questions:

1. *How do you see yourself now? (To what degree do you see yourself as confident? secure? worthwhile? accomplished? caring? open? accepting?)*

   _____

   _____

   _____

2. *How do you feel about the way you see yourself now? How would you describe this to a close friend in one concise sentence?*

   _____

   _____

   _____

3. *What is the difference between the way you see yourself now and the way you'd like to be? Do you feel hopeful about closing this gap?*

   _____

   _____

   _____

4. *Do others generally see you as you see yourself? What are some ways that others view you differently than you view yourself?*

   _____

   _____

   _____

5. *Who in your life has been most influential in shaping your self-concept, and how has he or she (they) affected your view of yourself? (Father? Mother? Friend? Teacher? Grandparents?)*

   _____

   _____

   _____

Adolescence: Identity versus Identity Diffusion

The years from 12 to 18 constitute a stage of transition between childhood and adulthood. For most people, this is a particularly difficult period. It is a paradoxical time: adolescents are not treated as mature adults, yet they are often expected to act as though they have gained complete maturity; they are typically highly self-centered and preoccupied with their subjective worlds, yet they are expected to cope with the demands of reality and to go outside of themselves by expanding their horizons.

Adolescence is a time for continually testing limits, and there is usually a strong urge to break away from dependent ties that restrict one's freedom. It is not uncommon for adolescents to be frightened and lonely, but they may mask their fears with rebellion and cover up their need to be dependent by exaggerating their degree of independence. Although young people are becoming increasingly aware of the extent to which they are the products of their own families, it seems extremely important for them to declare their uniqueness and establish a separate identity. Much of adolescents' rebellion, then, is an attempt to determine the course of their own lives and to assert that they are who and what *they* want to be, not what others expect them to be.

In this quest to define themselves, adolescents may tend to dismiss completely anything their parents stand for, because they are insecure about not achieving their own sense of uniqueness unless they do. It would be better to recognize that our parents, our family, and our history are a part of us, and that it's unrealistic to think that anyone can completely erase this influence. Instead of totally rejecting parental influences, young people could learn how to incorporate those values that could give their lives meaning, to modify those values that they deem in need of change, and to reject the ones that they choose not to live by. Those who go to the extreme of attempting to be totally different from their parents are really not free, because they are investing a great deal of energy in proving themselves and, by their overreaction, are continuing to give their parents undue importance in their lives.

According to White and Speisman (1977), adolescence is a time for integrating the various dimensions of one's identity that have been achieved in the past (pp. 21–22). As infants, we must learn to trust ourselves and others; as adolescents, we need to find a meaning in life and models in whom we believe. As toddlers, we begin to assert our rights as independent people by struggling for autonomy; as adolescents, we

make choices that will shape our future. As preschoolers, we engage in play and fantasize different roles; as adolescents, we commit ourselves by assuming new roles and identities. As schoolchildren, we try to achieve a sense of competence; as adolescents, we explore choices concerning what we want from life, what we can succeed in, what kind of education we want, and what career may suit us.

Adolescents must confront dilemmas similar to those faced by old people in our society. Both age groups must deal with finding a meaning in living and must cope with feelings of uselessness. Just as older people may be forced to retire and may encounter difficulty in replacing activities such as work, young people frequently feel that they are useless to society. They have not yet completed the education that will give them entry to many careers and they generally haven't had the chance to acquire the skills necessary for many occupations. Instead, they are in a constant process of preparation for the future. Even in their families, they may feel unneeded. Although they may be given chores to do, many adolescents do not experience much opportunity to be productive.

Adolescence is a critical period in the development of personal identity. For Erikson, adolescents' major developmental conflicts center on the clarification of who they are, where they are going, and how they are going to get there. A failure to achieve a sense of identity results in *identity diffusion*. Adolescents may feel overwhelmed by the pressures placed on them; if so, they may find the development of a clear identity a difficult task. They may feel pressured to make an occupational choice, to compete in the job market or in college, to become financially independent, and to commit themselves to physically and emotionally intimate relationships. In addition, they may feel pressured to live up to the standards of their peer group. Peer-group pressure is such a potent force that there is a danger that adolescents will lose their focus on their own identities and conform to the expectations of their friends and classmates. If the need to be accepted and liked is stronger than the need for self-respect, adolescents will most likely find themselves behaving in nongenuine ways, selling themselves out, and increasingly looking to others to tell them what and who they should be.

A further strain on adolescents' sense of identity is imposed by the conflict between their sense of expanding possibilities and society's narrowing of their options for action. As White and Speisman (1977) put it:

> While adolescents are telling themselves they can be anything they want to be, society is telling them, in very different terms, what they must do and who they must be if they are to succeed or even survive. Just when their thought broadens to include new perspectives and expectations, reality narrows the choices [p. 20].

The question of options is made even more urgent by the myth that the choices we make during adolescence bind us for the rest of our lives. Adolescents who believe this will be hesitant to experiment and test out many options. Too many young people yield to pressures to decide too early what they will be and what kind of serious commitments they will make. Thus, they may never realize the range of possibilities open to them. To deal with this problem, Erikson suggests a *psychological moratorium*—a period during which society would give permission to adolescents to experiment with different roles and values so that they could sample life before making major commitments.

Adolescents are also faced with choices concerning what beliefs and values will guide their actions; indeed, forming a philosophy of life is a central task of adolescence. In meeting this challenge, young people need adequate models, for a sense of moral living is largely learned by example. Adolescents are especially sensitive to duplicity, and they are quick to spot phony people who tell them how they *ought* to live while they themselves live in very different ways. They learn values by observing and interacting with adults who are positive examples, rather than by being preached to.

A particular problem adolescents face in the area of values concerns sexual behavior. Adolescents are easily aroused sexually, and everywhere they turn, whether in the media or in real life, they are saturated with sexual stimuli. At the same time, our society formally frowns on engaging in most types of sexual behavior before marriage. The resulting conflict can produce much frustration, anxiety, and guilt. Even apart from moral values in regard to sexuality, adolescents need to assess anew issues related to their sex-role identities. What is a woman? What is a man? What is feminine? What is masculine? What are the expectations we must live up to, and where do they originate? Wrestling with these difficult questions is part of the struggle of being an adolescent.

With all of these tasks and conflicts, it isn't surprising that adolescence is typically a turbulent and fast-moving period of life, and one that is often marked by loneliness. It is a time for making choices in almost every area of life—choices that, to a large extent, define our identities. The identities that we have developed during adolescence, while not necessarily final, have a profound effect on how we relate to future turning points throughout our adult lives.

Time Out for Personal Reflection

At this point it could be useful to review the choices open to adolescents, and especially to think of the choices that you remember having made at this time in your life. How do you think those choices have influenced the person you are today?

A few of the choices adolescents are faced with include:

What kind of identity will I choose, a positive or a negative one?

Will I choose to remain self-centered, or will I go beyond myself by developing an interest in the world and in others?

There is the choice to use drugs and alcohol excessively, to the point of escaping from reality, or the choice to face reality.

There is the choice to follow the crowd (to the extent of losing any sense of uniqueness), or to dare to be different (even if it means not being universally accepted).

How will I find meaning in the world? What will I look to for a sense of direction in life? Will religion be a part of this framework, and if so, what kind of religion will I embrace?

Will I merely accept the values I've been taught, or will I question them and eventually find values to live by that I've thought out? Will I let someone else decide how I should live, or will I draw my own blueprints and follow them?

1. *What major choices did you struggle with during your adolescent years?*

   _____

   _____

   _____

2. *If you could live your adolescent years again, what would you most like to change?*

   _____

   _____

   _____

3. *How do you think your adolescence affected the person you are today?*

   _____

   _____

   _____

   _____

Young Adulthood: Intimacy versus Isolation

The period of young adulthood extends from about age 18 to age 35. According to Erikson, we enter adulthood after we master the adolescent conflicts over identity and role confusion. However, our sense of identity is tested anew in adulthood by the challenge of intimacy versus isolation.

One characteristic of the psychologically mature person is the ability to form intimate relationships. Before we can form such relationships, we must be sure of our own identities. Intimacy involves a sharing, a giving of ourselves, a relating to another out of strength, and a desire to grow with the other person. Failure to achieve intimacy can result in isolation from others and a sense of alienation. The fact that alienation is a problem for many people in our society is evidenced by the widespread use of drugs and by other ways in which we try to numb our sense of isolation. On the other hand, if we attempt to escape isolation by clinging to another person, we rarely find success in the relationship.

Entering the Twenties

Whereas adolescence is a time of extreme preoccupation with internal conflicts and with the search for identity, young adulthood is a time for beginning to focus on external tasks, such as developing intimate relationships, getting established in an occupation, carving out a life-style, and perhaps marrying and starting a family. In *Passages*, Sheehy (1976) says that the tasks of this period are both enormous and exhilarating. During this time we create a dream, and this vision of ourselves generates tremendous energy and vitality. She writes that the "trying twenties" are characterized by an effort to do what we "should." Our "shoulds" are defined mainly by the media, by our family models, and by peer-group pressures. Some of these shoulds might be: "I should get married." "I should have children." "I should better myself by completing college." "I should be working to get ahead in the organization." "I should be saving money for a house."

During the twenties young people are faced with making a variety of profound choices. If you are in this age period, you are no doubt facing decisions about how you will live. Your choices probably include questions such as: Will I choose the security of staying at home, or will I struggle financially and psychologically to live on my own? Will I stay single, or will I get involved in some committed relationship? Will I stay in college full time, or will I begin a career? If I choose a career, what will it be and how will I go about deciding what I might do in the work world? If I marry, will I be a parent or not? What are some of my dreams, and how might I make them become a reality? What do I most want to do with my life at this time, and how might I find meaning?

Choices pertaining to work, education, marriage, family life, and a life-style are complex and deeply personal, and it is common to struggle over what it is we really want. There is the temptation to let others decide for us or to be overly influenced by the standards of others. But if we choose that path, we remain psychological adolescents at best. Gould (1978) puts the core task of the twenties in these words:

We learn that our parents' way will bring us results in some instances but not all. We learn that if we're frustrated, we can call for help, but we can't let anybody else take over. As the adult architects of our own existence, we must accept the new reality and the full responsibility. This is yet another stage of relinquishing the childhood consciousness illusion of absolute safety provided by omnipotent parents [p. 72].[1]

In short, we have the choice to live by parental rules, or we can leave home psychologically and decide for ourselves what our future will be. The following personal statements of individuals in their twenties illustrate the struggles of this period. A young man says:

I want to live on my own, but it's very difficult to support myself and go to college at the same time. The support and approval of my parents is surely something I want, yet I am working hard at finding a balance between how much I am willing to do to get their approval and how much I will live by my values. When I look at my parents, it scares me to see how limited their lives are, and I want my life to be different. I love my parents, yet at the same time I resent them for the hold they have on me due to my dependency needs. When I live differently than they think I should, I feel guilty.

Another person in her twenties expresses her desire for intimacy, along with her reservations and doubts:

While I realize that I want to be in a close relationship with a man, I know that I am also afraid of getting involved. I wonder if I want to spend the rest of my life with the same person. One thing that worries me is that if I allow myself to get close, he might leave, and I don't know if I'm ready for that hurt again. At other times I'm afraid I'll never find someone I can love who really loves me. I just don't want to give up my freedom, nor do I want to be dependent on someone.

[1]From *Transformations*, by Roger Gould, M.D. Copyright © 1978 by Roger Gould, M.D. This and all other quotations from this source are reprinted by permission of Simon & Schuster, a division of Gulf & Western Corporation.

Sheehy stresses that one of the terrifying aspects of the twenties is the conviction that the choices we make at this time are cast in cement. For instance, we might choose to "do nothing" for a time, or to go to graduate school, or to get married, or to get established in a career. Whatever we choose, we often fear that we will have to live with our choice for the rest of our lives. According to Sheehy, this fear is largely unjustified, for major changes are almost inevitable. As she puts it: "But since in our twenties we're new at making major life choices, we cannot imagine that possibilities for a better integration will occur to us later on, when some inner growth has taken place" (p. 86). However, she does indicate that, although our choices aren't irrevocable, they do set the stage for the choices we'll make later on.

Martha, age 23, typifies young people who are willing to allow themselves to dream and remain open about what they want in life. She is also a good example of Sheehy's conviction that the choices made during the twenties aren't irrevocable. Martha works for a savings and loan association, and she is about to begin full-time graduate study toward a counseling degree. Here is what she is looking forward to:

> At this time in my life I think I have a thousand choices open to me. I don't like my job as a loan officer that much, but it does provide me with security. I never want to stop learning, and I'm sure I want to be a vital person. At some time, though not yet, I'd like to be married. Eventually I'd like kids. I'd like to publish someday, as well as having a counseling practice.

When I asked Martha what she'd like to be able to say in her old age, she replied:

> I have a friend whose grandmother was 63 and she rode a pogo stick. I'd like to be as energetic in my old age as I am now. I never want to get bogged down with old ideas. Some people get set in their values, and they just won't change. I always want to evaluate and to be in the process of integrating new values in my life.

When I asked Martha if she saw herself as typical of those her age, her answer was:

> Most people between 18 and 23 don't look inward that much. I think they look to other people to make choices for

them. I hope I can do what feels right to me at the time. I'm uncertain now about many of my specific goals. I like taking life as it comes, but by that I'm not talking about being passive. I hope to be open to the possibilities that might eventually open up to me. I don't want to lose myself in someone else, but I would like to share my life with someone else.

Transition from the Twenties to the Thirties

According to Gould (1978), the transition from the late twenties to the early thirties is sometimes characterized by depression. It is a time of changing values and beliefs. For example, men who are switching careers or making changes within a career may be assuming that they will find a new direction in life. When their visions do not materialize, they may lapse into depression. Women who are married and have children may decide to work full time, and they may not find that this choice was what they were looking for. Gould talks about the thirties as a time for making a new contract—making basic changes in life-style, priorities, and commitments. It is during this period of unrest, disillusionment, depression, and questioning that people modify some of the rigid rules of their twenties. They also realize other facts: that their dreams do not materialize if they simply wish for things to happen; that there is no magic in the world; that life is not simple but, in fact, is complicated and bewildering; and that we can get what we want not by waiting and wishing passively but by working actively to attain our goals. As we open up in our thirties, a crisis can be precipitated when we discover that life is not as uncomplicated as we had envisioned it to be. The major challenge open to us as we realize these truths is put well by Gould (1978):

> Our disappointment at this information can send us into a tailspin, or we can discard our disillusion and gain a realistic view of what we must do to live as adults. That is, we must become responsible for our own growth and learn to shape our future based on a realistic view of what is inside us and the world around us [pp. 182–183].

Sheehy claims that we become impatient with living a life based on "shoulds" when we enter our thirties. Both men and women speak of feeling restricted at this time and may complain that life is narrow and dull. Sheehy asserts that these restrictions are related to the outcomes of the life-style choices we made during our twenties. Even if these personal and career choices have served us well during the twenties, in the thirties we become ready for some changes. This is a time for making new choices and perhaps for modifying or deepening old commitments. This process, which may involve considerable turmoil and crisis, relates to our desire for more out of life. We may find ourselves asking: "Is this all there is to life? What do I want for the rest of my life? What is missing from my life now?" Thus, a woman who has primarily been engaged in a career may now want to spend more time at home and with the children. A woman who has devoted most of her life to being a homemaker may now yearn to extend her horizon by getting established in a career. Men may do a lot of questioning about their work and wonder how they can make it more meaningful. If a man has been an "organization man" for a number of years, he might now consider breaking out of this mold by establishing his own business or changing careers. Single people may consider finding a partner, while those who are married may experience a real crisis in their marriage, which may be a sign that they cannot continue with old patterns.

Time Out for Personal Reflection

Think about a few of the major turning points in your young adulthood. Write down not more than three turning points, and then state how you think they were important in your life. What difference did your decisions at these critical times make in your life?

Turning point: _____

Impact of the decision on my life: _____

_____

_____

_____

Turning point: _____

Impact of the decision on my life: _____

_____

_____

_____

Turning point: _____

Impact of the decision on my life: _____

_____

_____

_____

Middle Age: *Generativity versus Self-Absorption or Stagnation*

The time between the ages of 35 and 60 is characterized by a "going outside of ourselves." It is a time for learning how to live creatively with ourselves and with others, and it can be the time of greatest productivity in our lives. For most of us, it is also the period when we reach the top of the mountain yet at the same time become aware that we must begin the downhill journey. In addition, we may painfully experience the discrepancy between our dreams of the twenties and thirties and the hard reality of what we have achieved.

According to Erikson, the stimulus for continued growth in middle age is the crisis of generativity versus stagnation. By *generativity*, Erikson meant not just fostering children but being productive in a broad sense—for example, through creative pursuits in a career, in leisure-time activities, in teaching or caring for others, or in some type of meaningful volunteer work. Two important qualities of the productive adult are the ability to love well and the ability to work well. Adults who fail to achieve a sense of productivity begin to stagnate, which is a form of psychological death.

When we reach middle age, we come to a crossroads in our lives. We reach the midpoint of our life's journey, and, even though we are in our prime, we begin to realize more acutely that life has a finishing point and that we are moving toward it. In *Passages*, Sheehy calls the time between the ages of 35 and 45 the "deadline decade." During this period, our physical powers may begin to falter, and the roles that we have used to identify ourselves may lose their meaning. We may begin to question what else is left to life and to reexamine or renew our commitments. Sheehy claims that at this time we face both dangers and opportunities. There are many dangers of slipping into deadening ruts and failing to make any real changes to enrich our lives. There are also opportunities for choosing to rework the narrow identities of the first half of our lives.

Sheehy contends that most of us encounter a mid-life crisis. We realize the uncertainty of life, and we discover more clearly that we are alone. We stumble on masculine and feminine aspects of ourselves that have previously been masked. We may also go through a grieving process, because many parts of our old selves are dying. This process does allow us to reevaluate and reintegrate an identity that is new and emerging, as opposed to an identity that is the sum of others' expectations. In Sheehy's words, "It is a dark passage at the beginning. But by disassembling ourselves, we can glimpse the light and gather our parts into a renewal" (1976, p. 30). A few of the events that might occur to contribute to the mid-life crisis are:

· We may come to realize that some of our youthful dreams will never materialize.
· We may begin to experience the pressure of time, realizing that now is the time to accomplish our mission.
· Coping with the aging process is difficult for many; the loss of some of our youthful qualities can be hard to face.
· The death of our parents drives home a truth that is difficult for many to accept—ultimately, we are alone in this life.
· There is the realization that life is not necessarily just and fair and that we often do not get what we had expected.
· There are marital crises and challenges to old patterns. A spouse may have an affair or seek a divorce.
· Our children grow up and leave home at this time. People who have lived largely for their children now may face emptiness.
· We may lose our jobs or be demoted, or we may grow increasingly disenchanted with our work.
· A woman may leave the home to enter the world of work and make this her primary interest.

Along with these factors that can precipitate a crisis, we may have the following choices available to us at this time:

· We can decide to go back for further schooling and gear up for a new career.
· We can choose to develop new talents and embark on novel hobbies, and we can even take steps to change our life-styles.
· We can look increasingly inward to find out what we most want to do with the rest of our lives and begin doing what we say we want to do.

Regardless of the crises, turning points, and choices that are associated with middle age, we are becoming increasingly clear that time is passing by, and we feel some urgency to evaluate our lives. We also realize that what we do or don't do has a bearing on the quality of our lives. "As we go from 35 to 45, it becomes clear, sometimes painfully clear, that we are the only, the final authority over the conduct of our own lives" (Gould, 1978, p. 221).

You may be some distance away from middle age, but I hope you don't stop reading at this point, determined that this will never happen to you! Now may be a good time for you to reflect on the way your life is shaping up and to think about the person you'd like to be when you reach middle age. To help you in making this projection, it could be useful to consider the lives of people you know who are over 40. Do you have any models available to you in determining what direction you pursue? Are there some ways you'd not want to live? Also, consider the following brief first-person accounts, all statements made by middle-aged people:

A man says that it's difficult to always be striving for success, and he shares some of his loneliness:

> So much of my life has been bound up in becoming a success. While I am successful, I continually demand more of myself. I'm never quite satisfied with anything I accomplish, and I continually look ahead and see what has to be done. It's lonely when I think of always swimming against the tide, and I fear getting dragged into deep water that I can't get out of. At the same time, I don't seem to be able to calm these waters down.

A woman says that she has stayed in a miserable marriage for 23 years. She finally recognizes that she has run out of excuses for staying. She must decide whether to maintain a marriage that is not likely to change much or decide on ending the marriage.

> I am petrified by the idea that I have to support myself and that I am responsible for my own happiness—totally. All these years, I've told myself that if *he* were different, then I'd feel much more fulfilled than I do in life. I also had many reasons that prevented me from taking action, even when it became very clear to me that he wasn't even slightly interested in seeing things change. I'm not afraid to go out

and meet people on a social basis, but I'm terrified of getting intimately involved with a man on a sexual or emotional basis. When I think of all those years in an oppressive marriage, I want to scream. I know I've kept most of these screams inside of me, for I feared that if I allowed myself to scream I'd never stop—that I might go crazy. Yet keeping my pain and tears inside of me has made my whole body ache, and I'm tired of hurting all the time. I want something else from life besides hurt!

A Middle-Age Woman's Delight and Pains in Growing

Let me present some of the highlights from an interview I conducted with one of my students—a woman of 44 years who has earned my respect and affection. Jill tells about some of the turning points in her life during the last few years and describes what she is looking forward to. Again, as with the other cases presented, let yourself think about what you would most hope to say about yourself when you reach middle age (if you aren't already there or beyond). It will help to think about your parents, relatives, and people you have known, as you form your own picture of what kind of life you'd like to create for yourself. Now, to Jill:

> About four years ago I knew I was frustrated in doing what I was. I began to ask myself if the rest of my life would be centered on playing tennis and all the other social things my friends were doing. I realized that I wanted more. I thought: Would I like to go back to work? I didn't know how to do a damn thing! Would I like to go back to college? That frightened me. While I was a good high-school student, my one and only year of college was devoted to partying. Finally, with fear and trepidation, I decided to return to college. I eventually got involved in Human Services and found that this was something that really interested me. I must say that I've been afraid at times, and there have been some setbacks. I've been tempted to go back to the tennis courts. I've set some friendships aside, and going to school has affected my marriage.
>
> I did not go to school because of pressure or necessity. Some women will go to college because they are left on their own, through divorce or death of a spouse. I got

involved in the program I'm in because it encouraged me to look at my own life, as well as think I could help the rest of the world. In looking at the changes I've made recently, I see that I have lots of choices, and I think that with choices come a lot more opportunities to make mistakes. If I have only two choices, then I have a 50% chance of being right. Yet the many options that are open to me also mean that I might regret some decisions I make. However, there is no way that I'd want to go back to what my life was like four years ago. I would rather not have gone through the struggles I did to get where I am, but that's not realistic. Looking back over these four years, I feel some sadness, and I've had to do some grieving. So, there is a combination of delight and pain. I've felt sad when I thought that I can't get back there again, but along with this is such a delight, such a feeling of freedom and a real good feeling of self, that I would never want that to be taken away from me.

Let me say that I didn't get much support from my friends on the tennis court for wanting to make life-style changes. I found that I had to step outside of this circle to begin a new life for myself. When I sat there four years ago, all I could see was sameness! And now when I look at life, I have no idea of where I'll be within two years from now, but I know it will be fun and exciting. I have a pretty good feeling about myself. If something is out there, I think I'll have a good chance of getting it. I'm not afraid of my age. Lots of women at school are afraid of their age, and they're discouraged from getting an advanced degree because they assume that the jobs will go to younger people. Sometimes I work myself up into a panic by "futurizing," and then I tell myself that I'll deal with issues as they come up instead of predicting them.

Being a married woman has made going to college a bit difficult, especially for my husband. Seeing my involvement with school and seeing a new world unfold before me have been threatening to him. And it's hard for me to say whether I think the changes I've made have been good or bad for our marriage. I do know that my grown kids have always been behind me and think it's great that I've found something that excites me.

While I'm in a good place today, I go through some pain with the changes in me and the choices I'm faced with. Not having any choices is real simple. I'd never sit here and tell you it's easy, but it's been worth it!

Time Out for Personal Reflection

If you have reached middle age, think about how the following questions apply to you. In your journal, you might write down your reactions to a few of the questions that have the most meaning for you. If you haven't reached middle age, think about how you'd like to be able to answer these questions when you reach that stage in your life. What do you need to do now in order to have your expectations met?

1. *Is this time one of "generativity" or "stagnation" for you? Think about some of the things you've done during this time of life that you feel the best about.*
2. *Do you feel productive? If so, in what ways?*
3. *Are there some things that you'd definitely like to change in your life right now? What prevents you from making these changes?*
4. *What questions have you raised about your life during this time?*
5. *Have you experienced a mid-life crisis? If so, how has it affected you?*
6. *What losses have you experienced?*
7. *What are some of the most important decisions that you have made during this time of your life?*
8. *Are you developing new interests and talents?*
9. *What do you look forward to in the remaining years?*
10. *If you were to review the major successes of your life to this point, what would they be?*

Later Life: Integrity versus Despair

After about the age of 60, our central developmental tasks include the following: adjusting to decreased physical and sensory capacities, adjusting to retirement, finding a meaning in life, being able to relate to the past without regrets, adjusting to the death of spouse or friends, accepting inevitable losses, maintaining outside interests, and enjoying grandchildren.

According to Erikson, the central issue of this age period is integrity versus despair. Persons who succeed in achieving *ego integrity* feel that their lives have been productive and worthwhile and that they have managed to cope with failures as well as successes. They can accept the course of their lives and are not obsessed with thoughts of what might have been and what they could or should have done. They can look back without resentment and regret and can see their lives in a perspective of completeness and satisfaction. Finally, they can view death as a natural part of the experience of life, even while living rich and meaningful lives to the day they die.

Unfortunately, some elderly people fail to achieve ego integration. Typically, such people fear death. They may develop a sense of hopelessness and feelings of self-disgust. They cannot accept their life's cycle, for they see whatever they have done as "not enough" and feel that they have a lot of unfinished business. They yearn for another chance, even though they realize that they cannot have it. They feel inadequate, for they think that they have wasted their lives and let valuable time slip by. These are the people who die unhappy and unfulfilled.

Old age does not have to be something that we look forward to with horror or resignation; nor must it be associated with bitterness. However, many elderly people in our society do feel resentment, because we have generally neglected them. Many of them are treated as members of an undesirable minority and are merely tolerated or put out to pasture in a convalescent home. Their loss is doubly sad, because the elderly can make definite contributions to society. Many elderly persons are still very capable, yet the prejudice of younger adults keeps them from fully using their resources. Perhaps we are afraid of aging (and death) and "put away" the elderly so that they won't remind us of our future.

In their book *Ageism*, Levin and Levin (1980) describe the various forms of prejudice and discrimination against the elderly. They see ageism like racism and sexism, as a negative evaluation toward old people in general. More specifically, ageism predisposes us to discriminate against old people by avoiding them or in some way victimizing them because of their age alone. The authors discuss the images of the aged by looking at common stereotypes. Asserting that the images of the aged are based more on myth than reality, they point out several fictions relating to growing old.

· The elderly are viewed as sexually inactive. Sex is typically thought of as unimportant for them.

- The public image of the elderly is generally associated with reduced job performance. Thus, old people are frequently discriminated against in the world of work and are often forced to retire while they are still capable of productive work.
- There is the view that, as one grows old, intelligence takes a downward trend. Childlike qualities are often attributed to the elderly.
- A pervasive stereotype is that the elderly are "set in their ways" and are highly conservative.
- The elderly are viewed as resisting change and welcoming a withdrawal from society.

Levin and Levin present research evidence that contradicts each of these stereotypes. These images are based on half-truths or outright fallacies, yet they are often used to justify the mistreatment of the elderly.

In addition to the stereotypes mentioned above, there are some other commonly held myths about the elderly, a few of which are:

- Most people who retire become depressed.
- Retirement is just a step away from death.
- It's disgraceful for an old person to remarry.
- Old people are not creative.
- An elderly person will die soon after his or her mate dies.
- Old people are no longer beautiful.

These are only a few of the myths that can render older people helpless if they accept them. I believe that the attitude an older person has about aging is extremely important. Like adolescents, the aged may feel a sense of uselessness because of others' view of them. Then it is easy for them to accept the myths of others and turn them into self-fulfilling prophecies.

Again, while most of you have not yet reached old age, I hope that you won't brush aside thinking about your eventual aging. Your observations of old people whom you know can provide you with information about what it is like to grow older. From these observations, you can begin to formulate some picture of the life you'd like to have as you get older.

Let me conclude this chapter with a brief example of an older person who is leading a simple and meaningful life in her old age. This woman, who is 70 years old, has lived alone since her husband died. She has a

routine that involves keeping up her garden, talking with friends, watching her favorite shows on television, and doing chores. At times she takes care of her grandchildren for a few days, but then she is eager to get back to her routine. When her grandchildren asked her if she didn't get lonely, she quickly responded by letting them know that she enjoys her solitude and that her days are full. She likes not having to answer to anyone but herself, and she looks forward to each day. She doesn't brood over the past, nor does she wish that things had been different. Instead, she accepts both her accomplishments and her mistakes, and she still derives pleasure in being alone as well as in being with those she loves.

Time Out for Personal Reflection

If you haven't yet reached old age, imagine yourself doing so. Think about your fears and about what you'd like to be able to say about your life—your joys, your accomplishments, and your regrets. To facilitate this reflection, you might consider the following questions:

- *What do you most hope to accomplish by the time you reach old age?*
- *What are some of your greatest fears of growing old?*
- *What kind of old age do you expect? What are you doing now that might have an effect on the kind of person you'll be as you grow older?*
- *What are some things you hope to do during the later years of your life? How do you expect that you will adjust to retirement? What meaning do you expect your life to have when you reach old age?*
- *How would you like to be able to respond to your body's aging? How do you think you'll respond to failing health or to physical limitations on your life-style?*
- *Assume that you will have enough money to live comfortably and to do many of the things that you haven't had time for earlier. What do you think you'd most like to do? With whom?*
- *What would you most want to be able to say about yourself and your life when you become elderly?*

In your journal, you might write down some impressions of the kind of old age you hope for, as well as the fears you have about growing older.

Chapter Summary

In this chapter, I've tried to clarify some of the principal conflicts and opportunities for choice that characterize each stage of personality development, and I've encouraged you to think about the critical turning points and choices in your own development. I want to stress that there are no neat marks to delineate one stage of development from another. There is a great deal of overlap between stages; moreover, we all experience each period of life in our own unique ways. I've also emphasized that the attainment of autonomy is a task that we are continually engaged in, and I've suggested some guidelines to help you assess the degree to which you're now an independent person.

The experiences and events that occur during each developmental stage are crucial in helping to determine our subsequent attitudes, beliefs, values, and actions regarding the important areas of our lives that will be discussed in the chapters to come: the body, sexuality, love, intimate relationships, work, loneliness and solitude, death and loss, and meaning and values. For this reason, I've devoted considerable attention to the foundations of our life choices. Understanding how we got where we are now is a critical first step in deciding where we want to go from here.

Now write down some of the ideas in this chapter that you most want to remember.

———————————————————————————

———————————————————————————

———————————————————————————

———————————————————————————

———————————————————————————

———————————————————————————

Activities and Exercises

1. Do you believe that you're able to make new decisions? Do you think that you're in control of your destiny? In your journal, write down some examples of new decisions—or renewals of old decisions—that have made a significant difference in your life.

2. Mention some critical turning points in your life. In your journal, draw a chart showing the age periods you've experienced so far and

indicate your key successes, failures, conflicts, and memories for each age period.

3. After you've described some of the significant events in your life, list some of the decisions that you have made in response to these events. How were you affected by some of these milestones in your life? Then think about what you've learned about yourself from doing these exercises. What does all of this tell you about the person you are today?

4. Many students readily assert that they are psychologically independent. If this applies to you, think about some specific examples that show that you have questioned and challenged your parents' values and that you have modified your own value system.

5. Talk with some people who are significantly older than yourself. For instance, if you're in your twenties, you could interview a middle-aged person and an elderly person. Try to get them to take the lead and tell you about their lives. What do they like about their lives? What have been some key turning points for them? What do they most remember of the past? You might even suggest that they read the section of the chapter that pertains to their present age group and react to the ideas presented there.

6. To broaden your perspective on human development in various cultural or ethnic groups, talk to someone you know who grew up in a very different environment from the one you knew as a child. You could find out how his or her life experiences have differed from yours by sharing some aspects of your own life. Try to discover whether there are significant differences in values that seem to be related to the differences in your life experiences. This could help you to reassess many of your own values.

Suggested Readings

Axline, V. *Dibs: In Search of Self.* New York: Ballantine, 1976. This book gives a touching account of a boy's journey from isolation toward self-awareness and self-expression and emphasizes the crucial effects of parent/child relationships on the development of a child's personality. It also describes how play therapy can be a tool for developing an autonomous individual.

Baruch, D. *One Little Boy.* New York: Dell (Delta), 1964. This is a fascinating account of one boy's feelings and problems and how his personal conflicts originated in the family dynamics, as revealed through play therapy. The book gives the reader a sense of appreciation for the kinds of struggles most children experience during early childhood in relationship with their parents.

Berne, E. *What Do You Say After You Say Hello?* New York: Bantam, 1975. Based on Transactional Analysis, this book demonstrates how we learn certain scripts that determine our present behavior. It discusses how we write our life scripts and how we can change them.

Bettelheim, B. *The Empty Fortress: Infantile Autism and the Birth of Self.* New York: Free Press, 1967. Three very interesting case studies are presented that give dramatic testimony concerning what can happen as a result of inadequate parenting during early childhood.

Bridges, W. *Transitions: Making Sense of Life's Changes.* Reading, Mass.: Addison-Wesley, 1980. This is a readable book designed to help people identify and cope with critical changes in their lives. The author describes the transition process and offers skills and suggestions for creatively dealing with each of the perilous passages of life.

Combs, A. W., Avila, D. L., & Purkey, W. W. *Helping Relationships: Basic Concepts for the Helping Professions* (2nd ed.). Boston: Allyn & Bacon, 1978. This is a good reference for learning more about the nature and development of the self-concept.

Egan, G., & Cowan, M. A. *Moving into Adulthood: Themes and Variations in Self-Directed Development for Effective Living.* Monterey, Calif.: Brooks/Cole, 1980. Chapters are devoted to topics such as identity, development of personality, friendship and intimacy, marriage and the family, love, work and career choice, leisure time, and life-style.

Erikson, E. *Childhood and Society* (2nd ed.). New York: Norton, 1964. Using a modified and extended version of psychoanalytic thought, Erikson describes a psychosocial theory of development. He delineates eight stages and their critical tasks.

Freud, S. *The Sexual Enlightenment of Children.* New York: Collier, 1963. The essays collected in this book show how Freud developed his theory of sexuality and applied it to the fantasies, fears, and experiences of children.

Gould, R. L. *Transformations: Growth and Change in Adult Life.* New York: Simon & Schuster (Touchstone Book), 1978. This is a well-written book on the life span, with descriptions of key tasks to be accomplished at the various stages, along with case examples. The author develops the theme that, as we grow, we take steps away from childhood and toward adulthood. At the same time, unfinished business from our past intrudes in the present and demands psychological work.

Havighurst, R. *Developmental Tasks and Education* (3rd ed.). New York: David McKay, 1972. Havighurst presents a brief description of the developmental tasks from infancy through later maturity.

James, M., & Jongeward, D. *Born to Win: Transactional Analysis with Gestalt Experiments.* Reading, Mass.: Addison-Wesley, 1971. This is a very readable guide to understanding how we develop a sense of whether we are "winners" or "losers." An overview of the principles of TA and a description of Gestalt experiments make up the core of the book, which deals with stroking, life scripts, injunctions, early decisions, parental messages, parenting, childhood, personal and sexual identity, game playing, adulthood, and autonomy. It is an excellent source for understanding parenting and learning how we are presently influenced by earlier childhood conditioning.

Kalish, R. *Late Adulthood: Perspectives on Human Development.* Monterey, Calif.: Brooks/Cole, 1975. A very readable account of problems facing the older person, with discussion of issues such as the aging process, the changing self-concept, attitudes toward the elderly, and physical and social environments for the elderly.

Levin, J., & Levin, W. C. *Ageism: Prejudice and Discrimination against the Elderly.* Belmont, Calif.: Wadsworth, 1980. The authors draw similarities between the elderly and minorities and women. They have a good section on myths and stereotypes associated with aging.

Levinson, D. J. *The Seasons of a Man's Life.* New York: Knopf, 1978. The author describes growth patterns from the viewpoint of the entire life span.

Nouwen, H., & Gaffney, W. *Aging: The Fulfillment of Life.* Garden City, N.Y.: Doubleday, 1976. A moving book in which the authors share their thoughts on what aging means to all of us, regardless of our age.

Sheehy, G. *Passages: Predictable Crises of Adult Life.* New York: Dutton, 1976. A very readable and interesting book that focuses on the crises of the various life stages. Excellent cases are presented to illustrate typical struggles as people pass from one stage of life to the next.

Steiner, C. *Scripts People Live: Transactional Analysis of Life Scripts.* New York: Bantam, 1975. One of the best accounts of life scripts is given in this very useful and interesting book.

Troll, L. *Early and Middle Adulthood.* Monterey, Calif.: Brooks/Cole, 1975. Many books on human development fail to include a discussion of middle age. This book deals with the issues, problems, and tasks of this period of life.

Twiford, R., & Carson, P. *The Adolescent Passage: Transitions from Child to Adult.* Englewood Cliffs, N.J.: Prentice-Hall (Spectrum), 1980. The authors explain the critical factors that shape the life of the adolescent, and they give practical strategies for relating to youth. Both normal and abnormal psychological development are discussed, as well as sexual interests and behaviors, drug abuse, and adolescent traumas.

White, K., & Speisman, J. *Adolescence.* Monterey, Calif.: Brooks/Cole, 1977. The authors do a good job of defining and describing many facets of the world of the adolescent. Chapters deal with change and identity, values, sex roles and sexuality, and problems of these years. The thinking of Erikson and of Piaget is applied to adolescent development.

Your Body

Prechapter Self-Inventory

This chapter's inventory is designed to help you determine whether you control your body or it controls you. It encourages you to take an honest look at your relationship to your body.

For each statement, indicate the response that most closely identifies your beliefs and attitudes. Use this code: 5 = I *strongly agree* with this statement; 4 = I *agree* in most respects; 3 = I am *undecided;* 2 = I *disagree* in most respects; 1 = I *strongly disagree.*

_____ 1. I experience a good deal of stress in a typical day.

_____ 2. I don't believe I can do much to reduce the stress in my life.

_____ 3. I don't ever feel really well and am bothered by headaches, upset stomach, and other minor irritations.

_____ 4. My body reacts negatively to the stresses I face.

_____ 5. I believe that my state of health is a result of my choices concerning the care of my body.

_____ 6. I'd characterize my life-style as a stressful one.

_____ 7. It is relatively easy for me to be able to fully relax.

_____ 8. I practice some form of meditation almost every day.

_____ 9. I have a regular exercise program.

_____ 10. Generally, I eat nutritious foods and avoid foods that are considered unhealthy.

_____ 11. When I look in the mirror, I am satisfied with my physical appearance.

_____ 12. I am satisfied with my weight.

_____ 13. To be honest, there are many ways in which I abuse and neglect my body.

_____ 14. I have tried weight control programs many times, but without much success.

_____ 15. If my body tells me that I am not taking care of it properly (through various symptoms), then I am willing to make some basic changes in my life-style to improve my health.

_____ 16. The way I live, I do worry at times about having a heart attack.

_____ 17. I am likely to take medications for minor physical illnesses.

_____ 18. If I am under considerable stress, I am willing to take a tranquilizer to ease the effects.

_____ 19. I have a routine physical examination about every year or so.

_____ 20. In all honesty, I take greater care in maintaining my car than I do my body.

Introduction

Your body—the physical you—is the subject of this chapter. If you look at your body carefully, you'll see that it reflects the significant choices you have made about yourself and your style of living. Do you take care of the physical you? Do you control your body, or do bodily states control you? Are you proud of your body, or are you ashamed of it? How do your feelings and attitudes about your body affect your choices in areas such as sexuality, love, and self-worth?

One of the most basic choices you have is to accept personal responsibility for your body—to decide whether you will control your body or whether you will let your body control you. Our bodies are indispensable; yet many of us devote more attention to maintaining our automobiles than to taking care of our own bodies. Some people are concerned more about the quality of the gasoline and oil they put into their cars than about the substances they put into their bodies! Those of us who delude ourselves into thinking that our bodies will never break down may ignore the messages our bodies are sending us. I hope this chapter, then, will increase your willingness to listen to what your body is telling you.

An honest examination of the choices you are making about your body can reveal a great deal concerning your feelings about your life. If you aren't taking care of your body, what beliefs and attitudes might be getting in the way? What resources do you need to begin modifying those parts of your life-style that affect your bodily well-being?

To address these issues, I devote much of this chapter to three basic questions that are of keen interest to many students: stress, weight control, and the use and abuse of drugs. Whether or not these topics represent problem areas for you, I hope you will find that the discussions can be applied to a wide range of issues concerning the body. As you become more aware of your body and of the feelings and attitudes you associate with it, you can begin to challenge those decisions that diminish the options in your life.[1]

The Age of Stress

The stress of modern times is largely a function of *change*, which can leave us dizzy and in a sense of shock. Rapid changes in social, cultural,

---

[1] I would like to acknowledge the contributions to this chapter of our friends Dr. Allan Abbott and his wife, Katherine, who consulted with Marianne and me and brainstormed many of the issues and ideas discussed.

political, and technological areas have led us to make psychobiological adaptations. These ways of dealing with ever-present stresses will be taken up later in the chapter. First, however, we will consider the consequences in our lives of accelerated change and the stress it creates.

Toffler (1970), in his provocative book *Future Shock*, argues that, unless we quickly learn to control the rate of change in our personal affairs as well as in society at large, we are doomed to a massive adaptational breakdown. Predicting that future shock may well be the most important disease of tomorrow, Toffler refers to this condition as the dizzying disorientation brought on by the premature arrival of the future.

In most places in the modern world stress is an inevitable part of life. Perhaps we cannot eliminate stress, but we can learn how to manage it. We don't have to allow ourselves to be victimized by the psychological and physiological effects of stress. It is true that there are external sources of stress, yet how we perceive and react to them is subjective and internal. By interpreting the events in our lives, we define what is and is not stressful, and thus we determine our levels of stress adaptation. Therefore, the real challenge is to learn how to recognize and deal constructively with the sources of stress, rather than trying to eliminate them.

Sources of Stress

Environmental sources.   Many of the stresses of daily life come from external sources. Consider for a moment some of the environmentally related stresses that you face at the beginning of a semester. You are likely to encounter problems just in finding a parking place on campus. Perhaps you must stand in long lines and cope with many other delays and frustrations. Some of the courses you need may be closed; simply putting together a decent schedule of classes may be next to impossible. There may be difficulties in arranging your work schedule to fit your school schedule, and these difficulties can be compounded by the external demands of friends and family and other social commitments. Financial problems and the pressure to work so that you can support yourself (and perhaps your family, too) make being a full-time student a demanding task.

Our minds and bodies are also profoundly affected by more directly physiological sources of stress. Illnesses, exposure to environmental pollutants, improper diet, lack of exercise, poor sleeping habits, and abusing our bodies in any number of other ways—all take a toll on us.

Psychological sources.   Stress is a subjective phenomenon in that how we label, interpret, think about, and react to those events that impinge on us has a lot to do with determining stress. In discussing the psychological sources of stress, Coleman (1979) identifies frustration, conflict, and pressure as the key elements. Consider each of these sources of stress by applying them to yourself and your situation.

Frustration results from a blocking of your needs and goals. External sources of frustration, all of which have psychological components, include accidents, delays, loss of loved ones, hurtful interpersonal relationships, loneliness, and isolation. Additionally, internal factors can hinder you in attaining your goals. These include a lack of basic skills, physical handicaps, and a lack of belief in yourself. What are some of the major frustrations you experience, and how do you typically deal with them?

Conflict is another source of stress. How many times have you been faced with two or more desirable choices and been forced to choose one path? And how many times have you had to choose between unpleasant realities? Perhaps your major conflicts involve your choice of a life style. For example, have you wrestled with the issue of being independent or blindly following the crowd? Of living a self-directed life or living by what others expect of you? Consider for a few minutes some of the major conflicts you've recently faced. How have these conflicts affected you? How do you typically deal with the stress you experience over value conflicts?

Pressure is part of the "hurry-sickness" of modern living. We may respond to the pressures placed on us by others at home, school, and work and in our social lives. Also, we continually place internally created pressures on ourselves. Many people are extremely demanding of themselves, driving themselves and never quite feeling satisfied that they've done all they could have or should have done. If you find yourself in this situation, consider some of the irrational and unrealistic beliefs that you might be living by. Are you overloading your circuits and heading for certain burnout? How do you experience and deal with the pressure in your daily life?

Stress and Your Body

Stress produces adverse physical effects, for in our attempt to cope with everyday living our bodies experience what is known as the "fight-or-flight" response. It is as though our bodies were on constant alert status, ready for aggressive action to combat the many enemies we face. If we subject our bodies to too many stresses, the biochemical changes that occur during the fight-or-flight response may lead to a situation of chronic stress and anxiety. This causes bodily wear and tear, which can lead to a variety of what are known as *psychosomatic*, or *psychophysiological*, disorders. These are real bodily disorders, manifested in disabling physical symptoms yet caused by emotional factors and the prolonged effects of stress. These symptoms range from minor discomfort to life-threatening conditions; most commonly they take the form of peptic ulcers, migraine and tension headaches, asthma and other respiratory disorders, high blood pressure, skin disorders, arthritis, digestive disorders, disturbed sleeping patterns, poor circulation, strokes, and heart disease.

We have a choice. Will we respond in positive ways to stress or in negative ways? Some people recognize that stress is a fact of modern life, and they learn how to deal with it directly by reducing stressful situations as much as possible. They also find creative ways of lessening the effects of stress on themselves through exercise, hobbies, meditation, and the like. Other people choose to escape from stress by excessively using drugs or liquor, by overeating, and by using a variety of medications to suppress symptoms. The abuse of drugs is widespread among people of all ages in our culture. It is interesting to note that the so-called "primitive" cultures restrict the use of various drugs to special ritualistic situations, while in our so-called "advanced" culture drugs have become an integral part of our life-style geared toward helping us escape from stress.

Dr. Allan Abbott and his wife, Katherine, spent some time treating primitive people in Peru. This experience stimulated their interest in the ways that stress affects our bodies. The Abbotts became especially interested in coronary-prone behavior, which is so characteristic of the North American way of life, when they observed that stress was not a part of the lives of these people. While the leading causes of death in North America are cardiovascular diseases and cancer (diseases the Abbotts relate to stress), they rarely cause the death of Peruvian Indians.

In Allan Abbott's view, our bodies are paying a high price for the materialistic and stressful manner in which we live. As a family-practice specialist, Abbott has come to believe that about 75% of the physical ailments he treats are psychologically induced or related to stress. As an aside, he asserts that 90% of what he does as a physician that makes a significant difference is psychological in nature, rather than medical.

According to him, belief in the doctor and the process and procedures a doctor employs has a great deal to do with curing patients. Taking a blood test, having an X ray done, getting a shot, and simple conversation with the physician are factors that appear to make patients improve. Indeed, faith healers work on this very principle of the role of belief and its effects on the body.

In agreement with Abbott is Albrecht (1979), who writes that many physicians have commented that 80% of their patients have emotionally induced disorders. A number of physicians treat their patients with medications such as tranquilizers, stomach remedies, sleeping pills, and pain killers. Instead of dealing with those factors that are producing the disorders, namely the life-styles of the patients, they treat the symptoms.

Accepting Responsibility for Your Body

Do you control your body? Or does your body control you? Not all physicians prescribe pills to alleviate the symptoms of what they see as a problematic life-style. Psychologically oriented physicians emphasize the role of *choice* and *responsibility* as critical determinants of our physical and psychological well-being. In their practices they challenge their patients to look at what they are doing to their bodies through the lack of exercise, the substances they take in, and other damaging behavior. While they may prescribe medication to lower a person's extremely high blood pressure, they inform the patient that medications can do only so much and that what is needed is a radical change in life-style.

However, doctors often find that most of the people they see are more interested in getting pills and in removing their symptoms than in changing a stressful life-style. These patients would much rather see themselves as the victims of heart attacks than as responsible for their heart trouble.

A growing number of doctors think in terms of an integrated concept of health. This view includes paying attention to personality patterns and life-styles. Perhaps the key principles underlying the integrated approach to health (also called the holistic health concept) is *responsibility*. In commenting on the responsibility we bear for our physical health, Albrecht (1979) makes several points that sum up the issue of who controls our bodies:

> [Responsibility] is the notion that one's health is almost entirely a function of what one does with one's body and one's thoughts. Poor health behaviors lead to poor health.

> Immature thinking and reacting lead to negative emotions and unnecessary stress. Overeating, oversmoking, overuse of tobacco, abuse of recreational drugs or patient medicines, and sedentary living are *choices* that one can make or unmake. By taking complete responsibility for your health, you become obligated to yourself to act and live in ways that will guarantee your own total wellness [p. 31].

As you can readily see, it makes a world of difference whether you see yourself as a passive victim or an active agent in the maintenance of your body. If you believe that you simply catch colds or are ill-fated enough to get sick, and if you don't see what you can do to prevent bodily illnesses, then your body is controlling you. But if you recognize that the way you are choosing to lead your life (including accepting responsibility for what you consume, how you exercise, and the stresses you put yourself under) has a direct bearing on your physical and psychological well-being, then you can be in control of your body. At this time in your life, how would you answer these central questions: Do you control your body? Or does your body control you?

High-Stress Life-Style and Your Heart

I, too, am guilty at times of not listening to signals my body is sending. A few years ago I was confronted with some heart pains. Tests showed irregular heart beats, and my cardiologist tried to give me a subtle message that I should look at my life-style and slow down a bit. Knowing that I was a psychologist, he did not give me a lecture on the relationship between stress and heart attacks, but he did ask me to read a book by Friedman and Rosenman (1974), *Type A Behavior and Your Heart.* At the very least, that incident taught me that I am not an indestructible machine.

Traditionally, medical experts have considered diet, hereditary factors, being overweight, smoking cigarettes, and a lack of exercise as the primary causes of heart disease. There is increasing evidence, however, that a high-stress life-style is causally linked to heart disease.

Studying the relationship of life-styles and personality behavioral patterns to heart attacks, Friedman and Rosenman concluded that the major cause of coronary disease is a complex of emotional reactions they call "Type A" behavior. Key characteristics of the Type A personality are a *time urgency,* a preoccupation with *productivity and achievement,* and a *competitive drive.* These people are aggressively involved in a chronic and incessant struggle to achieve more and more in less and less time. Possessed by a "hurry sickness," they strive to make more money and to produce as much as possible as fast as possible. Type A personalities do not accept the fact that they can become exhausted. Friedman and Rosenman (1974) write: "It is the Type A man's ceaseless striving, his everlasting *struggle* with time, that we believe so very frequently leads to his early demise from coronary heart disease" (p. 87).

Other behaviors of Type A personalities are as follows: Creating deadlines that they try to beat; assuming too many responsibilities and therefore becoming trapped in several stressful situations at once; being unable to really relax or to have fun; experiencing chronic stress; passively accepting high-stress situations and pressures; perceiving life as serious; being preoccupied with work and productivity, with little balance for solitude and meaningful social relationships; and being driven.

Thus, although all the evidence is not yet in, it appears that chronic, unrelieved stress is a primary cause of heart attacks. The contributions of Friedman and Rosenman challenge us to think about concrete ways to reduce stress, to learn to manage it better, and to make some basic changes in living that will lead to a low-stress life-style—becoming what they call the "Type B" person. Considering that each year over a million people in the United States suffer heart attacks (about two every minute), it is imperative that we learn to cope more successfully with stress.

Developing a Type B Personality

Developing a Type B orientation means making clear choices in organizing our lives so that we keep stress to a minimum. Transforming oneself from a Type A person entails learning a balance in life, especially between work and play. It involves changing basic attitudes and thoughts so that we do not react so intensely to situations and thus cause stress. Most of all, it demands that we accept full personal responsibility for how we are living—recognizing that our continual choices influence who we are and that we are not passively programmed and rigidly molded once and for all.

From a personal perspective, I know how difficult it is to make the transformation from Type A to Type B. I can't expect to cram my life with activities all semester, fragmenting myself with many stressful situations, and then expect a "day off" to rejuvenate my system. Instead, I am slowly learning that I need to acquire ways of cutting down on those situations that cause stress and to deal differently with the stresses that are inevitable. Taking a few moments out for quiet reflection, learning relaxation exercises, practicing some form of meditation, getting adequate sleep, having a sound diet, keeping physically fit, participating in a regular exercise program, and making other conscious choices that lead to a low-stress life-style are some avenues of maintaining a healthy body and mind.

I must add that making a *basic* change in life-style takes a tremendous degree of determination. As one person who has not yet succeeded at making the change from Type A to Type B, all I can say is "It ain't easy, but if this is a change I sincerely want, then I can do it."

In much of the remainder of this chapter we'll consider some practical, constructive ways to deal with stress. The roles of relaxation, exercise, and diet, three key factors in preserving our physical and psychological well-being, will be examined.

Time Out for Personal Reflection

Are you greatly increasing your chances of a heart attack by choosing coronary-prone behavior? The following survey is an adaptation of the characteristics of the Type A personality as described by Friedman and Rosenman (1974). Take this self-inventory to determine to what degree each of these behavioral traits is typical of you. Use this code: A = This is very much true of me; B = this is sometimes true of me; C = this is rarely true of me; and D = this is almost never true of me.

_____   *1. I tend to speak rapidly.*

_____   *2. My speech has an explosive quality to it, and I often accentuate many of my words.*

_____   *3. My voice often sounds irritated.*

_____   *4. Most of the time I walk and move with haste.*

_____   *5. I am a fast eater.*

_____   *6. When I eat, I generally read or watch television.*

_____   *7. I typically find myself trying to do more and more in less and less time.*

_____   *8. I persistently feel that I have unfinished projects, even though I work long and hard hours.*

_____   *9. If I have to wait in line or get caught in traffic, I tend to become upset and irritated.*

_____   *10. When others are speaking, I often get impatient in wanting them to make their point.*

_____   *11. Often I find myself trying to do too many things at once.*

_____ 12. Many times I attempt to maneuver the conversation around to a topic that interests me.

_____ 13. When others are speaking, I am generally thinking about what I will say next.

_____ 14. I feel guilty when I relax or do nothing for several hours or several days.

_____ 15. I am highly competitive.

_____ 16. At times I'm afraid to stop, for fear that I won't get enough done.

_____ 17. I measure my worth as a person by the number of my accomplishments.

_____ 18. Very often I set impossible tasks and deadlines for myself, and then I try to beat these deadlines.

_____ 19. There is an urge within me to continually get ahead, for I am never satisfied with where I am.

_____ 20. Time controls me; I do not control time.

A few suggestions for using this inventory:

· Look over the items that you rated as being true of you much of the time. Which of these traits would you most like to change? How can you begin to make these changes?

· Have someone else who knows you fairly well complete this inventory for you on the basis of how they perceive you. Don't show them how you responded until they finish rating you. Then, compare results and talk about any differences that interest either of you.

· If you are attempting to change from a Type A person to a Type B person, you could take this same inventory later in the course to see if you have made progress in any of the areas.

Three Ways of Dealing with Stress

A combination of factors contributes to our physical and psychological well-being. Thus, a holistic approach to health must pay attention to how people cause their own psychological distress. But it must also focus on their life-styles, including a range of specific factors: how they work and play, how they relax, what and how they eat, how they keep physically fit, their relationships with others, and their spiritual needs. In this section we will explore three aspects of dealing with the stresses of everyday life and taking care of our bodies: relaxation methods, exercise programs, and diet.

COULD HE CALL YOU BACK...HE'S
RELAXING BEFORE DINNER

Relaxation Methods

Before you continue reading, take a few moments to "relax" and to think about how you relax. Do you engage in certain forms of relaxation on a regular basis? What do you consider relaxing? Look over the following list and decide which forms of relaxation are for you. Think about the quality of each form of relaxation and how often you use it.

- sitting in a quiet place for as few as ten minutes each day and just letting your mind wander
- listening to music and fully hearing and feeling it (without making it the background of another activity)
- sleeping deeply and restfully
- being involved in a hobby that gives you pleasure
- engaging in sports that have the effect of calming you
- asking for and receiving a massage
- taking longer than usual in lovemaking

walking in the woods or on the beach
· closing your eyes and listening to the sounds in nature
· listening to the sounds of your breathing
· practicing some form of meditation each day
· relaxing in a hot tub
· allowing yourself to let go fully with friends
· regularly practicing muscle-relaxation exercises
· practicing some form of self-hypnosis to cut down stress and outside distractions

Ask yourself which of these or other ways you use to relax. Consider what gets in your way of achieving the level of relaxation you'd like as often as you'd like.

Barriers to relaxation. Some of us experience a great deal of difficulty in fully relaxing. For example, I approach relaxation with purpose and intensity. I often make the mistake of trying too hard to relax, which has the effect of making what I am doing one more burden. I can recall setting out for a vacation with my family saying "We *will* have a good time this week, and we *will* enjoy each other's company!" While I do a lot of walking in the woods, my mind is not often quiet. Frequently I return from such a solitary hike with many ideas for other projects. A constant struggle is to quiet myself enough to become aware of barriers that get in the way of unwinding.

In our complex society, many of us encounter obstacles in allowing ourselves to fully relax. Even if we take a few moments in a busy schedule to unwind, our minds may be reeling with thoughts of past or future events. Another problem is simply finding a quiet and private place where we can relax, and a time where we will be free from interruptions. Perhaps an important lesson to learn is how to let go for even a few minutes, to learn to unwind while waiting in a line or riding on a bus.

A *relaxation exercise.* Let me describe an exercise in self-relaxation that you can do by yourself. You can practice relaxation in many situations, and doing so can help you assume control of your own behavior, instead of being controlled by situations that produce tension within you. For a period of at least a week (and preferably much longer), engage in relaxation training for approximately 20 to 30 minutes daily. The purpose of the exercise is to teach you to become more aware of the distinction between tension states and relaxation states. A further objective is to reduce unnecessary anxiety and tension. The strategy for achieving muscular relaxation is to repeatedly tense and relax various muscle groups. To deepen your relaxation, auxiliary techniques such as concentrating on your breathing and imagining yourself in peaceful situations can eventually be added.

Here are some guidelines for your relaxation exercise. Make sure that you're in a peaceful setting and in a relaxed position. Tighten and relax the various parts of your body, beginning with your upper extremities and progressing downward to your lower extremities.

· Clench your fists tightly—so tightly that it hurts. Let go of the tension and relax.
· Stiffen the lower part of one arm. Tense it. Feel the tension. Let go of the tension.
· Tense the upper part of the arm. Tighten it until it begins to hurt. Relax it.
· Repeat the last two steps for your other arm.
· Wrinkle up your forehead. Wrinkle it tighter and tighter. Then relax and smooth it out. Picture your entire forehead and scalp becoming smoother and more relaxed.
· Raise your eyebrows as high as you can. Hold this position. Relax.
· Close your eyes as tightly as you can. Feel the tension. Close them even tighter, and feel that tension. Let go, and feel the relaxation around your eyes.
· Wrinkle your nose as tightly as you can. Relax.
· Clench your jaw, and bite your teeth together hard. Feel the pressure. Increase the tension in your jaw. Let your jaw and mouth become increasingly relaxed. Enjoy this relaxation.
· Smile in an exaggerated way, and hold it. Let go. Purse your lips as tightly as you can. Tighten your mouth muscles and feel the tension in your entire face. Let go of the tension. Relax.
· The exercise progresses with the neck, shoulders, and upper back; then the chest, abdomen, and lower back; then the rest of the body, down to the toes; and finally the entire body. During the entire exercise, keep your eyes gently closed. Cover all the major muscle groups. For each group, tense the muscles for several seconds and then relax them. Note the difference between the tension and relaxation states, and repeat the tension/release cycles at least once or twice for each muscle group.

With practice, you can become aware of tension in every part of your body, and you can learn to relax all the areas of your body, separately or together, without first having to tense them. Ultimately, the goal is to teach you to control your tension states by choosing to switch to a deep muscular-relaxation state.

I recommend that you review this relaxation exercise and practice it twice daily. It takes only about 20 minutes once you have learned the procedure, and you can call on it at those times in the day when you are under particular stress. Even closing your eyes for a few moments, concentrating on your breathing and the tension within your body, and telling yourself to "let go" are valuable tools in dealing with stress when you feel its effects on your body.

If you are like most people, you may not be consciously aware of the tension that you are carrying around in your body. People will sometimes give up too quickly as they are learning progressive-relaxation procedures, because they are not seeing immediate results. It may take several weeks of practice to really feel the tension in your body and to release it. However, once you master some skills of progressive relaxation, it will be possible to relax your entire body in a few moments.[2]

Breathing. Proper breathing is an antidote to stress, and it is essential to learning how to relax fully. Many of us busy ourselves so much that we literally forget to breathe. If you have developed poor breathing habits, one way to begin improving is simply to pay attention to how you breathe at any given moment. At times during the day you can actually stop and become aware of your breathing and spend a few minutes taking deep breaths. Breathing exercises can help reduce anxiety, irritability, muscular tension, depression, and fatigue.

Meditation. Meditation, one method of getting personally focused, is enjoying an increased popularity among people of all ages. For some people it still has an aura of mysticism, and they may shy away from it because it seems intricately bound up with elaborate rituals, strange language, strange clothing, and abstract philosophical and spiritual notions. But you don't have to wear exotic garb and sit in a lotus position in order to meditate. Simply sitting quietly and letting your mind wander or looking within can be a simple form of meditation.

---

[2]In their very helpful manual, *The Relaxation and Stress Reduction Workbook*, Davis, Eshelman, and McKay (1980) report that progressive relaxation has yielded excellent results in dealing with muscular tension, anxiety, insomnia, depression, fatigue, irritable bowel, muscle spasms, neck and back pain, high blood pressure, mild phobias, and stuttering.

As Davis, Eshelman, and McKay (1980) note, meditation can be practiced independently of any religious or philosophical orientation, purely as a means of reducing inner discord and increasing self-knowledge. They describe a variety of methods of meditation and urge readers to select one or more that suit them.

Meditation is effective in creating a deep state of relaxation in a fairly short time. It can be used to prevent or treat high blood pressure and heart disease. It can reduce anxiety and the effects of stress. However, most writers on meditation agree that exercises must be practiced for at least a month for meditation's more profound effects to be experienced.

Davis, Eshelman, and McKay (1980) outline four major components of meditation:

- a quiet place with a minimum of external distractions
- a comfortable position that can be held for about 20 minutes without causing stress
- dwelling on an object or a repetitive sound or word while letting thoughts simply pass by
- adopting a passive attitude, which includes letting go of thoughts and distractions and simply returning to the object you are dwelling on[3]

It's your choice.   Each of us has different sources and ways of relaxing. While I relax by quickly walking up mountain trails, you may find that the same activity wears you out. On the other hand, you may derive considerable pleasure from a card game, while I impatiently endure the game and think of other things I would rather be doing. Thus, we need to be honest with ourselves and determine if the activities we call "relaxing" are indeed that.

At times we might literally wear ourselves out in our attempts to provide relaxing times for our families and ourselves. For example, with the trend toward a shorter work week, many people drive for long distances, battling crowds on the freeway and then fighting the crowds when they finally arrive at their weekend spot. A couple of days later, they fight the same traffic getting home, catch up on house and yard chores, and then return to work the next day thoroughly exhausted from

---

[3]I recommend three books if you would like to do further reading or find a method of meditation that fits you: *The Relaxation and Stress Reduction Workbook*, by Davis, Eshelman, and McKay (1980); Shapiro's (1978) *Precision Nirvana;* and Ram Dass' (1978) *Journey of Awakening: A Meditator's Guidebook.*

their weekend "recreation." Your individual preferences are the determinants in this case, and you need to decide if you are getting what you
want from your times of relaxation.

Whatever forms your relaxation takes, the benefits are directly related
to reducing the negative effects of stress and in providing you with some
degree of mental tranquillity. You might ask yourself if you are doing
those things that you do find relaxing and if you are doing them as often
as you'd like. If not, you can begin to arrange your priorities and make
the time to renew yourself.

Exercise Programs

You will probably agree that exercise is essential for your physical and
psychological well-being. But you may also say how difficult it is to
commit yourself to a regular program. Having decided on a realistic
plan for exercising, we often come up with a list of "good excuses" why
we can't stick to it when it becomes inconvenient. Unfortunately, not
many people make exercises a priority in their lives, and still fewer are
willing to schedule their lives around an exercise program. For instance,
would you be willing to say that you could not schedule an appointment
at a certain time because that is the time you exercise?

Many corporations have come to realize the value of exercising as a
way of helping people manage stress and prevent burnout on the job.
While I'm not convinced that these corporations are primarily motivated by humanistic concerns, they apparently have found out prag-
matically that exercising pays off in terms of productivity. One such
organization encourages employees by using money as an incentive; it
pays 64 cents for each mile of swimming, 4 cents a mile for riding a
bicycle, and 15 cents a mile for jogging! If corporations recognize the
value of exercise in managing stress and increasing workers' output,
perhaps you can find some personal motivations for developing a program that you'd be willing to stick to.

Being honest with ourselves is essential, for sometimes we may
deceive ourselves into thinking that we are getting plenty of exercise in
walking up and down stairs or in walking around the office. While some
exercise programs may be fun and a source of joy, they typically entail
hard work, commitment, and self-discipline. For example, starting a
jogging program can be physically exhausting for most people and something they dread at the outset. If they push themselves beyond this initial
resistance, however, they may soon become addicted (Glasser, 1976;
Sheehan, 1975).

It is obviously helpful, therefore, to select a form of exercise that we enjoy. For example, I'm not much for competitive sports, yet I find pleasure in brisk walking, bike riding in high altitudes, and hiking, most of which can be solitary pursuits. If you like company in your exercising, you can find a friend to jog or go hiking with, or you can take part in team sports.

When you have found a program that appeals to you, it is essential to work out a plan that will enable you to stick to your goals. Recognize how easy it is to establish unrealistically high goals, in which case you might be setting yourself up for defeat. Most exercise books provide charts that give guidance on how to progress at a realistic rate, depending on your present physical condition and your age.

Diet and Nutrition

A third way of managing stress and taking care of your body is to develop a realistic diet and nutrition program. I will be using the term *diet* to include all the substances taken into the body, including food, drinks, medications, and drugs.

Should you decide to improve your diet and begin by looking for information, you are likely to find yourself overwhelmed and confused. Bookstores are filled with books on diets, nutrition, and holistic health. In reviewing these resources, you will probably find that much of the information is inconsistent on the issue of what constitutes a healthy diet. One "expert" will call another "expert" a charlatan. You have probably seen news reports pointing out that certain diet programs are dangerous to your health. With all the conflicting literature, you may not find an answer to what constitutes an adequate diet program. But this glut of words does indicate an obvious trend: people are becoming increasingly aware of what they put into their bodies.

Our frequent trips to see Marianne's parents, who live in a German village where a large percentage of the people still produce their own food, have sensitized us to the contrasts in taste and nutritional value between foods recently harvested and those that are prepackaged and stored. It is very difficult in a technologically advanced country to live close to the land, yet if one is interested one can find markets with fresh produce and organically grown food. Their popularity is increasing all over the country. This trend also points to the fact that many people are concerned about what they consume.

Marianne and I have read a variety of sources on diets, and we observe some common patterns that seem sensible to us. Our reading and our conversations with experts have helped us come up with some diet guidelines. We'd like to share them with you in the following "Time Out." We encourage you to think about what you are putting into your body and to take increasing responsibility for the effects on your body of the substances you are using.

Time Out for Personal Reflection

The following statements are guidelines for a healthful diet. It is a challenge to pay attention to what we eat and the substances we use. If we do, we can accept more responsibility for how we feel physically and psychologically. Perhaps the best expert on what constitutes a good personal diet is you—let your body tell you, and listen!

For the following statements, put a 1 in the space if you behave in this way most of the time, a 2 if you behave this way sometimes, and a 3 if you behave this way not very often.

_____   1. *I strive for a balanced diet with the six basic nutrients: water, protein, carbohydrate, fat, minerals, and vitamins.*

_____   2. *Typically, I watch my caloric intake.*

_____   3. *I tend to avoid eating foods with high levels of fats, oils, and cholesterol.*

_____   4. *I avoid eating sugar and salt as much as possible.*

_____   5. *I don't drink excessive amounts of coffee, tea, or soda pop.*

_____   6. *I eat many foods that contain fibers.*

_____   7. *As much as possible, I eat fresh food rather than preserved food.*

_____   8. *I watch the amount of red meat (beef, pork, and lamb) that I consume.*

_____   9. *I do not make a habit of using "junk" foods to satisfy my hunger.*

_____   10. *I usually sit down and take my time in eating.*

_____   11. *Before beginning a vitamin program, I decide if my body needs these supplements.*

_____   12. *My use of alcohol is very limited.*

_____   13. *I don't use hard drugs.*

_____   14. *I don't use tobacco.*

_____   15. *Typically, I eliminate (or keep to rare use) such drugs as aspirin, marijuana, tranquilizers, diet pills, laxatives, cold remedies, and pain pills.*

Some suggestions for using the inventory:

· *Are there any habits of diet and nutrition that you want and are willing to change?*
· *If you decide to make some specific changes, it might be best to focus on one target behavior at a time in order to lessen the chances of getting discouraged.*
· *In class, you might compare your responses with those of fellow students. What are your reactions to the pattern of your responses?*

Two Ways We Abuse Our Bodies

This section focuses on two common abuses to our body: the misuse of drugs and carrying around excessive weight.

Misuse of Drugs

We are conditioned to take an aspirin for a headache, to take a tranquilizer when we are anxious, to rely on stimulants to keep us up all night at the end of a term, and to use a variety of drugs to reduce other physical symptoms and emotional stresses. We are not so conditioned to use our own bodily resources to heal ourselves, which is a more positive means of achieving health. While all drugs are not necessarily dangerous in themselves, it is the misuse and abuse of them that is harmful to our body and soul. We all use drugs in some form or another. You might take an honest self-inventory to determine your drug intake and abuse.

It continually amazes me how many people persist in habitual use of a drug while being well-informed about its negative effects on their bodies. Nicotine is an example. Users may wake up with fits of coughing, their bodies may ooze of stale smoke, even a minimal amount of exercise may leave them short of breath, and they may well fear the increased risk of lung cancer.

Another interesting example is the increasing use of marijuana among people of all ages and social classes. Many will argue that there is no difference between a daily "joint" and a daily cocktail. Others will argue that there are differences, and that the regular use of marijuana has negative effects, both physiological and psychological. What I think is critical is that we be aware of our motivations and that we know the effects of using the drug.

There are some hazards associated with the daily use of marijuana, such as depression and lung cancer. While there is not enough scientific evidence to clearly specify the physical and psychological dangers, most experts agree that daily use is excessive. Aside from the physical health hazards, it is difficult to imagine how a person could smoke pot every day without eventually adversely affecting his or her job, schoolwork, or general productivity. Certainly alcoholics cannot get drunk every day without affecting their lives negatively.

It is time for us to take a serious and honest look at our lives when we depend on drugs of any kind (including alcohol) to feel a certain way. Some may argue that a sexual experience is intensified through using marijuana, that they feel less inhibited in social situations, that they feel more at one with the universe, that they are able to really laugh and feel great, and so forth. While I won't dispute these claims, I personally would like to be able to achieve these ends without having to rely on marijuana, alcohol, or any other drug. This seems even more critical when people say that they *cannot* feel elated, that they *cannot* have a good time, that they *don't* enjoy sex, and that they are *unable* to feel much of anything *without* using drugs. My hope is that we can rely on our own internal resources to experience "highs."

In the final analysis, people who are abusing their bodies through the misuse of drugs must honestly consider what they are getting from using drugs and the price they are paying for their decisions. They must determine for themselves whether the price in terms of their physical and psychological well-being is too high, and they need to balance that price against the price of giving up their habit.

Being Overweight

While eating in a restaurant in St. Louis, Marianne and I watched an extremely overweight man who was heaping butter on two small loaves of French bread. He also poured cream and lots of sugar into his coffee, devoured a large bowl of spaghetti, and topped off his dinner with a big serving of ice cream. All the while, he was perspiring and breathing heavily. Marianne remarked to me "I wonder why he wants to kill himself?"

Surely there is enough evidence from the medical profession to demonstrate that being overweight is not healthy. To have a trim body is more than a question of esthetics; it pertains to physical fitness and to health. While you are probably not in the category of the man in that restaurant, the problem of fighting against weight gain may be prominent in your mind. Perhaps you have said:

- "I have tried every program there is, and I just can't seem to stick to one."
- "I've lost extra pounds many times, only to put them on again."
- "I'm too occupied with school to think about losing weight."
- "I love to eat and I hate to exercise, yet I get disgusted with the shape of my body."

Can you think of other such statements that you've made about the condition and appearance of your body? Even if you are interested in taking off extra pounds, you might well encounter difficulty in regulating your eating habits and keeping yourself motivated to follow a regular exercise program. You might be lured into thinking that there is an easy solution to the problem of being overweight, and thus be easy prey for a succession of diet plans that promise quick and painless weight loss.

The chances are that you will not be able to eat all you want when you want and expect to effortlessly maintain an ideal weight for your body structure. Consequently, you'll need some degree of motivation for taking off excess weight and keeping it off. And you'll need to examine what stops you from following your plan.

In their excellent self-help book, *Toward a Self-Managed Life Style*, Williams and Long (1979) describe a behavioral approach to weight reduction that involves taking systematic steps to attain realistic goals. Cautioning that people are often lured by diet plans that promise quick, painless, and dramatic results, they emphatically make the point that such plans seldom produce long-lasting results and that weight reduction involves personal effort and a long-term commitment. I fully agree with the spirit of their message to those of us who are serious about weight control: "In a word, your style of eating must be changed. Any plan that fails to seek a permanent change in life style—a change you and your body can accept indefinitely—will produce, at best, only temporary results" (p. 89).

Thus, a basic change in attitudes and life-style seems important in successfully dealing with a weight problem. Fat people do not eat simply because they are hungry. They are typically more responsive to external cues in their environment. One of these is the acquiescence of well-meaning friends, who may joke with them by saying: "Oh, don't worry about those extra pounds. What's life without enjoyment of eating? Besides, there's more of you to love this way!" This kind of "friendship" can make it even more difficult to discipline ourselves by watching what and how much we eat.

In addition, our eating habits are largely determined by the accessibility of food. It is known that eating tends to be controlled by sight, smell, and taste, as well as having food readily available. Thus, if we hope to decrease our eating behavior, a basic approach is to reduce the range of stimuli that precipitate eating.

Do you want to change?   One good way to determine if you want to change is to look at yourself standing naked before a full-length mirror. If you are overweight, pretend that your body could speak. Could your body be saying any of the following?

· "I don't like myself."
· "My fat will keep me at a distance."
· "I am killing myself slowly."
· "I am burdened."
· "I don't get around much any more!"
· "I'm basically lazy and self-indulging."

Whatever condition your body happens to be in, let it "speak," and respect what it is "saying" by listening with care. If you determine that you are heavier than you'd like to be, it could prove useful to devote some time to thinking about why you are in the shape that you are in. While you are likely to say that you love to eat and hate to exercise, the truth of the matter may not be quite so obvious. You could begin by thinking about what you actually get from being overweight. Like it or not, there are certain "payoffs" to being fat, even if they are negative. Here are some possible reasons why people get and stay overweight:

· An overweight son or daughter may keep weight on as a way of getting constant parental attention, even if that attention consists of nagging to watch what he or she is eating.
· A girl may gain weight during adolescence because her father is threatened by her physical attractiveness.
· Overweight persons may convince themselves that they are being rejected for their fat, and thus not have to look at other dimensions of themselves.
· Some who are afraid of getting close to others may use their fat as a barrier.

• Those who are afraid of their sexuality and where it might lead them often get fat as a way of reducing their chances of becoming sexually involved.

You will also need to determine whether you are willing to exert the consistent effort that it takes to keep physically fit, as well as whether this is the right time for you to lose weight. Williams and Long (1979) have a few questions that help people make these determinations.

• Are you at least 10% overweight?
• Do you have problems interpersonally because of your weight?
• Does your present weight pose a health problem?
• Are you getting negative feedback because of your weight?
• Are you experiencing other problems that you consider more important than losing weight at this time?
• Are you able to find a support system that will help you stay with your weight-reducing program?

Some questions that I find useful to add to the list of Williams and Long in determining whether you're ready to do what is needed to lose weight are:

• Do *you* see yourself as having a weight problem?
• Is your self-image and self-respect negatively affected by your weight?
• Are you willing to look in the mirror and really experience your body? Do you like what you see? If not, are you willing to do anything to change it?
• Are you willing to do the hard work of eating sensibly and doing regular exercise to get yourself in physical shape?
• Are you willing to look beyond a simple answer for your being over-weight?
• Can you learn to reinforce yourself, even if you do not receive positive feedback and support from others in your environment?
• To what degree do you value your health, and what priority do you place on physical appearance?
• Are you willing to give up some of the fattening things you eat?

Strategies in weight control.   The following are some practical suggestions if you decide that losing weight and then maintaining an appropriate weight is a priority for you. If you are serious about this issue, review and consider these suggestions and see which of them make the most sense to you. Also, you will probably want to do some additional reading, especially in applying behavioral methods as a part of your self-directed program. With this in mind, consider the following strategies as a way of carrying out your choice.

1. Are you really overweight? Some thin people perceive themselves as being fat, while some people who are overweight by most objective standards may see themselves as just fine. In deciding if you are overweight you could ask yourself: Are there things you'd like to do but that you are prevented from doing because of your condition? Can you participate in sports? Can you exert yourself physically? Can you participate in satisfactory sex? Do you get overly tired?

2. If you decide to stand naked in front of the mirror, go through each of your body parts and "become each part," letting it "speak." For example, give your nose a personality, and pretend that your nose could speak. What might it say? If your legs were to speak, what do you imagine they'd say? (Do this for *every* part of your body, even if you find yourself wanting to bypass certain parts. In that case you might say: "I'm an ugly nose that doesn't want any recognition. I'd just like to hide, but I'm too big to be inconspicuous!")

3. If you are overweight, is your weight a barrier and a burden? For example, consider whether your fat is keeping you from doing what you want to do. Does it keep certain people away from you? You might pick up some object that is equivalent to the extra pounds you carry with you, letting yourself hold this object and begin to experience the excess weight.

4. Imagine yourself as looking more the way you'd like to. Let yourself think about how you might be different, as well as how your life would be different.

5. If you are overweight, are you blaming yourself and putting yourself down? Are you accepting personal responsibility for your condition and what you are doing now to contribute to that condition? What are you willing to do to change?

6. Are you paying attention to your *behavior* and not just to what you *say* you want to do or how you'd like to be different? (While some people say that they hate being fat and resolve to change, they also continue to eat fattening foods or large portions, and they fail to exercise. I tend to believe what people actually do rather than what they say.)

7. Have you had a thorough physical examination, and did you consult your physician about your plans to develop a weight-control program? If you are overweight, did you check first to see if there are some medical causes for the problem?

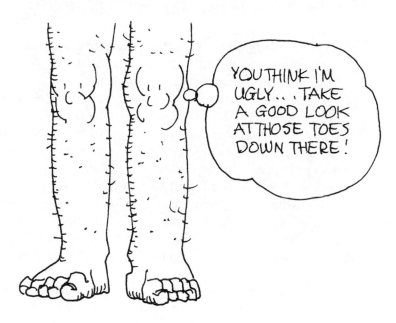

8. Are you familiar with some reading on diet, nutrition, and exercise? In addition to watching your diet, develop an exercise program that will work for you. In this way you are not only being calorie conscious but are also doing something to keep your body physically fit and burn off excess calories.

9. Beware of common methods of sabotage, including self-sabotage and others' attempts to thwart your plans. You might overeat when you feel depressed, have fattening food within reach, or decide to reward your progress by going on an eating binge. Others can sabotage your efforts with statements such as: "Forget the calories. You've worked hard so enjoy your dessert." "Oh hell, you can start dieting after this vacation." "Have a chocolate malt with me. I don't like to drink alone."

10. Apply some behavioral principles and procedures in your attempt to lose weight: Develop specific and realistic goals. Monitor your eating habits and keep records of what you eat, when you eat, how much you eat, and how you feel during and afterwards. Keep a record of your weight. And develop a system of reinforcements as an incentive to keep on your program.

11. Make a list of target foods that add to your weight problem. Eliminate one type of food at a time. For example, perhaps you can avoid dessert. As you make progress, then you can avoid other foods on your list.

12. Avoid eating fattening food as much as possible. Avoid snacking on candy and potato chips. Substitute fruits or raw vegetables.

13. Develop alternatives to overeating, such as physical activity. This form of substitution has obvious benefits.

14. Recognize that simply taking weight off, as difficult as it may be, does not mean that you have your problem solved. If you don't understand what your overeating and being overweight mean and the reasons for these behaviors, you could easily revert to self-defeating practices. Accept the reality that maintaining a healthy weight will entail continued work and commitment on your part.

15. After taking off the weight you wanted to remove, take another look at yourself standing naked in that full-length mirror. Let yourself go through the exercise of "becoming your body and speaking." What does it say? How do you feel as you see a new reflection in that mirror?

Group weight-control programs.   If you are thinking about supplementing your self-directed weight-control program with some type of group program that makes use of the "buddy system" for support and guidance, a word of caution is in order. There are far too many programs designed strictly for making money; some of them are dangerous to your health; and some of them foster dependency on others to the extent that you are likely to revert to old ways if you leave the program. Ideally, you should be able to make it on your own if something happens to the program. In general, the programs that seem to be the most successful have some of the following characteristics in common:

· Support groups are a part of the program.
· Attention is given to the psychological dynamics of being overweight and to why you put weight on in the first place.
· The program is well structured, and there is a form of observation and accountability.
· Attention is devoted to good nutritional habits and exercise.
· The program helps you become aware of what, when, how, how much, where, and why you eat.
· There is an encouragement for you to develop life-long proper eating habits, rather than fostering a crash diet.
· The program teaches you to develop responsibility and self direction and to create a self-management program based on a system of positive reinforcement.

As with other programs that have been discussed in this chapter, simply getting into a structured weight-control program alone is not the answer to weight loss. It takes a good deal of motivation on your part and commitment to follow through with the program, particularly when the going gets rough.

Time Out for Personal Reflection

1. *The following are some common rationalizations that people use for not changing patterns of behavior that affect their bodies. Look over these statements and decide what ones, if any, you use. What others do you sometimes use that are not on this list?*

   _____   *I don't have the time to exercise every day.*

   _____   *No matter how I try to lose weight, nothing seems to work.*

   _____   *I sabotage myself, and others sabotage me, in my attempts to lose weight.*

   _____   *I'll stop smoking as soon as my life becomes less stressful.*

   _____   *When I have a vacation, then I'll relax.*

   _____   *Even though I drink a lot (or use other drugs), it calms me down and has never interfered with my life.*

   _____   *I need a drink (or a marijuana cigarette) to relax.*

   _____   *Food isn't important to me; I eat anything I can grab fast.*

   _____   *I simply don't have the time to eat three balanced meals a day.*

   _____   *Food has gotten so expensive, I just can't afford to eat decent meals any more.*

   _____   *If I stop smoking, then I'll surely gain weight.*

   _____   *I simply cannot function without several cups of coffee.*

   _____   *If I don't stop smoking, then I might get lung cancer or die a little sooner, but we all have to go sometime.*

   What other statements could you add to this list?

   _____

   _____

2. *What is your reaction when somebody says "There is really no difference between having an evening drink or two and smoking a joint to unwind"?*

   _____

   _____

   _____

3. *Many people begin weight-control programs and do lose some weight but then revert to old patterns and gain their weight back. What are your ideas on why this is so? Is this true of you?*

_____

_____

4. *Complete the following sentences with the first word or phrase that comes to mind:*
   a. *One way I abuse my body is* _____
   b. *One way I neglect my body is* _____
   c. *When people notice my physical appearance I think that* _____

   _____

   d. *When I look at my body in the mirror I* _____
   e. *I could be healthier if only* _____
   f. *One way I could cut down the stress in my life is* _____

   _____

   g. *If I could change one aspect of my body it would be my* _____
   h. *One way that I relax is* _____
   i. *I'd describe my diet as* _____
   j. *For me, exercising is* _____

5. *What are your attitudes toward your body? Take some time to study your body, and become aware of how you look to yourself and what your body feels like to you. Try standing naked in front of a full-length mirror, and reflect on some of these questions:*

   · *Is your body generally tight or relaxed? What parts tend to be the most unrelaxed?*
   · *What does your face tell you about yourself? What kind of expression do you convey through your eyes? Are there lines on your face? What parts are tight? Do you force a smile?*
   · *Are there any parts of your body that you feel ashamed of or try to hide? What aspects of your body would you most like to change? What are the parts of your body that you like the best? The least?*

6. *After you've done the exercise just described (perhaps several times over a period of a few days), record a few of your impressions below, or keep an extended account of your reactions in your journal.*

a. *How do you view your body, and how do you feel about it?*

_____

_____

b. *What messages do you convey to others about yourself through your body?*

_____

_____

c. *Are there any decisions you are now willing to make about changing your body?*

_____

_____

Your Body Image and Life Choices

Your view of your body and the decisions you have made about it have much to do with the choices that we are about to study in the rest of this book. In my view, people are affected in a very fundamental way by how they perceive their bodies and how they think others perceive their bodies.

If you feel basically unattractive, unappealing, or in some other way physically inferior, these self-perceptions are likely to have a powerful effect on other areas of your life. For example, you might be very critical of many of your physical characteristics. You may think that your ears are too big, that your nose is ill-shaped, that you have an ugly complexion, that you're too short, that you're not muscular enough. Perhaps some part of you believes that others will not want to approach you because of your appearance. If you *feel* that you are basically unattractive, you may well tell yourself that others will see your defects and will not want to be with you. Because of this feeling, you might contribute to the reactions that others have toward you by the messages you send to them. You may be perceived by others as aloof, distant, or judgmental. Even though you may want to get close to people, you may also be frightened of the possibility of meeting with their rejection.

If something like this is true of you, I challenge you to look at the part you might be playing in contributing to the reactions you get from others. How does your state of mind influence both your view of yourself and the view others have of you? Do you take even less care of your body because you're unhappy with it? Why should others approach you, if you continue to tell them that you are not worth approaching? Will others think more of you than you think of yourself?

You may say that there is little you can do to change certain aspects of your physical being, such as your height or basic build. Yet you *can* look at the attitudes you have formed about these physical characteristics. How important are they to who you are?

Consider also whether you made some decisions about your body early in life, or during adolescence, that still affect you. Did you feel embarrassed about certain of your physical characteristics? As you have matured physically, these characteristics might have changed—or become less important to others—yet you may still be stuck with some old perceptions and feelings. Even though others may think of you as an attractive person, you may react with suspicion and disbelief, for you continue to tell yourself that you are in some way inferior. By examining where you picked up some of your attitudes about your body, you can begin to challenge yourself with respect to the evidence that justifies your current self-perception.

In the next few chapters we consider the topics of sexuality, love, and intimate relationships. I encourage you to consider now how your perceptions of your body affect these areas of your life. Do you shy away from the opposite sex because of your fears about how others will react to your physical being? Might you keep yourself in a self-imposed prison, unwilling to initiate positive contact with others, simply because you assume they won't like the way you look? Does your body express your feelings of tenderness, anger, enthusiasm, and so on, or does it tend to be rigid and under control? By examining these questions, you can widen the brackets of freedom in these other areas of your life.

I end this chapter with an invitation to make an honest assessment of how you see your body and how you feel about it, as well as the many ways in which your views influence your behavior. Your subjective evaluation of your body is at least as powerful as your objective physical traits—and it is open to change.

Chapter Summary

The purpose of this chapter has been to stimulate you to think about how you are treating your body and how you might improve your physical and psychological well-being. Two questions were themes in the chapter: Do you control your body? Or does your body control you?

Stress was discussed within the framework of our modern civilization. We cannot realistically expect to eliminate stress from our lives, but we can modify our thinking and our life-styles to reduce stressful situations and manage stress more effectively.

The topic of stress highlighted the importance of a willingness to accept responsibility for what you are doing to your body. A central message was developed: listen to your body and respect what you hear.

An integrated approach of relaxation, exercise, and diet was proposed as a model for effectively dealing with the negative aspects of stress and as a way of taking care of your body. Again, you were asked to think about your patterns in these areas and to consider whether you are willing to make any changes. We also looked at some common ways that we abuse our bodies, especially through the misuse of drugs and through being overweight. Finally, we considered how your body image is centrally related to many other life choices in areas such as sexuality, intimate relationships, love, and loneliness.

I hope you will apply the specific examples emphasized in this chapter to whatever areas of your life concern you with respect to your body. Even if you are not presently concerned with the problems of stress, drug abuse, or weight control, you may have discovered certain attitudes about your body that are self-defeating. A theme of this chapter has been to examine what might be keeping you from really caring about your body—or acting on the caring that you say you have. The basic choice is more than a matter of smoking or not smoking, of exercising or not exercising; the basic choice concerns how you feel about yourself and about your life. By accepting responsibility for the feelings and attitudes you have developed about your body, you begin to free yourself from feeling victimized by your body.

Activities and Exercises

1. You may have become motivated enough to want to actively work at changing a pattern of behavior that is related to the health of your body. Some examples of self-directed programs you might want to set up for yourself include eliminating smoking (or some drug); reducing or eliminating alcoholic beverages; designing an effective exercise program; developing a systematic approach to losing weight and maintaining an appropriate weight; and making specific changes in your life-style in the direction of reducing stress. Begin by consulting a book such as Williams and Long (1979) or Watson and Tharp (1981)

for the details of setting up a program for self-directed behavior change. Then, you might want to read other books in the "Suggested Readings" to help you with the specific program you'd like to develop.

2. In your journal, keep an account of the stressful situations that you encounter for about a week or so. After each entry, you might note items such as: To what degree was the situation a stressful one because of your cognitions (or thoughts, beliefs, and assumptions pertaining to the events)? How were you affected? Do you see any ways of dealing with these stresses more effectively?

3. Consider making a written contract, with yourself and some other person, about changing a specific behavior. You could pledge to eliminate snacking, agree to keep a stress journal for a month, or make a contract to begin an exercise program. Check with the person you've signed the contract with frequently to appraise your progress.

4. In your journal, record for one week all the activities that are healthy for your body as well as those that are unhealthy. It could be valuable to record things such as what you eat, stress patterns, smoking and drinking, sleeping habits, exercise, relaxation, and so forth. After you've done this for a week, look over your list and determine whether there are areas that you'd be willing to work on during this semester.

5. Consider some of the following questions as a basis for self-examination on the issue of how your body image affects other aspects of your life. If you want, seek out a close friend and tell that person some of your answers to the following questions; then ask for honest feedback as one way of checking out your own perceptions of your body. Or you might form a small group in your class to share some of your reactions to your own bodies and the ways in which your feelings have influenced your behavior.

- Look at your face in a mirror, and carefully study your facial characteristics. What does your face tell you and others about your personal history? Does your face seem alive and inviting? Or does it reflect fear and tend to keep others away from you?
- What messages do you express to others through your body?
- When you look at your body, what does it tell you about the degree of caring you have for yourself? If you say that you care about yourself, yet your body belies this statement, what do you suppose is keeping you from acting on the caring you say you have?
- When you were a child or adolescent, did your body image keep you from doing certain things that you wanted to do? Do traces of some

earlier feelings about your body get in the way of doing what you'd like to do now? If so, what are some initial steps you can take to change?

Suggested Readings

Albrecht, K. *Stress and the Manager.* Englewood Cliffs, N.J.: Prentice-Hall, 1979. If you were to select just one book on stress management, this would be my top recommendation. The author has many sound ideas and practical suggestions for changing to a low-stress life-style.

American Heart Association Cookbook (3rd ed.). New York: Ballantine, 1979. A helpful guide on cooking tips and methods. This book is designed to help consumers buy, prepare, and serve proper proportions of the foods that will maintain ideal weight and reduce the amount of animal fat and cholesterol.

Brown, B. *New Mind, New Body.* New York: Bantam, 1974. The author presents evidence on how the technique of biofeedback can be used to control muscle relaxation, tension headaches, heartbeat rate, blood pressure, and the effects of stress.

Coates, T. J. *How to Sleep Better: A Drug-Free Program for Overcoming Insomnia.* Englewood Cliffs, N.J.: Prentice-Hall (Spectrum), 1977. This is an interesting, helpful, and systematic account of ways to sleep and to relax without the aid of drugs. The book has an excellent description of progressive relaxation techniques, and it contains charts to record behavioral progress.

Coleman, J. *Contemporary Psychology and Effective Behavior* (4th ed.). Palo Alto, Calif.: Scott, Foresman, 1979. Chapters 5–8 contain excellent reading on life stress and effective methods of coping with it.

Cooper, K. H. *The New Aerobics.* New York: Bantam, 1970. Good material on physical fitness testing, tips and safeguards in exercising, and the values of various exercise programs.

Dass, R. *Journey of Awakening: A Meditator's Guidebook.* New York: Bantam, 1978. Readers who want to know more about ways of meditating, along with a directory of further resources, will find this book a helpful place to begin.

Davis, M., Eshelman, E. R., & McKay, M. *The Relaxation and Stress Reduction Workbook.* Richmond, Calif.: New Harbinger Publications, 1980. This is an excellent manual for those who want to learn how to relax. Contains practical exercises in body awareness, progressive relaxation, meditation, self-hypnosis, ways of disputing irrational ideas, assertiveness training, time management, and biofeedback.

Friedman, M., & Rosenman, R. H. *Type A Behavior and Your Heart.* Greenwich, Conn.: Fawcett, 1974. This pioneering medical team conducted research into the relationship between high-stress life-styles and heart attacks. They've translated their findings in simple and interesting style. *Must reading* for those who are thinking of changing to a less stressful way of living.

Glasser, W. *Positive Addiction.* New York: Harper & Row, 1976. Glasser has good chapters on running and meditation as pathways to health. He cites many examples of people who have become positively addicted to these activities and who have incorporated them into their life-styles.

Kottler, J. *Mouthing Off: A Study of Oral Behavior, Its Causes, and Treatments.* New York: Libra, 1981. The book is a definitive investigation of why we are so orally fixated, what problems this behavior presents, and how to take better control of our lives by more responsibly and intelligently "mouthing off." Several helpful self-control strategies are provided.

Pritikin, N., with McGrady, P. M. *The Pritikin Program for Diet and Exercise.* New York: Grosset & Dunlap, 1979. Contains some useful information on various aspects of a diet, including the role of fats, cholesterol, protein, carbohydrates, fiber, food balancing, salt, alcohol, caffeine, and smoking. The values of walking and jogging are also discussed in a clear way. A useful book for those who are considering improving their diets.

Rudestam, K. E. *Methods of Change: An ABC Primer.* Monterey, Calif.: Brooks/Cole, 1980. An excellent guide for those who want to develop a self-help program in learning to relax, to meditate, and to get centered. Includes cognitive-behavioral techniques to produce change.

Shapiro, D. H. *Precision Nirvana.* Englewood Cliffs, N.J.: Prentice-Hall (Spectrum), 1978. The author provides helpful guidelines by combining Eastern and Western cultures. Readers who want to learn more about meditation will find this a valuable source.

Sheehan, G. *Dr. Sheehan on Running.* Mountain View, Calif.: World Publications, 1975. This is the author's account of a decision he made to change his lifestyle. He discusses the values of running as a way of releasing creativity as well as staying physically fit.

Smith, R. P. *The La Costa Diet and Exercise Book.* New York: Grosset & Dunlap, 1977. Contains useful information for readers interested in learning more about physical fitness and diet. Specific exercises are given for women and men.

Toffler, A. *Future Shock.* New York: Bantam, 1970. This book describes what happens to people when they are subjected to rapid changes. It is designed to help readers come to terms with the future by learning how to cope both personally and socially with the stress of change.

Watson, D. L., & Tharp, R. G. *Self-Directed Behavior: Self-Modification for Personal Adjustment* (3rd ed.). Monterey, Calif.: Brooks/Cole, 1981. For those who want to set up a self-directed program designed to control smoking, eating, or drinking or to promote regular exercise, this book offers useful guidelines in systematically making behavioral changes.

Williams, R. L., & Long, J. D. *Toward a Self-Managed Life Style* (2nd ed.). Boston: Houghton Mifflin, 1979. This is an excellent source for those who want to set up a behavioral program for themselves to deal with areas such as weight control, smoking and drinking, or exercise.

Prechapter Self-Inventory

For each statement, indicate the response that most closely identifies your beliefs and attitudes. Use this code: 5 = I *strongly agree* with this statement; 4 = I *agree* in most respects; 3 = I am *undecided*; 2 = I *disagree* in most respects; 1 = I *strongly disagree*.

_____ 1. Men are by nature more sexually aggressive than women and enjoy sex more than women do.

_____ 2. Sex-role definitions and stereotypes get in the way of mutually satisfying sexual relations.

_____ 3. Concern over sexual performance is quite common.

_____ 4. Psychologically healthy people don't experience any guilt over their sexual activities.

_____ 5. If a woman doesn't experience orgasm, it is generally because the man has not been sensitive enough to her needs.

_____ 6. If a man experiences impotence, it is generally because of the woman's lack of appreciation of his manhood.

_____ 7. In a sexual relationship, it is the job of each partner to make the other feel like a woman or a man.

_____ 8. Getting in touch with our sexual attractions and feelings toward others generally leads to overt sexual behavior.

_____ 9. The quality of a sexual relationship is usually parallel to the quality of the partners' relationship in general.

_____ 10. Sexual freedom implies doing whatever consenting adults agree to.

_____ 11. If we want to, we can reeducate ourselves so that we can experience sexual relationships with numerous partners without feeling guilty.

_____ 12. Sexual freedom ought to be counterbalanced by sexual responsibility.

_____ 13. We will probably be no more sexually attractive to others than we are to ourselves.

_____ 14. Discussing sexual wants and needs generally leads to mechanical and unspontaneous sex.

_____ 15. Extramarital sex inevitably causes dissatisfaction in the marital relationship.

_____ 16. Today's generation is really unconcerned about being sexually inadequate.

_____ 17. Most people who are intimate with each other find it relatively easy to talk openly and honestly about the intimate details of sexuality.

_____ 18. The key to improving sexual satisfaction is to master sexual techniques and skills.

150

—————   19. **Sex** without love is unsatisfying.

—————   20. Most people today rarely experience guilt or shame over sexuality.

Introduction

In this chapter, I encourage you to think critically about sex-role stereotypes and to form your own standards of what it means to be a woman
or a man. Since most of us have been exposed to many years of powerful
conditioning concerning what a man or a woman should be, it may be
difficult to quickly change some of our ingrained attitudes. Nevertheless,
we can make a good beginning toward freeing ourselves from limiting
roles if we're willing to question our attitudes and if we're truly interested in expanding our consciousness about men and women as persons.

Another goal of this chapter is to introduce the idea of learning how
to recognize and openly express our sexual concerns. Too many people
suffer from needless guilt, shame, worries, and inhibition, merely
because they keep their concerns about sexuality secret, largely out of
embarrassment. Moreover, keeping their concerns to themselves can
hinder their efforts to determine their own values regarding sex. In this
chapter, I ask you to examine your values and attitudes toward sexuality
and to determine what choices *you* want to make in this area of your
life.

The Man in Hiding

The All-American Male

I believe that many men in our society live restricted and deadening
lives because they have "bought" some cultural myths of what it means
to be a male. Unfortunately, too many men are caught in rigid roles and
expect sanctions when they deviate from what is supposedly "manly."
In this way they become so involved in the many roles they play that
they eventually become strangers to themselves. They no longer know
what they are like inside, because they put so much energy into maintaining an acceptable male facade.

What is the stereotype of the all-American male, and what aspects of
themselves do many males feel they must hide in order to conform to
it? In general, the stereotypic male is cool, detached, objective, rational,
and strong. A man who attempts to fit himself to the stereotype will
suppress most of his feelings, for he sees the subjective world of feelings

as being essentially feminine. Goldberg (1976, 1979), Jourard (1971), Deaux (1976), Pleck and Sawyer (1974), Mornell (1979), Basow (1980), and others have discussed these issues and identified characteristics that a man living by the stereotype may attempt to suppress or deny. Among these characteristics are:

- *Dependence.* Rather than admit that he needs anything from anyone, he may live a life of exaggerated independence. He feels he should be able to do by himself whatever needs to be done, and he finds it hard to reach out to others.
- *Passivity.* He feels he must be continually active, aggressive, assertive, and striving. He views the opposites of these traits as signs of weakness, and he fears being seen as weak.
- *Fears.* He won't express his fears, and most likely he won't even allow *himself* to experience them. He has the distorted notion that to be afraid means that he lacks courage, so he hides his fears from himself and from others.
- *His inner self.* He doesn't disclose himself to women, because he is afraid that they will think of him as unmanly if they see his inner core. He keeps himself hidden from other men because they are competitors and, in this sense, potential enemies.
- *Vulnerability.* He cannot make himself vulnerable, as is evidenced by his general unwillingness to disclose much of his inner experiences. He won't let himself feel and express sadness; nor will he cry. To protect himself, he becomes emotionally insulated and puts on a mask of toughness, competence, and decisiveness. He finds it difficult to express warmth and tenderness.
- *Bodily self-awareness.* He doesn't recognize bodily cues that may signal danger. He drives himself unmercifully and views his body as some kind of machine that won't break down or wear out. He may not pay attention to his exhaustion until he collapses from it.
- *Closeness with other men.* Although he may have plenty of acquaintances, he doesn't have very many male friends he can confide in.
- *Failure.* He hides from failure, and he must at all times put on the facade of the successful man. He feels he's expected to succeed and produce, to be "the best," to get ahead and stay ahead. He has to win, which means that someone else has to lose.
- *"Feminine" qualities.* Because he plays a rigid male role, he doesn't see how he can still be a man and at the same time possess (or reveal) traits that are usually attributed to women. Therefore, he is very controlled,

shutting out much of what he could experience and leading an impoverished life as a result.

· *A need for or enjoyment of physical contact.* He has a difficult time touching freely. He thinks that he should touch a woman only if it will lead to sex, and he fears touching other men because he doesn't want to be perceived as a homosexual.

From the standpoint of an observer, other characteristics are typical of the stereotypic male. A few of these characteristics are:

· *Rigid perceptions.* Such men see men and women in rigid categories. Women should be weak, emotional, and submissive; men are expected to be tough, logical, and aggressive.

· *Drive to perform.* The masculine imperative is to live up to the ideal of what a man should be, and there is a pressure to always give a better performance.

· *A slave to his work.* Many men put much of their energy into external signs of success. Thus, little is left over for their wives and children. They often grew up in an environment where women were not given a high value and where relationships were not important. Instead, success, achievement, and productivity were valued.

· *Alive at work, dead at home.* Many men are aggressive and dynamic on the job but lose most of this vitality when they walk in the door at home. This type of man is often at his best when there is a challenging task to be completed, a problem to be solved, or some opposition to wage battle against.

· *Denial of emotions.* Most emotions are seen as "feminine," and thus this man either denies or distorts feelings. He often will not allow himself to realize how he is affected emotionally by his self-destructive path toward achievement and success. While he may engage in self-deception by telling himself that "everything is under control," he may block out any feelings that indicate that living stoically does demand a price. For him, a "real man" can forge ahead fearlessly and tirelessly toward attaining goal after goal. Thus, to *express* emotion is a sign of weakness. If he ever allowed himself to cry, he'd most likely do it alone! This kind of man may say that he'd rather die than show feelings, and he often does. By holding in a range of feelings and pretending they don't exist, he is likely to eventually explode or collapse.

· *Burnout.* Since he treats himself like a machine (and expects it to constantly function without breaking down), this man eventually burns out, and *then* he may wonder what he's been doing with his life.

The Price Men Pay for Remaining in Hiding

What price must a man pay for denying most of his inner self and putting on a false front? First, he loses a sense of himself because of his concern with being the way he thinks he should be as a male. Writing on the "lethal aspects of the male role," Sidney Jourard (1971) contends that men typically find it difficult to love and be loved. They won't reveal themselves enough to be loved. They hide their loneliness, anxiety, and hunger for affection, thus making it difficult for anyone to love them as they really are.

Another price the guarded male must pay for his seclusion is that he must always be vigilant for fear that someone might discover what is beneath his armor. Jourard puts this point well:

> He may, in an unguarded moment, reveal his true self in its nakedness, thereby exposing his areas of weakness and vulnerability. Naturally, when a person is in hostile territory, he must be continually alert, tense, opaque, and restless. All this implies that trying to seem manly is a kind of work, and work imposes stress and consumes energy. Manliness, then, seems to carry with it a chronic burden of stress and energy expenditure which could be a factor related to man's relatively shorter life span [pp. 35–36].

In his excellent book *The Hazards of Being Male*, Goldberg (1976) cites evidence showing that men tend to die at an earlier age than women do, that they suffer from cardiovascular problems more than women do, that boys do more poorly than girls in school, that men are involved in more crime than women are, and that the suicide rate is higher for males than for females. Goldberg makes the point that all the statistics that point to the hazards of being male actually constitute a description of the crises faced by males in our society. He contends that "the male has become an artist in the creation of many hidden ways of killing himself" (p. 189) and calls for a "revolution" in male consciousness.[1]

In a later book, *The New Male*, Goldberg (1979) develops the idea that, if men continue to cling to the traditional masculine blueprint, they will end their lives as pathetic throwaways who are abandoned and asleep. He describes such men as alive at 20, machines at 30, and burned out by 40. During their twenties, most of their energies are directed toward

---

[1]From *The Hazards of Being Male*, by H. Goldberg. Copyright 1976 by Nash Publishing Company. Reprinted by permission.

"making it" while denying important needs and feelings. At 20, these men are typically urgently sexual, restless and passionate about converting their ideas into reality, eager to push themselves to their limits (if they recognize any), curious and adventurous, and optimistic about the possibilities for living. In his early twenties the traditional male is driven by societal pressures to prove his manliness, long before he is aware of who he is and what it is that he really wants for himself. Therefore, he locks himself into a cage and becomes trapped in his life situation, with few apparent choices. At 30 he has convinced himself that he is not a person but a machine that has to function so the job can get done. By his forties, he may experience a "male menopause" as his functioning begins to break down. Goldberg sees this decline as the result of years of repression and emotional denial, which makes him a danger to both himself and to others. Because his anxiety would be too much to deal with if he were to accept that he had been a self-destructive conformist, he may urge other young men to pay the same dues as he did for entry into the "macho" club.

Some Men Are Coming Out of Hiding

It needs to be acknowledged that at least some men are challenging the conditioning that directs them to fall passively into the traditional male role. I am thinking of several men who *did* recognize that they had allowed themselves to become machines and who became aware that they were slaves to a hollow image of themselves. For example, Leroy told me the following:

> I was a driving and driven man who was too busy to smell the flowers. My single goal in life was to prove myself and become a financial and business success. I was on my way to becoming the president of a corporation, and I was thinking that I had it made. When I got my W-2 form, I became aware that I had made more money than was in my plan for success, yet I had had a miserable year. I decided that I wanted to experience life, to smell more flowers, and to not kill myself with a program that I never consciously chose for myself.

Leroy's decision did not come easy. It was, and continues to be, a real struggle for him to admit that he is only human. It is not easy for him to allow himself to experience and express feelings, yet he is making fine strides at becoming a very sensitive, caring, and expressive man. Leroy

is actively "talking back" to "inner voices within him" that tell him he *must* keep driving himself, that he *must* constantly set and conquer new goals, and that he does not have the time to enjoy and savor life. For him a turning point was landing in the hospital and almost dying. This jarred him into accepting that he was not an indestructible machine. Commenting on the impact of this experience, Leroy said:

> To me, life was a constant struggle, and I could never let down. Life was a series of performances that involved me pleasing others and then waiting for the applause to come. The applause was never enough, because I prostituted myself. I was always disappointed by the applause, because I felt empty when the applause would die down. So I continued to push myself to give more performances. But out of my illness I began to look at my life and slow down, and I realized there is a world out there that does not solely involve my work. I decided to work no more than 50 hours a week; before getting sick I was working 70 to 90 hours a week. With that extra time, I decided to smell life—there

are a lot of roses in life, and the scent is enticing and exciting to me, and I'll thrive on it as long as I can breathe it.

At 37 years of age, Leroy is showing the courage to reverse some of the self-destructive patterns that were killing him. He is deciding for himself what kind of man he wants to be, rather than living by an image of the man that others thought he should be. Leroy says that he likes roses because of the scent, even though they do have thorns that hurt. He is now convinced that the scent makes up for the thorns. While he experiences more emotional pain than he ever allowed himself to feel before, he also experiences joy and sharing that he never knew before.

The Emerging Woman and Changing Sex Roles

Like men, women in our society have suffered from a sexual stereotype. Typically, women have been perceived as weak, fragile, unambitious, helpless, unintelligent, designed by nature for the role of homemaker and mother, unassertive, noncompetitive, and unadventurous. This rigid viewpoint is in the process of changing as many women actively fight the stereotype of the passive, dependent female.

In comparing the male and female stereotypes, Kay Deaux (1976) notes that the stereotypic woman *is* accorded some redeeming traits:

These traits generally reflect warmth and expressiveness. Women are described as tactful, gentle, aware of the feelings of others, and able to express tender feelings easily. Men, in contrast, are viewed as blunt, rough, unaware of the feelings of others, and unable to express their own feelings [pp. 13–14].

Nevertheless, Deaux adds, men are generally perceived as having more positive traits than women, and in our society such "male" values as competence and success are more highly prized than the supposedly female qualities of warmth and expressiveness.

How are these sexual stereotypes formed? Deaux cites evidence that boys and girls are conditioned early in life to accept predetermined sex roles. She indicates, for example, that boys are often seen as curious, active, and independent, while girls are seen as lacking in curiosity, having little initiative, and needing help from boys. Not long ago, reading primers showed men as the ones who solved problems and went to work, while the women were typically shown in the kitchen. Deaux also cites a study showing how television and magazines influence children to accept sex-role stereotypes. Men usually appear in advertisements and commercials when figures who suggest authority are needed; by contrast, women are usually the principal figures when commercials deal with the use of household products. In summary, Deaux makes the point that "parents and other socializing agents convey certain expectations to their children as to what grown-up men and women are like. These impressions may form the basis of stereotypes that are found much later in life" (1976, p. 20).

Are these stereotypes changing? According to Deaux, if children have good models in the home, and if they see changes in male and female images in the media, the stereotypes may well change in the future, but for now "we must conclude that stereotypes are still alive and doing reasonably well in our culture" (p. 21).

In summarizing studies done on sex-role stereotypes, Basow (1980) cites considerable research evidence supporting their existence. Sex-role studies have found strong agreement among people about the differing characteristics of women and men. The following are some of the stereotypic sex-role differentiations commonly held by people:

Men, on the one hand, are viewed as exhibiting the following behaviors or possessing the following traits more than women do: aggressiveness, independence, objectivity, dominance, active and competitive orientation toward the world, directness and a logical way of dealing with problems, adventurousness, self-confidence, ambition, and the ability to separate feelings from ideas. On the other hand, women, more so than men, are seen as exhibiting these qualities: gentleness, sensitivity, ability to express feelings, tactfulness, religiosity, and interest in relationships. Some of these traits are the ones that both sexes often associate with being "feminine" or being "masculine."

Brooks-Gunn and Matthews (1979), in their book, *He and She: How Children Develop Their Sex-Role Identity*, write that stereotypes still persist and continue to affect the way we are perceived by others. Sex-role stereotypes influence societal practices, discrimination, individual beliefs, and sex-related behavior itself. The authors contend that sensitizing ourselves to the process of sex-role development can help us to make choices about modifying the results of our socialization.

Women in Revolt

Despite the staying power of sexual stereotypes, increasing numbers of women are rejecting limited views of what a woman is expected to be. Women are discovering that they can indeed have many of the traits traditionally attributed to them yet at the same time take a new view of themselves. In particular, many women are in revolt against the pressures put on them to find their satisfactions exclusively or primarily in marriage and the raising of a family. Contending that "earth mother is dead," Goldberg (1976) writes that contemporary women are showing their true identities. They are no longer willing to conspire with men in fostering the image of themselves as weak, helpless, and designed primarily to take care of men's needs and the needs of their children.

Goldberg views this assertiveness on the part of women as liberating not only for themselves but for men as well, because it frees men from the need to live up to the macho image. When both men and women are free of restrictive roles and thus free to be the persons they *could* be, they can develop authentic relationships with one another based on their individual strengths instead of on a game in which one must be weak so that the other can be strong. In Goldberg's words, "When she is she in her genuine, total, strong femaleness and personhood and he is he in his maleness and personhood, they can begin to revel in the realities and joys of an authentic, interdependent, and genuinely fulfilling interaction" (1976, p. 32).

Although I like this ideal picture, I do see a trend that disturbs me. Many women seem so caught up in their revolt against traditional expectations that they have difficulty accepting any of the qualities traditionally attributed to them, regardless of whether the qualities are positive ones that they may in fact possess as individuals. For example, a woman might be embarrassed to admit that she does derive fulfillment from being a homemaker and a mother, even if that happens to be true of her. In short, by going to the extreme of denying any traits that might traditionally be associated with the female stereotype, some women run the risk of losing the independent sense of themselves that they are trying to achieve. I question the degree of freedom achieved by a movement if we allow it to dictate our standards. Although a movement can and should raise our level of consciousness, it seems critically important that we choose what we want for ourselves. After all, that's what being liberated really means.

An Increase of Options

Women today have more options than women in past decades did, but this increase brings with it an increase in anxiety. Well-defined roles can be restrictive, but they can also be secure, and many contemporary women experience difficulty when they look inward and attempt to decide what they want. Moreover, many of these women actually feel uncomfortable with choices that will lead to success. They have been conditioned for so long *not* to experience success in the outside world that they have a real fear of succeeding. Deaux (1976) describes research suggesting that, even though women may have a need to achieve, they may also have a motive to *avoid* achieving too much. They have learned to expect negative social consequences if they do succeed. Deaux indicates that the percentage of women who fear success does not appear to be decreasing greatly.

Certainly, to maximize her options, a woman needs to be alert to the danger of keeping herself locked into old roles and denying her talents. She must avoid the pitfall of blaming the dissatisfaction she feels on circumstances outside herself. At the same time, she can recognize that stepping out of old roles can be frightening, and she can try to become aware of what her fears and anxieties are. Just as she can question the traditional female stereotype, she can also question the myth that a successful and independent woman doesn't need anyone and can make it entirely on her own. This trap is very much like the trap that many males fall into and may even represent an assimilation of traditionally male values. Hopefully, a woman can learn that she can achieve independence, exhibit strength, and succeed while at times being dependent and in need of nurturing. Real strength allows either a woman or a man to be needy and to ask for nurturing without feeling personally inadequate.

Some women experience a lack of support and an actual resistance from the men in their lives when they do step outside of traditional roles and exercise some of their options. Basow (1980) notes that, since men typically have been the dominant sex, with most of the power, it is difficult for them to share this power with women.

In her counseling practice Marianne finds that many women struggle with attempting to balance a career outside of the home with their career at home. Their husbands, who sometimes see themselves as liberated, are put to the test when they are expected to assume an increasing share in the responsibilties at home. They may say that they want their wives to "emerge and become fulfilled persons," yet they may also send messages such as: "Don't go *too* far!" "Don't abandon the ship by throwing aside the traditional expectations." "Have a life outside of the home, but don't give up any of what you are doing at home." In addition, some of the problems that women experience in going beyond their traditionally expected roles are simply the result of having added an unrealistic load of responsibilities on themselves. While women may have to fight their husbands' resistance to their changes, the major fight is frequently with themselves. Their internal wars may be far more intense than their confrontations with others. They may say to themselves one of the following sentences, some of which are rational and others, irrational:

· "I must be a good mother, a good wife, and a good housekeeper."
· "If I don't take care of the kids, who will?"
· "If I'm not around to see that the house is kept up, the place will become unlivable."
· "If I were competent, I could manage both careers, without anything or anyone in my life suffering."

Both husband and wife may need to look at how realistic it is to expect that she can have a career while at the same time retaining all of her responsibilities for cleaning the house, cooking the meals, and being primarily responsible for the children. No easy answers are available, but a continuing redefinition and renegotiation of what either partner is and is not willing to do is essential.

The situation in which many women are finding themselves is well illustrated by the following letter, written by a woman in her early forties and used with her permission. It expresses her awareness that she has been what Goldberg calls an "earth mother" to her family and her realization that her confinement to this role has stunted not only her emotional growth but also the well-being of her family. Now she is asserting her need to achieve an identity as more than a wife and a mother. In becoming aware of her choices, she has become able to declare that she will pay attention to her own needs as well as to the needs of her family.

> Dear John:
>
> It strikes me as humorous that you are getting a "Dear John" letter from your mother. I am tired of playing the role of "mother" and I want to try my wings. When you come home I feel frustrated and trapped back into a role that I am trying to shed. I am determined to be a different person. I no longer am challenged by my role as mother. I've done the best I can, and I am proud of what I have accomplished. But you are all leaving the nest, and I must find and develop other parts of myself so that I can continue to function as a happy, healthy human being.

The battle to change how other people see me is a hard one. My own family is the most resistant to my change. Sometimes I am merely annoyed by their resistance, but other times I feel like a gopher trapped in a hole just waiting for the poison to come and render him helpless. I don't want to be dominated by the family needs. I want to be free to develop the new me. I feel unused potential stirring inside of me, battling to get out, to be expressed. As long as I am the servant keeping everything nice and neat for the rest of you, picking up after you, doing things you don't want to do, I don't have time to develop my own potential.

I can really be SOMEBODY in this world. I am worth more than a chief cook and bottle washer. And I am determined to be much, much more than that. If the rest of you won't allow me to change, then I shall have to dump you. I don't want these anchors dragging me down. I have challenged you to be more than mediocre—to self-actualize yourself. I have willingly sacrificed for you, but now it is my turn. Any help I give you now is destructive to both you and me. To you by not encouraging you to stand on your own two feet; to me by denying my own needs and desires.

I'm not sure exactly where I'm going, but my direction is becoming more focused. I am determined to take the time to find out the best development for me. If you come home this summer, you will have to take care of yourself and not be a burden financially, emotionally or time-wise on me. I'm not sure yet if I will be attending summer school or working or not doing either this summer. But I will be working on where I best fit in this big wide world. I need lots of time to do that. And I am not going to sacrifice myself for the rest of you.

You personally are the biggest complainer about what a lousy mother I am—I don't fill your definition of the role. Too bad! Marry a woman who will, if you can, but don't expect me to be that woman. I can't respect myself when I am that woman. . . . All my life I have been trying to fulfill other people's expectations of what I am. Now I am determined to find out what I am and what I can be. I am going to earn a good salary. I am going to be respected. I am going to be well-known in my field. I am going to think thoughts that other people don't—I already do. I see from my own perspective and put together large patterns and see how different ideas fit together in a way that other people often don't see. Somehow this has got to be useful to me and to the world. I want to find out how.

I am bursting with energy and excitement in this drive to find myself and to free myself from old conventions. I want to be what I *can* be. I am bitter that my family does not want to hear. My change forces all of you to change, and you are afraid. Afraid of the unknown. I am afraid, too. But I am more afraid of staying where I am at. Do you really want me to be a dependent person, like my mother? Or do you want me to be a happy person who can carry her own weight, like Aunt Alice?

The time for change is NOW. I can't wait. My greatest fear is that my family will gang up to pressure me into remaining as the "rescuer"—the one who does what others do not want to do. I love you all. I care about what you think of me. I am afraid I won't have the courage to stand up to all of you and the pressure you put on me. You, my family, bring me the greatest terror and the greatest joy.

Women and Sexual Liberation

Sexual liberation is a part of the freeing of women from significant traditional stereotypes. Increasingly, women are recognizing and expressing their sexual wants and desires. They are freeing themselves of the myths that their role is to be sexually passive or coy and to please their male partners while depending on them for their own achievement of orgasm. In short, they are freeing themselves to say yes when they want to say yes and no when they want to say no.

The widely read *Hite Report*, a nationwide study of female sexuality by Shere Hite (1976), contains much detailed information gathered from over 3000 women, from teenagers to the elderly. In this book, women discuss such matters as what they like and don't like; the experience of orgasm, with and without intercourse; their reactions to what they like and don't like in men; the greatest pleasures and frustrations in their sex lives; the importance of clitoral stimulation; and their views of sexual liberation and sexual slavery. The book can help liberate both sexes from some damaging myths; in addition, it can be a catalyst for discussion between partners about sexual attitudes and practices.

I often hear women complain that their men don't satisfy them sexually. Yet many of these women claim that they do not talk about sex with the men in their lives, asserting that if they were really loved and appreciated, these men would intuitively know what to do to satisfy them. I challenge the assumption that someone else knows what we like or need. Both sexes can take more initiative in talking about their sexual relationships and making clear what, if anything, they would like to be different.

Liberation for Both Women and Men

The increasing liberation of women has also stimulated to some degree the liberation of men. Warren Farrell (1975) contends that, if a man were freed of the responsibility of being the primary breadwinner, he would probably have far fewer fears about losing his job and feel freer to pursue a line of work that interested and excited him. He might feel less pressured to be the sole source of his spouse's happiness, less hassled by staying afloat in competition, and more open to deriving satisfaction from something other than his work. He might be more interested in spending time with his children, in pursuing hobbies, and in developing relationships based on feelings rather than on security. Finally, he would probably experience less anxiety about his sex role and might develop a set of values that gave a new richness to living.

I want to emphasize that both sexes need to remain open to the other and to change their attitudes if they are interested in releasing themselves from stereotyped roles. People of both sexes seem to be in a transitional period in which they are redefining themselves and ridding themselves of old stereotypes; yet too often they are needlessly fighting with each other, when they could be helping each other to recognize that they have *both* been conditioned for many years and that they need to be patient as they each learn new patterns of thought and behavior.

Many women and men want the same thing—to loosen the rigid sex-role expectations that have trapped them. Many men recognize a need to broaden their view of themselves to include capacities that have been traditionally stereotyped as feminine and that they have consequently denied in themselves. Many women are seeking to give expression to a side of themselves that has been associated with males. As men and women alike pay closer attention to attitudes that are deeply ingrained in themselves, they may find that they haven't caught up emotionally with their intellectual level of awareness. Although we might well be "liberated" intellectually and *know* what we want, many of us experience difficulty in *feeling* OK about what we want. The challenge consists in getting the two together!

Alternatives to Rigid Sex Roles

The fact that certain male and female stereotypes have been prevalent in our culture doesn't mean that all men and women live within these narrow confines. Nevertheless, many people have uncritically accepted rigid definitions of their roles, while others just as uncritically reject them; and probably even liberated people are affected by some vestiges of sexual stereotypes. Fortunately, there is much challenging of traditional perspectives among the college students I come in contact with. For instance, more and more men are apparently realizing that they can combine self-confidence, assertiveness, and power with tenderness, warmth, and self-expressiveness. The macho male doesn't seem to be admired or respected by either the men or the women I encounter on the university campus.

The alternative to living according to a stereotype is to realize that we can actively define our own standards of what we want to be like as women or as men. We don't have to blindly accept roles and expectations that have been imposed on us or remain victims of our early conditioning. We can begin to achieve autonomy in our sexual identities by looking at how we have formed our ideals and standards and who our models have been; then we can decide whether these are the standards we want to use in defining ourselves now.

One appealing alternative to rigid sex-role stereotypes is the concept of *androgyny,* or the coexistence of male and female characteristics in the same person. We all secrete some male and female hormones, and many psychologists postulate that we also have both feminine and masculine psychological characteristics. For example, Carl Jung developed the notions of the *animus* and the *anima,* which refer to the (usually hidden) feminine and masculine aspects within us. Taken together, the *animus* and the *anima* reflect Jung's conception of humans as bisexual in nature. Since women share in some of the psychological characteristics of men (through their *animus*), and since men possess some feminine aspects (through their *anima*), both are better enabled to understand the opposite sex. Jung was very insistent that women and men must express both dimensions of their personality. Failure to do so

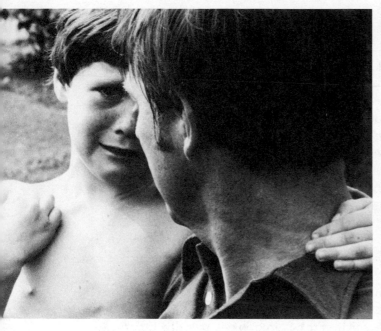

results in one-sided development. Thus, becoming fully human entails the expression of the full range of these personality characteristics.[2]

Deaux (1976) cites research indicating that an androgynous person has a wider range of capacities than a person who lives by sex-typed expectations. For example, an androgynous person can show "masculine" assertiveness or "feminine" warmth, depending on what a situation calls for. For Deaux, androgyny is a promising concept that deserves further attention. One of the central themes of her book *The Behavior of*

[2]For those who wish to pursue Jung's ideas further, a good basic book is *A Primer of Jungian Psychology* (Hall & Nordby, 1973).

Women and Men is that there are relatively few characteristics in which women and men consistently differ:

> Men and women both seem to be capable of being aggressive, helpful, and alternately cooperative and competitive. In other words, there is little evidence that the nature of women and men is so inherently different that we are justified in making stereotyped generalizations [Deaux, 1976, p. 144].

Basow (1980), in her book *Sex-Role Stereotypes: Traditions and Alternatives*, writes that androgyny does not imply being neuter or, indeed, anything else about one's sexual orientation. Rather, it refers to a person's flexibility in sex-role behaviors. Thus, androgynous people may perceive themselves as being understanding, affectionate, and considerate *and* self-reliant, independent, and firm.

According to Basow, the ultimate goal is to move toward androgyny *and beyond* by transcending traditional sex-role polarities to reach a new level of synthesis. Thus, a person is able to move freely in a variety of situations. The same person could be compassionate with a friend, assertive with a fellow worker, and tender with a child. In this view, the world is not divided into polarities of masculinity and femininity; rather, people have a range of potentials that can be adapted to a range of situations.

In his stimulating book, *Passive Men, Wild Women*, Mornell (1979) calls for us to learn to accept all sides of our complex personalities. He discourages looking for easy answers that speak about dependence *or* independence, tenderness *or* tough-mindedness, dominance *or* submissiveness, and being a work person *or* a home person. For Mornell,

> the ultimate answer . . . *begins* with our refusing to accept the man as passive and the woman as wild, and in our seeing the problem for what it is. Let us accept and even enjoy our basic differences. Let us learn with and from each other what we may have never learned from our own fathers, mothers, or our society: how to accept our human differences and still be strong individuals, active partners, and involved lovers [1979, p. 94].

The real challenge is for us to choose the kind of woman or man we want to be and not be determined by passive acceptance of a cultural stereotype or blind identification with some form of rebellion.

━━━━━━━━━━━━━━━━━━━

Time Out for Personal Reflection

1. There are common myths and misconceptions associated with being a woman and being a man. Take the following inventory by writing an A in the blank on the left if you agree more than you disagree with the statement or a D in the blank if you disagree more than agree. Then, in the next space, answer the statement in the way you think most of your friends and associates of the same sex as you would be likely to respond.

Statements about men:

____ ____ *a. Men are defined by what they achieve.*

____ ____ *b. Men are basically aggressive by nature.*

____ ____ *c. Men have a need to feel superior.*

____ ____ *d. Men should have more social freedom than women.*

____ ____ *e. Men should always display courage and be strong.*

____ ____ *f. Men should protect women.*

____ ____ *g. Men are primarily concerned about the world of work.*

____ ____ *h. Men ought to make women feel important.*

____ ____ *i. Men ought to respond rationally rather than emotionally.*

____ ____ *j. Men have a basic need to be competitive.*

Statements about women:

____ ____ *a. Women by nature have a need to have and take care of children.*

____ ____ *b. Women should be less active than the men in their lives.*

____ ____ *c. Women define themselves by giving to others.*

____ ____ *d. Women should make a primary commitment to the home.*

____ ____ *e. Women should make the men in their lives feel important.*

____ ____ *f. Women should not have a career if it jeopardizes their family life.*

____ ____ *g. Women should be faithful to the men in their lives.*

____ ____ *h. Women are typically hurt very easily.*

____ ____ *i. Women, by nature, are more emotional than logical.*

____ ____ *j. Women should not be too assertive and surely not aggressive.*

Some suggestions:

Now, compare your responses with those of others in your class, both men and women. Are there many differences? Also, you could discuss the degree to which your attitudes concerning sex roles might have been influenced by your environment. A lively discussion could be geared around determining which of the above statements are perceived as myths and misconceptions and which are seen as "facts of life."

2. The following statements may help you assess how you see yourself in relation to sex roles. Place a T before each statement that generally applies to you and an F before each one that generally doesn't apply to you. Be sure to respond *as you are now*, rather than as you'd like to be.

_____ I'd rather be rational than emotional.
_____ I'm more an active person than a passive person.
_____ I'm more cooperative than I am competitive.
_____ I tend to express my feelings rather than keeping them hidden.
_____ I tend to live by what is expected of my sex.
_____ I see myself as possessing both masculine and feminine characteristics.
_____ I'm afraid of deviating very much from the customary sex-role norms.
_____ I'm adventurous in most situations.
_____ I feel OK about expressing both negative and positive feelings.
_____ I'm continually striving for success.
_____ I fear success as much as I fear failure.

Now look over your responses. Which characteristics, if any, would you like to change in yourself?

_____

_____

_____

3. What are some of your reactions to the changes in women's view of their sex role? What impact do you think the women's liberation movement has had on women? On men?

_____

_____

_____

_____

4. What do you think of the concept of androgyny? Would you like to possess more of the qualities you associate with the opposite sex? If so, what are they? Are there any ways in which you feel limited or restricted by rigid sex-role definitions and expectations?

_____

_____

_____

_____

_____

Sexuality and Personality Development

Learning to Talk Openly about Sexual Issues

One might expect that young people today would be able to discuss openly and frankly the concerns they have about sex. Students will discuss attitudes about sexual behavior in a general way, but they show considerable resistance to speaking of their own sexual concerns, fears, and conflicts. I've come to believe that it can be a great service simply to provide a climate in which people can feel free to examine their personal concerns. A particularly valuable technique is to give women and men an opportunity to discuss sexual issues in separate groups and then come together to share the concerns they've discovered. Typically, both men and women appreciate the chance to explore their sexual fears, expectations, secrets, and wishes, as well as their concerns about the normality of their bodies and feelings. Then, when the male and female groups come together, the participants usually find that there is much common ground, and the experience of making this discovery can be very therapeutic. For instance, men may fear becoming impotent, not performing up to some expected standard, being lousy lovers, or not being "man enough." When the men and women meet as one group, the men may be surprised to discover that women worry about having to achieve orgasm (or several of them) every time they have sex and that they, too, have fears about their sexual desirability. When people talk about these concerns in a direct way, much game playing and putting on of false fronts can be dispensed with.

My work with therapeutic groups continues to teach me how much we need to learn how to talk with each other about sexual concerns. Many people suffer from unrealistic fears that they are alone in their feelings and concerns about their sexuality. If we could learn how to initiate open discussion of these issues, we might find that genuine sexual freedom is possible. We could shed many of the tears that needlessly hamper our joy in freely experiencing sex.

At this point, let me describe some of the typical concerns that are openly aired by both men and women in discussion groups I've participated in. These concerns might be expressed as follows:

- "I often wonder what excites my partner and what that person would like, yet I seldom ask. I suppose that it's important for me to learn how to initiate by asking and also by telling the other person what *I* enjoy."
- "So often I doubt my capacity as a lover. I'd like to know what my partner thinks. Perhaps one thing that I can learn to do is to share this concern with him (her)."
- "I worry about my body. Am I normal? How do I compare with others? Am I too big? Too small? Am I proportioned properly? Do others find me attractive? Do I find myself attractive? What can I do to increase my own appeal to myself and to others?"
- "Am I responsible if my partner's dissatisfied?"
- "Sex can be fun, I suppose, but often I'm much too serious. It's really difficult for me to be playful and to let go without feeling foolish—and not just in regard to sex. It isn't easy for me to be spontaneous."
- "There are many times when I feel that my spouse is bored with sex, and that makes me wonder whether I'm sexually attractive to her (him)."
- "There are times when I desire sex and initiate it, and my husband (wife) lets me know in subtle or even direct ways that he (she) isn't interested. Then I feel almost like a beggar. This kind of experience makes me not want to initiate any more."
- "As a woman, I'd really like to know how other women feel after a sexual experience. Do they normally feel fulfilled? What prevents them from enjoying sex? How do they decide who's at fault when they don't have a positive experience?"
- "As a man, I frequently worry about performance standards, and that gets in the way of my making love freely and spontaneously. It's a burden to me to worry about doing the right things and being sexually powerful, and I often wonder what other men experience in this area."
- "There seem to be two extremes in sex: we can be overly concerned with pleasing our partners and therefore take too much responsibility for their sexual gratification, or we can become so involved with our own pleasure that we don't concern ourselves with our partners' feelings or needs. I ask myself how I can discover a balance—how I can be selfish

enough to seek my own pleasure yet sensitive enough to take care of my partner's needs."

- "Sometimes I get scared of women (men), and I struggle with myself over whether or not I should let the other person know that I feel threatened. Will I be perceived as weak? Is it so terrible to be weak at times? Can I be weak and still be strong?"
- "I frequently feel guilty over my sexual feelings, but there are times when I wonder whether I really want to free myself of guilt feelings. What would happen if I were free of guilt? Would I give up all control?"
- "I worry a lot about being feminine (masculine) and all that it entails. I'm trying to separate out what I've been conditioned to believe about the way a woman (man) is supposed to be, yet I still have a hard time in deciding for myself the kind of woman (man) I want to be. I want to find my own standards and not be haunted by external standards of what I should be and feel."
- "Can sex be an attempt to overcome my feelings of isolation and separation? There are times when I think I'm running into a sexual relationship because I feel lonely."
- "I've wondered whether or not we are by nature monogamous. I know I'd like to experience others sexually, but I surely don't want my mate to have these same experiences."
- "There are times lately when I don't seem to be enjoying sex much. In the past year, I haven't been able to experience orgasm, and the man

that I'm living with thinks it's his fault. What's happening? Why am I not as sexually responsive as I used to be with him?"

· "I feel very open and trusting in talking about my sexuality in this group, and I'd very much like to experience this with my partner. I want to be able to be direct and avoid getting involved in sexual games. I need to learn how to initiate this kind of open dialogue."

· "There are times when I really don't crave intercourse but would still like to be held and touched and caressed. I wish my partner could understand this about me and not take it as a personal rejection when for some reason I simply don't want intercourse."

· "I really felt humiliated when I became impotent—I was sure she saw me as unmanly. I'm glad to learn that this is a common experience with other men and that I'm not abnormal."

Learning to Enjoy Sensuality and Sexuality

As we've seen, performance standards and expectations often get in the way of people's sensual and sexual pleasure, particularly in the case of men. Many men report that they feel a need to perform "up to standard," and they burden themselves with the stress of worrying about what is expected of them. Some men are not content to be themselves but think they must be *supermen*, particularly in the area of sexual attractiveness and performance. They measure themselves by unrealistic standards and may greatly fear losing their sexual power. Instead of enjoying sexual and sensual experiences, they become orgasm oriented. They often place heavy expectations on women to climax as well, in order to reaffirm their view that they are more than sexually adequate. With this type of orientation toward sex, it is no wonder that these men fear two problems in particular: impotence and premature ejaculation.

I like the way Goldberg (1976) deals with the meaning these sexual problems often have. In a chapter entitled "The Wisdom of the Penis," Goldberg says that impotence can really be a message that a man doesn't want to have sex with this particular woman at this particular time; it doesn't necessarily mean that he has lost his power in general. Goldberg makes a strong case that men should have sex only when they are genuinely aroused and excited; otherwise, they are inviting impotence. "The penis," he writes, "is not a piece of plumbing that functions capriciously. It is an expression of the total self. In these days of overintellectualization it is perhaps the only remaining sensitive and revealing barometer of the male's true sexual feelings" (p. 39). In similar fashion, Goldberg interprets premature ejaculation as the body's way of saying "I really don't want to do this, but, if I must, let's get it over with as fast as possible." In short, if we can learn to pay attention to what our bodies are telling us, they can teach us ways of enjoying a sensual and sexual life. Much the same point is made by Jourard (1971) in writing on the delight and ecstasy that a sexual experience can bring. The body, says Jourard, doesn't lie: "If she wants me and I don't want her, I cannot lie. My body speaks the truth. And I cannot take her unless she gives herself. Her body cannot lie" (p. 53).

It should be added that sexual dysfunction can occur for any one of a number of reasons, including, in some cases, physical ones. However, in the majority of cases, a problem such as impotence is due to psychological factors. For example, in addition to the lack of desire to have sex with a certain person at a certain time, impotence may result from feelings of guilt, prolonged depression, anxiety about personal adequacy, or a generally low level of self-esteem. Most men for whom impotence becomes a problem might be well advised to ask "What is my body telling me?"

Paying attention to the messages of our bodies is only a first step. We still need to learn how to express to our partners *specifically* what we like and don't like sexually. I've found that both men and women tend to keep their sexual preferences and dislikes to themselves instead of sharing them with their partners. They've accepted the misconception that their partners should know intuitively what they like and don't like, and they resist telling their partners what feels good to them out of fear that their lovemaking will become mechanical or that their partners will only be trying to please them. I'm thinking of the man who said that he felt "very uptight" because he considered oral sex morally wrong and thought of it as a type of perversion. He engaged in it anyway, without much enthusiasm, because he felt his wife expected it and because he thought that, if he didn't, she would be disappointed in him as a man. It would have been very important for him to openly express his reluctance to her, instead of keeping it a secret.

Often, a woman will complain that she doesn't derive as much enjoyment from sexual intercourse as she might because the man either is too concerned with his own pleasure or is orgasm oriented and sees touching, holding, and caressing only as necessary duties he must perform to obtain "the real thing." Thus, she may say that he rolls over in bed as soon as he is satisfied, even if she's left frustrated. Although she may require touching and considerable foreplay and afterplay, he may not recognize her needs. For this reason, she needs to express to him what it feels like to be left sexually unsatisfied, without attacking him, which only raises his defenses. Hite (1976) makes this point clearly: "You have to care about yourself and *want* to please yourself, and you have to feel that it is your *right*. You have to do it, whatever it is—or ask for it, very clearly and very specifically" (p. 302).

Here is an exercise that many sex therapists recommend to clients who want to increase their enjoyment of sensuality and sexuality. The first step is to devote some time to *talking* with your partner about what you each like, what feels good, and so on. Then, to avoid the type of goal-oriented sex that is aimed exclusively at orgasm, you might decide *not* to have sexual intercourse, while taking turns in being the receiver and the giver of sensual touching. For example, the woman might be the receiver for five or ten minutes, and during this time her only task is to ask for what she wants, to direct her partner to what feels good for her, and to enjoy the experience. Then she becomes the giver, and he asks for what he wants and gives her feedback. Although this kind of approach might sound simple, it's surprising how many couples have never tried it. These people have restricted the pleasure they could give to their partners and receive for themselves, merely because they didn't think it was right to ask directly for what they wanted.

Shame Related to Our Bodies

As children, and even more so as adolescents, many of us learn to associate parts of our body with shame. Small children may be oblivious to nudity and to their bodies, but as they run around nude and are made the objects of laughter and jokes by other children and by adults, they gradually become more self-conscious about their bodies and tend to hide them. Sometimes the sense of shame remains with people into adulthood. The following brief cases represent some typical difficulties:

- A woman painfully recalls the onset of menstruation. Since no one had really taken the time to prepare her for this event, she became mildly frantic the first time it happened. Her immediate reaction was that she was being punished for having evil thoughts.
- A man finally shares his concern over the size of his penis, which he thinks is small. His anxiety about this has caused him extreme embarrassment when he has showered with other men, and it has inhibited him in his sexual relations with women. He is convinced that women have been silently laughing at him or have viewed him as sexually inadequate.

- A young, attractive woman relates that she walked stoop-shouldered as an adolescent, trying to conceal her large breasts. She actually felt a sense of shame over being, as she put it, so "well built." Now, as an adult, she frequently feels that men are interested in her only for her physical qualities. She doubts their sincerity in finding her interesting apart from her body.

- A man is convinced that his body is dirty and his impulses vile. He is preoccupied with fears of sinning. He learned early in life to associate shame with his sexual and sensual feelings, and now this attitude prevents him from experiencing his body.

Guilt over Sexual Feelings

Most of us have learned certain taboos about sex. We commonly feel guilty about our *feelings*, even if we don't act on them. Guilt is commonly experienced in connection with homosexual fantasies and impulses, feelings of sexual attraction toward members of one's family, sexual feelings toward people other than one's spouse, enjoyment of sexuality, and too much (or too little) desire for sex. Even though we intensely fear such feelings, we can and should learn to accept them as legitimate. Moreover, simply having feelings doesn't mean that we're impelled to act on them.

As is the case of shame over our bodies, we need to become aware of our guilt and then to reexamine it to determine whether we're needlessly burdening ourselves. Not all guilt is unhealthy and irrational, of course, but there is a real value in learning to challenge guilt feelings and to rid ourselves of those that are *unrealistic*.

For many of my earlier years, I experienced a great deal of guilt over my sexual feelings and fantasies. I believe that my guilt was largely due to the influence of a strict religious education that took a strong stand on sexual morality. Even though I've consciously struggled to overcome some of this influence, I still experience traces of old guilt. As in so many other areas, I find that early lessons in regard to sex are difficult to unlearn. Consequently, it has been important for me to continue to challenge old guilt patterns that interfere with my sexual enjoyment, while at the same time developing a personal ethical code that I can live by with integrity and self-respect.

Many people express some very real fears as they begin to recognize and accept their sexuality. A common fear is that, if we recognize or accept our sexual feelings, our impulses will sweep us away, leaving us out of control. It's important to learn that we can accept the full range of our sexual feelings yet decide for ourselves what we will *do* about them. For instance, I remember a man who said that he felt satisfied with his marriage and found his wife exciting but was troubled because he found other women appealing and sometimes desired them. Even though he had made a decision not to have extramarital affairs, he still experienced a high level of anxiety over simply having sexual feelings toward other women. At some level, he believed that he might be more likely to *act* on his feelings if he fully accepted that he had them. In my opinion, he was torturing himself needlessly. I saw it as important that he learn to discriminate between having sexual feelings and deciding to take certain actions and that he learn to trust his own decisions.

In making responsible, inner-directed choices of whether to act on sexual feelings, many people find questions such as the following to be helpful guidelines: Will my actions hurt another person or myself? Will my actions limit another person's freedom? Will my actions exploit another's rights? Are my actions consistent with my commitments? Of course, each of us must decide on our own moral guidelines, but it seems unrealistic to expect that we can or should control our feelings in the same way that we can control our actions. By controlling our actions, we define who we are; by trying to deny or banish our feelings, we only become alienated from ourselves.

Guilt over Sexual Experiences

While some people are convinced that in these "modern times" college students do not suffer guilt feelings related to sexual behaviors, my observations show me that this is not the case. College students, whether single or married, young or middle-aged, often report a variety of experiences over which they feel guilty. Guilt may be related to masturbation, extramarital (or "extrapartner") affairs, homosexual behavior, sexual practices that are sometimes considered deviant, and the practice of having sex with many partners.

Sources of guilt feelings.   Sex therapists emphasize early sexual learning as a crucial factor in one's later sexual adjustment. They assume that current guilt feelings often stem from both unconscious and conscious decisions that were made in response to verbal and nonverbal messages about sexuality.

In their comprehensive volume, *Sexual Choices*, Nass, Libby, and Fisher (1981) discuss the sources of sexual information and its relationship to developing guilt feelings. They write that our early recollections of where we learned about sex are typically fuzzy. Although we may remember selected incidents, where and when we developed certain attitudes and feelings about sex are often not a part of our consciousness. According to these authors, some of the major sources of basic information on sexual matters are parents, peers, the media, and sex-education programs.

Nass, Libby, and Fisher see parents as the earliest shapers of sexual attitudes. For example, erotic activities such as masturbation and sex play may result in punishment, or they may not be given any labels that children can understand. This process of "nonlabeling" of erotic activities and body parts can lead children to deny their own sexuality. If children are not given words for their sexual experiences, they can easily develop inaccurate beliefs and guilt feelings pertaining to natural feelings and behavior. If parents restrict their vocabulary by referring to the genitals as simply organs of excretion, then children are likely to assume that sexual pleasure is "dirty" or unnatural. Such distortions or omissions of information create a hidden attitude toward sexuality through which later sex information is bound to be filtered.

Peers often fill the void left by parents. However, reliance on the same-sex peer group usually results in learning inaccurate sexual information, which can later lead to fears and guilt over sexual feelings and activities. Most sex information from the peer group is imparted during the early teen years. Many distorted notions are incorporated, such as: "If you masturbate, your penis will fall off." "Kissing may lead to getting pregnant."

Movies, television, magazines, and newspapers provide information that is often a source of negative learning about sexuality. Material dealing with rape, violent sex, and venereal disease is blatantly presented to children. This slanted information often produces unrealistic and unbalanced attitudes about sexuality and ultimately fosters fears and guilt that can have a powerful impact on the ability to enjoy sex as an adult.

The main point is that we acquire a sense of guilt over sexual feelings and experiences as a result of a wide diversity of sources of information and *mis*information. As was mentioned, becoming aware of early verbal and nonverbal messages about sexuality is essential if we hope to free ourselves of guilt.

An example: Incest guilt.   In our therapeutic groups Marianne and I find that the participants have a difficult time in working through the guilt they feel over certain sexual experiences. As a common illustration, I'll use the example of incest.

In groups designed for personal growth and for relatively well-functioning people, we find a startling number of women who report incidents of incest and sexual experimentation with fathers, uncles, stepfathers, grandfathers, and brothers. Many women will bring up the matter because they feel burdened with guilt, rage, hurt, and confusion over having been taken advantage of sexually. Some are confused and guilty both, because even though they may feel like a victim (and in most cases they were), at the same time they may see themselves as a conspirator. They may believe that they were at least partly to blame in that they led the man on or enjoyed the act (as well as fearing it at the same time). Typically, these experiences happen in childhood or early adolescence; the women remember feeling helpless at the time, not knowing how to stop the man and also being afraid to tell anyone. Once they bring out these past experiences, intense, pent-up emotions surface, such as feelings of hatred and rage for having been treated in such a way, feelings of having been imposed on, and feelings of having been raped and used.

The effects of these early childhood experiences can be far reaching and contemporary, in that a woman's ability to form sexually satisfying relationships may be impaired by events that she has kept inside of herself for many years. She may resent all men, associating them with the father or other man who initially took advantage of her. If she couldn't trust her own father, then what man can she trust? She may have a hard time trusting men's feelings of affection for her, thinking that they are merely trying to get her to have sex with them. She may keep control of relationships by not letting herself be open with men or be sexually playful and free with them. Her fear is that, if she gives up her control, she will be hurt again. She may rarely or never allow herself to fully give in to sexual pleasure during intercourse. Her guilt over sexual feelings and her negative conditioning prevents her from being open to enjoying a satisfying sexual relationship. She may still blame men for her feelings of guilt and her sexual nonresponsiveness.

We've found that it is therapeutic for most of these women to simply share this burden that they've been carrying alone for so many years. In a climate of support, trust, care, and respect, these women can *begin* a healing process that will eventually allow them to shed needless guilt. Before this healing can occur, they generally need to fully express bottled-up feelings, usually of anger and hatred. We stress that what is important is that this catharsis occur in the group in *symbolic* ways; it is not necessarily recommended that they confront the men who initiated sexual activities with them. Sometimes the man in question will no longer be alive, or the woman might decide that she does not want to go to her uncle and discuss the times he took advantage of her when she was 11 years old. Through role playing, release of feelings, and sharing of her conflicts with others in the group, she often finds that she is not alone in her plight, and she begins to put these experiences into a new perspective. While she will never forget these experiences, she can begin the process of letting go of feelings of self-blame. In doing so, she is also freeing herself of the control these sexual experiences (and the feelings associated with them) have had over her ability to form intimate relationships with men.

Ways in Which We Use Sex

Increasing our sexual awareness can include becoming more sensitive to the ways in which we sometimes use sex as a means to some end. For instance, sexual activity can be used as a way of actually preventing the development of intimacy. It can also be a way of avoiding experiencing our aloneness, our isolation, and our feelings of distance from others. Sex can be an escape into activity, a way of avoiding inner emptiness. When it is being used in any of these ways, it can take on a driving or compulsive quality that detracts from its spontaneity and leaves us unfulfilled. Sex used as a way of filling inner emptiness becomes a mechanical act, divorced of any passion, feeling, or caring. Then it only deepens our feelings of isolation and detachment.

It appears that the pendulum has swung from one extreme to the other. At one time, people typically invested a lot of energy in denying sex while stressing love; now, the ideal for some is to have sex without the attachment of love. As Rollo May (1969) observes, "The Victorian person sought to have love without falling into sex; the modern person seeks to have sex without falling into love" (p. 46). Yet in my work with many college students, I find that this kind of unfeeling sex isn't what most of them are looking for. Many of those who have experienced it to any significant degree feel increasingly removed from their partners and from themselves as well.

It might be well to reflect on how sex can be used to either enhance or diminish ourselves and our partners as persons. We can ask ourselves such questions as: Are my intimate relationships based on a need to conquer or exert power over someone else? Or are they based on a genuine desire to become intimate, to share, to experience joy and pleasure, to both give and receive? Asking ourselves what we want in our relationships and what uses sex serves for us may also help us avoid the overemphasis on technique and performance that frequently detracts from sexual experiences. Although technique and knowledge are important, they are not ends in themselves, and overemphasizing them can cause us to become oblivious to the *persons* we have sex with. An abundance of anxiety over performance and technique can only impede sexual enjoyment and rob the experience of genuine intimacy and caring.

Myths and Misconceptions about Sex and Sexuality

As in other areas of life, we sometimes saddle ourselves with beliefs about sex that we have not given much thought to. Open discussion with those you are intimate with, as well as an honest exchange of views in your class, can do a lot to help you challenge the basis of some myths and misconceptions about this significant area of your life. What follows are some illustrations of statements that I consider to be misconceptions. As you read over this list, ask yourself what your attitudes are and where you developed these beliefs. Are they working for you? Could any of the following statements apply to you? How might some of these statements affect your ability to make free choices concerning sexuality?

- If I allow myself to become sexual, then I'll get into trouble.
- Women should be less active than men in sex.
- Women are not as sexy when they initiate.
- As you get older, you're bound to lose interest in sex.
- If my partner really loved me, I would not have to tell him or her what I liked or wanted; knowing what I need intuitively without my asking is a sign of love.
- If I had negative conditioning regarding sex as I was growing up, I can't hope to overcome this limitation and am doomed to never fully enjoy sexual experiences.
- Acting without any guilt or restrictions is what is meant by being sexually free.
- The more a person knows about the mechanics of sex, the more he or she will be satisfied with sexual relationships.
- I am not responsible for the level of my sexual satisfaction.
- My partner would be offended and hurt if I told him or her what I liked and wanted.
- Some people find that the only place they get along well together is in bed.
- Being sexually attracted to a person other than my partner implies that I don't really find my partner sexually exciting.

- There is only one right person for me.
- Multiple sexual relationships enhance a primary relationship.
- An exclusive relationship ensures a greater degree of emotional and sexual intensity than is true of an open relationship.
- The inability or unwillingness to engage in multiple sexual relationships indicates a lack of trust in oneself or at least a basic insecurity.
- The more physically attractive a person is, the more sexually exciting he or she is.
- With the passage of time, any sexual relationship is bound to become less exciting or grow stale.

What are a few sexual myths or misconceptions you think ought to be added to this list?

_____

_____

_____

_____

_____

Time Out for Personal Reflection

1. *Do you tend to deny your sexuality? If so, in what ways? Check any statements that fit you:*

_____ *I'm overweight.*

_____ *I usually wear unattractive clothes that tend to hide my bodily features.*

_____ *I tend to retreat into my intellect and neglect my body.*

_____ *I generally don't let myself experience my sexual feelings.*

_____ *I don't see myself as a sexual person.*

2. *List some other ways in which you deny your sexuality:*

_____

_____

_____

3. *Are there any steps you'd like to take toward learning to accept your body and your sexuality more than you do now? If so, what are they?*

_____

_____

_____

4. *Do you experience guilt over sexual feelings? If so, what specific kinds of feelings give rise to guilt for you?*

_____

_____

_____

5. *How openly are you able to discuss sexuality in a personal way? Would you like to be more open in discussing your sexuality or sexual issues? If so, what is preventing this openness?*

_____

_____

_____

_____

_____

6. *What are some personal issues relating to sex that you're willing to discuss in your class group? What are some areas that you would not be willing to share or explore?*

_____

_____

_____

_____

_____

Developing Our Own Sexual Values

During the past couple of decades, a change has occurred in our society that many people term a sexual revolution. Certainly, there has been an open questioning of society's sexual standards and practices, accompanied by the growing belief that individuals can and should decide for themselves what acceptable sexual practices are. Previously, many people did not have to struggle to decide what was moral or immoral, since they took the standards of sexual behavior from external sources. This is not to say that they were necessarily moral, even by their own standards, for they may have been more secretive about their sexual activities and may also have suffered more guilt than do many people today.

Although I believe that it's desirable for people to bring sexual issues into the open and talk freely without the guilt and shame their parents may have experienced, I also believe that we need to form consistent value systems on which to base our behavior, including our sexual behavior. The change in sexual attitudes can give us the freedom to be sexually responsible—to determine our own values and govern our own behavior.

For much of the earlier part of my life, I looked outside myself for the answers to sexual issues. Instead of struggling to find values that would be my own, I accepted the guidelines that came ready-made from my church. Although it was comfortable for me at the time, I now see this acceptance of external standards as an avoidance of my responsibility to define my own sexual ethics, as well as an avoidance of the anxiety I would have experienced in attempting to do so. Since then, I've come to recognize the importance of dealing with sexual issues in a way that has meaning for me and that I can live with.

I frequently get the impression that it isn't in vogue to talk about sexual values and ethics; many people seem to prefer to follow their spontaneous impulses without weighing the place of values in their decisions. Of course, designing a personal and meaningful set of sexual ethics is not an easy task. It can be accomplished only through a process of honest questioning. Our questioning can start with the values we presently have: What is their source? Do they fit in with our views of ourselves in other areas of our life? Which of them can we incorporate in our lives in order to live responsibly and with enjoyment? Which do we think we should reject? Achieving freedom doesn't have to mean shedding all our past learnings or values. Whether we keep or reject them in whole or in part, we can refuse to allow someone besides ourselves to make our decisions for us. It can be tempting to allow others (whether past authorities or present acquaintances) to tell us what is right and wrong and design our lives for us, for then we don't have to wrestle with tough decisions ourselves. Whenever we yield to that temptation, however, we surrender our autonomy and run the risk of becoming alienated from ourselves.

In *Existential Sexuality*, Koestenbaum (1974) describes the journey from "sexual prison" to "sexual paradise," encouraging us never to sell out on our sexual freedom by losing sight of our own power to choose. For Koestenbaum, although sex is a natural urge, the place that sex occupies in our lives and the attitudes we have toward it are very much a matter of free choice. We are free to answer for ourselves such basic questions as: Does sex necessarily have to include love? Can we have love without sex? Are love and sex the foundations for marriage? What is the purpose of sex? Should love precede sex? Many other questions could be added to this list, depending on what issues are central for us. For Koestenbaum, the important point is that these questions cannot be answered objectively by experts or authorities. As he puts it, "Sex seen as a choice, not a need, frees us from the tyranny of 'experts'—moral and medical—returning our bodies and the life of our bodies to the rightful owner: the inwardness residing within each of us" (p. 45). I like

the way he expresses the concept of sexual liberation: "It removes the strictures of guilt and opens us up to the spaciousness and grace of our lives. When you realize that the 'whether' and the 'how' of sex is your own decision, you are truly liberated" (p. 45).

Developing our own values means assuming responsibility for ourselves, which for me includes taking into consideration how others may be affected by our choices while allowing them to take responsibility for theirs. I make the assumption that, in an adult relationship, the parties involved are capable of taking personal responsibility for their own actions. Consequently, I think it's difficult to be used or manipulated unless we allow others to use or manipulate us. Generally, we cannot be exploited unless we collaborate in this activity. For example, in the case of premarital or extramarital sex, each person must weigh such questions as: Do I really want to pursue a sexual relationship with this person at this time? Is the price worth it? What are my commitments? Who else is involved, and who could be hurt? Might this be a positive or a negative experience? How does my decision fit in with my values generally?

In summary, it's no easier to achieve sexual autonomy than it is to achieve autonomy in the other areas of our lives. While challenging our values, we need to take a careful look at ways in which we could easily engage in self-deception by adjusting our behavior to whatever we might desire at the moment. We also need to pay attention to how we feel about ourselves in regard to our past sexual experience. Perhaps, in doing so, we can use our level of self-respect as one important guide to our future behavior. That is, we can each ask "Do I feel enhanced or diminished by my past experience?"

Homosexuality as an Alternative Life-Style

Homosexual relationships are becoming the avowed preference of an increasing number of people in our society. Although an in-depth discussion of this topic falls outside the scope of this book, several themes that have been running through this chapter are applicable to the choice of homosexuality as a way of life.

Nass, Libby, and Fisher (1981) report that sociologists now view homosexuality not as a perversion or deviance but as an orientation that is neither good nor bad in itself. Homosexuality can be regarded as another style of expressing sexuality; this style can be healthy or unhealthy, depending on the person and the social and psychological dynamics. Sociologists hold that the fact that homosexuality is minority behavior is not a sufficient reason for denying it acceptance.

In the past, many people felt ashamed and abnormal because of homosexual preferences. Heterosexuals frequently categorized them as deviates and as sick or immoral. For these and other reasons, many homosexuals were forced to conceal their preferences, perhaps even to themselves. Today, the gay-liberation movement is actively challenging the stigma attached to this alternative life-style, and those who choose it are increasingly asserting their right to live as they choose, without discrimination. Nevertheless, much of the public continues to cling to stereotypes, prejudices, and misconceptions regarding homosexual behavior.

In their book *Counseling with Gay Men and Women*, Woodman and Lenna (1980) define the gay-liberation movement as a demand for equal rights and equal protection under the law. These rights include the right to choose how to live creatively and socially. As a part of the liberation effort there are two aims: (1) the recognition of homosexuality as not abnormal or aberrant; and (2) the dismantling or restructuring of discriminatory social institutions. This movement has implications on both the individual and collective levels. As individuals, many gay people are no longer willing to remain passive when others define reality in ways that are contrary to their feelings and experiences. Collectively, gay people are banding together by forming organizations to fight institutionalized oppression. Woodman and Lenna provide the following picture of an alternative life-style:

> The contemporary gay perspectives are that homosexual life-styles are not only alternative but also totally positive and legitimate. Being gay is not seen as merely engaging in homosexual behavior but as a gestalt of personal feelings and a network of social relationships in which sexual and affectional preferences play a role [1980, p. 9].

In basic agreement with the perspective described by Woodman and Lenna is the concept of "homosexuality as beyond deviance" as advocated by Nass, Libby, and Fisher (1981). They write that homosexuals have organized to free themselves from the fears and stigmas of the past, mainly by trying to reeducate the public. According to them, these organized efforts have promoted greater acceptance of homosexual choices by some people, and many gays have been helped to develop a more positive self-image.

A further problem consists in the labeling done by both heterosexuals and homosexuals. Nass, Libby, and Fisher contend that applying labels to people can restrict their possibilities in developing an identity. They suggest the phrasing "He is now involved in a homosexual relationship" as preferable to "He *is* a homosexual." The former statement allows for the possibility that one's gender preference is a choice subject to change, rather than a permanent condition. Also, a person has many other dimensions besides sexual orientation, and the label of "gay" or "homosexual" can easily reduce a person's identity to a merely sexual one.

Moses and Hawkins (1982) take the position that labeling people as "lesbian" or "homosexual" often leads others to react negatively to them on the basis of the label. They argue for a move away from slapping labels on people—labels that often become a part of their self-concepts.

These authors also summarize research that has found homosexuality to be not pathological in itself, and they conclude that the illness model of homosexuality is no longer viable. Instead, the main difference between homosexuals and heterosexuals is their *choice* of affectional and sexual preference. Consequently, counselors who work with homosexual people should place emphasis on assisting them to recognize and accept their sexual identity and on helping them to value this identity in a predominantly heterosexual society. Often such counseling may include an exploration of the possibilities of increasing the client's sexual repertoire, but this choice should rest with the client.

In categorizing relationships as heterosexual or homosexual, we sometimes forget that sex is not the only aspect of a relationship. Here I would only urge the same points I've made earlier in this chapter—namely, that whatever choice we make, we need to examine the bases for it, whether it is the best choice for us, and whether it is compatible with our own values. Just as I'm concerned that people might choose or reject certain sex roles because of others' expectations, so too I am concerned that people may reject a gay life-style merely because others condemn it or adopt it merely because they are unquestioningly following a liberation movement. For me, what is most important is that we define ourselves, that we assume the responsibility for our own choices, and that we feel that we can live out our choices with inner integrity.

Time Out for Personal Reflection

1. *What influences have shaped your attitudes and values concerning sexuality? In the following list, indicate the importance of each factor by placing a 1 in the blank if it was very important, a 2 if it was somewhat important, and a 3 if it was unimportant. For each item that you mark with a 1 or a 2, indicate briefly the nature of that influence.*

———————— *parents* ————————————————————————————

———————— *church* ————————————————————————————

———————— *friends* ————————————————————————————

———————— *siblings* ————————————————————————————

———————— *movies* ————————————————————————————

———————— *school* ————————————————————————————

_____   *books* _____

_____   *television* _____

_____   *spouse* _____

_____   *grandparents* _____

_____   *your own experiences* _____
             other influential factors:

             _____

             _____

2. Look over the following list, quickly checking the words that you associate with sex.

____ fun   ____ dirty   ____ routine
____ ecstasy   ____ shameful   ____ closeness
____ procreation   ____ joy   ____ release
____ beautiful   ____ pressure   ____ sinful
____ duty   ____ performance   ____ guilty
____ trust   ____ experimentation   ____ vulnerability

Now look over the words you've checked and see whether there are any significant patterns in your responses. What can you say by way of summary about your attitudes toward sex?

_____

_____

_____

_____

3. *Try making a list of specific values you hold regarding sexual issues. As a beginning, you might respond to the following questions:*

   a. *How do you feel about promiscuity?*

   _____

   _____

   b. *What is your view of sex outside of marriage?*

   _____

   _____

c. *Do you think it's legitimate to separate love and sex?*

_____

_____

d. *How do you feel about having sex with a person you don't like or respect?*

_____

_____

e. *List other specific values or convictions you have concerning sexual behavior.*

_____

_____

4. *What are your reactions to those people who choose homosexuality as an alternative life-style?*

_____

_____

_____

5. *How do you feel about homosexual experiences for yourself?*

_____

_____

_____

6. *What are your views concerning the gay-liberation movement? Do you believe that the rights of homosexuals have been denied? Do you think that people who openly profess a gay life-style have rights equal to those of heterosexuals and should not be denied a specific job because of their sexual preference alone?*

_____

_____

_____

_____

_____

Chapter Summary

In this chapter, I've encouraged you to think about your attitudes and values concerning sexuality and sex roles and to take a close look at where and how you developed them. I've indicated that many of us tend to keep our questions and concerns about sexuality to ourselves and that many of our exaggerated fears and misconceptions can be cleared up if we learn how to discuss sexuality with others. Finally, in asking you to examine the basis of your sex-role expectations, your concept of what constitutes a woman or a man, and your views about sexual behavior, I've stressed the idea that you can decide for yourself what kind of woman or man you want to be, instead of following the expectations of others.

Activities and Exercises

1. Write down some of your major questions or concerns regarding sexuality. You might consider discussing these issues with a friend, your partner (if you're involved in an intimate relationship), or your class group.
2. Write down the characteristics you associate with being a woman (or feminine) and being a man (or masculine). Then think about how you acquired these views and to what degree you're satisfied with them.
3. Select a book on sexuality from the reading list at the end of the chapter, and pick out some sections that you'd like to discuss with a friend or your partner. Read some of these selections together, and discuss how they apply to each of you.
4. Make a list of sex-role stereotypes that apply to men and a list of those that apply to women. Then select people of various ages, and ask them to say how much they agree or disagree with each of these stereotypes. If several people bring their results to class, you might have the basis of an interesting panel discussion.
5. For a week or two, pay close attention to the messages that you see transmitted on television, both in programs and in commercials, regarding sex roles, expectations of women and men, and sexuality. Record your impressions in your journal.
6. In your journal, trace the evolution of your sexual history. What were some important experiences for you, and what did you learn from these experiences?
7. Discuss with some friends various aspects of homosexuality as a lifestyle. What trends do you see regarding acceptance or rejection of

those who choose homosexual relationships? As a starting point for your discussion, you might respond to the following words taken from Patricia Warren's novel *The Front Runner* (1974), which depicts the psychological experience of a homosexual:

> I did not pray to be miraculously changed back into a heterosexual. I prayed for knowledge to know myself, and accept myself totally. Being gay, I now realized, was not merely a question of sex—it was a state of mind. Society had told me I was a disease, but I was now convinced that I had come to homosexuality by natural inclination [p. 33].

Suggested Readings

Basow, S. A. *Sex-Role Stereotypes: Traditions and Alternatives.* Monterey, Calif.: Brooks/Cole, 1980. This book is aimed at exploring these questions: How did sex-role stereotypes originate? How are they maintained and transmitted? How can one break free from them and change? Breaking free of stereotypes is aided by the concept of androgyny, which aims at a flexible integration of masculine and feminine attributes in one person.

Brooks-Gunn, J., & Matthews, W. Schempp. *He and She: How Children Develop Their Sex-Role Identity.* Englewood Cliffs, N.J.: Prentice-Hall (Spectrum), 1979. This is a thought-provoking and personal book that challenges readers to examine patterns of socialization and the bases upon which they learned to become "feminine" or "masculine." The development of sex-role identity is traced from infancy through adolescence. The book contains a comprehensive bibliography for those who wish to pursue their study further.

Deaux, K. *The Behavior of Women and Men.* Monterey, Calif.: Brooks/Cole, 1976. A very informative work that deals with both stereotypes and self-evaluations of women and men. The book also includes an excellent treatment of the concept of androgyny.

Farrell, W. *The Liberated Male.* New York: Bantam, 1975. This book challenges men to examine ways of freeing themselves from the bonds of rigid sex-role definitions.

Filene, P. *Men in the Middle: Coping with the Problems of Work and Family in the Lives of Middle-Aged Men.* Englewood Cliffs, N.J.: Prentice-Hall (Spectrum), 1981. This book contains autobiographical essays by eight middle-class men who explain how they have coped with two disruptive forces in their lives: the equalization of male and female roles in contemporary society, and the passages into middle age.

Friedan, B. *The Feminine Mystique.* New York: Dell, 1975. Friedan argues that social change in the way women are perceived and treated is a must, and she takes the position that women can affect society as well as be affected by it.

Her contention is that both women and men have the power to choose and that in so doing they can make their own heaven or hell.

Goldberg, H. *The Hazards of Being Male.* New York: Nash, 1976. This book is an excellent treatment of the stereotypes of masculinity. The author describes the traps males have fallen into and ways of getting out of them.

Goldberg, H. *The New Male.* New York: New American Library (Signet), 1979. The author writes about how changes in both sexes affect the other. He describes the crisis of the contemporary male and makes some suggestions for how to stop being a machine and become a person.

Gordon, S., & Libby, R. W. *Sexuality Today and Tomorrow.* North Scituate, Mass.: Duxbury Press, 1976. The authors acquaint readers with the major social, political, and personal issues related to sexuality and sex roles. They present a wide range of interesting articles on a variety of life-styles, on social ethics and personal morals, and on the future of sexuality. Interesting and stimulating reading.

Hall, C. S., & Nordby, V. J. *A Primer of Jungian Psychology.* New York: New American Library (A Mentor Book), 1973. A basic outline of Carl Jung's view of the structure of personality, the dynamics and development of personality, psychological types, and dreams and symbols. This is a good beginning place for readers interested in Jungian psychology.

Hite, S. *The Hite Report.* New York: Dell, 1976. This book gives the results of a nationwide study of female sexuality. Women give a subjective view of their feelings about all the aspects of sex, and the author discusses a cultural interpretation of female sexuality. An informative and valuable book for both women and men.

Jourard, S. *The Transparent Self* (2nd ed.). New York: Van Nostrand, 1971. The book contains a series of personal articles on love, sex, marriage, the healthy personality, and the lethal aspects of the male role.

Koestenbaum, P. *Existential Sexuality: Choosing to Love.* Englewood Cliffs, N.J.: Prentice-Hall (Spectrum), 1974. A thoughtfully written book that stresses the freedom and responsibility you have to choose your kind of sex and to give meaning to sex.

Lewis, R. A. (Ed.). *Men in Difficult Times: Masculinity Today and Tomorrow.* Englewood Cliffs, N.J.: Prentice-Hall, 1981. A varied collection of articles on topics such as the high costs of traditional male roles, socialization into male roles, the impact of feminism on men, nurturance by and for males, ways men can change, and innovative patterns for the new man.

May, R. *Love and Will.* New York: Norton, 1969; Dell, 1974. This is a powerful book that deals with many aspects of love: the paradoxes of love and sex, love and death, the relation of love and will, the meaning of caring, and our capacity for love.

McCarthy, B., Ryan, M., & Johnson, F. *Sexual Awareness: A Practical Approach.* San Francisco: Boyd and Fraser Publishing Co. and The Scrimshaw Press,

1975. This book emphasizes attitudes and techniques for couples who want to understand and enhance their sexual feelings and functioning. Some of the issues dealt with include self-expression and experiencing one's sexuality, increasing arousal and sexual response, sexual expression, and the concept of sex therapy. The book has exercises for each chapter.

Mornell, P. *Passive Men, Wild Women*. New York: Ballantine, 1979. The author makes the point that men and women keep reacting to and bringing out one another's worst side. In a clear style, he outlines the problem of men who are alive at work and dead at home and talks about the problems of passionate women who live with passive men.

Moses, A. E., & Hawkins, R. O. *Counseling Lesbian Women and Gay Men: A Life-Issues Approach*. St. Louis, Mo.: C. V. Mosby, 1982. A comprehensive and well-written book that describes the gay experience and deals with special issues in counseling gay clients. The authors offer some specific suggestions for positive intervention with gay people. Contains a very comprehensive bibliography for those who wish to pursue further study of the subject of homosexuality.

Nass, G. D., Libby, R. W., & Fisher, M. P. *Sexual Choices: An Introduction to Human Sexuality*. Monterey, Calif.: Wadsworth, 1981. A fairly complete and comprehensive textbook on human sexuality. Some of the topics discussed are developing a sexual identity and sexual relationships, early sexual learning, homosexual and bisexual preferences, marriage and alternative lifestyles, intimacy and the elderly, women's liberation and sexual choices, sexual assault, enhancing sexual health, wanted and unwanted conception, and birth control.

Pengelley, E. *Sex and Human Life*. Reading, Mass.: Addison-Wesley, 1974. This is a well-written and informative book about the physiological aspects of sexuality. It contains information on sexual intercourse, sexual difficulties, sexuality and aging, variations of sexual behavior, and cultural aspects of sex.

Pleck, J., & Sawyer, J. (Eds.). *Men and Masculinity*. Englewood Cliffs, N.J.: Prentice-Hall (Spectrum), 1974. This book includes a series of articles dealing with issues in male liberation. It shows how men in consciousness-raising groups can help one another to go beyond the limits of the male stereotype. The book describes how the male stereotype is learned, how it restricts men, and how men are freeing themselves from traditional roles.

Safilios-Rothschild, C. *Love, Sex, and Sex Roles*. Englewood Cliffs, N.J.: Prentice-Hall (Spectrum), 1977. Some interesting chapters include those on women as objects, men as objects, the perils of transition, and the future of love and sex.

Sheehy, G. *Passages: Predictable Crises of Adult Life*. New York: Bantam, 1976. Sheehy gives some excellent case studies illustrating the struggles of men and women at all ages. She also describes the relationship problems that can arise because of changes in either the man or the woman.

Warren, P. N. *The Front Runner*. New York: Bantam, 1974. This popular novel about homosexual love describes the psychological and physical experience of a gay person and explores struggles and conflicts that many homosexuals experience.

Woodman, N. J., & Lenna, H. R. *Counseling with Gay Men and Women: A Guide for Facilitating Positive Life-Styles*. San Francisco: Jossey-Bass, 1980. The problems discussed in this book include the recognition and acceptance of a gay identity and a gay life-style. The book provides an approach for resolving problems involving both inner conflicts and relationships with others.

Chapter Six

Love

Prechapter Self-Inventory

For each statement, indicate the response that most closely identifies your beliefs and attitudes. Use this code: 5 = I *strongly agree* with this statement; 4 = I *agree* in most respects; 3 = I am *undecided*; 2 = I *disagree* in most respects; 1 = I *strongly disagree*.

_____ 1. Love demands exclusivity. Loving more than one person of the opposite sex diminishes our capacity to be deeply involved with another person.

_____ 2. Genuine love is unconditional, which means fully accepting the other person without demanding that he or she become something different.

_____ 3. My ability to love others stems from (and is limited to) my love for myself. Unless I love myself, I cannot love others.

_____ 4. It is abnormal to fear losing others' love.

_____ 5. If I experience hurt or frustration in love, the chances are that I won't continue to risk loving.

_____ 6. If I genuinely love another, I'll make myself known and transparent to that person.

_____ 7. Women are more capable than men of achieving intensity and depth in loving relationships.

_____ 8. Our society makes it extremely difficult to express loving feelings toward members of the same sex.

_____ 9. Commitment is essential to authentic loving.

_____ 10. If I sometimes experience indifference toward those I say I love, then I can hardly say I love them.

_____ 11. Most people are at least as afraid of being accepted as they are of being rejected.

_____ 12. Children who don't feel loved by their parents probably won't be able to accept or give love later in life.

_____ 13. I have to take some risks if I'm to open myself to loving.

_____ 14. Jealousy is one sign of love.

_____ 15. True love implies selflessness, in the sense of putting the other person's needs above my own.

_____ 16. In a loving relationship, there is complete trust and a total absence of fear.

_____ 17. Love means simply accepting another person, without challenging him or her to change in any way.

_____ 18. The presence of love in a relationship means that there is continuous excitement and joy with each other.

_____ 19. My ability to experience and express negative feelings (hate, anger, hostility, and so on) toward another is a sign that love does exist between us.

_____ 20. Love implies constant closeness and intimacy.

Introduction

In this chapter, I invite you to look carefully at your style of loving by examining your choices and decisions concerning your ability to give and receive love. Often I hear people claim either that they have love in their lives or that they don't. I make the assumption that the issue is not as clear-cut as this and that we all have the capacity to become better lovers. We can look at the situations that we put ourselves in and that we create for ourselves and then consider how conducive these are to the sharing of love. We can also look at our attitudes toward love. Some of the questions we can examine are: Is love active or passive? Do we fall in and out of love? How much are we responsible for creating a climate in which we can love others and receive love from them? Do we have romantic and unrealistic ideals of what love should be? If so, how can we challenge them? In what ways does love change as we change?

As you read this chapter, I hope that you'll try to apply the issues I discuss to your own experience of love and that you'll consider the degree to which you're now able to appreciate and love yourself. I also hope that you'll review your own need for love as well as your fears of loving and that you may come to recognize whether there are barriers within yourself that prevent you from experiencing the level of love you're capable of.

Our Need to Love and to Be Loved

I believe that, in order to fully develop as a person and enjoy a rich existence, we need to care about others and have them return this care to us. To me, a loveless life is characterized by a joyless isolation and alienation. Our need for love includes the need to know that, at least in one person's world, our existence makes a difference. If we exclude ourselves from physical and emotional closeness with others, we pay the price of experiencing emotional and physical deprivation.

People express their need to love and to be loved in many ways, a few of which are revealed in the following statements:

- "I need to have someone in my life I can actively care for. I need to let that person know he (she) makes a difference in my life, and I need to know I make a difference in his (her) life."
- "I want to feel loved and accepted for who I am now, not for what the other person thinks I should be in order to be worthy of acceptance."
- "Although I enjoy my own company, I also have a need for people in my life. I want to reach out to certain people, and I hope they'll want something from me."
- It's true that loving and being loved is frightening, but I'd rather open myself up and risk what loving entails than close myself off from this experience."
- "I'm finding out that I'm a person who does need others and that I have more of a capacity to give something to others than I thought I had."
- "I'm beginning to realize that I need to learn how to love myself more fully, for up until now I've limited myself by discounting my worth. I want to learn how to appreciate myself and accept myself in spite of my imperfections. Then maybe I'll be able to really believe that others can love me."
- "There are times when I want to share my joys, my dreams, my anxieties, and my uncertainties with another person, and at these times I want to feel heard and understood."

Of course, there are many ways to harden ourselves so that we won't experience a need for love. We can close ourselves off from needing anything from anybody; we can isolate ourselves by never reaching out to another; we can refuse to trust others and to make ourselves vulnerable; we can cling to an early decision that we are basically unlovable. It's important to recognize, however, that *we* make these decisions about love—and *we* pay the price.

Still another way of protecting ourselves is pointed out by Marshall Hodge (1967) in *Your Fear of Love*. He maintains that there are two alternatives to being fully open to love. One alternative is to cut ourselves off completely from the experience of love by not allowing anyone to make a difference in our lives. The second alternative is to love with caution by remaining reserved and guarded; in this way, we don't disclose much of ourselves to anyone and thus attempt to protect ourselves from our need for love without cutting ourselves off from love entirely. In whatever way we deaden ourselves to our own need for love, the question is: Is the safety we achieve worth the price we pay for it?

Barriers to Loving and Being Loved

Self-Doubt and Lack of Self-Love

Despite our need for love, we often put barriers in the way of our attempts to give and to receive love. One common obstacle consists of the messages we sometimes send to others concerning ourselves. If we enter relationships convinced that nobody could possibly love us, we will give this message to others in many subtle ways. We thus create a self-fulfilling prophecy, whereby we make the very thing we fear come true by telling both ourselves and others that life can be no other way.

If you are convinced that you're unlovable, your conviction is probably related to decisions you made about yourself during your childhood or adolescent years. At one time, perhaps, you decided that you wouldn't be loved *unless* you did certain expected things or lived up to another's design for your life. For example, one such decision is: "Unless I produce, I won't be loved. To be loved, I must produce good grades, become successful, and make the most of my life." Such a decision can make it difficult to convince yourself later on in life that you can be loved even if you're not productive.

People sometimes have a difficult time believing that they are lovable for *who* they are, and they may discount the love others give them as being contingent on a single characteristic of their personality. For example, think for a moment of how many times you have completed this sentence in any of the following ways: People love me only because I am . . . pretty, bright and witty, famous, good in sports, a good student, a fine provider, attractive, accomplished, cooperative and considerate, a good father (mother), a good husband (wife), and so forth.

If you limit your ability to receive love from others by telling yourself (and by convincing others) that you are loved primarily for a single trait, it would be well to challenge this assumption. For example, if you say "You only love me because of my body," you might try to realize that your body is *one* of your assets. You can learn to appreciate this asset without assuming that it is all there is to the person you are. If you have trouble seeing any desirable characteristics besides your physical attractiveness, you are likely to give others messages that your primary value is bound up in appearances. Ideally, you will come to accept that being a physically attractive person makes it easier for others to notice you and want to initiate a contact with you. However, you don't need to limit yourself by depending exclusively on how you look, for you can work at developing other traits. The danger here consists of relying on physical attractiveness as a basis for building and maintaining a relationship. Regardless of the characteristic, if you rely exclusively on it as a source of gaining love from others (or from yourself), your ability to be loved is in a tenuous state.

In my own life I have had to struggle for a long time in recognizing and accepting my lovability. It would be easy for me to say "People love me only because I'm productive—because I write books, am an energetic teacher, am a good organizer, and work hard." The truth is, my productivity may attract certain people to me, and it may have something to do with the reasons others love me. However, it would be a faulty assumption to equate my total worth as a person with my productivity. It has taken me a long time to begin to believe that others love me for something other than my accomplishments; in fact, they may love me *despite* my drivenness and my own need to produce. I continue to learn that my compulsive energy and drive often put distance between those people who love me (and those I love) and myself. Thus, a lesson that I'm continuing to learn is that the very thing I sometimes believe I *must* do or be in order to be loved actually gets in the way of others' loving me.

My point here is not just that we sometimes imagine that *other people* have expectations we must meet in order to be loved; we often obstruct our ability to love and receive love by *our own* unwillingness to accept what we actually are, as opposed to what we think we should be. For instance, I think it's essential for me to remember that I have difficulty in feeling worthy apart from my productivity. It's not always easy for me to acknowledge this difficulty to myself, and I have a tendency to distort or overlook it. I can easily convince myself that I *should* have worked this issue out by now, that I really should be beyond this limitation and should think and feel different. However, my only hope for changing this early decision about my self-worth is to recognize how I actually feel, think, and behave. Once I accept some of my self-limiting attitudes as part of me, I can actively be alert for manifestations of them, and I can challenge their validity.

Thus, a real limitation of our ability to love others is the degree to which we are unable to love and appreciate ourselves. I find over and over that, as we begin to learn to appreciate ourselves, we have some basis for actively loving others and accepting their love. A major stumbling block for many people is that they refuse to look at themselves, focusing instead on what they can do to "give" to others. I believe that we can give the most when we recognize our own worth and our own limitations. However, I also want to stress that early decisions about ourselves aren't easy to erase. In many subtle ways, they continue to manifest themselves. Consequently, we must continually challenge the validity of our assumptions and be alert for the obstacles we put in the way of our loving and being loved.

Learning to love and appreciate ourselves.   Some people are reluctant to speak of their self-love, because they have been brought up to think that self-love is purely egocentric. Yet unless we learn how to love ourselves, we'll encounter difficulties in loving others and in allowing them to express their love for us. We can't very well give to others what we don't possess ourselves. And if we can't appreciate our own worth, how can we believe others when they say that they see value in us?

Having love for ourselves doesn't imply having an exaggerated picture of our own importance or placing ourselves above others or at the center of the universe. Rather, it implies having respect for ourselves, even though we're imperfect. It entails caring about our lives and striving to become the persons we are capable of becoming. Once we can respect, appreciate, and care for ourselves, we open up the possibility of respecting, appreciating, and caring for others.

Many writers have stressed the necessity of self-love as a condition of love for others. In *The Art of Loving*, Erich Fromm (1956) describes self-love as a respect for our own integrity and uniqueness, and he maintains that it cannot be separated from love and understanding of others. In his beautiful book, *Love*, Buscaglia (1972) also writes that to love others we must first love ourselves, for we cannot give what we haven't ourselves learned and experienced. Buscaglia describes the loving of oneself as "the discovery of the true wonder of you; not only the present you, but the many possibilities of you" (p. 99).

The question of how we can learn to love ourselves is raised by Hodge (1967) in his excellent and moving book, *Your Fear of Love*. According to him, we can begin by realizing that it's impossible to become completely self-accepting. Then we can enjoy the fascinating experience of moving in the direction of learning to love and appreciate ourselves, which is a lifelong adventure.

As we grow to treat ourselves with increasing respect and regard, we increase our ability to fully accept the love that others might want to give us; at the same time, we have the foundation for genuinely loving others. I agree with Hodge when he says: "Love of one's self is not antagonistic to having satisfying relationships. On the contrary, we are free to love others only as we become free to love ourselves" (p. 221).[1] Mayeroff (1971) agrees, saying in *On Caring*, "If I am unable to care for myself, I am unable to care for another person" (p. 49).[2] To care for ourselves, Mayeroff adds, we need to be responsive to our own needs for growth; we also need to feel at one with ourselves rather than estranged from ourselves. Furthermore, caring for ourselves and caring for others are mutually dependent: "I can only fulfill myself by serving someone or something apart from myself, and if I am unable to care for anyone or anything separate from me, I am unable to care for myself" (p. 48).

In counseling situations, I often ask clients who only give to others, and who have a difficult time taking for themselves, questions such as: "Do *you* deserve what you so freely give to others?" "Could you begin to consider being as kind to yourself as you are to others?" "If your own well runs dry, will you be able to give to others?"

Our Fear of Love

There are other barriers to love besides a lack of self-love. Despite our need for love, we often fear loving and being loved. Our fear can lead us to seal off our need to experience love, and it can dull our capacity to care about others. Love doesn't come with guarantees; we can't be sure that another person will always love us, and we do lose loved ones. As Hodge (1967) insists, we can't eliminate the possibility that we will be hurt if we choose to love. Our loved ones may die or be injured or become painfully ill; they may simply be mistrustful of our caring. In Hodge's words, "These are painful experiences, and we cannot avoid them if we choose to love. It is part of the human dilemma that love always includes the element of hurt" (p. 266).

We can choose not to accept the risk of loving and thus protect ourselves from being hurt, but if we do, we pay the price of excluding love from our lives. Loving demands courage, for there are always risks involved. I like the way Hodge expresses it:

> If we postponed the experience and expression of love until we no longer feared it, we would postpone it forever. Some people do appear to use their fear of love as a perpetual excuse for stalemated living—loving and trembling seem

[1]This and all other quotations from this source from *Your Fear of Love*, by M. Hodge. Copyright 1967 by Doubleday & Company, Inc. Reprinted by permission.
[2]This and all other quotations from this source from *On Caring*, by M. Mayeroff. Copyright © 1971 by Harper & Row, Publishers, Inc. Reprinted by permission of the publishers, Perennial Library.

to go together. If we desire love we must learn to love in spite of our fears [pp. 267–268].

There are some common fears of risking in love. Most of them are related to rejection, loss, the failure of love to be reciprocated, and uneasiness with intensity. Some of them might be expressed as follows:

· "Since I once got badly hurt in a love relationship, I'm not willing to take the chance of trusting again."
· "I fear allowing myself to love others because of the possibility that they will be seriously injured, contract a terrible illness, or die. I don't want to let them matter that much; that way, if I lose them, it won't hurt as much as if they really mattered."
· "My fear is that love will never be as good as I imagine it to be—that my ideal notions will never be matched in reality."
· "I'm afraid of loving others because they might want more from me than I'm willing to give, and I might feel suffocated."
· "I'm afraid that I'm basically unlovable and that, when you really get to know me, you'll want little to do with me."
· "My fear is that I'm loved not for who I am but for the functions that I perform and the roles that I serve. If I ceased doing these things, I would no longer be loved. It's hard for me to imagine that I'm loved simply for myself."
· "Emotional closeness is scary for me, because, if I care deeply for a person, and I permit her to care about me, then I'm vulnerable."
· "One great fear is that people in my world will be indifferent to me—that they simply won't give a damn about my existence."
· "In many ways it's easier for me to take rejection than acceptance. It's hard for me to accept compliments or to be close and intimate. If people tell me that they want to care for me, I feel I've taken on a burden, and I'm afraid of letting them down."
· "I've never really allowed myself to look at whether I'm lovable. My fear is that I will search deep within myself and find little for another to love. What will I do if I discover that I'm grotesque, or hollow and empty, or incapable of giving or receiving?"

Time Out for Personal Reflection

   1. *Who are some of the people that have made the most difference in your life, and in what ways were they important?*

       a. _____

b. _____

c. _____

d. _____

e. _____

2. *Who are some of the people you've been significant for, and in what ways?*

a. _____

b. _____

c. _____

d. _____

e. _____

3. *How do you express your love to others? Check the responses that apply to you, and add any other ways in which you show love, affection, and caring.*

_____   a. *by telling the other person that I love him or her*
_____   b. *through touching and other nonverbal means*
_____   c. *by doing special things for the person*
_____   d. *by making myself known to the person*
_____   e. *by becoming vulnerable and trusting*
_____   f. *by buying the person gifts*

g. _____

_____

_____

_____

4. *How do you express to another person your own need to receive love, affection, and caring?*

_____   a. *by telling him or her that I need to be loved*
_____   b. *by being open and trusting*
c. _____

_____

_____

5. List some specific fears that you have concerning loving others.

_____

_____

_____

_____

6. List some specific fears you have concerning allowing others to love you.

_____

_____

_____

_____

7. Mention some barriers within yourself that prevent you from fully loving others. (Examples: extreme selfishness, lack of caring, fear of vulnerability, fear of being responsible for another.)

_____

_____

_____

_____

8. Mention some barriers within yourself that prevent others from loving you or that prevent you from fully receiving their love. (Examples: being overly suspicious, refusing to accept others' love, feeling a lack of self-worth, needing to return their love.)

_____

_____

_____

_____

9. List some qualities you have that you deem lovable. (Examples: my ability to care for others, my sense of humor.)

_____

_____

_____

_____

10. *List some specific ways in which you might become a more lovable
    person. (Examples: increasing my feelings of self-worth, trusting
    others more, taking better care of my physical appearance.)*

_____

_____

_____

_____

11. *What did you learn about yourself from these exercises? Are there
    ways in which you're willing to change? If so, how might you go
    about it?*

_____

_____

_____

_____

_____

_____

Myths and Misconceptions about Love

There are many myths and misconceptions about love that inhibit our
ability to love fully and to receive love from others. Some of the more
common beliefs that need to be challenged are discussed below.

The myth of eternal love.   I believe that the notion that love will endure
forever is nonsense. This idea can deceive us into feeling a sense of security that simply has no basis in reality. There are no guarantees that our
love (or another's love for us) will last a lifetime. That would be true
only if we never changed. On the contrary, I think that the intensity and
the degree of our love changes as we change. We may experience stages
of love with one person, deepening our love and finding new levels of
richness; there is also the chance that each of us will grow in different
directions or outgrow the love we once shared.

DO YOU GUARANTEE THAT ?

The myth that love is fleeting. On the opposite end of the spectrum is the notion that love is strictly temporary. I am thinking of one person who found himself to be in love with different women as often as his moods changed. One day he would claim that he loved Sara and wanted to be committed to her in an exclusive relationship, but in a short while he would grow tired of Sara and find himself in love with Peggy and would maintain that he wanted an intense and exclusive relationship with her. For him, love was strictly a here-and-now feeling. I don't believe that such changeable feelings constitute real love. In most intense, long-term relationships, there are times when the alliance is characterized by deadness, frustration, strife, or conflict. There inevitably are times when we feel "stuck" with a person, and at such times we may consider dissolving the relationship. If our attitude is "I'll stay while things are rosy, but as soon as things get stormy or dull, I'll split and look elsewhere for something more interesting," then it's worth asking what kind of love

"OF COURSE I LOVE YOU SARA — UH-H PEGGY!
UH-H-H... HELLO? ...HELLO?"

it is that crumbles with the first crisis. For me, authentic love means recognizing when we're stuck in an unsatisfying place but being willing to challenge the reasons for the deadness and caring enough about the other person to stay and work on breaking through the impasse.

The myth that love implies constant closeness. I feel strongly that most of us can tolerate only so much closeness and that the other side of this need is our desire for distance. I am fond of Kahlil Gibran's words in *The Prophet:* "And stand together yet not too near together: For the pillars of the temple stand apart, and the oak tree and the cypress grow not in each other's shadow."[3]

---

[3]This and all other quotations from this source reprinted from *The Prophet*, by Kahlil Gibran, with permission of the publisher, Alfred A. Knopf, Inc. Copyright 1923 by Kahlil Gibran; renewal copyright 1951 by Administrators C.T.A. of Kahlil Gibran Estate, and Mary G. Gibran.

There are times when a separation from our loved ones can be very healthy. At these times we can renew our need for the other person and also allow ourselves to become centered again. If we fail to separate ourselves from others when we feel the need to do so, we'll surely strain the relationship. I'm thinking now of a man who refused to spend a weekend without his wife and children, even though he said he wanted some time for himself. The myth of constant closeness and constant togetherness in love prevented him from taking private time just for himself. It might also have been that the myth covered up certain fears. What if he discovered that his wife and children managed very well without him? What if he found that he couldn't stand his own company for a few days and that the reason for "togetherness" was to keep him from boring himself?

The myth that we fall in and out of love.   A common notion is that we "fall" in love—that we passively wait for the right person to come along and sweep us off our feet. According to this view, love is something that happens *to* us. In contrast, I see love as being *active,* as something we ourselves create. *We* make love happen.

Numerous writers have discussed this concept of love as an activity. Mayeroff (1971) asserts that patience is an important part of loving, for it enables others to grow in their own way and at their own pace. He adds "Patience is not waiting passively for something to happen, but is a kind of participation with the other in which we give fully of ourselves" (p. 17). In *Let Me Live!,* Lyon (1975) writes that love is a *verb* that implies *acts* of loving. Active lovers, he says, are *greedy* in the sense that they want much from life and from love. "To achieve this goal they are willing to gamble. As gamblers, they are ready to play for high stakes by committing themselves first and fully" (p. 80). To Lyon, the "one basic fact of life" is that, in the long run, we get from life and love what we deserve:

> If you choose to fall in love, you will fall—or be pushed—out of love. If you live as an alien, yours will be a life of alienation. If you passively wait for love to happen to you, you will wait an eternity. But should you reach, grab, seek, act, risk—then you will find that there *is* life after birth [p. 81].

Buscaglia (1972) also criticizes the phrase "to fall in love." He contends that it's more accurate to say we *grow* in love, which implies an activity of choosing: "Love is active, not passive. It is continually engaged in the process of opening new doors and windows so that fresh ideas and questions can be admitted" (p. 69). For Buscaglia, love is like a "continual feast to be nourished upon. It sets an appetizing, attractive, gourmet table, but it cannot force anyone to eat. It allows each the freedom to select and reject according to his taste" (p. 69). In *The Art of Loving*, Fromm (1956) also describes love as an active agent: "Love is an activity, not a passive affect; it is a 'standing in,' not a 'falling for.' In the most general way, the active character of love can be described by stating that love is primarily *giving*, not receiving" (p. 22).[4]

People often say "I love you" and at the same time are hard pressed to describe the active way in which they show this love. Declaring "I love you just because . . ." may not be enough. Words can be easily overused and become hollow. The loved one may be more convinced by actions than by words.

In summary, active love is something that we can choose to share with others. We don't lose love by sharing it but rather increase it. This thought leads me to the next myth.

The myth of the exclusiveness of love.   We sometimes think of love as a limited quantity that we must carefully dole out and conserve. In *Love Today*, Herbert Otto (1973) counters this idea with the statement "Deep within some core of our being, most of us recognize that although we are led to believe we have only so much love to offer, *the more love we give, the more we have to give*" (p. 273). Similarly, we may believe that we are capable of loving only one other person—that there is one right person for each of us and that our fate is to find this singular soul. However, I believe that one of the signs of genuine love is that it is expansive rather than exclusive. By opening myself to loving others, I open myself to loving one person more deeply. The need to restrict love to just one person seems irrationally based on our need to feel that we are irreplaceable.

In some senses, though, we may choose to make our love exclusive or special. For example, two people may choose not to have sexual relationships with others, because they realize that doing so might interfere with their capacity to freely open up and trust each other. Nevertheless, their sexual exclusivity does not have to mean that they cannot genuinely love others as well.

Jealousy is an issue that can be mentioned here. For example, Joe may feel insulted if he discovers that his wife, Carol, finds certain other men

---

[4]This and all other quotations from this source from *The Art of Loving*, by E. Fromm. Copyright © 1956 by Harper & Row, Publishers, Inc. Reprinted by permission of the publishers.

sexually attractive. Even if Carol and Joe have an agreement not to have sexual relationships with others, Joe might be threatened and angry over the mere fact that Carol has sexual *feelings* for other men. He may wrongly assume: "What is the matter with me that Carol has to look at other men? If I were enough of a man for her, then I should be able to satisfy all of her needs, and she would not find other men sexually attractive. Her interest in other men is a sign that something is wrong with me!" Jealousy can easily get out of proportion when it controls the person, instead of the person controlling it. On the other hand, I think it is a mistaken assumption to equate an absence of jealousy with an absence of love. Carol might be upset if Joe did not display any jealousy toward her, insisting that this meant that he was indifferent to her or that he had come to take her for granted.

The myth that true love is selfless.   We may have been conditioned to believe that genuine love implies that we forget ourselves. It is a myth that true love means giving selflessly. For one thing, love also means *taking*. If you cannot allow others to give to you and cannot take their expressions of love, you are likely eventually to become drained or to become resentful of your continual giving. For another thing, in giving to others we do meet many of our own needs, and I see nothing wrong in this, as long as we can admit it. For example, a mother who never says no to any demands made by her children may not be aware of the ways that she has conditioned them to depend on her. They may be unaware that she has any needs of her own, for she hides them so well. In fact, she may set them up to take advantage of her out of her need to feel significant. In other words, her "giving" is actually an outgrowth of her need to feel like a good mother, rather than an honest expression of love for her children.

I am not implying that giving to others or the desire to express our love to others is necessarily a problem. Rather, I hope to stress that we should recognize our own needs and should allow others to take care of us and return the love we show to them.

Authentic and Inauthentic Love

"Love" that Stifles

It isn't always easy to distinguish between authentic love, which enhances us and those we love, and the kind of "love" that diminishes ourselves and those to whom we attempt to give it. Certainly, there are forms of pseudo-love that parade as real love but that have the effect of crippling not only ourselves but also those we say we love. Later in this section, I describe my view of genuine love; here, I want to list some signs of what I consider inauthentic love. This list isn't rigid or definitive, but it may give you some ideas you can use in thinking about the quality of your love.

I believe my love is inauthentic when:

· I have an inordinate need to control the other person.
· I cannot allow my loved ones the freedom to decide for themselves but in many ways dictate how they should be in order to be loved by me.
· There are threats attached to my loving.
· I really don't trust the other person or let the other person trust me.
· I refuse to allow the other person to grow and change, because I fear that I won't know how to respond to his or her new self.
· I treat the loved one like a possession.
· I expect or demand that the other person do for me things I'm unwilling to do for myself.
· My expectations are unrealistic.
· I expect the other person to fill my emptiness, while I avoid doing much about filling myself.
· I refuse to make any type of commitment, keeping myself free but at the same time keeping the other person uncertain about my intentions.
· I won't share my thoughts, my feelings, and my soul with the other person.
· I expect the other person to be an open book to me, while I remain closed.

I'm quite sure that all of us can find some of these manifestations of inauthentic love occurring in our relationships, and I don't think that means our love is necessarily phony. For instance, at times we might be reluctant to let another person into our private lives, might have excessive expectations, or might attempt to impose our agendas on others "for their own good." What is essential is to be honest with ourselves and to recognize when we are doing things that are not expressions of genuine love, for then we can change these patterns.

Some Meanings of Authentic Love

So far, I've discussed mostly what I think love is *not*. Now I'd like to share some of the positive meanings love has for me.

Love means that I *know* the person I love. I'm aware of the many facets

of the other person—not just the beautiful side but also the limitations, inconsistencies, and flaws. I have an awareness of the other's feelings and thoughts, and I experience something of the core of that person. I can penetrate social masks and roles and see the other person on a deeper level.

Love means that I *care* about the welfare of the person I love. To the extent that it is genuine, my caring is not a smothering of the person or a possessive clinging. On the contrary, my caring liberates both of us. If I care about you, I'm concerned about your growth, and I hope you will become all that you can become. Consequently, I don't put up roadblocks to your personal growth, even though it may result in my discomfort at times.

Love means having *respect* for the *dignity* of the person I love. If I love you, I can see you as a separate person, with your own values and thoughts and feelings, and I do not insist that you surrender your identity and conform to an image of what I expect you to be for me. I can allow and encourage you to stand alone and to be who you are, and I avoid treating you as an object or using you primarily to gratify my own needs.

Love means having a *responsibility* toward the person I love. If I love you, I'm responsive to most of your major needs as a person. This responsibility does not entail my doing for you what you are capable of doing for yourself; nor does it mean that I run your life for you. It *does* imply acknowledging that what I am and what I do affects you, so that I am directly involved in your happiness and your misery. A lover does have the capacity to hurt or neglect the loved one, and in this sense I see that love entails an acceptance of some responsibility for the impact of my way of being on you.

Love means *growth* for both myself and the person I love. If I love you, I am growing as a result of my love. You are a stimulant for me to become more fully what I might become, and my loving enhances your being as well. We each grow as a result of caring and being cared for; we each share in an enriching experience that does not detract from our being.

Love means making a *commitment* to the person I love. This commitment does not entail surrendering our total selves to each other; nor does it imply that the relationship is necessarily permanent. It does entail a willingness to stay with each other in times of pain, uncertainty, struggle, and despair, as well as in times of calm and enjoyment.

Love means a *sharing with* and an *experiencing with* the person I love.

My love for you implies that I want to spend time with you, share meaningful aspects of your life with you, and experience with you what is meaningful in your life.

Love means *trusting* the person I love. If I love you, I trust that you will accept my caring and my love and that you won't deliberately hurt me. I trust that you will find me lovable and that you won't abandon me; I trust the reciprocal nature of our love. If we trust each other, we are willing to be open to each other and can shed masks and pretenses and reveal our true selves.

Love means that I am *vulnerable*. If I open myself up to you in trust, then I am also vulnerable to experiencing hurt and rejection and loss. Since you aren't perfect, you have the capacity to hurt me; and, since there are no guarantees in love, there is no real security that your love will last forever.

Love is *freeing*. Love is freely given, not doled out on demand. At the same time, my love for you is not contingent on whether you fulfill my expectations of you. Authentic love does not imply "I'll love you when you become perfect or when you become what I expect you to become." Nevertheless, love is not *unconditional*. Although genuine love is not based on whether we live up to each other's expectations, this does not imply that I will be loved and accepted regardless of what I do or who I become. I can destroy or lessen your love for me, just as I can work to enhance it.

Love is *expansive*. If I love you, I encourage you to reach out and develop other relationships. Although our love for each other and our commitment to each other might preclude certain actions on our parts, we are not totally and exclusively wedded to each other. It is a pseudo-love that cements one person to another in such a way that he or she is not given room to grow.

Love means having a *want* for the person I love without having a *need* for that person in order to be a separate identity. If I am nothing without you, then I'm not really free to love you. If I love you and you leave, I'll experience a loss and be sad and lonely, but I'll still be able to survive. If I am overly dependent on you for my meaning and my survival, then I am not free to challenge our relationship; nor am I free to challenge and confront you. Because of my fear of losing you, I'll settle for less than I want, and this settling will surely lead to feelings of resentment.

Love means *identifying* with the person I love. If I love you, I can empathize with you and see the world through your eyes. I can identify with you because I'm able to see myself in you and you in me. This closeness does not imply a continual "togetherness," for distance and separation are sometimes essential in a loving relationship. Distance can intensify a loving bond, and it can help us rediscover ourselves, so that we are able to meet each other in a new way.

Love is *selfish*. I can only love you if I genuinely love, value, appreciate, and respect myself. If I am empty, then all I can give you is my emptiness. If I feel that I'm complete and worthwhile in myself, then I'm able to give to you out of my fullness. One of the best ways for me to give you love is by fully enjoying myself with you.

Love can tolerate *imperfection*. In a love relationship, there are times of boredom, times when I may feel like giving up, times of real strain, and times I experience an impasse. Authentic love does not imply perpetual happiness. However, I can stay during rough times, because I can remember what we had together in the past, and I can envision what we will have together in our future if we care enough to face our problems and work them through.

I would like to conclude this discussion of the meanings authentic love has for me by sharing a few thoughts from Fromm's *The Art of Loving* (1956). I'm fond of Fromm's description of mature love, which for me sums up the essential characteristics of authentic love:

> Mature love is union under the condition of preserving one's integrity, one's individuality. Love is an active power in man; a power which breaks through the walls which separate man from his fellow men, which unites him with others; love makes him overcome the sense of isolation and separateness, yet it permits him to be himself, to retain his integrity. In love this paradox occurs that two beings become one and yet remain two [pp. 20–21].

Is It Worth It to Love?

Often I hear people say something like "Sure, I need to love and to be loved, but is it *really* worth it?" Underlying this question is a series of other questions: Can I survive without love? Is the risk of rejection and loss worth taking? Are the rewards of opening myself up as great as the risks?

It would be comforting to know an absolute answer to these questions, but I fear that each of us must struggle to decide for ourselves whether it's worth it to love. It seems to me that our first task is to decide whether we prefer isolation to intimacy. Of course, our choice is not between extreme isolation and constant intimacy; surely there are degrees of both. But we do need to decide whether to experiment with extending our narrow worlds to include significant others. We can increasingly open ourselves to another and discover for ourselves what that is like for us; alternatively, we can decide that people are basically unreliable or not worth the risk and that it's better to be safe and go hungry emotionally. We can also decide how far we choose to trust and how important loving and being loved will be in our lives.

Suppose now that you feel unable to love or to give love and thus feel isolated, but that you'd like to learn how to become more intimate. You might begin by acknowledging this reality to yourself, as well as to those in your life with whom you'd like to become more intimate. In this way, you can take some significant beginning steps.

In answering the question of whether it's worth it to you to love, you can also challenge some of your attitudes and beliefs concerning acceptance and rejection. I've encountered many people who believe that it isn't worth it to love because of the possibility of experiencing rejection. If you feel this way, you can decide whether to stop at this barrier. You can ask yourself: "What's so catastrophic about being rejected? Will I die if someone I love leaves me? Can I survive the emotional hurt that comes with disappointment in love?"

Hodge (1967) claims that, as adults, we're no longer helpless and that we can do something about rejection and hurt. We can choose to leave relationships that aren't satisfying; we can learn to survive hurt, even though it may be painful; and we can realize that being rejected by a person doesn't mean that we are fundamentally unlovable. I very much like the last line in Hodge's *Your Fear of Love,* and I ask you to consider how it may apply to you: "We can discover for ourselves that it is worth the risk to love, even though we tremble and even though we know we will sometimes experience the hurt we fear" (p. 270).

Time Out for Personal Reflection

1. *The following are some possible reasons for thinking that it is or isn't worth it to love. Check the ones that fit your own thoughts and feelings.*

    It's worth it to love, because

_____   *of the joy involved when two people love each other.*
_____   *the rewards are greater than the risks.*
_____   *a life without love is empty.*
List other reasons:

_____

_____

It isn't worth it to love, because

_____   *of the pain involved when love is not returned.*
_____   *the risks are not worth the possible rewards.*
_____   *it's better to be alone than with someone you might no longer love (or who might no longer love you).*
List other reasons:

_____

_____

2. What is your answer to the question of whether it's worth it to love?

_____

_____

_____

3. Review my list of the meanings love has for me, and then list some of the meanings love has for you.

_____

_____

_____

_____

4. *Think of someone you love. What specifically do you love about that person? (Example: I love his sensitivity.) Then, list specific ways that you show your love to this person? (Example: I spend time with her. I enjoy doing things that make her happy.)*

_____

_____

_____

_____

_____

5. *What are some questions you have regarding the ideas discussed so far in this chapter? Which ones would you most like to hear the others in your class respond to?*

_____

_____

_____

_____

Love and Sexuality

Although I treat the issues of love, sex, and intimacy in different chapters, these topics cannot really be completely separated. So I hope you'll try to make some connections by integrating the ideas of the three chapters and by applying them to yourself. The following exercises should help get you started.

Time Out for Personal Reflection
A Personal Inventory on Love and Sexuality

After you've worked through the following questions and indicated the responses that actually apply to you now, you might want to take the inventory again and give the responses that indicate how you'd like to be. Feel free to circle more than one response for a given item or to write your own response on the blank line. You may want to take the inventory again at the end of the course to see whether, or to what degree, any of your beliefs, attitudes, and values concerning love and sexuality have changed.

1. *As far as my need for love is concerned,*
   a. *I can give love, but it's difficult for me to receive love.*
   b. *I can accept love, but it's difficult for me to give love.*

c. *Neither giving nor accepting love is especially difficult for me.*
d. *Both giving and accepting love are difficult for me.*

e. _____

2. *I feel that I have been loved by another person:*
    a. *only once in my life.*
    b. *never in my life.*
    c. *many times in my life.*
    d. *as often as I've chosen to open up to another.*

    e. _____

3. When it comes to self-love and appreciation of myself,
    a. *I have a healthy regard and respect for myself.*
    b. *I find the idea of self-love objectionable.*
    c. *I encounter great difficulty in appreciating myself.*
    d. *I'm generally able to love myself, but there are parts of myself that I dislike.*

    e. _____

4. *I love others because:*
    a. *I want their love and acceptance in return.*
    b. *I fear being alone if I don't.*
    c. *I like the feeling of loving another.*
    d. *I derive joy from giving to another person.*

    e. _____

5. *To me, love is best described as:*
    a. *giving to another out of my fullness as a person.*
    b. *thinking more of the other person than I do of myself.*
    c. *relating to another in the hopes that I'll not feel so empty.*
    d. *caring for another to the same degree that I care about myself.*

    e. _____

6. *My greatest fear of loving and being loved is:*
    a. *that I will have nothing to give another person.*
    b. *that I will be vulnerable and may be rejected.*
    c. *that I might be accepted and then not know what to do with this acceptance.*
    d. *that I will feel tied down and that my freedom will be restricted.*

    e. _____

7. In regard to commitment in a loving relationship, I believe that:
   a. without commitment there is no real love.
   b. commitment means I love that person exclusively.
   c. commitment means that I stay with the person in times of crisis and attempt to change things.
   d. commitment is not necessary for love.

   e. _____

8. For me, the relationship between love and sex is that:
   a. love often develops *after* a sexual relationship.
   b. sex without love is unsatisfying.
   c. the two must always be present in an intimate relationship with another person of the opposite sex.
   d. sex can be very exciting and gratifying without a love relationship.

   e. _____

9. I could become more lovable by:
   a. becoming more sensitive to the other person.
   b. learning to love and care for myself more than I do now.
   c. doing what I think others expect of me.
   d. being more genuinely myself, without roles and pretenses.

   e. _____

10. If I loved a person who did not love me in return, I would:
    a. never trust another love relationship.
    b. feel devastated.
    c. convince myself that I really didn't care.
    d. feel hurt but eventually open myself to others.

    e. _____

11. In love relationships, generally I:
    a. settle for what I have with the other person as long as things are comfortable.
    b. constantly seek to improve the relationship.
    c. am willing to talk openly about things I don't like in myself and in the other person.
    d. am able to express positive feelings but unable to express negative feelings.

    e. _____

12. *When it comes to talking about sexuality:*
    a. *I encounter difficulty, especially with my partner.*
    b. *I feel free in discussing sexual issues openly.*
    c. *I usually become defensive.*
    d. *I'm willing to reveal my feelings if I trust the other person.*

    e. _____

13. *My attitudes and values toward sexuality have been influenced principally by:*
    a. *my parents.*
    b. *my friends and peers.*
    c. *my church.*
    d. *my school experiences.*

    e. _____

14. *I think that social norms and expectations:*
    a. *encourage the dichotomy between male and female roles.*
    b. *impose heavy performance standards on men.*
    c. *make it very difficult to develop one's own ideas about what constitutes normal sexuality.*
    d. *clash with my own upbringing.*

    e. _____

15. *I think that sexual attitudes could be improved by:*
    a. *giving children more information while they are growing up.*
    b. *teaching principles of religion.*
    c. *increasing people's knowledge about the physical and emotional aspects of sexuality.*
    d. *allowing people to freely discuss their sexual values and conflicts in small groups.*

    e. _____

Here are a few suggestions of things you can do after you've finished this inventory:

1. *You can use any of the items that strike you as points of departure for your journal writing.*
2. *If you're involved in an intimate relationship, you can ask the other person to take the inventory and then share and compare your responses. Your responses can be used as a basis for dialogue on these important issues.*

3. You can write down other questions that occurred to you as you took this inventory, and you can bring these questions to class.

4. Your class can form small groups in which to discuss the items that had the most meaning for each person. In this way, you can get the perspective of others in your class.

A Sentence-Completion Exercise on Love and Sex

Complete the following sentences by quickly writing down your immediate response.

1. My greatest fear of love is _____

2. To me, love without sex is _____

3. To me, love with sex is _____

4. To me, sex without love is _____

5. I need love because _____

6. I feel most loved when _____

7. One lovable quality about me is _____

8. I could increase my ability to love others by _____

_____

9. I express my love for others primarily by _____

10. To me, love means primarily _____

11. If nobody loved me, _____

12. For me, the greatest risk in loving others is _____

13. For me, the greatest risk in letting others love me is _____

_____

14. When I'm with those I love, I _____

_____

15. When I'm separated from my loved ones, I _____

_____

_____

_____

Chapter Summary

This chapter has explored some basic issues related to our ability to give and to receive love, including our need for love, our fear of love, barriers to loving and being loved, whether it's worth it to love, early decisions about our own ability to love and to be loved, authentic versus inauthentic love, myths about love, and meanings of authentic love. A few key points to remember are:

1. Loving others and receiving love from them does entail some risk. There are no guarantees in loving.
2. Unless we love ourselves, we cannot really love others. Our ability to care for others is based largely on our ability to care for ourselves.
3. We must each decide for ourselves whether it's worth it to love.
4. By recognizing our attitudes about loving, we can increase our ability to choose the ways in which we behave in our love relationships.

Now list some of the ideas that seemed most significant to you or that you'd most like to remember.

Activities and Exercises

1. Mention some early decisions that you made regarding your own ability to love or to be loved, such as:

   · "I'm not lovable unless I produce."
   · "I'm not lovable unless I meet others' expectations."
   · "I won't love another because of my fears of rejection."
   · "I'm not worthy of being loved."

   Write down some of the messages that you've received and perhaps accepted uncritically. How has your ability to feel loved or to give love been restricted by these messages and decisions?
2. Ask several people to give their responses to the question "Is it worth it to love?" Bring these responses to class, and share them with others.
3. For a period of at least a week, pay close attention to the messages

conveyed by the media concerning love. What picture of love do you get from television? What do popular songs portray about love? Make a list of some common myths regarding love that you see promoted by the media. Some of these myths might include:

· Love means that two people never argue or disagree.
· Love implies giving up one's identity.
· Love implies constant closeness and romance.
· Love means rarely having negative feelings toward those you love.

4. How much do you agree with the proposition that you can't fully love others unless you first love yourself? How does this apply to you? In your journal, you might want to write some notes to yourself concerning the situations in which you don't appreciate yourself. You might also keep a record of the times and events when you do value and respect yourself.

5. How important is love in your life right now? Do you feel that you love others in the ways you'd like to? Do you feel that you're loved by others in the ways you want to be?

6. Are you an active lover or a passive lover? You might try writing down the ways in which you demonstrate your caring for those you love and then ask them to read your list and discuss with you how they see your style of loving.

Suggested Readings

Buscaglia, L. *Love*. Thorofare, N.J.: Charles B. Slack, 1972. This is a very personal and beautiful book of random thoughts on the meanings of love.

Coutts, R. *Love and Intimacy: A Psychological Approach*. San Ramon, Calif.: Consensus, 1973. A very readable and personal book that deals mostly with how to recognize and how to overcome unrealistic social inhibitions or personal problems that interfere with living and with intimate relationships. Coutts believes that, if love and intimacy needs are satisfied, sexual intimacy will follow.

Fromm, E. *The Art of Loving*. New York: Harper & Row (Colophon), 1956; paperback edition, 1974. Love in all its aspects is the subject of this book. Fromm presents a philosophy of love in a book that can be read several times for new insights.

Gibran, K. *The Prophet*. New York: Knopf, 1923. A rich, poetic treatment of many facets of life, including love, marriage, giving, work, freedom, children, death, friendship, self-knowledge, and so on.

Hodge, M. *Your Fear of Love*. Garden City, N.Y.: Doubleday, 1967. This is a very useful and easy-to-read book that describes how fears originate and how they can prevent us from loving. Hodge gives a personal and down-to-earth treatment of topics such as freedom, anger, sex, manhood, and womanhood. He also explores the concept of living to be ourselves, which includes learning to love ourselves and to live spontaneously.

Jourard, S. *The Transparent Self: Self-Disclosure and Well-Being* (2nd ed.). New York: Van Nostrand, 1971. Jourard contends that we have many ways of concealing our real selves and that we use masks and roles to keep from being open. He makes a case for the value of being transparent in human relationships. The book includes some excellent essays on love, sex, marriage, and the lethal aspects of male roles.

Lyon, W. *Let Me Live!* (Rev. ed.). North Quincy, Mass.: Christopher, 1975. The author's chapter on love makes a case for learning how to be an active lover. Lyon also deals with other topics, such as sex, masculinity, femininity, and marriage, in an interesting and provocative manner.

May, R. *Love and Will.* New York: Norton, 1969; Dell, 1974. Presenting much insightful material, May discusses paradoxes of love and sex, sex without love, love and death, the relationship of love and will, and the meaning of caring.

Mayeroff, M. *On Caring.* New York: Harper & Row, 1971. This is a sensitive book on the philosophy of caring as a dimension of loving. Mayeroff discusses how caring can give meaning to life and help both oneself and the other person to grow.

Otto, H. (Ed.). *Love Today.* New York: Dell (Delta), 1973. A book of articles on various aspects of love that gives a good overview of issues related to intimacy, creativity, and sharing.

Paul, J., & Paul, M. *Free to Love.* New York: Pyramid, 1975. The authors, who are also a marriage counseling team, share what they've learned about love and intimacy through the experience of their own marriage.

Powell, J. *Why Am I Afraid to Tell You Who I Am?* Nile, Ill.: Argus, 1969. In this sequel to the author's popular *Why Am I Afraid to Love?* the theme of growing through open relationships is explored.

Rosenman, M. *Loving Styles: A Guide for Increasing Intimacy.* Englewood Cliffs, N.J.: Prentice-Hall (Spectrum), 1979. While the focus of this book is on man/woman intimacy, the concepts described could often apply to other forms of intimacy. There are many exercises and case studies to help readers identify their personal style of loving and examine how they can make their relationships work better.

Safilios-Rothschild, C. *Love, Sex, and Sex Roles.* Englewood Cliffs, N.J.: Prentice-Hall, 1977. The author contends that, because of the drastically unequal social positions of men and women, fulfilling and mature love is almost impossible. Her thesis is that, as love, sexuality, and marriage become free options for people rather than instruments in the pursuit of security, both sexes may discover how to love each other in many different types of intimate relationships.

Intimate Relationships

For each statement, indicate the response that most closely identifies your beliefs and attitudes. Use this code: 5 = I *strongly agree* with this statement; 4 = I *agree* in most respects; 3 = I am *undecided*; 2 = I *disagree* in most respects; 1 = I *strongly disagree*.

_____ 1. An absence of conflict and crisis is one sign of a growing relationship.

_____ 2. It's difficult to have many intimate relationships at one time.

_____ 3. It's a good idea to explore a variety of life-styles besides the traditional marriage.

_____ 4. One sign of a good relationship is that both parties remain basically the same.

_____ 5. If I'm involved in a satisfactory intimate relationship, I won't feel attracted to others besides my partner.

_____ 6. Marriage should last forever if we choose the right partner.

_____ 7. If one partner in an intimate relationship expresses a need for privacy or time alone, the relationship must be unsatisfactory in some way.

_____ 8. The traditional marriage is obsolete and is bound to give way to alternative life-styles.

_____ 9. One mark of a successful relationship is that each person feels able to survive without the other.

_____ 10. Divorce or other ending of the relationship is generally a good solution if a couple is experiencing boredom or difficulties.

_____ 11. Most people would like to find intimacy with one other person.

_____ 12. Wanting too much from another person can cause difficulties in a relationship.

_____ 13. Commitment, in the sense of a willingness to stay with a person in rough times as well as good times, is essential in an intimate relationship.

_____ 14. By its very nature, an exclusive relationship is bound to become dull, predictable, and unexciting.

_____ 15. I know what I'm looking for in a relationship.

_____ 16. It's essential that the partners each retain their separate identity if a relationship is to be a good one.

_____ 17. I feel free to choose the kind of life-style I want.

_____ 18. In a meaningful relationship, I forget my needs and devote myself to the other person.

_____ 19. I have what I want in terms of intimacy with others.

_____ 20. I can be emotionally intimate with another person without being physically intimate with that person.

Introduction

Much of this chapter focuses on marriage as one typical form of intimate relationship. Although many students either aren't married or are actively involved in some alternative life-style, there seems to be ample reason to dwell on this type of intimate relationship. Marriage is still one of the most widely practiced life-styles in our society, particularly if the term *marriage* is construed broadly to include the many couples who consider themselves committed to an intense relationship even though they are not legally married as well as those who are creating marriages that are different in many respects from the traditional kind. I do want to stress, however, that, whether we choose to marry or not, we can be involved in many different types of intimate relationship, and much of what is true for marriage is true for these other types as well. Allowing for the differences in relationships, the signs of growth and meaningfulness are much the same and so are the problems. Consequently, whatever life-style you choose, you can use the ideas in this chapter as a basis for thinking about the role of intimacy in your life.

Types of Intimacy

I've mentioned that there are many types of intimate relationship. One significant type is the relationship between parents and children. Many of the ideas in this chapter can be applied to bettering your relationships with your parents or your children. You can take a fresh look at these relationships, including both their frustrations and their delights, and you can think about how you might initiate some changes.

I'm thinking now of David, who told me about how little closeness he had experienced with his father. David saw his father as a "rock," yet he deeply wished that he could be physically and emotionally close to him. David made the difficult decision to talk to his father and tell him exactly how he felt and what he wanted. Instead of the cold rebuff he had expected, he found that his father reached out to him and admitted that he, too, wanted to be close but that he felt awkward in asking for it—and that he had feared *David's* rejection!

The experience David had with his father could have occurred in any intimate relationship. We can experience feelings of awkwardness, unexpressed desires, and fears of rejection with our friends, lovers, spouses, parents, or children. Thus, many of the suggestions I make in this chapter in regard to couples apply also to other significant relationships. In particular, you can use the ideas about growth and change to improve

your relationship with your parents or children, especially if you recognize that either you or they have outgrown the relationship you had previously.

Deep and meaningful friendships with persons of either sex are another type of intimacy. In my own life, I feel very fortunate in having four close male friends. With all these men I feel the freedom to be fully myself, which includes being vulnerable, trusting them, caring for them, enjoying my time with them, and knowing that each of the relationships is a two-way street. I believe it's important to think about how free we feel with our closest friends, the respect we give them and the respect we receive from them, and the degree to which we feel enriched by each friendship. As you read this chapter, I hope you'll reflect on the quality of your friendships and on what you can do to make them better.

The intimacy we share with another person can be emotional, intellectual, physical, spiritual, or any combination of these. It can be exclu-

sive or nonexclusive, long-term or brief. For example, many of the participants in the personal-growth groups that Marianne and I conduct become very emotionally involved with one another. During the space of a week in which they share their struggles, they develop a closeness that is real and meaningful, even though they may not keep in touch once the week is over. At the same time, I've observed how reluctant many people are to open themselves up emotionally in such short-term situations as a weekend personal-growth group, because they want to avoid the sadness of parting. They might say "What if we do get close and really care for one another here? I hate to see all this intimacy come to an end when the workshop is over!" Bonds of intimacy and friendship can be formed in a short period, however, and subsequent distance in space and time need not diminish the quality of the friendships we form. For example, Marianne and I are very close with a couple who live 500 miles away. Even though we see one another only for several days each year, our contact is meaningful, and we experience a continuity in the relationship when we're together. We don't need to engage in small talk, and we have very personal conversations and intimate moments. To take another example, several years ago Marianne met a foreign-exchange student from Norway. They had a relatively short time together, but they developed a genuine friendship that they keep alive through correspondence, and both of them have benefited from their exchanges.

Experiences such as the ones I've just described convince me that we only rob ourselves when we avoid intimacy. We may pass up the chance to really get to know neighbors and new acquaintances, because we fear that either we or our new friends will move and that the friendship will come to an end. Similarly, we may not want to open ourselves to intimacy with sick or dying persons, because we fear the pain of losing them. Although such fears may be natural ones, too often we allow them to cheat us of the uniquely rich experience of being truly close to another person. We can enhance our lives greatly by daring to care about others and fully savoring the time we can share with them now.

I'd like to give one more example of intimacy—this time, of an intellectual kind. After I had written the manuscript of this book, my editors at Brooks/Cole sent it to a number of reviewers, both instructors and students, for a careful reading. Then the reviewers and editors joined Marianne and me for a weekend seminar at our home in Idyllwild, California, to discuss the book chapter by chapter. The group was composed of very diverse personalities. Most of the participants were professors who had taught courses in personal growth and adjustment and, in some cases, had written successful books in this field. All in all, I felt before our meeting that our group had the potential for stuffiness and that the seminar might give rise to unproductive arguments and other friction. Instead, the entire group jelled very quickly, and I was amazed at our productivity. We listened carefully to one another and demonstrated genuine respect for one another. We engaged in extremely open, highly stimulating exchanges. Even though most of us had not met previously, a closeness was generated among us by our common task of offering suggestions for the improvement of the book and by our involvement in honest discussions about the issues raised in these chapters. I felt that we all left the seminar feeling excited and very close to one another, and the consensus seemed to be that everyone there had gained something from the time we spent together.

As you read the remainder of this chapter, I hope that you'll spend time thinking about the quality of all the various kinds of intimacy you experience in your life now. Are you involved in the kinds of intimate relationships that you want to be involved in? How can you enhance your relationships? What are *you* willing to do to improve them? What is your view of a growing relationship? I also hope that you'll think of ways to apply the themes I discuss in connection with couples to the many types of relationship in your life.

The one idea I most want to stress is that you can choose the kinds of intimate relationship you want to experience. Often, we fail to make our own choices and instead fall into a certain type of relationship because we think "This is the way it's *supposed* to be." For example, I wonder how many people marry who in reality might prefer to remain single— particularly women, who often feel the pressure to marry and have a family because it's "natural" for them to do so. Instead of blindly accepting that relationships must be a certain way or that only one type of life-style is possible, you have the choice of giving real thought to the question of what types of intimacy have meaning for you.

Time Out for Personal Reflection

1. *What do you look for in a person you'd like to marry or form an intimate relationship with? For each item, put a 1 in the space if the quality is very important to you, a 2 if it is somewhat important, and a 3 if it is not very important.*

———————	intelligence
———————	character (a strong sense of values)
———————	physical appearance and attractiveness
———————	money and possessions
———————	charm
———————	prestige and status
———————	a strong sense of identity
———————	expressiveness and tendency to be outgoing
———————	a sense of humor
———————	caring and sensitivity
———————	power
———————	independence
———————	a quiet person
———————	someone who will make decisions for me
———————	someone I can lean on
———————	someone who will lean on me
———————	someone I can't live without
———————	someone who works hard and is disciplined

_____   *someone who likes to play and have fun*
_____   *someone who has values similar to mine*
_____   *someone I'd like to grow old with*

Now list the three qualities that you value most in a person when you are considering an intimate relationship.

_____

_____

_____

2. *Why do you think a person might want an intimate relationship with you? Look over the qualities listed above, and then list the qualities you see yourself as having.*

_____

_____

_____

_____

3. *Identify the kinds of intimate relationships you have chosen so far in your life. If you aren't presently involved in any significant intimate relationships, would you like to be?*

_____

_____

_____

_____

4. *What do you get from being involved in a significant relationship? Check the responses that apply to you, and add your own on the lines provided.*

_____   *a feeling of being cared for*
_____   *a sense of importance*
_____   *joy in being able to care for another person*
_____   *excitement*
_____   *the feeling of not being alone in the world*
_____   *sharing and companionship*

Other:

_____

_____

_____

_____

Meaningful Relationships: A Personal View

In this section, I list some of the characteristics that I judge to be parts of a meaningful couple relationship. As you look over my list, you might adapt it to the different kinds of intimacy in your life and add the qualities that *you* think are important in an intimate relationship.

I see intimate relationships as most meaningful when they are dynamic and evolving rather than fixed or final. Thus, there may be periods of joy and excitement followed by times of struggle, pain, and distance. Unless two persons have settled for complacency, there are probably not too many long periods in which they are the same with each other. As long as they are growing and changing, both separately and as a couple, their relationship is bound to change as well. As I look at intimacy from this growth-and-change perspective, the following are some of the qualities of a relationship that seem most important to me.

Each person in the relationship has a separate identity; they each give and receive without losing their separateness. I like the way Kahlil Gibran (1923) expresses this thought in *The Prophet:* "But let there be spaces in your togetherness, and let the winds of the heavens dance between you" (p. 16).

Although each person desires the other, each can survive without the other. They are not so tightly bound together that, if they are separated, one or the other becomes lost and empty. For example, there are those couples who are rarely apart. They may labor under the myth that a desire for time alone is an indication that something is amiss in their relationship. They may not realize the potential strain on their relationship if they see their identity only as a couple (without separate identities). Some couples split up because they eventually feel suffocated. They did not give each other the distance necessary to develop as individuals.

Each is able to talk openly with the other about matters of significance to the relationship. They are willing to engage in dialogue about the quality of what they have together. They can openly express grievances and let each other know what changes they desire.

Each person assumes responsibility for his or her own level of happiness and refrains from blaming the other if he or she is unhappy. Of course, in a close relationship, the unhappiness of one person is bound to affect the other, but no one should expect another person to *make* him or her happy, fulfilled, or excited.

The two persons are willing to work at keeping their relationship alive. Meaningful relationships are not easy to come by. Nor are they stagnant. If we hope to keep a relationship vital, we must reevaluate and revise our way of being with each other from time to time. Like a book, relationships need to be updated. Some experimentation is needed, and this entails effort.

The two persons are able to have fun and to play together; they enjoy doing things with each other. It is easy to become so serious that we forget to take the time to enjoy those we love. One way of changing drab relationships is to become aware of the infrequency of playful and light moments and then determine what things are getting in the way of enjoying life.

Each person is growing, changing, and opening up to new experiences. I believe that, if we cannot make it alone, we cannot make it with another person. When we rely on others for our personal fulfillment and confirmation as persons, then we are in trouble. For me, the best way to build solid relationships with others is to work on developing our own centeredness and to be willing to do what is necessary to grow as individuals.

If the relationship contains a sexual component, each person makes some attempt to keep the romance alive. They may not always experience the intensity and novelty of the early period of their relationship, but they can devise ways of creating a climate in which they can experience romance and closeness. They may go places they haven't been to before or otherwise vary their routine in small ways. They recognize when their sex life is getting dull and look for ways to rejuvenate the boring aspects of their life together. In their lovemaking, they are sensitive to each other's needs and desires; at the same time, they are able to ask each other for what they want and need.

The two persons are equal in the relationship. People who feel that they are typically the "givers" and that their partners are usually unavailable when they need them might question the balance in their relationships. Also, each person might ask whether he or she feels OK in the presence of the other. In some relationships, one person may feel compelled to assume a superior position relative to the other—for example, to be very willing to listen and give advice yet unwilling to go to the other person and show any vulnerability or need.

Each person actively demonstrates concern for the other. In a vital relationship, the partners do more than just talk about how much they value each other. The actions they perform show their care and concern more eloquently than any words.

Each person finds meaning and sources of nourishment outside the relationship. Their lives did not begin when they met each other; nor would their lives end if they should part.

Each avoids manipulating, exploiting, and using the other. They each respect and care for the other and are willing to see the world through the other's eyes.

Each person is moving in a direction in life that is personally meaningful. They are each excited about the quality of their lives and their projects. Both of them basically like who they are and what they are becoming.

If they are married, they stay married out of choice, not simply for the sake of their children, out of duty, or because of convenience. They choose to stay together even if things get rough or if they sometimes experience emptiness in their marriage. They share a commitment a look at what is wrong in their relationship and to work on changing undesirable situations.

Each person recognizes the need for solitude and is willing to create the time in which to be alone. Moreover, each recognizes the other's need for private times.

Each avoids assuming an attitude of ownership toward the other. Although they may experience jealousy at times, they do not demand that the other person deaden his or her feelings for others.

Each shows some flexibility in role behavior. They are willing to share chores and activities rather than to refuse on the ground that a certain activity isn't "masculine" or "feminine." They may even reverse roles at times.

They do not expect each other to do for them what they are capable of doing for themselves. They don't expect the other person to make them feel alive, take away their boredom, assume their risks, or make them feel valued and important. Each is working toward creating his or her own autonomous identity. Consequently, neither person depends on the other for confirmation of his or her personal worth; nor does one walk in the shadow of the other.

Each discloses himself or herself to the other. They need not indiscriminately share every secret, but they are able to share whatever is germane to the relationship. They are each willing to make themselves known to the other in significant ways, which may include sharing joy, expectations, frustrations, dreams, fears, boredom, excitement, and other personal feelings.

Each allows the other a sense of privacy. Because they recognize each other's individual integrity, they avoid prying into every thought or manipulating the other to disclose what he or she wants to keep private.

Each person has a desire to give to the other. They have an interest in each other's welfare and a desire to see that the other person is fulfilled. Thus, they go beyond thinking only of what the other person can do for them.

They encourage each other to become all that they are capable of becoming. Unfortunately, people often have an investment in keeping those with whom they are intimately involved from changing. Their expectations and needs may lead them to resist changes in their partners and thus make it difficult for their partners to grow. However, if they recognize their fears, they can challenge their need to block their partners' progress. On the other hand, people sometimes hinder their partners' growth by refusing to give them a chance to change or refusing to believe in their ability to do so. They can encounter this tendency in themselves by expressing their own desires, without nagging and faultfinding, and by caring enough to challenge their partners when it seems appropriate to do so.

Each has a commitment to the other. The more I work with couples, the more I see commitment as a vital part of an intimate relationship. By commitment, I mean that the people involved have an investment in their future together and that they are willing to stay with each other in times of crisis and conflict. Although many people express an aversion to any long-term commitment in a relationship, I wonder how deeply they will allow themselves to be loved if they believe that the relationship can be dissolved on a whim when things look bleak. Perhaps, for some people, a fear of intimacy gets in the way of developing a sense of commitment. Loving and being loved is both exciting and frightening, and we may have to struggle with the issue of how much anxiety we want to tolerate. Commitment to another person involves risk and carries a price, but it is an essential part of an intimate relationship.

One of the reviewers of this book made the comment that the single major interest among college students is creating and maintaining friendships, especially intimate relationships. There is no single or easy prescription for success in this case, but I do think that developing meaningful relationships entails the willingness to struggle.

I am struck with how many college students encounter difficulties in keeping intimate relationships alive. There are some choices you can make that I think will increase your chances of developing lasting friendships. These choices include: being tolerant of differences between your friends and yourself; learning to become aware of conflicts and dealing with them constructively; being willing to let the other person know how you are affected in the relationship; staying in the relationship, even though you may experience a fear of rejection; checking out your assumptions with others, instead of deciding for them what they are thinking and feeling; being willing to make yourself vulnerable and to take risks; keeping yourself open about how you feel about your relationships with others; and avoiding the temptation to live up to others' expectations instead of being true to yourself.

In summary, creating and maintaining friendships and intimate relationships requires hard work and the willingness to ride out hard times. Further, in order to be a good friend to another, you must first be a good friend to yourself, which implies knowing yourself and caring about yourself. The following "Time Out" asks you to focus on some of the ways in which you see yourself as an alive and growing person, which is the foundation of building meaningful relationships.

Time Out for Personal Reflection

1. *What are some ways in which you see yourself as growing? In what ways do you see yourself as resisting personal growth by sticking with old and comfortable patterns, even if they don't work? To facilitate your reflection, look over the following statements, and mark each one with a T or an F, depending on whether you think it generally applies to you.*

———————   *I keep myself attractive.*
———————   *If I'm involved in an intimate relationship, I tell the other person what I want.*
———————   *I'm willing to try new things.*

———————   *Rather than settling for comfort in a relationship or in life, I ask for more.*

———————   *If I'm involved in an intimate relationship, I tell the other person what I'm feeling.*

———————   *I'm engaged in projects that are meaningful to me.*

2. *List other ways in which you're growing:*

———————————————————————————————

———————————————————————————————

———————————————————————————————

3. *List some ways in which you resist personal growth:*

———————————————————————————————

———————————————————————————————

———————————————————————————————

4. *In what ways do you see the person with whom you're most intimate growing and/or resisting growth?*

———————————————————————————————

———————————————————————————————

———————————————————————————————

———————————————————————————————

5. *If you're involved in a couple relationship, in what ways do you think you and your partner are growing closer? In what ways are you going in different directions?*

———————————————————————————————

———————————————————————————————

———————————————————————————————

———————————————————————————————

6. *Are you satisfied with the relationship you've just described? If not, what would you most like to change? How might you go about it.*

———————————————————————————————

———————————————————————————————

———————————————————————————————

7. *What did you learn from doing these exercises?*

_____

_____

_____

_____

A suggestion for using this "Time Out": If you're involved in a couple relationship, have your partner respond to the questions on a separate sheet of paper. Then compare your answers and discuss areas of agreement and disagreement.

Sources of Conflict in Intimate Relationships

A major problem that arises in intimate relationships is boredom or a sense of predictability. Regardless of how exciting and innovative a person or a couple might be, it seems inevitable that a feeling of staleness will set in at times. When this occurs, the couple can try to avoid confronting their boredom by denying its existence, or they can frankly recognize it and share it with each other. In my own experience, I find that accepting my share of responsibility for my boredom, as opposed to making my wife responsible for it, gives me a place to begin dealing with it. In general, if I'm not bored with myself, the chances are that our relationship will not *remain* dull, even though we sometimes experience a feeling of stagnation with each other.

In an address he gave a meeting of the American Association of Marriage and Family Counselors, Sidney Jourard described marriage as a dialogue that ends as soon as habitual ways of acting set in. He maintained that people are frequently not very creative when it comes to finding new ways of living with each other and that they tend to fall into the same ruts day after day, year after year. Moreover, many people—whether married or living together—seem to seek only superficial relationships in order to avoid risk. In Jourard's words: "The silent shrieks of pain deafen me. To be married is for many boredom or hell. To be unmarried, legally or unlegally, as many experience it is hell and despair."[1] To this lethal image of marriage and living together, Jourard proposed an alternative, life-giving model. His theme was that "Mar-

[1] From "Marriage Is for Life," by Sidney Jourard. *Journal of Marriage & the Family*, July 1975, pp. 199–208.

riage Is for Life"—not in the sense of having to last a lifetime, but in the sense of giving life to the people involved. As a way of freeing ourselves from deadening ways of living together, Jourard suggested that we might have several different "marriages" with the same person. We could recognize that, at its best, marriage is a relationship that generates change through dialogue. Instead of being threatened by change, we could welcome it as necessary for keeping the relationship alive.

For Jourard, therefore, we can have a series of marriages with the same person by divorcing ourselves from dead patterns and taking our dissatisfaction as a sign that it is time for new growth. In this way, we may be able to establish a new relationship with the same person. Jourard emphasized that divorce often means that one or the other partner has made a decision not to live in the same manner as before. The meaning of a decision to divorce can thus be similar to the meaning of a suicide, in the sense that people who contemplate suicide often are saying, in part, that they are no longer willing to live in the same way as they have been living. Similarly, the changes that occur in an intimate relationship can lead one or both parties to feel that they are at an impasse and that ending the relationship is the only way out.

Personal Reflections on a Marriage

One of the signs of a growing marriage might well be that the two partners have "married and divorced" each other several times, in the sense that they see their marriage as a process of reevaluating old roles and arrangements. They separate themselves from archaic ways of being with each other and are open to a "new marriage" through renegotiation of their relationship. In this way, a marriage can be seen as something that evolves, not as a static entity.

Recently, when Marianne and I were on a vacation, we talked about the evolution and development of our marriage. At the time of our first meeting, she was a German foreign-exchange student who would soon return home, and I was her high-school English teacher. We both initially resisted involvement with each other, because we feared intimacy and commitment. We were sure that the relationship would eventually end.

However, things did not work out as we had expected. Over a long period of struggle and internal conflict, we made a decision to marry. Part of what made this decision difficult was our differing religious and cultural backgrounds. During our first year of marriage, we each defined (or simply fell into) our respective traditional roles, which we did not challenge. Marianne modeled her vision of what a wife should be after her own parents; I was very much influenced by my parents' marriage. I found comfort in the fact that Marianne saw her primary function as taking care of the house and cooking. Control was very much of an issue for each of us, and we had our share of conflicts over our need for control of the other.

We were also in different places emotionally. Marianne was experiencing sadness and loss over leaving her country and her family, and she had not yet found a new identity. At the same time I was excited about completing my doctoral studies and getting involved in my new teaching career. I was impatient with her for not quickly resolving her difficulties and finding her own source of nourishment.

A turning point in our marriage was having a child, and then another one 18 months later. Having children brought up the issue of how we wanted to rear them, as well as our feelings about being parents. Becoming parents was something that we never really examined, for we both simply assumed that one of the reasons for marrying was to have children.

Another turning point involved Marianne's decision to go to college. She did what she had never dreamed of doing—namely, getting an advanced education. She challenged her conditioning, which did not include college in her plan for life. Encouraged by both the American family she had lived with, other close friends, and myself, she eventually got her master's degree in counseling and a license as a marriage and family therapist.

Marianne and I have found a common interest by sharing many professional activities, including writing books together, leading groups and workshops, and having both joint and independent professional practices. Our professional cooperation has enhanced our marriage, as we are able to share in work that has a great deal of meaning to both of us.

I do not want to imply that we have worked through all of our sources of conflicts once and for all; we frequently have our differences and difficulties. Associated with the development of our marriage, there have been a number of crises, conflicts, and battles over control. We have had to learn to accept each other's differences, to decide what kind of parents each of us would be, to renegotiate roles and functions, and to evaluate and set priorities. We both recognize that our involvement in home and work differs. Marianne struggled in particular with the issue of balancing her duties as a student and, later, as a professional with those of a mother and a wife. While it seems easier for her now to balance her professional life with her family life, this continues to be a struggle for me.

Although there continue to be bumps in our relationship, we are willing to talk about what we want changed and how to do it. We each realize how easy it is to get so involved in our separate lives that we fail to see the impact on our marriage and family life; we continue to learn the value of taking time to put our lives in perspective, to evaluate our ways, and to make some new choices.

I want to point out that neither of us has put our primary focus on our relationship with each other, this has been a significant focus for us both. In the past and especially during the early part of our marriage, each of us participated in individual therapy, as well as many group counseling experiences, as a vehicle for dealing with blocks within us that prevented us from being the persons we could be. We realize that we need to know ourselves and develop our separate identities if we hope to have a meaningful relationship with each other. And while we value this relationship and continue to grow from it, we do not depend on the other for our survival as individuals.

A Case Illustration of Conflicts in Marriage

In our couples' workshops, Marianne and I frequently see conflicts that arise when one person is excited about growing and the other isn't. For example, a woman becomes engaged in meaningful projects and decides that she wants more from all aspects of her life. In her enthusiasm, she wants more from and for her husband. However, these changes may be accompanied by an increase in anxiety; for example, she might be frightened of what her increasing strength will do to her marriage. Thus, she may experience a deep inner conflict: on the one hand, she feels committed to her own growth; on the other hand, she fears that her demands will be threatening to her husband and disrupt or even destroy their relationship. The following example illustrates this kind of conflict.

Sue and Hal dated in high school and married shortly after graduation. During the first few years of their marriage, Sue stayed home, reared children, and generally depended on Hal to take care of most of her needs. She had few friends, and she didn't cultivate many outside interests. In many respects, Hal fit the picture of the "macho" male. He defined himself by competing and succeeding in the business world and by buying a lavish house. Their relationship was fine, as he saw it, but eventually Sue became disenchanted with her dependence. She initiated marriage counseling, which Hal participated in reluctantly, and she also obtained personal counseling for herself. She made significant new decisions: to get a well-paying job, to go to college part time, and to be generally more demanding of Hal and less willing to tolerate what she saw as his male chauvinism. Whereas Sue had once been willing to let Hal be the superior one in their relationship, she now began to insist on being treated like a full and equal person.

As a result of these changes, Hal felt a real panic. When Sue became sexually assertive with him on a few occasions, he only felt more inadequate. He believed that men should always be the initiators, while women should merely submit passively. Not knowing how to handle Sue's new assertiveness and strength, he became sexually impotent, and he began to feel that his world was coming apart. He had always defined his power in terms of Sue's dependence on him. Now, if she liked other men and found them interesting and attractive, he reasoned that she must not like him or find him attractive. The more success she enjoyed, the more self-doubt he suffered.

The challenge facing Hal and Sue was to determine whether they could modify some of their long-established patterns and create a relationship in which Sue would be free to become a mature person and Hal could feel confident in his own right. Their predicament was quite typical; I've observed many men who feel threatened when the women they live with exercise power as a person. However, I've also seen men like Hal initially resist any positive changes in their partners and yet eventually come to like and respect them for the courage they manifest in changing.

With this challenge, however, comes risk. For example, although it was true that Hal might eventually have found Sue more attractive because of her growth, he might also have become increasingly defensive and attempted to tighten his control on her thinking and behavior. He might even have left because of his fear. She would then have been faced with a decision. Would she be willing to accept this kind of life? Would she back down and become the person she once was—the person Hal had been comfortable with? Would she remain nominally married while seeking a relationship with another man? Would she push Hal to initiate a divorce, so that he would bear the responsibility; or would she initiate a divorce herself if that was what she wanted?

The case of Sue and Hal illustrates a few of the unknowns and risks involved when one person is eager to change and the other person wants things to remain the same. Hal and Sue experienced a painful struggle

as they tried to decide whether they wanted to remain together and as they tried to clarify what they wanted with each other. Eventually, Hal realized that their original motivations for marrying could be different from their motivations for staying married. Through counseling, he recognized that much of their relationship had been based on Sue's need to have someone take care of her and his own need to be dominant and superior. Ultimately, both Hal and Sue discovered that they could change individually while finding new reasons for staying together.

Time Out for Personal Reflection

The following questions are designed for people who are involved in couple relationships. If you're not involved in such a relationship, you can apply them to whatever relationship is most significant to you right now (for instance, with your parents, children, or closest friend).

1. *What are some sources of conflict in your relationship? Check any of the following items that apply to you, and list any other areas of conflict on the lines provided.*

_____   *spending money*
_____   *use of free time*
_____   *what to do about boredom*
_____   *investment of energy in work*
_____   *interest in others of the opposite sex*
_____   *outside friendships*
_____   *wanting children*
_____   *how to deal with children*
_____   *differences in basic values*
_____   *in-laws*
_____   *sexual needs and satisfaction*
_____   *expression of caring and loving*
_____   *power struggles*
_____   *role conflicts*

Other areas of conflict:

_____

_____

2. *How do you generally cope with these conflicts in your relationship? Check the items that most apply to you.*

_____   *by open dialogue*
_____   *by avoidance*
_____   *by fighting and arguing*
_____   *by compromising*
_____   *by getting involved with other people or in projects*

List other ways in which you deal with conflicts in your relationship:

_____

_____

3. *Mention one conflict that you would like to resolve, and write down what you'd be willing to do in order to help resolve it.*

The conflict is _____

To attempt a resolution, I'm willing to _____

_____

_____

4. *List some ways in which you've changed during the period of your relationship. How have your changes affected the relationship?*

_____

_____

_____

_____

5. *To what extent do you have an identity apart from the relationship? How much do you need (and depend) on the other person? Imagine that he or she is no longer in your life, and write down how your life might be different.*

_____

_____

_____

_____

_____

6. *If you were to develop a marriage contract (or a living-together arrangement), what specific points would you most want to include?*

_____

_____

_____

_____

Divorce and Separation

Earlier in this chapter, I mentioned Jourard's concept of establishing new marriages with the same person and suggested that a crisis doesn't have to mean that a relationship must or should end. In fact, an impasse can become a turning point that enables two people to create a new way of life together. If they both care enough about their investment in each other, and if they are committed to doing the work that is necessary to change old patterns and establish more productive ones, a crisis can actually save their relationship.

People often decide on divorcing without really giving themselves or their partners a chance to face a particular crisis and work it through. For example, a man begins to see how deadening his marriage is for him and to realize how he has contributed to his own unhappiness in it. As a result of changes in his perceptions and attitudes, he decides that he no longer wants to live with a woman in this deadening fashion. However, rather than deciding to simply end the marriage, thinking that divorce will bring him a new life, he might allow his partner to really see and experience him as the different person he is becoming. Moreover, he might encourage her to change as well, instead of giving up on her too quickly. His progress toward becoming a more integrated person might well inspire her to work actively toward her own internal changes. This kind of work on the part of both persons takes understanding and patience, but they may find that they can meet each other as new and changing persons and form a very different kind of relationship.

Sometimes, of course, ending a relationship is the wisest course. Divorce can then be an act of courage that makes a new beginning possible. My concern is only that too many couples may not be committed enough to each other to stay together in times of crisis and struggle. As a result, they may separate at the very time when they could be making a new start.

How do two people know when a divorce is the best solution? No categorical answer can be given to this question. However, before two people do decide to split up, they might consider at least the following questions:

· Has each of them sought personal therapy or counseling? Perhaps their exploration of themselves would lead to changes that allow them to renew or strengthen their relationship.

· Have they considered marital counseling as a couple? Have they attended a couples' group or workshop to explore alternatives for their future? If they do get involved in marriage counseling of any type, are they each doing so willingly, or is one of them merely going along to placate the other?

· Are both parties really interested in preserving their marriage? Perhaps one or both are not interested in keeping the *old* relationship, but it is vital that they both at least want a life together. I routinely ask both members of a couple in difficulties to decide whether they even want to live with the other person. Some of the responses people give include: "I don't really know. I've lost hope for any real change, and at this point

I find it difficult to care whether we stay together or not." "I'm sure that I don't want to live with this person any more; I just don't care enough to work on improving things between us. I'm here so that we can separate cleanly and finish the business between us." "Even though we're going through some turmoil right now, I would very much like to care enough to make things better. Frankly, I'm not too hopeful, but I'm willing to give it a try." Whatever their responses, it's imperative that they each know how they feel about the possibility of renewing their relationship.

• Have they each taken the time to be alone, to get themselves in focus, and to decide what kind of life they want for themselves and with others?

• As a couple, have they taken time to be with each other for even a weekend? I'm continually surprised at how few couples arrange for time alone with each other. It's almost as if many couples fear discovering that they really have little to say to each other. This discovery in itself might be very useful, for at least they might be able to do something about the situation if they confronted it; but many couples seem to arrange their lives in such a way that they block any possibilities for intimacy. They eat dinner together with the television set blasting, or they spend all their time together taking care of their children, or they simply refuse to make time to be together.

• What do they each expect from the divorce? Frequently, problems in a marriage are reflections of internal conflicts within the individuals in that marriage. For this reason, I usually recommend that couples involved in marital counseling also engage in their own personal therapy or counseling. In general, unless there are some changes within the individuals, the problems they experienced may not end with the divorce. In fact, many who do divorce with the expectation of finding increased joy and freedom discover instead that they are still miserable, lonely, depressed, and anxious. Lacking insight into themselves, they may soon find new partners very much like the ones they divorced and repeat the same dynamics. Thus, a woman who finally decides to leave a man she thinks of as weak and passive may find a similar man to live with again, unless she comes to understand why she needs or wants to align herself with this sort of person. Or a man who contends that he has "put up with" his wife for over 20 years may find a similar person unless he understands what motivated him to stay with his first wife for so long. It seems essential, therefore, that each come to know as clearly as possible why they are divorcing and that they look at the changes they may need to make in themselves as well as in their circumstances.

Sometimes one or both members of a couple identify strong reasons for separating but say that, for one reason or another, they are not free to do so. This kind of reasoning is always worth examining, however, since an attitude of "I couldn't possibly leave" will not help either partner to make a free and sound choice. Some of the reasons people give for refusing to divorce include the following:

• "I have an investment of 15 years in this marriage, and to leave now would mean that these 15 years have been wasted." A person who feels this way might ask himself or herself: "If I really don't see much potential for change, and if my partner has consistently and over a long period of time rebuffed any moves that might lead to improving our relationship, should I stay another 15 years and have 30 years to regret?"

• "I can't leave because of the kids, but I do plan on leaving as soon as they get into high school." I often think that this kind of thinking burdens children with unnecessary guilt. In a sense, it makes them responsible for the unhappiness of their parents. I would ask: Why place the burden on them if *you* stay in a place where you say you don't want to be? And will you find another reason to cement yourself to your partner once your children grow up?

• "Since the children need both a mother and a father, I cannot consider breaking up our marriage." True, children do need both a father and a mother. But it's worth asking whether they will get much of value from either parent if they see them despising each other. How useful is the model parents present when they stay together and the children see how little joy they experience? Might they not get more from the two parents separately? Wouldn't the parents set a better and more honest example if they openly admitted that they no longer really chose to remain together?

• "I'm afraid to divorce because I might find that I would be even more lonely than I am now." Certainly, loneliness is a real possibility. There are no guarantees that a new relationship will be established after the divorce. However, we might be more lonely living with someone we didn't like, much less love, than we would be if we were living alone. Living alone might bring far more serenity and inner strength. Moreover, whether a new relationship can be established depends to a great degree on a person's self-perception. The more people become attractive to themselves, the greater the chance that others will see them as attractive.

• "One thing that holds me back from separating is that I might discover that I left too soon and that I didn't give us a fair chance." To avoid this regret, a couple should explore all the possibilities for creating a new relationship *before* making the decision to dissolve their marriage. However, there does come a point at which a person must finally take a stand and decide, and then I see it as fruitless to brood continually over whether he or she did the right thing.

In summary, we limit our options unnecessarily whenever we tell ourselves that we *can't possibly* take a certain course of action. Before deciding to terminate a relationship, we can ask whether we've really given the other person (and ourselves) a chance to establish something new. By the same token, if we decide that we want to end the relationship but can't, it's worth asking whether we're not simply evading the responsibility for creating our own happiness. Neither keeping a relationship alive and growing nor ending one that no longer is right for us is easy, and it's tempting to find ways of putting the responsibility for our decisions on our children, mates, or circumstances. We take a real step toward genuine freedom when we fully accept that, whatever we decide, the choice is ours to make.

Time Out for Personal Reflection

Complete the following sentences by writing down the first responses that come to mind. Suggestion: Ask your partner or a close friend to do the exercise on a separate sheet of paper; then compare and discuss your responses.

1. *To me, intimacy means* _____

2. *The most important thing in making an intimate relationship successful is* _____

3. *The thing I most fear about an intimate relationship is* _____

   _____

4. *When an intimate relationship becomes stale, I usually* _____

   _____

5. *One of the reasons I need another person is* _____

   _____

6. One conflict that I have concerning intimate relationships is _____

_____

7. In an intimate relationship, it's unrealistic to expect that _____

_____

8. To me, commitment means _____

_____

9. My views about marriage have been most influenced by _____

_____

10. I have encouraged my partner to grow by _____

_____

11. My partner has encouraged me to grow by _____

_____

On Choosing the Single Life

While this chapter has so far focused on the intimacy we share with others through relationships, let us not forget the importance of intimacy with ourselves. I fear for the security of those people who depend exclusively on others to be friends to them, while neglecting the value of learning to make friends with themselves.

In this regard, there are some people who choose to remain single (for a time or throughout their lives). Some decide that marriage or any other type of committed relationship is not for them. Unfortunately, society has tended to be more accepting of this as a life-style for men than for women. Many single women are told by others that they *should* be getting married, and under this pressure some of them begin to question their own worth. Even though they enjoy their single life-style, they may eventually "choose" marriage because they begin to wonder what is wrong with them.

More women today are resisting this pressure to get married and have a family, and more women are waiting until later in life to get involved in a committed relationship. There are intrinsic values and limitations in both a marriage and a single life. Yet what I think is critical is that we weigh the pros and cons of each and freely make the choice of how we most want to live, rather than passively following someone else's script for us.

The following case typifies the problems and challenges many young women face if they choose a single life-style. June likes the advantages of being single, yet she struggles with nagging doubts over whether she is missing more by not getting married, particularly when she has someone in mind whom she is fond of.

June has a successful teaching career at age 27. She earns a good salary, is living in her own house, is free to pursue additional education, and enjoys the freedom of traveling in many countries of the world. June has nobody to answer to in terms of considering changing her career. She says that her many male and female friends provide nourishment to her. She also enjoys many sports and other leisure activities. She feels a sense of accomplishment and independence, something that few people her age do.

At times June struggles with the internal pressure that she will never get married. She also feels external pressure from the man she is now having a close relationship with. But she is also very afraid to give in to his urgings to get married. While she enjoys the intimacy with him, she does not feel ready to commit herself to marriage. Though she does tell herself that she really *should* be ready at her age to take this step, she realizes that the price of getting married would be giving up much of what she values in her single life-style.

June judges herself as being too selfish to make compromises and consider her friend's needs and demands. She tells herself at times that perhaps she should be willing to give up more of what she wants so that she could share a life with him. She wonders about her chances for ever marrying if she fails to take this opportunity. Her family is also applying pressure to her to marry and not spoil a good relationship. At this time June is still searching within herself for her answer. Does she really want to get married? Who is telling her that she should get married? Does she equate being single with a lonely life? And does she want to get married because she is afraid of being seen as a spinster?

Chapter Summary

In this chapter, I've encouraged you to think about what characterizes a growing, meaningful relationship and to ask yourself such questions as: Do I have what I want in my intimate relationships? Do I desire more (or less) intimacy? What changes would I most like to make in my intimate relationships? In each of my relationships, can both the other person and I maintain our separate identities and at the same time develop a strong bond that enhances us as individuals?

It's important to stress that the picture I've drawn of a growing relationship is not a dogmatic or necessarily complete one; nor will our relationships, however good they are, always approximate it. I've tried to say what I think intimacy is like at its best, and my hope is that these reflections will stimulate your own independent thinking. You can begin by honestly assessing the present state of your intimate relationships, and recognizing how they really are (as opposed to how you wish they were). Then you can begin to consider the choices that can lead to positive change in those areas you're dissatisfied with. Throughout this chapter, I've emphasized that we must actively work on recognizing problems in ourselves and in our relationships if we are to make intimacy as rewarding as it can be. Finally, I've stressed that you can choose the kinds of intimacy you want in your life.

Now list some key ideas that you want to remember.

Activities and Exercises

Some of the following activities are appropriate for you to do on your own; others are designed for two persons in an intimate relationship to do together. Select the ones that have the most meaning for you, and consider sharing the results with the other members of your class.

1. In your journal, write down some reflections on your parents' relationship. Consider such questions as the following:

· Would you like to have the same kind of relationship your parents have had? What are some of the things you like best about their relationship? What are some features of their relationship that you would not want to have in your own marriage?

· How have your own views, attitudes, and practices regarding marriage and intimacy been affected by your parents' relationship? Discuss the impact of their relationship on your own marriage, intimate relationship, or views about marriage and intimacy.

2. How much self-disclosure, honesty, and openness do you want in your intimate relationships? In your journal, reflect on how much you would share your feelings concerning each of the following with your partner. Then discuss how you would like your partner to respond to this same question.

- your sexual fantasies about another person
- your secrets
- your need for support from your partner
- your angry feelings
- your dreams
- your desire for an affair with someone else
- your behavior if you did decide to have an affair
- your friendships with persons of the opposite sex
- your ideas on religion and your philosophy of life
- the times when you feel inadequate as a person
- the times when you feel extremely close and loving toward your partner
- the times in your relationship when you feel boredom, staleness, hostility, detachment, and so on

After you've answered this question for yourself, think about how open you want *your partner* to be with *you*. If your partner were doing this exercise, what answers do you wish he or she would give for each of the preceding items?

3. Over a period of about a week, do some writing about the evolution of your relationship, and ask your partner to do the same. Consider issues such as: Why were we initially attracted to each other? How have we changed since we first met? Do I like these changes? What would I most like to change about our life together? What are the best things we have going for us? What are some problem areas we need to explore? If I could do it over again, would I select the same person? What's the future of our life together? What would I like to see us doing differently? After you've each written about these and any other questions that are significant for you, read each other's work and discuss where you want to go from here. This activity can stimulate you to talk more openly with each other and can also give

each of you the chance to see how the other perceives the quality of your relationship.

4. Here is another activity for a couple to do together. Select a book dealing with the themes of love, sex, intimacy, or related issues. (See the reading list at the end of the chapter for suggestions.) Read the book separately, and write down some notes about ideas or feelings that have an impact or special meaning. Then get together and share your reactions and notes, and relate them to your own relationship.

5. Make up a list of specific suggestions for ways of experimenting with your intimate relationships. What are some concrete things you'd like to try with another person? If you're involved in a couple relationship, ask your partner to make up his or her own list; then share your results, and discuss some possibilities for action.

6. Often, we engage in unacknowledged conspiracies with another person in order to keep a relationship secure. For the sake of this exercise, assume that there are some conspiracies going in your intimate relationships, and see whether you can detect them. For instance, does one of you have to be a winner and one of you a loser? Does either of you need to be helpless in order for the other to feel powerful? Are you a mother or father to the other person? Are you the other person's "child"? Are you the other's security blanket? Are you the other's policeman? Try to be as honest as you can. If you're involved in a couple relationship, ask your partner to do the exercise as well; then share your results.

7. Interview some friends, associates, neighbors, and acquaintances to determine their views concerning intimacy. To get started, you might ask them to respond to some of the specific questions raised in this chapter.

8. As you look at various television shows, keep a record of the messages you get regarding marriage, family life, and intimacy. What are some common stereotypes? What sex roles are portrayed? What myths do you think are being presented? After you've kept a record for a couple of weeks or so, write down some of the attitudes that you think you may have incorporated from television and other media about marriage, family life, and intimacy.

Suggested Readings

Ables, B. S., in collaboration with Brandsma, J. M. *Therapy for Couples*. San Francisco: Jossey-Bass, 1977. The topics here include the phases of couple therapy, facilitating couple communication, reeducation, and often specific problems. The case is made for the need of a couple-treatment approach distinct from either individual counseling or family therapy.

Bach, G., & Wyden, P. *The Intimate Enemy: How to Fight Fair in Love and Marriage*. New York: Morrow, 1969. This book deals with a wide range of marital games and proposes guidelines for "fighting fair."

Bernard, J. *The Future of Marriage*. New York: Bantam, 1973. Bernard discusses many timely issues concerning the present state and the future of marriage, such as: Is marriage obsolete? When is a marriage too secure? Will we have group marriages in the future? Are marriage contracts realistic?

DeLora, J. S., & DeLora, J. R. (Eds.). *Intimate Life Styles: Marriage and Its Alternatives* (2nd ed.). Pacific Palisades, Calif.: Goodyear, 1975. This is a book of readings that deal with alternatives to traditional marriage, future intimate life-styles, stresses in a changing society, and sex as a personal and interpersonal concern.

Gibran, K. *The Prophet*. New York: Knopf, 1923. Gibran's poetic book has much to say about the meaning of intimacy.

Herrigan, J., & Herrigan, J. *Loving Free*. New York: Ballantine, 1975. This book tells the story of one couple's marriage and struggles: the problems they faced, how they worked at their marriage, and how they improved it. The authors write: "We're not professionals nor are we psychologists. We're two people who love each other and believe there is something worth fighting for in marriage. After thirteen years of marriage we still believe that love is the best shot we've got. We're still willing to put our all into it, and are more enthusiastic than ever about our life together—in or out of bed."

Lasswell, M., & Lobsenz, N. *No-Fault Marriage: The New Technique of Self-Counseling and What It Can Help You Do*. New York: Ballantine Books, 1976. This book is designed to help couples look at their own marriages and apply some of the counseling and communication skills that they can learn in marriage counseling. The authors point out why "winning" doesn't work in marital situations.

O'Neill, N., & O'Neill, G. *Open Marriage, a New Life Style for Couples*. New York: Avon, 1973. This book recommends a flexible concept of marriage that allows each couple to draw on their particular qualities as individuals and develop a relationship that is uniquely suited to them. Although it has sometimes been misinterpreted as an endorsement for open sexual relationships, the book is really focused on how two persons can grow both individually and as a couple.

Paolino, T. J., & McCrady, B. S. (Eds.). *Marriage and Marital Therapy: Psychoanalytic, Behavioral and Systems Theory Perspectives*. New York: Brunner/Mazel, 1978. A series of articles deals with trends in marriage and marital therapy and a comparative view of different therapy systems.

Schwartz, R., & Schwartz, L. J. *Becoming a Couple: Making the Most of Every Stage of Your Relationship*. Englewood Cliffs, N.J.: Prentice-Hall (Spectrum), 1980. This book provides some useful ideas that can help couples recognize the various stages of marital development. The focus is on a no-fault structure within which couples avoid the pitfalls of playing blaming games.

Smith, J. R., & Smith, L. G. (Eds.). *Beyond Monogamy: Recent Studies of Sexual Alternatives in Marriage*. Baltimore: Johns Hopkins University Press, 1974. This book contains a variety of articles on topics such as mate swapping, infidelity, group sex, and "swinging."

Chapter Eight

Work

For each statement, indicate the response that most closely identifies your beliefs and attitudes. Use this code: 5 = I *strongly agree* with this statement; 4 = I *agree* in most respects; 3 = I am *undecided;* 2 =I *disagree* in most respects; 1 = I *strongly disagree.*

_____ 1. Work affects all aspects of a person's life.

_____ 2. Most people wouldn't work if they didn't need the money.

_____ 3. Work is one very important way in which I can express my creativity.

_____ 4. Most people aren't really that happy in their careers.

_____ 5. Most people will change their jobs several times during their lives.

_____ 6. It's more important to me to have a secure job than it is to have one that's exciting.

_____ 7. The thought of retirement petrifies me.

_____ 8. Generally, a change of jobs will cure job dissatisfaction.

_____ 9. If I'm unhappy in my job, the cause for my unhappiness is most likely within me, not in the job itself.

_____ 10. It's never too early to choose a vocation.

_____ 11. It is unrealistic to expect that a woman can work in a career or a job and also assume the responsibilities of homemaker and mother.

_____ 12. I expect that I will have to take some steps to prevent getting burned out in my job.

_____ 13. Taking tests, coupled with some career counseling, sounds as though it could be useful in helping me make a vocational choice.

_____ 14. Just about anyone can get a job if he or she is motivated enough.

_____ 15. Most people I know are dissatisfied with their line of work.

_____ 16. With some imagination, most people could find ways to make changes within their jobs that could lead to markedly improved job satisfaction.

_____ 17. If the members of a couple are working in jobs outside of the home, I think they should share equally in the responsibilities in the home (cleaning, cooking, taking care of children).

_____ 18. Most people I know who are retired are able to find meaningful things to do, and they enjoy their retirement.

_____ 19. Most people just passively fall into a job, rather than actively making a choice that will be best for them in the long run.

_____ 20. I expect my work to fulfill many of my needs and be an important source of meaning in life.

Introduction

Freud saw the goals of *lieben und arbeiten* as core characteristics of the healthy person; that is, to him the freedom "to love and to work" and to derive satisfaction from loving and working was of paramount importance. It is my belief that work is intimately related to the topics discussed in earlier chapters. The quality of our marriages and other intimate relationships, our ability to love ourselves and others, and our physical and psychological well-being are influenced by the level of satisfaction we derive from our work.

Most working people ignore the impact their work has on their lives in general. Work is a good deal more than an activity that takes up a certain number of hours each week. If you feel creative and excited about your work, the quality of your life will be improved. If you hate your job and dread the hours you spend on it, your relationships and your feelings about yourself are bound to be affected.

If you are not yet engaged in your life's work, you can increase the relevance of this chapter by thinking about your expectations about work. You could talk to people in your immediate environment about their level of satisfaction in their work and use these observations to help you decide on your eventual career. If you let others' expectations or attitudes determine how you feel about your work, however, you'll surrender some sense of the autonomy and power to control your life that rightfully belong to you. Consequently, it's important to discover your own attitudes about work if you're to exercise real choice in this large part of your life.

The Place of Work in Our Lives

"A man doesn't know what he has until he loses it," sings a character in the musical *Damn Yankees*—and, though he is singing about love, the idea can be applied to work as well. Sometimes it is not until we lose our jobs that we understand the many ramifications of work for our lives as a whole. The following letter from a woman I'll call Judy is a good illustration:

> I am a 46-year-old white female with seven years of college, trained for a very specialized occupation. Almost one year ago, after working in the same place for 12 years, I quit my job to follow my husband to a new and exciting resort area. While my husband became busy at his job, I

thought I wanted to start my own business. This required personal selling, something that I quickly learned I was not very good at. So I started applying for jobs that were a little out of my field and writing resumes to warp my experience and education to fit various occupations. Fourteen rejection letters later, I am still without a job. Openings directly in my field are extremely rare in this area.

Not having a job seems to be something like hunger. When you are not hungry, you don't think about not having food. The "content" feeling is something you take for granted. When my job materializes, and it will eventually, I don't expect that it will make me happy, but it will keep me from having that empty feeling. . . .

One of the hardest things to adjust to has been not being able to spend money on our grown children or to think of taking a vacation. I now realize how *very* important being able to continue to help my children is to me, as well as having money for vacations. Cutting back hurts psychologically, and feels like deprivation.

What am I going to do with the rest of my life? Right now I don't know. But I realize that there is a lot of time in a day that needs to be filled in a meaningful way. Tennis, church, square dancing, taking classes, walking on the beach, all meaningful experiences, can only be pleasurable for so long. Work helps the time pass. The money from work gives me some personal power and choices. And right now I am not contributing to anything or anyone outside of my husband. That doesn't feel good at all; and the personal isolation is the pits. I don't have to consult with anyone on a project, because there aren't any projects or co-workers. I wonder if I had always been a housewife instead of a professional woman, would I feel content? I know I hate it when someone says "Do you work?"—and I have to say "No."

Clearly, work meant an important source of income to Judy, but it also provided human contact and a sense of worth that she missed greatly when she found herself without a job. How central her work was in her life became even more evident when I received another letter from her a few weeks later:

Miracles! I have just landed a fantastic job at excellent pay. Suddenly I feel as if I have rejoined the human race. I am going to be a part of a team, working on projects. I will be consulting with others, having human give and take. I will get to use my hard-won professional skills. The sky is bluer. No longer sort of numb, I can feel the steering wheel of the car in my hand better. The flowers are prettier. I will have some money to spend on the people I love, including myself. I have regained some power and control. I can look others in the eye and tell them where I work when they ask. I have challenges to look forward to. I feel so happy I think I'll burst. *And am I terrified of retirement!*

The Effects of Work in My Own Life

My professional life is varied, and these diverse work experiences provide me with excitement, stimulation, challenge, the chance to learn from others, and the inspiration to develop new projects.

I would find it very difficult to stay in a job simply because it provided financial security. I have made several career choices and at times given up tenured positions or security to get involved with programs that offered more meaning and challenge. When I assess my work activities, I become aware of how much energy I devote to them and how heavily I depend on them to structure my life. In many respects, my life is my work, and my work is my life. At times it still frightens me to consider what my life would be like if I were not working as much as I am.

My work style has both positive and negative effects on my life. On the good side, I feel creative in my work, I derive a deep sense of personal satisfaction from my projects, and I'm doing them because I want to. I'm not writing books because of the pressure to "publish or perish" but because writing them is one way to express myself personally and professionally. Similarly, if I do additional consulting or teaching of graduate courses, it's not primarily because of the financial rewards but because I like being associated with counselor-education programs at this level. My work is generally fun and a source of vitality, and it gives me a sense of fulfillment and challenge.

Yet there are negative effects too. One disadvantage of my work style is that I tend to rely too heavily on work as a source of nourishment and to neglect other possible ways of giving and being nourished. I must be careful not to be consumed by my work. Too often I find myself missing the present moment because I'm busy thinking about some future proj-

W-O-R-K — W-O-O-R-R-K!
... I GOTTA HAVE W-O-R-K!!!

ect. Moreover, so much of my life is bound up with work that I find it difficult to really live when I'm not being "productive." During semester breaks or vacations, I feel uneasy unless I'm accomplishing some form of significant work.

Other people are affected by my work-style as well. Often I feel at a loss concerning what to say to someone when I don't talk about work. At times my family suffers from my investment in work, and I cheat myself out of contact with them and with many of the simple joys of life. While my family does share in my involvement with work, they are also willing to let me know when my overextension causes them pain. And our friends have pointed out to us that, while Marianne works very hard and enjoys her professional work, she seems much less driven than I. While I often say yes to an attractive offer for a workshop or a weekend conference (and then later find myself overextended), Marianne is more likely to say "It sounds exciting; let me think about it."

When all is said and done, however, I do feel fortunate in having work that I find meaningful, exciting, and fulfilling. I know that not everyone feels the way I do about work, so some of my struggles in this area may be different from yours. I know that I have choices to make about how I'll structure my life and that I must assess the price I pay for my investment in work. For me, the struggle comes in learning how to really *let go* and forget work at times and still feel that I'm alive and valuable.

A Physician Who Is Not Wedded to His Work

Here's an example of a professional whose work style is different from mine. While this man does work to live, he is also able to get away from his profession of medicine by becoming fully involved in a number of unrelated hobbies.

Dr. Allan Abbott (whom I referred to earlier, in the chapter on "Your Body") has had a wide range of experiences as a physician, and he continues to be open to many different aspects of his profession. He practiced as an anesthesiologist until he decided that he wanted more contact with his patients than putting them to sleep. He worked with his wife, Katherine, a registered nurse, in the wilds of Peru. He went around the world as a ship's physician for a "floating high school." He conducted research on coronary-prone behavior that was stimulated by his observations of a primitive culture where heart disease was absent. He developed a family practice with his wife in the mountain community of Idyllwild, California, for three years. And he recently accepted a position as an associate professor that entails supervising residents in the specialty of family practice in a hospital.

Although Dr. Abbott is very dedicated to his work, he devotes much time to diverse interests that could easily become careers in themselves. For example, one of his hobbies is the designing, building, and racing of aerodynamic bicycles. He has twice broken the world's speed record. His other talents and interests include painting, sculpturing, and home construction. Although his professional work could be all-consuming, he has chosen to provide time to cultivate his other areas of interest.

Choosing an Occupation or Career

What do you expect from work? What factors do you give the most attention to in selecting a career or an occupation? In my work at a university counseling center, I've discovered that many students haven't really thought seriously about why they are choosing a given vocation. For some, parental pressure or encouragement is the major reason for their choice. Others have idealized views of what it will be like to be lawyers, engineers, or doctors. Many people I've counseled regarding career decisions haven't looked at what they value the most and whether these values can be attained in their chosen vocations. In choosing your vocation (or evaluating the choices you've made previously), you may want to consider which factors really mean the most to you.

Job decisions are very often based on a desire for some type of financial or psychological security. The security a job affords is a legitimate consideration for most people, but you may find that security alone isn't enough to make your job meaningful. On the other hand, the security of a job can actually enhance its meaningfulness. For example, security in your job may free you to concentrate your time and energies in a creative direction.

Other factors that are often considered in connection with vocational choices include the opportunities for challenge and advancement, self-expression, service to others, financial rewards, status, and prestige, to mention only a few. Not everyone has a need to be challenged in his or her job, and not everyone works well under pressure to move upward in a job. Although the opportunity for self-expression is a priority for some people, others may consider it relatively unimportant or may find it outside their jobs. For some people, prestige and status are important considerations; if their jobs failed to provide these things, they would not be happy with them. One common pitfall is that we often allow others to determine what constitutes the "prestige" attached to a particular job. You can decide for yourself what makes a job important. Is it the amount of money you make that defines your status? Is it the opportunity to exceed quotas or to compete and win? Is it the feeling of actually producing something? Is it how hard you work? Is it the opportunity to serve others' needs?

Of course, the factors I've mentioned are only a few of the many considerations involved in selecting a vocation. Since so much time and energy are devoted to work, it's extremely important to decide for ourselves what weight each factor will have in our thinking. If you value being of service to others and working with people in a personal way, you may be disappointed if you decide on a well-paying job that gives you little opportunity to work with people. If you place a high value on meeting new people and seeing new places, you may regret settling for a more secure position that offers little chance for adventure. Too often, the motivating factor in choosing a job or a career is the money and status associated with it. I hope you'll ask yourself "Is the price of status and money worth the possible psychological distress of a job I don't like?" Thus, in considering a line of work, you might also ask yourself how much time you will have left over for leisure and for learning.

In short, *you* stand a greater chance of being satisfied with your work if you put time and thought into your choice and if you actively take steps toward finding a career or an occupation that will bring more

"I THINK I'M GOING TO BE PSYCHOLOGICALLY DISTRESSED BY THIS".

enrichment to your life than it will disruption. Ultimately, *you* are the person who can best decide what you want in your work. In this regard, I like the suggestion given by Bolles (1978):

> You are in charge of your life. No matter how many forces there may be which seem to influence or even dictate part of your life, there is always that part over which you have control. You can increase that control. If you decide what it is that you want out of your Learning, and out of your Working, and out of your Playing, you will be infinitely less *powerless* and *"victimizable"* [p. 58].

Ways of Making Wise Vocational Choices

The question you may be asking yourself now is "How can I go about deciding what will be a meaningful line of work?" A good place to begin is the counseling center or career-development center on your campus. A career counselor can be a great help to you in starting the process of your life and work planning. Other resources typically available at the center include interest inventories and personality assessments. Tests and inventories do not give answers, but they can provide guidelines in helping you to look at how your interests, personality traits, and values might be related to various career options. Ultimately, you still have to make choices, but these inventories may show you some alternatives that you hadn't considered before. Rather than relying on one test alone, I typically suggest several, including some of the following:

The Edwards Personal Preference Schedule. The questions in this inventory are designed to identify 15 dimensions of a person's personality: the needs for achievement, deference, order, exhibition, autonomy, affiliation, intraception, succorance, dominance, abasement, nurturance, change, endurance, heterosexuality, and aggression. This device can help us to see more clearly how certain of our needs are related to vocational choices, and it can also help us understand why we are drawn to certain types of people and not to others.

The Myers-Briggs Personality Type Indicator. This personality assessment device gives us some indication of a variety of personality orientations (such as extraversion and introversion). While the results, which yield a certain "personality type," may not be significant in themselves, this information could be useful background for a discussion of what kinds of personality might fit various careers and occupations.

The Strong-Campbell Interest Inventory. Designed as an objective measurement of interest patterns, this inventory gives clues to whether a person would be most satisfied working with data, things, or people. It is not an assessment of abilities or aptitudes, but rather a measurement of likes and preferences as compared with those of people in many different occupations. It usually points to several possible occupations that the person could consider.

The Kuder Occupational Interest Survey. This is an alternative to the Strong-Campbell interest inventory, geared mainly to the same objectives.

The Allport-Vernon-Lindsey Study of Values. This is a useful device designed to clarify value orientations. For example, it will show whether your central values are in the social area, the political area, or the economic area. Considering your values and how they are related to various occupations is an important part of career counseling.

In addition to making use of the counseling and testing center on your campus, here are some other things you might do to aid your work planning.

• Talk to people in the career or occupation that you think you want to pursue. What is it like for them to be in this type of work? What advice could they offer you? Would they make the same choice again? What are the advantages and disadvantages of their job? What do they get from their work? What specific skills are needed? What does the job market look like in the near future? Talking with a number of people in the same line of work could be one of your best resources. Again, as with interest and personality inventories, these people will not give you an answer concerning the "right" decision for you, but they can give you valuable data to use in making a better choice for yourself.

• If you have several careers in mind, try to get involved with them in some way as soon as possible. Part-time jobs during the school year that are related to a job that interests you, or a full-time job in the summer, could shed some realistic light on your situation. For example, our daughter Heidi is thinking of becoming a veterinarian. While she knows that she loves animals, she doesn't know if she'd actually like to work with sick animals. Marianne suggested that she spend a summer working in an animal clinic as one way of checking out her interests. Also, she just finished a high school course in Animal Care, which she liked very much. Yet she does not look forward to the dissection of frogs and cats in biology class next year!

• Read *What Color Is Your Parachute?* by Richard Bolles (1981). This book is a practical manual for job hunters and career changers. It is the distillation of the experience of millions of successful job hunters of all ages in all types of work. It provides a wealth of practical information that should give you some clear direction in choosing jobs.

Bolles stresses that career and life planning is a continuous process, not a single event that is finished for all time. He also makes the point that only you can decide what you want to do. He encourages readers to adopt an active stance toward selecting and getting a job:

> We believe that you will improve your effectiveness and your sense of yourself as a person 300% if you can learn to think (or if you already think) of yourself as *an active agent* helping to mould your own present environment and your own future, rather than a passive agent, waiting for your environment to mould you [p. 74].

Perhaps one of the major factors that will prevent you from becoming active in the process of life and work planning is the temptation to put off doing what needs to be done to *choose* your work. If you merely "fall into a job" somewhat as you might "fall in love," you will probably be disappointed with the outcomes. You might consider Bolles's sound advice: "I hate to tell you this, but the time to figure out where your parachute is, what color it is, and strap it on, is *now*—and not when your vocational airplane that you are presently in is on fire and diving toward the ground" (p. 70).

It must be cautioned that you should strike a balance between waiting too long to select a job and deciding too soon. The important point is that *you* have a choice.

One other consideration is worth mentioning in connection with career choices. One of the reviewers of this book recently called my attention to predictions that there will be five to seven occupational changes in a typical working lifetime during the last part of the century. It therefore seems that, if you're at the beginning of your working life, you can anticipate having a series of jobs. Thus, it could well be a mistake to think about selecting *one* occupation that will last a lifetime. Instead, it may be more fruitful to think about selecting a general type of work or a broad field of endeavor that appeals to you. With a broad goal in mind, you can consider your present job as a means of gaining experience and opening doors to new possibilities, and you can focus on what *you* want to learn from this experience. It can be liberating to realize that your decisions about work can be part of a developmental process and that your jobs can change as you change. If you see your job choices in this developmental way, you can remain open to making changes and integrating them with other changes in your life-style.

The Dangers of Choosing an Occupation Too Soon

So much emphasis is placed on what we will do "for a living" that there is a real danger of feeling compelled to choose an occupation or a career before we're really ready to do so. The pressure to identify with some occupation begins in childhood with the often-heard question "What are you going to be when you grow up?" (Part of the implication of this question is that we're not grown up until we've decided to *be* something.) If freshman year in high school isn't too early to start worrying about acceptance to college, then no grade is too early to start worrying about acceptance to the right high school! Thus, the pressure is applied at a very early age to decide on what you basically intend to do with your life—before you've really had a chance to sample either the life out there in the world or the life within you.

One of my students decided early in his high school career to major in Business Administration when he got to college. Joe also decided to follow in his father's footsteps and become a successful accountant. Eventually, he did graduate from college with high grades in his Business-Administration major. Before graduating, however, he took a few electives in the Human Services program for his own enrichment and in the process discovered the difference between taking courses only because they were required and pursuing courses that excited him personally. As a result, he went on to earn a second bachelor's degree, this time in Human Services. As Joe put it, this second degree was for himself, whereas his first one had been for his father.

Today, Joe is struck by how unaware he initially was of why he was even in college and pursuing the kind of life he once did. It frightens him to think that he could have become an accountant simply because his father had an accounting firm and was pushing him in that direction. Joe realizes that his father had good intentions; after all, as his son, Joe would have had a natural place in his firm and wouldn't ever have had to worry about security. Nevertheless, Joe sees now that these plans were his father's and not his own. So he has made the choice to follow a less certain path and to explore an area that he has discovered is exciting to him. In doing so, he gives up the security of his father's clear design for his future, but he envisions other types of rewards.

I admire Joe's willingness to question his motivation for being in college and his courage in making a new decision that was his own. I think it is critically important that Joe realized first that he was being pushed too soon to make his career decision; with this awareness, he was able to make his own choices.

Recently, I hired a young man of 22 to do some painting and carpentry work in my house. Paul went to a community college for a year in the Midwest, but he dropped out because he needed to work to support himself. Then he and a friend decided to travel and experiment with whatever jobs they could find. They traveled over 1000 miles by bicycle, doing odd jobs along the way. For a while, they picked apples in the Northwest and really enjoyed that work. Afterwards, Paul wound up in Idyllwild to stay for a time.

Although Paul said that he wasn't really in a hurry to find a job, he found that he soon had plenty of work. He met a carpenter and became an apprentice, and he says that he has never enjoyed work as much as he does now. Previously, most of his jobs had been chores that he performed just to make money. Now he's doing something he likes while learning skills and making living money besides.

Paul has avoided committing himself to a vocation before he has a chance to experience life, the world of work, and his own interests and capabilities. Some people might see Paul as being aimless and as wasting valuable time, but I respect what he's doing, and I believe that he's really expanding his choices and eventually will find work that will be meaningful to him. Besides, he seems to be having an exciting time living right now, without worrying about preparation for the future.

Joe and Paul are young men who ultimately resisted the pressure to select vocations too early in life. Although different people may make appropriate career decisions at different times, I think it is generally a disservice to young people to pressure them to make crucial life decisions concerning what they want to be "when they grow up." I believe most of us need an opportunity to experiment with a diverse range of occupations, to clarify our interests, and to test our abilities. Although taking the time we need to make choices for ourselves can produce anxiety for all concerned, it can also lead to greater satisfaction in the long run.

Special Concerns of Women in Choosing a Life's Work

Women often face some special considerations as they make choices in the world of work. There is no doubt that women are often discriminated against on the basis of their sex. Despite protests and legislation, equal pay for equal work is far from a reality in most fields. I was talking recently with several women about their experiences in the world of work. They strongly believed that their chances of finding jobs they wanted were limited because they were married and had children. One said "An interviewer told me that he was not interested in hiring a wife and mother because she doesn't have the time and energy to devote to the job that a single person would." Other women are expressing their anger over the difficulty in being promoted to manager or supervisor, especially if men are involved in the picture.

A particularly difficult area for many women is successfully balancing the many responsibilities of a dual career—one outside of the home and another at home. Following is a first-person account of some of the struggles that Marianne experiences in trying to combine her many roles—as a therapist, author, mother, homemaker, friend, consultant, community worker, lecturer, wife, teacher, traveler, and hostess, just to mention a few! Her struggle typifies those of other women who also juggle many roles.

When I look at the list of my multiple roles it does not surprise me that I recently stuck my finger in the garbage disposal and absent-mindedly turned on the wrong switch. Although my hand was hurt, my emotional pain was greater than the physical pain. This incident forced me to look at how many things I was attempting to do in one day.

Just to review that day! I got two daughters off to school beginning at 6:00 A.M., I straightened up the house, I had a cup of coffee and watched some news on the *Today* show, and I spent several hours writing and revising books with Jerry—which was interrupted by my doing laundry, answering phone calls, running errands in town, organizing and beginning to pack for my daughters' summer trip to Germany, and picking up the kids from school.

To top it off, I had three individual counseling sessions with clients in the afternoon. Immediately after the last one, I began to prepare the evening meal. I was still preoccupied with the last client, and I was thinking of all the details of making the arrangements for someone to stay with the girls while Jerry and I would be on a consulting trip/vacation out of the country. I was anticipating helping one of the girls with her homework—while Jerry was in the background asking "When is dinner ready?"

While this is not the way my typical day goes, there are times when it happens more than I would like. Looking at my activities, I find that I enjoy most of the things that I do, but their diversity often fragments me. Through my contact with women friends and clients, I find that I share a common struggle in combining many conflicting roles involved in having a career and also taking the role of mother and homemaker seriously.

The process of delicately balancing many different and sometimes conflicting roles has been a struggle for many years, and it seems to be a continuing one. I am very aware of my parental programming, which entailed the traditional conditioning of women. Growing up in a small German village for 19 years had a significant impact on me. It was not an easy task to break out of this traditional pattern, to risk my parents' disapproval, to pursue higher education, and eventually to become involved in a professional career. Over the years I have certainly modified many of my parents' designs for me, yet I have come to the realization that many of their values are ones that I have consciously chosen and am now choosing to live by. At this point in my life, I am not willing to give up my professional career. However, it is at least equally important for me to be a good wife, mother, and homemaker and above all to have a significant positive involvement in my children's lives.

I pride myself in being efficient in the many different things that I do. Yet this at times comes home to haunt me, because I am slow in learning to ask for help or to delegate work. I have conditioned Jerry, our children, and our friends to rely on my need to be efficient in all that I do, and they gladly let me be this way! I am aware that many of these tasks are self-appointed responsibilities; it is up to me to know my limits, to set them, and to let others know what I will and will not do. When I have worked myself into a panic, it is much easier for me to let off steam and complain about the people around me who make too many demands on me. When all is calm and I take time to reflect, I often come up with the reality that it is my responsibility to negotiate, to ask for what I want or need, and to directly and clearly specify my limits before I overextend myself— even if delegating certain routine tasks does not come easy to me.

I find that many women, and I am one of them, see it as unfair that our husbands delight in our professional endeavors yet at the same time rely on us to perform the traditional role of homemaker. When I am not angry about this fact, I am able to recognize that there are changes taking place. Both men and women are slowly reconditioning themselves and not rigidly sticking to predefined roles. I realize that I must make the time to evaluate and arrange my priorities and that ultimately I am the one who chooses how I spend my days. Nevertheless, there are many times that I feel that I am performing a juggling act, and at times I get dizzy and feel overextended.

While women may be capable of doing any one of several tasks well, attempting to do *all* of them at the same time can be unrealistic. In her excellent book *Workaholics*, Marilyn Machlowitz (1980) discusses the expectations of the so-called "Superwoman" who attempts to live up to the roles of Supermom, Superwife, and Superworker. Of course, there is never enough time or energy to fulfill Superwoman's self-expectations, and thus she suffers from a sense of guilt. A woman like this needs to ask herself whether the physical and psychological price she is paying to maintain the Superwoman image is worth it.

In their book *Burnout: From Tedium to Personal Growth*, Pines, Aronson, and Kafry (1981) conclude that dual-career women need to accept the reality that they have two full-time jobs. A dual-career woman is often overburdened, harrassed, guilt-ridden, and a likely candidate for burnout. To combat these dangers, she needs to exercise her power of choice:

> She must be aware that she will face daily struggles for priorities of her time and energy. The home/career woman must define her goals in each of her different roles and distribute her mental, physical, and emotional energy accordingly. A decision to combine family and career means making compromises. The woman herself must decide how these compromises will be made, both between and within her roles [p. 98].

Time Out for Personal Reflection

This "Time Out" is intended to be a survey of your basic attitudes, beliefs, values, and interests in regard to occupational choices. Complete each statement by circling the letters of the response or responses that most apply to you or by writing your own response on the blank line.

1. *Most of the jobs I've had so far*
   a. *have been very rewarding.*
   b. *have been unsatisfying.*
   c. *have primarily been a means to survival.*
   d. *have been of my own choosing.*

   e. _____

2. *For me, the most important consideration in selecting a vocation is*

  a. *the financial rewards.*
  b. *the prestige.*
  c. *the promise of advancement.*
  d. *the chance to be of service to others.*

  e. _____

3. *In choosing a career, I would give top priority to obtaining*
  a. *a secure position.*
  b. *a position that would challenge me.*
  c. *a position that would allow me to work with people.*
  d. *a position that offers variety.*

  e. _____

4. *I think of the financial aspects of a job as*
  a. *extremely important.*
  b. *important, but not decisive.*
  c. *not very important.*
  d. *one of my least important considerations.*

  e. _____

5. *In considering a career, I rank such factors as the status and prestige of the job as*
  a. *the most important considerations.*
  b. *very important.*
  c. *somewhat important.*
  d. *of little or no importance.*

  e. _____

6. *In considering a job, I consider security to be*
  a. *extremely important.*
  b. *important, but not decisive.*
  c. *one of my top five considerations.*
  d. *one of my least important considerations.*

  e. _____

7. *When I think of working, the opportunity to use and develop my creativity and to express myself as a person is*
  a. *extremely important to me.*
  b. *important, but not a main factor.*
  c. *of some value to me.*

    d. *of little or no importance to me.*

    e. _____

8. *In choosing a career, I think of the opportunity to make a significant difference in the lives of other people as*
    a. *my most important consideration.*
    b. *important, but not a top priority.*
    c. *slightly important.*
    d. *of little or no importance.*

    e. _____

9. *I would most like a job in which*
    a. *I could be my own boss.*
    b. *I could work for others who would assume primary responsibility.*
    c. *I had a great deal of power and influence.*
    d. *I could work at my own pace.*

    e. _____

10. *In regard to choosing my own occupation, I believe that*
    a. *I can be whatever I choose to become.*
    b. *my choice is severely limited by the job market.*
    c. *fate will determine what kind of work I do.*
    d. *my choices, while limited, are nevertheless real and significant.*

    e. _____

11. *I think that work satisfaction is related to satisfaction in other areas of my life*
    a. *to a very high degree.*
    b. *to a considerable degree.*
    c. *to some degree.*
    d. *only to a very slight degree.*

    e. _____ .

   After you've completed this survey, look it over to see whether there are significant patterns in your responses. What can you say by way of summary about your attitudes and values as they relate to selecting a career?

_____

Work and the Meaning of Your Life

Whether or not you've already decided on an occupation or career, it's important to consider what you find or expect to find through work and how work can either contribute to or detract from the meaning and quality of your life. If you expect your work to provide you with a primary source of meaning, and if your life isn't as rich with meaning as you'd like, you might begin to tell yourself "If only I had a job that I liked, *then* I'd be fulfilled." This "If only, then . . ." type of thinking can lead you to believe that somehow the secret of finding a purpose in your life depends on something outside yourself.

In his book *The Doctor and the Soul*, Frankl (1965) contends that "no one occupation is the sole road to salvation." He talks about people who try to deceive themselves by thinking that they *would* be fulfilled now *if only* they had gone into another occupation. Frankl states that, on the contrary, if an occupation doesn't lead to fulfillment, the fault may be in the person rather than in the work: "The work in itself does not make the person indispensable and irreplaceable; it only gives him the chance to be so" (p. 95).

Frankl describes a patient who found her life meaningless and who believed that, if she had a job that fulfilled her, her life would be meaningful. Frankl pointed out to her that her attitude toward her work and the manner in which she did her work were more important than the job itself. He showed her that the way a person approaches a job and the special things he or she does in carrying out that job are what make it meaningful.

The Dynamics of Discontent in Work

It is certainly true that, if you're dissatisfied with your job, one recourse you have is to seek a new one. However, change alone might not produce different results. In general, I think it's a mistake to assume that change necessarily cures dissatisfactions, and this very much applies to changing jobs. To know whether a change of jobs would be helpful, you need to understand as clearly as you can why your present job isn't satisfactory to you. Consequently, I'd like to talk about some of the external factors that can devitalize us in our jobs and the very real pressures and stresses our jobs often create. Then I'd like to focus attention on the importance of looking *within ourselves* for the source of our discontent. The emphasis will be on what *you* can do about changing some of these factors in the job and in yourself. Often we blame external factors for our unhappiness and, in so doing, fail to look at how our own attitudes and expectations might be contributing to our discontent. The focus of much of the rest of the section is on what you can do *within* the job to lessen dissatisfaction, if not ensure thriving.

You may like your work and derive satisfaction from it yet at the same time feel drained because of irritations produced by factors that aren't intrinsic to the work itself. Such factors might include low morale among fellow workers, or actual conflict and disharmony among them; authoritarian supervisors who make it difficult for you to feel any sense of freedom on the job; or organizational blocks to your creativity. There are also countless pressures and demands that can sap your energy and lead you to feel dissatisfied with your job. These include having to meet deadlines and quotas; having to compete with others instead of simply doing your best; facing the threat of losing your job; feeling stuck in a job that offers little opportunity for growth or that you deem dehumanizing; dealing with difficult customers or clients; and having to work long hours or perform exhausting or tedious work. A stress that is particularly insidious—because it can compound all the other dissatisfactions you might feel—is the threat of cutbacks or layoffs, an anxiety that becomes more acute when you think of your commitments and responsibilities. In addition to the strains you may experience on the job, there may also be the daily stress of commuting to and from work. You may be tense before you even get to work, and the trip home may only increase the level of tension or anxiety you bring home with you. One real problem for many of us is that our relationships with others are negatively affected by this kind of life-style. If our work drains and deenergizes us, we may have little to give to our children, spouses, and friends, and we may not be receptive to their efforts to give to us.

All the factors I've mentioned can contribute to a general discontent that robs our work of whatever positive benefits it might otherwise have. In the face of such discontent, we might just plod along, hating our jobs and spoiling much of the rest of our lives as well. The alternative is to look at the specific things that contribute to our unhappiness or tension and to ask ourselves what we can do about them. We can also ask what we can do about our own attitudes toward those pressures and sources of strain that we can't influence directly.

One way in which we frequently limit our choice of attitudes toward our jobs is by overemphasizing the *job itself* and other external realities as the cause of our discontent. As long as we project all our troubles outside ourselves, we can make the job or the boss or the customers convenient scapegoats, but we prevent ourselves from looking at what *we* can do to change. Some people, for instance, adopt a perfectionist attitude, blaming their unhappiness on the failure of others to meet their high standards. They may change jobs again and again, hoping that, this time, things will be exactly right, which of course they never are. The trouble is that they are looking outside of themselves instead of at the unrealistically high aspirations they impose on themselves and others. Until they begin to accept that they are contributing to their own discontent, no amount of changing jobs will effect a satisfactory solution.

Meaninglessness in Work

In *Working,* a fascinating report on the everyday lives of working people, Studs Terkel (1975) gives a penetrating inside view of the material and spiritual hardships that many workers experience in their struggle to make a living. He describes scores of interviews with people in many occupations, including a strip miner, a telephone operator, a bookbinder, a garbage man, a spot welder, a bus driver, a car salesman, a mail carrier, an interstate truck driver, a janitor, a waitress, and many others. Many of these first-person accounts testify to the meaninglessness of the workers' lives.

Clearly, many, if not most, working people do not find their jobs personally meaningful or see them as opportunities for self-expression and self-actualization. Thus, many of them do not identify themselves with their jobs, despite the time and energy they must devote to them. To these people, work must simply be made as tolerable as possible. No one can say what an enormous toll this attitude must take on the quality of their lives and their sense of self-respect.

All of us will probably find certain aspects of our work to be boring, or at least unexciting. Every occupation has its tedious and routine chores. For example, although I greatly enjoy most of my work projects,

I generally find reading papers to be a chore; I detest making out grades; I never look forward to writing the many letters of recommendation that I write in a semester; and attending meetings gets old for me very fast. I even get bored with some of my classes (or my lectures) once in a while. Even in play and recreation, most of us must learn to tolerate some monotony. I play tenor saxophone in our community swing band, and I very much enjoy playing for groups in the park or at a dance. I also enjoy the fellowship associated with our weekly band practices. Still, there are times of boredom when I must practice a piece of music over and over or do certain exercises that will keep me in the band. So I see it as vital for me to recognize that some boredom is a part of life but that I have some choice in how I relate to this boredom. Besides, once I recognize the things that are chores for me, I can think of ways to make them more tolerable—or even fun.

Apart from the boredom that might creep into any job, however, there are undoubtedly occupations in which most of the time on the job is merely endured. In *Working*, Terkel documents the quiet desperation experienced by many people in service occupations. He found that certain themes tended to run through his interviews: we need to be needed; we need to feel that our work (and we) are of some significance; we need and want to be remembered; we search for "daily meaning as well as daily bread"; we work for "recognition as well as cash." In Terkel's words, "To be remembered was the wish, spoken and unspoken, of the heroes and heroines in this book" (1975, p. xiii).[1] Terkel concludes that merely surviving the day is a victory for many who are among the "walking wounded" in the world of work. As he says, "The scars, psychic as well as physical, brought home to the supper table and the TV set, may have touched, malignantly, the soul of our society" (p. xiii).

In the automated age in which we live, many people feel as if their work could be done better by machines. Indeed, many of the people Terkel interviewed talk about feeling like robots, objects, or machines. They speak in their own way of being depersonalized—faceless, anonymous, interchangeable cogs in a gigantic machine. For example, an 18-year-old telephone operator complains that she is missing any personal touch in her work. People put coins in a machine, and she responds: "You're there to perform your service and go. You're kind of detached" (p. 65). Even though she'd like to be more personal in her job, and even

[1]From *Working: People Talk about What They Do All Day and How They Feel about What They Do*, by S. Terkel. Copyright 1974 by Pantheon Books, a division of Random House, Inc. Reprinted by permission.

though there are times when she'd like to engage callers in conversations or brief exchanges, she realizes that in her role she can't be much more than a programmed machine. "I'm a communications person," she says with eloquent irony, "but I can't communicate" (p. 66). Instead, she is reduced to repeating a few acceptable and anonymous responses day after day, such as: "Good morning, may I help you?" "What number do you want?" "I have a collect call from Bill; will you accept the charges?" Apart from such standard phrases, she cannot interact with others in a human way without risking her supervisor's disapproval and perhaps her job itself.

If you find your work meaningless, what can you do about it? What can you do if, instead of energizing you, your job drains you physically and emotionally? What are your options if you feel stuck in a dead-end job? Are there some ways that you can constructively deal with the sources of dissatisfaction within your job?

One way of dealing with the issue of meaninglessness and dissatisfaction in work is to look at how you really spend your time. It would be useful to keep a running account for a week to a month of what you do and how you relate to each of your activities. Which of them are draining you, and which are energizing you? While you may not be able to change everything about your job that you don't like, by keeping a record of day-by-day activities within your job, you might be surprised by the significant changes you can make to increase your satisfaction. People often adopt a passive and victimlike position in which they complain about everything and dwell on those aspects that they believe they cannot change. Instead, a more constructive approach is to focus on those factors within your job that you *can* change.

Perhaps, too, you can redefine the hopes you have for the job. Of course, you may also be able to think of the satisfactions you'd most like to aim for in a job and then consider whether there is a job that more nearly meets your needs and what steps you must take to obtain it. You might be able to find ways of advancing within your present job, making new contacts, or acquiring the skills that eventually will enable you to move on. The important thing is to look carefully at how much the initiative rests with *you*—your expectations, your attitudes, and your sense of purpose and perspective.

In making changes within a job, Bolles (1978) suggests, we should turn negative statements concerning our past into some positive statements concerning the future we would like to have. For example, on the left side of a sheet of paper you can list what you don't like in the world of work, both past and present; on the right side you can list what you'd like to have, either within your present job or in any future job. Your list might look like:

· getting little or no recognition for accomplishments and efforts	· getting recognition from others and giving myself recognition
· being oversupervised	· receiving a reasonable degree of supervision, with some latitude to use my judgment
· doing too many stressful things in a day	· decreasing some of the stressful activities and taking more time to relax between tasks
· too many demands made on me	· deciding if I am willing to accept all the demands
· not being challenged enough	· finding a way to increase the challenges and to grow on the job

Identifying positive wants in this way can provide you with clues for constructive change—and help you become an *agent* rather than a *victim*.

Job Burnout: Some Ways of Staying Alive

The phenomenon of job burnout is receiving increasing attention. What is burnout? What are some of its causes? What can be done to prevent it? How can it be overcome?

Burnout is a state of physical, emotional, and mental exhaustion. It is the result of repeated emotional pressures, often associated with intense involvement with people over long periods of time. People who are burned out are characterized by physical depletion and by feelings of hopelessness and helplessness. They tend to develop negative attitudes toward themselves, others, work, and life (Pines, Aronson, & Kafry, 1981).

The problem of burnout is especially critical for people working in the human-services field. With the emphasis in this kind of work on giving to others, often there is not enough focus on giving to oneself. According to Pines, Aronson, and Kafry (1981), people who perform human services share three basic characteristics: (1) they are involved in emotionally taxing work; (2) they tend to be sensitive to others' problems and have a desire to relieve suffering; and (3) they often see their work as a calling to be givers to those who need help. Unfortunately, some who enter the helping professions have high hopes that are never realized. If they meet with constant frustration, see almost no positive change in their clients, and encounter obstacles to meeting their goals of helping others, their hopes may eventually be replaced by a sense of hopelessness.

Marianne and I regularly serve as consultants in training and supervision workshops for the employees in a state mental hospital (most of whom lead groups with patients). We have found that most of the staff members comment on the extreme demands of the job and on how draining their day-to-day work is. Their most frequent complaints center on a lack of recognition or positive appreciation for the demanding work they do in a week. While their supervisors frequently point out their limitations, they are slower to recognize their contributions. Also, many of the treatment staff (psychiatric technicians, psychologists, and social workers) feel that they do not make a difference in the lives of their patients. Certainly, their degree of discouragement has an impact on their level of effectiveness in treating the patients. Many of these mental-health workers say that they look forward to the end of the day, and even more so to Friday. They also talk about how difficult it is to maintain enthusiasm for any length of time. The bleakness of the physical surroundings and their contacts with fellow workers and patients are typically depressing to them. When they are enthusiastic, their fellow workers may skeptically remark with something like: "You hang around here for a few years more and you'll learn what we have to face. You'll get burned out like the rest of us!" It takes a lot of extra effort and energy to thrive (or even maintain) in such a depressing environment. The atmosphere causes a strain among the staff, and it contributes to interpersonal conflicts within the wards. This makes an already draining and taxing type of work even more difficult.

Short of leaving the job, what can the staff members do to make their work more pleasant? They do have the choice of increasing their misery by focusing on everything that is negative about their job and by dwelling on what they are unable to change in the system as a whole. While some of these workers are global in their criticism, they are often hard pressed to come up with suggestions that would lead to positive change. Too often they look to management for approval and recognition, instead of finding a way to work for their own approval.

Some of these staff members have found a way to actively take charge of their lives and increase their sense of personal power. They refuse to wait forever for the praise that may never come from management. Rather than allowing themselves to get burned out through the discouragement that comes from focusing on all that cannot readily be changed within the system, they have developed ways to make small changes in a certain part of the system. For example, a number of them have organized support groups with their peers. These groups meet regularly to discuss difficulties and stresses of the job and ways to manage matters more effectively. One suggestion involved the importance of "warming up" slowly at the beginning of the day. This meant allowing a few minutes to make contact with fellow workers and to think about their patients and how they'd like their day to be. Getting themselves psychologically ready for their work seems to have lowered the stress they experience. Some of them have exchanged job duties, or they have exchanged wards and worked with different treatment programs. All of these are ways of breaking the monotony of a routine and of increasing contact with fellow workers in other parts of the hospital.

Of course, job burnout is a problem in other fields besides human services. Occupational tedium is quite prevalent among those who work in bureaucracies. Work overload, stresses and pressures associated with achieving, lack of autonomy, and lack of recognition and rewards are all related to burnout, particularly among those who work for large organizations. A few preventive measures workers can consider include: thinking of ways to bring variety into their work; finding interests besides work; taking stock to determine whether what they are doing is meaningful or draining; finding ways of incorporating their interests within the job; and talking with fellow workers about the kinds of changes that they *can* make within the organization if they are willing to take the initiative. An important antidote to burnout is feeling some degree of personal power and control in the world of work.

Your Job versus Your Work

Although I derive much satisfaction from the work I'm paid to do, I hope that I'd be able to achieve a sense of productivity and fulfillment even if my jobs did not provide me with the opportunity to do so. In that event, I might think of my *work* or *calling* as something different from my *job*.

This distinction between a *job* and a *work* is made by Robert Strom (1978). He notes that we tend to associate our identities, status, and

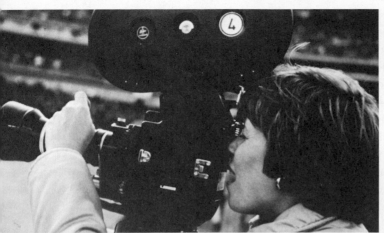

sense of potency with the activities we're paid for performing. As we have seen, however, many jobs offer little scope for personal creativity or fulfillment, particularly in an increasingly automated society. Moreover, our society seems to be moving in the direction of more and more leisure time, shorter work weeks, and earlier retirement—trends that can make it even more difficult to derive our sense of identity and worth from our jobs. In this situation, one option we have is to find our fulfillment primarily in other activities. In Strom's words:

> If a distinction between job and work were generally accepted, the result would be in everyone's best interest. We could enlarge our inquiry of self and others from "What is your job?" to "What is your *work*?" In other words, "What

is your mission as a person, the activity you pursue with a sense of duty and from which you derive self-meaning and a sense of personal worth?" It would be understood that, given the meaninglessness of some jobs, numerous people would necessarily identify their work as something different from their employment. This would release them from the self-delusion and guilt that come from working at a job they abhor but from which they are expected to gain satisfaction [1978, p. 234].

The idea that we *are* what we do for a living is so pervasive that society at large may be slow to make the distinction Strom suggests. However, we don't have to wait for others to change their views in order to decide for ourselves how much we will find our sense of meaning and purpose in our employment; nor do we have to despair or become apathetic if, despite our best efforts, we don't find jobs that are meaningful to us. To a great extent, we are the ones who decide how much we contribute to and derive from our jobs. If we feel an emptiness or lack of fulfillment in our lives, it's up to us to create our own meaning, to the extent our circumstances allow, instead of blaming our jobs for failing to provide it.

If you decide that you must remain in a job that allows little scope for personal effort and satisfaction, you may need to accept the fact that you won't find much meaning in the hours you spend on the job. It's important, then, to be aware of the effects the time spent on the job has on the rest of your life and to minimize them. More positively, it's crucial to find something outside the job that fulfills your need for recognition, significance, productivity, and excitement. By doing so, you may develop a sense of your true work as something different from what you're paid to do; you may even come to think of your job as providing the means for your *work*—that is, the productive activities you engage in away from the job, whether they take the form of hobbies, creative pursuits, volunteer work, the spending of time with friends and family, or whatever the case may be. The point is to see whether things can be turned around so that you are the master rather than the victim of your job. Too many people are so negatively affected by their jobs that their frustration and sense of emptiness spoil their eating, recreation, family lives, sex lives, and relationships with friends. If you can reassume control of your own attitudes toward your job and find dignity and pride elsewhere in your life, you may be able to do much to lessen these negative effects.

Time Out for Personal Reflection

Take a few minutes now to think about any dissatisfactions you have concerning your work.

1. A major dissatisfaction in my work is:

_____

_____

2. What I'd most like to have different in the future is:

_____

_____

3. Some specific steps I could take now to begin making this change are:

_____

_____

4. If you are not now working, you might ask people in various occupations what they find in their work that keeps them vital or that creates dissatisfaction for them. How meaningful are their jobs? What, if anything, could they do to make the changes they'd like in their jobs? List below the persons you are willing to contact to discuss their jobs.

_____

_____

Changing Jobs or Careers

Certainly, we have the option of changing jobs in order to increase our satisfaction with work, but changing jobs after a period of years can entail even more risk and uncertainty than making our first job selection. The key when we consider a vocational choice is to become clear about our own expectations and wants.

An illustration is provided by Ralph, a 34-year-old truck driver. Ralph tells me that he knows now that he became a truck driver because he always felt like a loner. He thought that truck driving was one occupa-

tion in which he could spend a lot of time alone and not have to deal
with people. As he looks back on his decision, he sees that he took the
job because he didn't feel that he had the confidence to interact with
people. He felt inferior in most areas of his life, but he felt that he could
handle trucking. And he adds that he gets some sense of power from
driving a huge, noisy truck. However, things are changing within Ralph.
He realizes now that he doesn't have to limit his life by staying in an
occupation that he doesn't really *want* to stay in. He has resumed college,
and he has begun to challenge his self-limiting notion that he is stupid
and could never be anything else but a trucker. He says that what he
really wants to do is work with adolescents who get themselves into
trouble, because he feels a kinship with them. He still drives a truck in
order to make a living, but at the same time he is taking steps to prepare
himself for a change.

Even though Ralph had done well financially as a trucker, he no longer
found his work satisfying. He realized that he had at least three alternatives: he could remain a trucker, he could do some kind of volunteer
work in addition to his trucking, or he could prepare himself for another
job while keeping his trucking job temporarily. Ultimately, Ralph chose
the last option, but the first crucial step was his recognition of his
motivations for choosing trucking in the first place. With this awareness,
he was able to see clearly that he did want a change and that he had the
potential to be something different.

It's important to realize that we may be enthusiastic about some type
of work for years and yet eventually become dissatisfied because of the
changes that occur within us. With these changes comes the possibility
that a once-fulfilling job will become monotonous and draining. If we
outgrow our jobs, we can learn new skills and in other ways increase
our options. Because our own attitudes are crucial, when a feeling of
dissatisfaction sets in, it's wise to spend time thinking about what we
ourselves want from our jobs and how we can most productively use our
talents.

Changing Careers in Mid-Life
The notion that we're stuck with our original career choices is increasingly being challenged, particularly by people in middle age. As I discussed in Chapter 3, many people experience a mid-life crisis—a time
when they question the meaning of their work, the quality of their relationships, and the direction of their lives. There is a danger at this time
of slipping into a deadening rut; and there can be the difficult recogni-

tion that we may not accomplish all the goals we set for ourselves earlier in life. However, the mid-life crisis can also be a challenge to renew and revitalize our commitments or to branch out in new directions.

The awareness of options can be an important asset at this time in life. Most of the people I know have changed their jobs several times; you might think whether this pattern fits the people you know as well. And, whether or not you've reached middle age, you might ask yourself what your own beliefs and attitudes toward changing careers are. Although making large changes in our lives is rarely easy, it can be a good deal harder if our own attitudes and fears are left unquestioned and unexamined.

A common example of mid-life change is the woman who decides to return to college or to the job market after her children reach high school age. Many community colleges and state universities are enrolling women who realize that they want more fulfillment at this time in their lives. They may still value their work at home, but they are looking forward to developing new facets of themselves.

I'm thinking of one of my students, Nancy. She entered college at age 47 with a lot of mixed feelings. She wanted to meet new people, tap some of her unused resources, take new and challenging courses, and prepare herself for a career in the helping professions. She felt good when she was at school, and a completely new dimension of herself began to blossom as she followed through with her choice to involve herself in activities that were challenging and nourishing for her. She did some field work in the community, working with parents and their children, and she felt excited over the contribution she was making. Despite these positive feelings, however, she frequently felt guilty for not being at home enough and for not being as available to her children and her husband as they wanted her to be. Now, even though she realizes that she needs to be a person in her own right, she still suffers doubts about her choice, and she is struggling to combine her different roles.

Despite the struggle involved, I respect the refusal of women like Nancy to allow themselves to stagnate. They are making their own choices to do something different.

This phenomenon is not unique to women. I know of many men who are deciding in middle age to quit jobs they've had for years, even if they're successful, because they want new challenges. Men often define themselves by the work they do, and work thus becomes a major source of the purpose in their lives. If they feel successful in their work, they may feel successful as persons; if they become stagnant in work, they may feel that they are ineffectual in most areas of their lives.

Such is the case with John, a 52-year-old aerospace engineer who finally decided that too much of his identity was wrapped up in his profession. He decided to keep his job in industry as a consultant to various engineering firms while at the same time starting a master's-degree program in counseling. His interest in counseling stemmed from some marriage counseling he and his wife had received. He had experienced a new realm of feelings, and he decided that he didn't always have to be detached, thing-oriented, logical, and unemotional. Eventually, John received his degree in counseling, and even though he hasn't switched from engineering to counseling as a profession, it has been important for him to know that he has the qualifications to assume a new career if he so chooses. In this way he experiences more freedom in the world of work, because he knows that he is in engineering because he *wants* to be now, not because he *has* to be.

People such as Nancy and John are finding new directions and new dimensions of meaning in their lives because they're willing to question long-standing assumptions about themselves and about work. Although such self-awareness is always relevant and helpful, it is particularly so during mid-life, when we can either renew ourselves or set the stage for a life of doing a job simply to survive.

Time Out for Personal Reflection

1. *Mention a few of the most important benefits that you get (or expect to get) from work.*

_____

_____

_____

2. *What kind of work would you most like to be involved in? Why?*

_____

_____

_____

3. *What kind of work would you least like to be involved in? Why?*

_____

_____

_____

4. *List the aspects that you most look for in selecting a field of work (such as security, opportunities for self-expression, financial rewards, contact with co-workers, and so on).*

   _____

   _____

   _____

5. *What nonwork activities have you been involved in that you liked, because in doing them you felt creative, happy, or energetic?*

   _____

   _____

   _____

6. *Could you obtain a job that would incorporate some of the activities you've just listed? Or does your job already account for them?*

   _____

   _____

   _____

7. *What do you think would happen to you if you couldn't work? Write what first comes to mind.*

   _____

   _____

   _____

8. *Some people experience a good deal of anxiety over making choices dealing with work. Check any of the following factors that you feel create anxiety for you:*

   _____ *I feel that I must make a career choice too early.*
   _____ *I don't know what my abilities are.*
   _____ *Once I make a choice, I think that I must stay with it.*
   _____ *I fear that my choice will be wrong and that I'll be stuck with a miserable job.*
   _____ *I'm afraid that I won't be able to find the kind of work I really want.*
   _____ *I'm afraid that I'll become consumed by my work.*
   _____ *I'm concerned that I'll select a line of work because I've been influenced by others and that I'll be living up to their expectations rather than my own.*

9. *Mention any other anxieties you are aware of concerning your decisions about work:*

_____

_____

_____

10. *If you could quit your job and still have all your needs met, what would you do with your time?*

_____

_____

_____

Retirement

Retirement from a job can be traumatic for many people. How can people who have relied largely on their jobs for meaning or structure in their lives deal with their retirement? Must they lose their sense of self-worth when they are forced to retire? Can they find a sense of purpose and value apart from their occupations?

I remember talking to a woman who was close to 65 and who was feeling abandoned because she was being forced to retire as a junior high school teacher. She loved interacting with the students, and her principal made it clear that she was still a fine teacher. Deeply saddened by what she described as "being put out to pasture," she gradually assumed a hopeless stance and became depressed. Of course, she did have some choice in regard to her response to this situation; instead of remaining depressed, she could have gone on to search for other ways to give of herself, perhaps through some form of volunteer work. The difficulty she had in envisioning any other possibilities for herself illustrates how difficult retirement can be for people who have had meaningful and fulfilling careers. Still, it was unquestionably sad that, because of the school district's policy, her age alone deprived her of the chance to do what she loved doing. As a result, both she and the students were cheated by her forced retirement.

Of course, there are people who initiate retirement for themselves and continue to find meaning in their lives by involving themselves in substitute activities. Lester is an example of this kind of person. Although he is formally retired, he says that he continues to work by doing household repairs and remodeling, because he "couldn't stand to do nothing." Although the income he derives from this work is small, he takes satisfaction in the feeling of being needed.

Lester originally had managed a resort before changing jobs during his middle years. Although he had found the work at the resort exciting, he decided to quit because of his disenchantment with the commercial aspects of the job. He then took the risk of accepting a job as chief maintenance man at a hospital. As it turned out, he liked that job immensely. Lester is an example of a person who chose to make a couple of major job changes before his retirement, which perhaps made it easier for him to refuse to be idle once he did retire. Now he actively creates jobs that not only help people but at the same time give him a sense of being a productive member of the community.

The question of retirement is inseparable from the typical issues and conflicts of later life. Like adolescents, older people may have difficulty feeling that they are contributing something valuable to society. Unlike adolescents, however, they have had the opportunity to prepare for this time in their lives. What happens to us when we retire depends to a great extent on how well we've resolved the conflicts and issues of the previous stages in our lives. I think it's very unfortunate that so many of us live for the future, deluding ourselves into thinking that we will find what we want once we retire. We may find that, if we haven't achieved a sense of creativity, identity, and purpose in our earlier years, we'll feel a sense of inadequacy, emptiness, and confusion once retirement arrives. If we haven't defined for ourselves during our years on the job the place work has in our lives and the meaning we find away from the job, we'll be poorly equipped to deal with the questions of meaning and purpose in later life.

In thinking ahead to our own retirement, we can make use of the distinction mentioned earlier in this chapter between a job and a "work." As adults, we can, if we choose, find a sense of identity and purpose in activities other than those we're paid to perform. We can decide during our working lives on the extent to which we identify ourselves and our work with our jobs. If we're alive to these issues during our young and middle adulthood, we'll be in a much better position to handle the experience of retirement.

Very often we're advised to prepare for retirement in a material sense by saving money, investing, and enrolling in some sort of retirement plan. No doubt this is good advice, but it's equally necessary to think of preparing ourselves for retirement in a spiritual or emotional sense. Probably the best way to do that is to work at being aware of the role our jobs play in our lives and the extent to which we find our sense of meaning in them. If we keep in mind the distinction between a job and a work, we may agree with Strom (1978) when he says that, whether a person never holds a job or retires at age 60, "nothing framed by a period shorter than a lifetime can be termed a person's work" (p. 236).

Time Out for Personal Reflection

1. *How do you react to the idea of mandatory retirement at a certain age (say, 65)? At this time in your life, do you think you'd want to continue working when you reach "retirement age"?*

_____

_____

_____

2. *Imagine yourself as a retired person now. What are some of the things you expect to do with a typical day or week? How will you make use of your leisure time? Do you want to continue some type of part-time employment? If so, what?*

_____

_____

_____

_____

3. *What can you do during your working life to anticipate and prepare for the retirement stage of your life?*

_____

_____

_____

_____

4. *Do you know any retired people? If so, do you think they are leading*

happy lives? In what ways have they found or failed to find fulfillment in this stage of life?

_____

_____

_____

_____

5. *What are your present attitudes about retirement? Check each statement with which you find yourself more in agreement than disagreement.*

_____ *People shouldn't be forced to retire against their will.*

_____ *Most people are lost without work.*

_____ *We need to be educated to make the optimum use of leisure time.*

_____ *Most people look forward to their retirement.*

_____ *I believe in saving money during the earlier stages of life so that I'll be secure after I retire.*

_____ *I see myself as preparing emotionally for the time when I'll retire.*

_____ *I see myself as preparing financially for the time when I'll retire.*

_____ *When I retire, I'd like to travel to various parts of the world and experience different ways of life.*

_____ *I expect retirement to be a lonely and frustrating experience more than a creative and meaningful one.*

Chapter Summary

In this chapter, I've stressed that our jobs are important in part because our level of job satisfaction often carries over into the other areas of our lives. I've also stressed that, although work can be an important source of meaning in our lives, it is not the job itself that provides this meaning. The satisfaction we derive depends to a great extent on the way we relate to our jobs, the manner in which we do them, and the meaning that we ourselves attribute to them. If we find ourselves in occupations that we don't like, and if our opportunities for changing jobs are limited, we still retain the capacity to choose our own attitudes toward our circumstances. Often this realization is a powerful factor that can lead to change.

Perhaps the most important idea in this chapter is that we must look to ourselves if we're dissatisfied with our work. It's easy to blame circumstances outside of ourselves when we feel a lack of purpose and meaning. Even if our circumstances are difficult, this kind of stance only victimizes us and keeps us helpless. We can increase our power to change our circumstances by accepting that we are the ones responsible for making our lives and our work meaningful, instead of expecting our jobs to bring meaning to us.

Now write down some of the ideas you found especially significant in this chapter.

Activities and Exercises

1. Interview a person you know who dislikes his or her career or occupation. You might ask questions such as the following:

   · If you don't find your job satisfying, why do you stay in it?
   · Do you feel that you have much of a choice about whether you'll stay with the job or take a new one?
   · What aspects of your job bother you the most?
   · How does your attitude toward your job affect the other areas of your life?

2. Interview a person you know who feels fulfilled and excited by his or her work. Some questions you might ask are:

   · What does your work do for you? What meaning does your work have for the other aspects of your life?
   · What are the main satisfactions for you in your work?
   · How do you think you would be affected if you could no longer pursue your career?

3. You might interview your parents and determine what meaning their work has for them. How satisfied are they with the work aspects of their lives? How much choice do they feel they have in selecting their work? In what ways do they think the other aspects of their lives are affected by their attitudes toward work? After you've talked with them, determine how your attitudes and beliefs about work have been influenced by your parents. Are you pursuing a career that your parents can understand and respect? Is their reaction to your career choice important to you? Are your attitudes and values concerning work like or unlike those of your parents?

4. If your college has a vocational-counseling program available to you,

consider talking with a counselor about your plans. You might want to explore taking vocational-interest and aptitude tests. If you're deciding on a career, consider discussing how realistic your vocational plans are. For example, you can pursue such issues as:

- What are your interests?
- Do your interests match the career you're thinking about pursuing?
- Do you have the knowledge you need to make a career choice?
- Do you have the aptitude and skills for the career you have in mind?
- What are the future possibilities for you in the work you're considering?

5. Here is another suggestion for an interview. If you're considering a particular occupation or career, seek out a person who is actively engaged in that type of work and arrange for a time to talk with him or her. Ask personal questions concerning the chances of gaining employment, the experience necessary, the satisfactions and drawbacks of the position, and so on. In this way, you can make the process of deciding on a type of work more realistic and perhaps avoid disappointment if your expectations don't match reality.

Suggested Readings

Bolles, R. N. *The Three Boxes of Life*. Berkeley, Calif.: Ten Speed Press, 1978. This excellent book on the subject of life and work planning focuses on three areas: education, working, and leisure. It is a fine resource for lifelong learning, for developing a balanced life in the world of work, and for enjoying leisure.

Bolles, R. N. *What Color Is Your Parachute?* Berkeley, Calif.: Ten Speed Press, 1981. If you were to select just one book as a guide for career planning, this would be my recommendation. The author writes that the book is an attempt to empower job hunters or career changers to learn a process that they can use no matter how many times they change jobs. Practical hints are given for deciding on a vocation and then securing the job you want. It is an excellent resource guide to other books in the area of work, to securing professional help, and to keeping current in the job market.

Carney, C. G., Wells, C. F., & Streufert, D. *Career Planning: Skills to Build Your Future*. New York: D. Van Nostrand Co., 1981. The focus of this book is on the lifelong process of career development and the identification of the personal qualities that are applicable to the world of work. There are helpful self-assessment inventories for clarifying interests, abilities, and values. The authors' aim is to provide material that will lead to the self-awareness and practical skills necessary for creating a future in a changing world.

Day, J. *A Working Approach to Human Relations in Organizations.* Monterey, Calif.: Brooks/Cole, 1980. This text/workbook is written from the point of view of the employee—as future manager. It includes a combination of theory and practical applications for such topics as finding the right job, motivation on the job, communication, relationships with co-workers, and organizational change.

Dunnette, M. D. (Ed.). *Work and Nonwork in the Year 2001.* Monterey, Calif.: Brooks/Cole, 1973. A collection of readings on the future of work. The book includes discussions of work from historical, intercultural, and institutional perspectives.

Frankl, V. *Man's Search for Meaning.* New York: Washington Square Press, 1963. (Pocket Books edition, 1975.) In this book, Frankl develops the idea that we are always free to decide on our attitudes toward any set of circumstances— a freedom that has applications to the way in which we relate to our jobs.

Frankl, V. *The Doctor and the Soul.* New York: Bantam, 1965. This book has an excellent section on the relationship of work to the meaning of life.

Machlowitz, M. *Workaholics: Living with Them, Working with Them.* Reading, Mass.: Addison-Wesley, 1980. An interesting book that describes the personality characteristics of workaholics and the effects of their work style on their families and on their own level of happiness. Some suggestions are given for maximizing the pleasures and minimizing the pressures of workaholism.

Pines, A. M., & Aronson, E. (with D. Kafry). *Burnout: From Tedium to Personal Growth.* New York: Free Press, 1981. This book describes burnout and tedium, discusses the causes of these syndromes, and explores some ideas for dealing with them. The authors give special attention to burnout among people working in large bureaucracies and in the human-services field. They also discuss special issues of concern to dual-career women.

Pirsig, R. *Zen and the Art of Motorcycle Maintenance.* New York: Bantam, 1976. Finding meaning and value in an increasingly technological culture and taking pride in our work are among the themes of this book. Pirsig also has some thoughts about the "gumption traps" that can sap our energy and block our creativity.

Rubin, L. *Worlds of Pain: Life in the Working-Class Family.* New York: Basic Books, 1976. In this sensitive book, the author captures the experience of working-class people in their jobs, their marriages, and their leisure time. Her chapters on work and its meaning and the quality of leisure are excellent. She shows how work influences many other important aspects of life.

Strom, R. *Growing Together: Parent and Child Development.* Monterey, Calif.: Brooks/Cole, 1978. Strom's chapter on "Educating for Leisure" discusses the distinction between job and work and argues that, although not everyone must have a job, everyone should have work. He also discusses the constructive use of leisure time and has a chapter on "The Future of Grandparents" that is of interest in connection with the problems surrounding retirement.

Terkel, S. *Working*. New York: Avon, 1975. This magnificent book gives penetrating views of what work means to many people in our society, how they deal with feelings of helplessness and meaninglessness, and how their jobs influence the rest of their lives.

Toffler, A. *Future Shock*. New York: Bantam, 1971. This book deals with the rapid change that our society is undergoing and with the effects this accelerated change has on us. "Future shock" has many implications for the world of work.

Chapter Nine

Loneliness and Solitude

Prechapter Self-Inventory

For each statement, indicate the response that most closely identifies your beliefs and attitudes. Use this code: 5 = I *strongly agree* with this statement; 4 = I *agree* in most respects; 3 = I am *undecided;* 2 = I *disagree* in most respects; 1 = I *strongly disagree.*

_____ 1. Loneliness is a condition that needs to be cured.

_____ 2. Experiencing aloneness gives us a sense of strength and power.

_____ 3. Loneliness is generally intensified during our adolescent years.

_____ 4. Our culture provides many ways of escaping the experience of aloneness.

_____ 5. If we don't feel valuable as persons when we're alone, we probably won't feel valuable when we're with others.

_____ 6. Experiencing solitude is an essential way of rediscovering ourselves.

_____ 7. People who seek to be alone usually are escaping from intimacy with others.

_____ 8. It's very possible to be lonely in a crowd.

_____ 9. The popularity of encounter groups stems from our need to overcome our isolation and alienation.

_____ 10. The experience of loneliness can be a path to personal renewal and self-discovery.

_____ 11. We cannot escape loneliness completely.

_____ 12. Trying to avoid any experience of loneliness can lead to alienation from ourselves and others.

_____ 13. There is little value in experiencing loneliness.

_____ 14. We don't have much control over the circumstances that can cause loneliness; so, if we're lonely, there's not much we can do except suffer through it.

_____ 15. My childhood was a lonely period in my life.

_____ 16. My adolescent years were lonely ones for me.

_____ 17. Older people are necessarily lonely.

_____ 18. Older people, like people of any age, can choose how they will respond to lonely circumstances in life.

_____ 19. Loneliness is a problem for me in my life now.

_____ 20. I generally arrange for time alone so that I can gain some perspective on what is important and what is unimportant in my life.

Introduction

One of the greatest fears many people have is the fear of loneliness. Because we may associate the lonely periods in our lives with pain and struggle, we may think of loneliness only as a condition to be avoided

306

as much as possible. Furthermore, we may identify being alone with being lonely and actively avoid having time by ourselves or else fill such time with distractions and diversions. Paradoxically, out of fear of rejection and loneliness, we may even make ourselves needlessly lonely by refusing to reach out to others or by holding back parts of ourselves in our intimate relationships.

In this chapter, I encourage you to think of loneliness as a natural—and potentially valuable—part of human experience. I also encourage you to distinguish between being lonely and being alone. In a real sense, all of us are ultimately alone in the world, and appreciating our aloneness can actually enable us to enrich our experience of life. Moreover, we can use times of solitude to look within ourselves, renew our sense of ourselves as the centers of choice and direction in our lives, and learn to trust our inner resources instead of allowing circumstances or the expectations of others to determine the course of our lives. Finally, if we fundamentally accept our aloneness and recognize that no one can take away *all* our loneliness, we can deal more effectively with our experiences of loneliness and give ourselves to our projects and relationships out of our freedom instead of running to them out of our fear.

Our Ultimate Aloneness

With the existentialist thinkers, I believe that, ultimately, we are alone. Although the presence of others can surely enhance our lives, no one else can completely become us or share our unique worlds of feelings, thoughts, hopes, and memories. In addition, none of us knows when our loved ones may leave us or die, when we will no longer be able to involve ourselves in a cherished activity, or when the forest we love will be burned or cut down. We come into the world alone, and we will be alone again when the time comes to leave it.

This awareness of our ultimate aloneness—like the awareness of our freedom or of our mortality—can be frightening. Just as we may shrink from recognizing our freedom out of fear of the risks involved or resist thinking about our eventual death, so too we may avoid experiencing our ultimate aloneness. We may throw ourselves into relationships, activities, and diversions and depend on them to numb our sense of aloneness. Certainly, our society provides many distractions and escapes for those who choose to avoid the experience of aloneness. However, I believe that we cannot deny something we deeply feel to be true without becoming alienated from ourselves.

Perhaps we fear our aloneness because we identify it with extreme loneliness. I think it's important to recognize that experiencing our aloneness is not the same as being without friends or loved ones or pondering something depressing or morbid. On the contrary, it can be an invaluable and positive experience. Throughout this book, I have stressed the theme of *choice* and encouraged you to think about ways of directing your life according to your own inner standards, desires, values, and ethics. My premise has been that each of us is an individual, unique being and that whatever meanings we discover in our lives have their sources within our individual selves. This means, in part, that each of us creates a unique world by our own choices and experiences—a world that has never existed before and never will again. If we dare to experience our ultimate aloneness, we can strengthen our awareness of ourselves as the true centers of meaning and direction in our lives. In times of solitude, we can restore our perspective on life and return to our projects and relationships refreshed and renewed. By experiencing our aloneness, we can become more fully aware that, although nothing we cherish is permanent, it is our free choice that makes it valuable and unique. In these ways, our freedom and aloneness come together as the twin sources of meaning in our lives.

Escaping from Our Aloneness versus Confronting It

Just as we may look to others to make our choices for us, so we may become dependent on others for protection from fears of aloneness. Instead of confronting the fears we may have of being bored, empty, or lost if we are left to ourselves, we can allow these fears to determine the choices we make. In so doing, we risk becoming alienated from our inner selves and thus actually increasing our anxiety over aloneness.

Some of the ways in which we may try to escape the experience of aloneness include the following:

- We can busy ourselves in work and activities, so that we have little time to think or to reflect by ourselves.
- We can schedule every moment and overstructure our lives so that we have no opportunity to think about ourselves and what we are doing with our lives.
- We can surround ourselves with people and become absorbed in social functions, in the hope that we won't have to feel alone.
- We can try to numb ourselves with television, loud music, alcohol, or drugs.
- We can immerse ourselves in helping others and in our "responsibilities."

- We can eat compulsively, hoping that doing so will fill our inner emptiness and protect us from the pain of being alone.
- We can make ourselves slaves to routine, becoming machines that don't feel much of anything.
- We can find plenty of trivial things to occupy our attention so that we never really have to focus on ourselves.
- We can go to bars and other centers of activity, trying to lose ourselves in a crowd.

Most of us lead hectic lives in crowded, noisy environments. We are surrounded by entertainments and escapes. Paradoxically enough, in the midst of our congested cities and with all the activities available to us, we are often lonely because we are alienated from ourselves. The predicament of many people in our society is that of the alienated man described by the Josephsons in their book *Man Alone: Alienation in Modern Society:* "The alienated man is everyman and no man, drifting in a world that has little meaning for him and over which he exercises no power, a stranger to himself and to others" (Josephson & Josephson, 1962, p. 11).

If we want to get back in touch with ourselves, we can begin by looking at the ways in which we have learned to escape the fear of being alone. We can examine the values of our society and question whether they are contributing to our estrangement from ourselves and to our sense of isolation. We can ask whether the activities that fill our time actually satisfy us or whether they leave us hungry and discontented. I believe that we can begin to feel connected with ourselves and with others, but it may take an active effort on our part to resist the pressures of our lives and take the time to be with ourselves.

The Values of Loneliness and Solitude

Loneliness and solitude are different experiences, each of which has its own potential value. Loneliness generally results from certain situations that occur in our lives—the death of someone we love, the decision of another person to leave us for someone else, a move to a new city, a long stay in a hospital. Loneliness can occur when we feel set apart in some way from everyone around us. And sometimes feelings of loneliness are simply an indication of the extent to which we've failed to listen to ourselves and our own feelings. However it occurs, loneliness is generally something that happens to us, rather than something we choose to experience; but we *can* choose the attitude we take toward it. If we allow ourselves to experience our loneliness, even if it is painful, we may be surprised to find within ourselves the sources of strength and creativity.

Unlike loneliness, solitude is something that we often choose for ourselves. In solitude, we make the time to be with ourselves, to discover who we are, and to renew ourselves. In her beautiful and poetic book, *Gift from the Sea*, Anne Morrow Lindbergh (1975) describes her own need to get away by herself in order to find her center, simplify her life, and nourish herself so that she can give to others again. She describes how her busy life, with its many and conflicting demands, had fragmented her, so that she felt "the spring is dry, and the well is empty" (p. 47).[1] Through solitude, she found replenishment and became reacquainted with herself:

> When one is a stranger to oneself then one is estranged from others too. If one is out of touch with oneself, then one cannot touch others. . . . Only when one is connected to one's own core is one connected to others. . . . For me, the core, the inner spring, can best be refound through solitude [pp. 43–44].

If we don't take time for ourselves but instead fill our lives with activities and projects, we run the risk of losing a sense of centeredness. As Lindbergh puts it, "Instead of stilling the center, the axis of the wheel, we add more centrifugal activities to our lives—which tend to throw us off balance" (1975, p. 51). Her own solitude taught her that she must remind herself to be alone each day, even for a few minutes, in order to keep a sense of herself and give of herself to others. I like the way she expressed this thought in words addressed to a seashell she took with her from an island where she had spent some time alone:

> You will remind me that I must try to be alone for part of each year, even a week or a few days; and for part of each day, even for an hour or for a few minutes, in order to keep my core, my center, my island-quality. You will remind me that unless I keep the island-quality intact somewhere within me, I will have little to give my husband, my children, my friends or the world at large [p. 57].

In much the same way as Lindbergh describes solitude as a way of discovering her core and putting her life in perspective, Clark Moustakas

[1]This and all other quotations from this source from *Gift from the Sea*, by A. M. Lindbergh. Copyright 1955 by Pantheon Books, a Division of Random House, Inc.

(1977) relates that a critical turning point in his life occurred when he discovered that loneliness could be the basis for a creative experience. He came to see that his personal growth and changed relationships with others were related to his feelings of loneliness. Accepting himself as a lonely person gave him the courage to face aspects of himself that he had never dared to face before and taught him the value of listening to his inner self. For him, solitude became an antidote to loneliness. He writes: "In times of loneliness, my way back to life with others required that I stop listening to others, that I cut myself off from others and deliberately go off alone, to a place of isolation" (p. 109). In doing so, Moustakas became aware of how he had forsaken himself and of the importance of returning to himself. This process of finding himself led him to find new ways of relating to others: "In solitude, silent awareness and self-dialogues often quickly restored me to myself, and I was filled

with new energy and the desire to renew my life with others in real ways" (p. 109).

Solitude can thus provide us with the opportunity to sort out our lives and gain a sense of perspective. It can give us time to ask significant questions, such as: How much have I become a stranger to myself? Have I been listening to myself, or have I been distracted and overstimulated by a busy life? Am I aware of my sense experiences, or have I been too involved in doing things to be aware of them?

One way to become aware of how much experience you ordinarily shut out is to do the following simple exercise. Choose a relatively quiet place where you can be alone. Close your eyes. Listen carefully to all the sounds about you. What are you aware of hearing? Do you hear sounds you usually don't hear? Become aware of smells. Become aware of touch. Try to experience all your senses. How much do you hear, feel, smell, and see that you ordinarily miss because of the hectic pace of your life?

Another value of taking time to be alone is that solitude can help us find new purpose and meaning when life begins to lose its vitality. As Moustakas (1975) says in *The Touch of Loneliness*, we can contemplate life and discover its meaning for us by experiencing the depths of our own being when the external world fails to alleviate our inner suffering or satisfy our hunger. When life seems empty, we can renew ourselves by taking time alone to look within for our answers, instead of to others. We can realize new dimensions of ourselves and examine the patterns that may be causing our lives to be empty, or at least not as rich as they might be. In Moustakas's words, "In such times it is essential that the person look within, detached and isolated, that he or she be open to the unknown resources of energy in life and in the universe" (1975, p. 105). According to Moustakas, in order to experience this self-discovery and self-renewal we must be willing to accept that we are basically alone in our lives, even though we may be comforted by the presence of others. This experience of our aloneness can be a source of power, insight, and creativity.

Many of us fail to experience solitude because we allow our lives to become more and more frantic and complicated. Unless we make a conscious effort to be alone, we may find that days and weeks go by without our having the chance to be with ourselves. Moreover, we may fear that we will alienate others if we ask for private time, so we alienate ourselves instead. Perhaps we fear that others will think us odd if we express a need to be alone. Indeed, others may sometimes fail to understand our need for solitude and try to bring us into the crowd or "cheer us up."

People who are close to us may feel vaguely threatened, as if our need for time alone somehow reflected on our affection for them. Perhaps their own fears of being left alone will lead them to try to keep us from taking time away from them. Thus, claiming what we need and want for ourselves can involve a certain risk; however, if we fail to take that risk, we give up the very thing solitude could provide—a sense of self-direction and autonomy.

I think that most of us need to remind ourselves that we can tolerate only so much intensity with others and that ignoring our need for distance can breed resentment. For instance, a mother and father who are constantly with each other and with their children may not be doing a service either to their children or to themselves. Eventually they are likely to resent their "obligations." Unless they take time out, they may be there bodily and yet not be fully present to each other or to their children.

In summary, I hope that you will welcome time alone. Once we fully accept it, our aloneness can become the source of our strength and the foundation of our relatedness to others. Taking time to *be* alone gives us the opportunity to think, plan, imagine, and dream. It allows us to listen to ourselves and to become sensitive to what we are experiencing. In solitude we can come to appreciate anew both our separateness from, and our relatedness to, the important people and projects in our lives.

Time Out for Personal Reflection

1. *Do you try to escape from your aloneness? In what ways? Check any of the following statements that you think apply to you.*

_____   *I bury myself in work.*

_____   *I constantly seek to be with others.*

_____   *I drink excessively or take drugs.*

_____   *I schedule every moment so that I'll have very little time to think about myself.*

_____   *I attempt to avoid my troubles by watching television or listening to loud music.*

_____   *I eat compulsively.*

_____   *I sleep excessively to avoid the stresses in my life.*

_____   *I become overly concerned with helping others.*

_____   *I rarely think about anything if I can help it; I concentrate on playing and having fun.*

List other specific ways in which you sometimes try to avoid experiencing your aloneness:

_____

_____

_____

_____

2. Would you like to change any of the patterns you've just identified? If so, what are they? What might you do to change them?

_____

_____

_____

_____

3. Would you be willing to devote even ten minutes a day to being alone, without distractions? During these periods you might record in your journal the date, the time, and what you think about. Right now, take the time to list some things that you would like to do or reflect on when you're alone.

_____

_____

_____

_____

4. Do you agree or disagree with the idea that we are ultimately alone in the world? Why?

_____

_____

_____

5. Do you see time spent alone as being valuable to you? If so, in what ways?

_____

_____

_____

6. *Have you experienced periods of creative solitude? If so, what were some of the positive aspects of these experiences?*

_____

_____

_____

7. *List a few of the major decisions you've made in your life. Did you make these decisions when you were alone or when you were with others?*

_____

_____

_____

_____

A journal suggestion: If you find it difficult to be alone, without distractions, for more than a few minutes at a time, try being alone for a little longer than you're generally comfortable with. During this time, you might simply let your thoughts wander freely, without hanging on to one line of thinking. In your journal, describe what this experience is like for you.

Loneliness and Life Stages

How we deal with feelings of loneliness can depend to a great extent on our lonely experiences in childhood and adolescence. Later in life, we may feel that loneliness has no place or that we can and should be able to avoid it. It's important to reflect on our past experiences, because they are often the basis of our present feelings about loneliness. In addition, we may fear loneliness less if we recognize that it is a natural part of living in every stage of life. Once we have accepted our ultimate aloneness and the likelihood that we will feel lonely at many points in our lives, we may be better able to take responsibility for our own loneliness and recognize ways in which we may be contributing to it.

Loneliness and Childhood

Reliving some of our childhood experiences of loneliness can help us come to grips with present fears about being alone or lonely. The following are some typical memories of lonely periods that people I've worked with in therapy have relived:

- A woman recalls the time her parents were fighting in the bedroom and she heard them screaming and yelling. She was sure that they would divorce, and in many ways she felt responsible. She remembers living in continual fear that she would be deserted.
- A man recalls attempting to give a speech in the sixth grade. He stuttered over certain words, and children in the class began to laugh at him. Afterwards, he developed extreme self-consciousness in regard to his speech, and he long remembered the hurt he had experienced.
- A Black man recalls how excluded he felt in his all-White elementary school, and how the other children would talk about him in derisive ways. As an adult, he can still cry over these memories.
- A woman recalls the fright she felt as a small child when her uncle made sexual advances toward her. Although she didn't really understand what was happening, she remembers the terrible loneliness of feeling that she couldn't tell her parents for fear of what they would do.
- A man recalls the boyhood loneliness of feeling that he was continually failing at everything he tried. To this day, he resists undertaking a task unless he is sure he can handle it, for fear of rekindling those old lonely feelings.
- A woman vividly remembers being in the hospital as a small child for an operation. She remembers the loneliness of not knowing what was going on or whether she would be able to leave the hospital. Since no one talked with her or allowed her to talk out her fears, she was all alone with them.

As we try to relive these experiences, we should remember that children do not live in a logical, well-ordered world. Our childhood fears may have been greatly exaggerated, and the feeling of fright may remain with us even though we may now think of it as irrational. Unfortunately, being told by adults that we were foolish for having such fears may only have increased our loneliness while doing nothing to lessen the fears themselves.

At this point, you may wonder "Why go back and recall childhood pain and loneliness? Why not just let it be a thing of the past?" I feel convinced that we need to reexperience some of the pain we felt as children to see whether we are still carrying it around with us now. We can also look at some of the decisions we made during these times of extreme loneliness and ask whether these decisions are still appropriate.

Frequently, strategies we adopted as children remain with us into adulthood, when they are no longer appropriate. For instance, suppose that your family moved to a strange city when you were 7 years old and that you had to go to a new school. Kids at the new school laughed at you, and you lived through several months of anguish. You felt desperately alone in the world. During this time you decided to keep your feelings to yourself and build a wall around yourself so that others couldn't hurt you. Although this experience is now long past, you still defend yourself in the same way, because you haven't *really* made a new decision to open up and trust some people. In this way, old fears of loneliness might contribute to a real loneliness in the present. If you allow yourself to experience your grief and work it through, emotionally as well as intellectually, you can overcome past pain and create new choices for yourself.

Time Out for Personal Reflection

Take some time to decide whether you're willing to recall and relive a childhood experience of loneliness. If so, try to recapture the experience in as much detail as you can, reliving it in fantasy. Then reflect on the experience, using the following questions as a starting point.

1. *Describe in a few words the most lonely experience you recall having as a child.*

    _____

    _____

    _____

2. *How do you think the experience affected you* then?

    _____

    _____

3. *How do you think the experience may still affect you* now?

    _____

    _____

Journal suggestions: Consider elaborating on this exercise in your journal. Here are a few questions you might reflect on: How did you cope with your loneliness as a child? How has this influenced the way you deal with loneliness in your life now? If you could go back and put a new ending on your most lonely childhood experience, what would it be? You might also think about times in your childhood when you enjoyed being alone. Write some notes to yourself about what these experiences were like for you. Where did you like to spend time alone? What did you enjoy doing by yourself? What positive aspects of these times do you recall?

Loneliness and Adolescence

For many people, loneliness and adolescence are practically synonymous. Adolescents often feel that they are all alone in their world, that they are the first ones to have the feelings they do, and that in some real way they are separated from others by some abnormality. Bodily changes and impulses are alone sufficient to bring about a sense of perplexity and loneliness, but there are other stresses to be undergone as well. Adolescents are developing a sense of identity. They strive to be successful yet fear failure. They want to be accepted and liked, but they fear rejection, ridicule, or exclusion by their peers. They are curious about sex yet often frightened to experiment or constrained from doing so. Most adolescents know the feeling of being lonely in a crowd or among friends, and many of the young people I've worked with report the loneliness they feel as a result of keeping their own convictions private and adopting the views and morals of their group, out of fear of being ostracized. Conformity can bring acceptance, and the price of nonconformity can be steep for those who have the courage to decide for themselves how they will think and behave.

As you recall your adolescent years—and, in particular, the areas of your life that were marked by loneliness—you might reflect on the following questions:

· Did I feel included in a social group? Or did I sit on the sidelines, afraid of being included and wishing for it at the same time?
· Was there at least one person whom I felt I could talk to—one who really heard me, so that I didn't feel desperately alone?
· What experience stands out as one of the most lonely times during these years? How did I cope with my loneliness?
· Did I experience a sense of confusion concerning who I was and what I wanted to be as a person? How did I deal with my confusion? Who or what helped me during this time?

·   How did I feel about my own worth and value? Did I believe that I had anything of value to offer anyone or that anyone would find me worth being with?

As you reflect on your adolescence, add your own questions to the list I've suggested. Then try to discover some of the ways in which the person you now are is a result of your lonely experiences as an adolescent. Do you shrink from competition for fear of failure? In social situations, are you afraid of being left out? Do you feel some of the isolation you did then? If so, how do you deal with it?

Time Out for Personal Reflection

1. *To help you recollect your adolescent years, reflect on the following pairs of statements, and check the one that best fits your experience. If neither response fits you, you can write in your own on the line provided.*

_____   a. *I felt included in a social group.*
_____   *I generally sat on the sidelines and feared being included, while wishing for it at the same time.*

_____

_____   b. *There was at least one person whom I felt I could talk to—someone who really heard me and made me feel less alone.*
_____   *I generally felt that there was nobody who really understood or listened to me.*

_____

_____   c. *I felt little value or worth as a person.*
_____   *I believed that I had value and that others valued me and wanted to be with me.*

_____

2. *Describe the most lonely experience of your adolescent years.*

_____

_____

_____

_____

3. How did you cope with the loneliness you've just described?

_____

_____

_____

_____

4. What effect do you think the experience you've described has on you today?

_____

_____

_____

_____

5. Recall some times as an adolescent when you chose to be alone. What were these times like for you? Were there times when you enjoyed being alone?

_____

_____

_____

_____

Loneliness and Young Adulthood

In our young-adult years, we are engaged in experimenting with ways of being and in establishing life-styles that may remain with us for many years. We may be struggling with the question of what to do with our lives, what intimate relationships we want to establish, and how we will chart our futures. Dealing with all the choices that face us in this time of life can be a lonely process.

How we come to terms with our own aloneness at this time can have significant effects on the choices we make—choices that, in turn, may determine the course of our lives for years to come. For instance, if we haven't learned to listen to ourselves and to depend on our own inner resources, we might succumb to the pressure to choose a relationship or a career before we're really prepared to do so, or we might look to our projects or partners for the sense of identity that we ultimately can find only in ourselves. Alternatively, we may feel lonely and establish patterns that only increase our loneliness. This last possibility is well illustrated by the case of Saul.

Saul was in his early twenties when he attended college. He claimed that his chief problem was his isolation, yet he rarely reached out to others. His general manner seemed to say "Keep away." Although he was enrolled in a small, informal class in self-awareness and personal growth, he quickly left after each session, depriving himself of the chance to make contact with anyone.

One day, as I was walking across the campus, I saw Saul sitting alone in a secluded spot, while many students were congregated on the lawn, enjoying the beautiful spring weather. Here was a chance for him to do something about his separation from others; instead, he chose to seclude himself. He continually told himself that others didn't like him and, sadly, made his prophecy self-fulfilling by his own behavior. He made himself unapproachable and, in many ways, the kind of person people would avoid.

In this time of life, we have the chance to decide on ways of being toward ourselves and others as well as on our vocations and future plans. If you feel lonely on the campus, I'd like to challenge you to ask yourself what *you* are doing and can do about your own loneliness. Do you decide in advance that the other students and instructors want to keep to themselves? Do you assume that there already are well-established cliques to which you cannot belong? Do you expect others to reach out to you, even though you don't initiate contacts yourself? What fears might be holding you back? Where do they seem to come from? Are past experiences of loneliness or rejection determining the choices you make now?

Often we create unnecessary loneliness for ourselves by our own behavior. If we sit back and wait for others to come to us, we give them the power to make us lonely. As we learn to take responsibility for ourselves in young adulthood, one area we can work on is taking responsibility for our own loneliness and creating new choices for ourselves.

Loneliness and Middle Age

Many changes occur during middle age that may result in new feelings of loneliness. Although we may not be free to choose some of the things that occur at this time in our lives, we *are* free to choose how we relate to these events. Among the possible changes and crises of middle age are the following:

- Our spouses may grow tired of living with us and decide to leave. If so, we must decide how we will respond to this situation. Will we blame ourselves and become absorbed in self-hate? Will we refuse to see any of our own responsibility for the breakup and simply blame the other person? Will we decide never to trust anyone again? Will we mourn our loss and, after a period of grieving, actively look for another person to live with?

- Our lives may not turn out the way we had planned. We may not have enjoyed the success we'd hoped for, we may feel disenchanted with our work, or we may feel that we passed up many fine opportunities earlier. But the key point is what we can do about our lives *now*. What choices will we make in light of this reality? Will we slip into hopelessness and berate ourselves endlessly about what we could have done and should have done? Will we allow ourselves to stay trapped in meaningless work and empty relationships, or will we look for positive options for change?

- Our children may leave home, and with this change we may experience emptiness and a sense of loss. If so, what will we do about this transition? Will we attempt to hang on? Can we let go and create a new life with new meaning? Will our will to live leave with our children? Will we look back with regret at all that we could have done differently, or will we choose to look ahead to the kind of life we want to create for ourselves now that we don't have the responsibilities of parenthood?

These are just a few of the changes that many of us confront during the middle years of living. Although we may feel that events are not in our control, we can still choose the ways in which we respond to these life situations. To illustrate, I'd like to present a brief example that reflects the loneliness many people experience after a divorce and show how the two persons involved made different decisions about how to deal with their loneliness.

Amy and Gary were married for over 20 years before their recent divorce, and they have three children in their teens. Amy is 43; Gary is 41. Although they have both experienced a good deal of loneliness since their divorce, they have chosen different attitudes toward their loneliness. For his part, Gary felt resentful at first and believed that somehow they could have stayed together if only Amy had changed her attitude. He lives alone in a small apartment and sees his teenagers on weekends. He interprets the divorce as a personal failure, and he still feels a mixture of guilt and resentment. He hates to come home to an empty apartment, with no one to talk to and no one to share his life with. In some ways, he has decided not to cultivate other relationships, because he still bears the scars of his "first failure." He wonders whether women would find him interesting, and he fears that it's too late to begin a new life with someone else.

Gary declines most of his friends' invitations, interpreting their concern as pity. He says that at times he feels like climbing the walls, that he sometimes wakes up at night in a cold sweat and feels real pangs of abandonment and loneliness. He attempts to numb his lonely feelings by burying himself in his work, but he cannot rid himself of the ache of loneliness. Gary seems to have decided on some level not to let go of his isolation. He has convinced himself that it isn't really possible for him to develop a new relationship. His own attitude limits his options, because he has set up a self-fulfilling prophecy: he convinces himself that another woman would not want to share time with him, and, as a consequence, others pick up the messages that he is sending out about himself.

For her part, Amy had many ambivalent feelings about divorcing. After the divorce, she experienced feelings of panic and aloneness as she faced the prospect of rearing her children and managing the home on her own. She wondered whether she could meet her responsibilities and still have time for any social life for herself. She wondered whether men would be interested in her, particularly in light of the fact that she had three teenagers. She anguished over such questions as "Will I be able to have another life with someone else?" "Do I want to live alone?" "Can I take care of my emotional needs and still provide for the family?" Unlike Gary, Amy decided to date several people—when she felt like it, and because she felt like it. At first she was pressured by her family to find a man and settle down. She decided, however, to resist this pressure, and she has chosen to remain single for the time being. She intends to develop a long-term relationship only if she feels it is what she wants after she has had time to live alone. Although she is lonely at times, she doesn't feel trapped and resists being a victim of her lonely feelings.

Experiences like those of Gary and Amy are very common among middle-aged people. Many find themselves having to cope with feelings of isolation and abandonment after a divorce. Some, like Gary, may feel panic and either retreat from people or quickly run into a new relationship to avoid the pain of separation. If they don't confront their fears and their pain, they may be controlled by their fear of being left alone for the rest of their lives. Others, like Amy, may go through a similar period of loneliness after a divorce, yet refuse to be controlled by a fear of living alone. Although they might want a long-term relationship again some day, they avoid rushing impulsively into a new relationship in order to avoid any feelings of pain or loneliness.

Loneliness and the Later Years

Our society emphasizes productivity, youth, beauty, power, and vitality. As we age, we may lose some of our vitality and sense of power or attractiveness. Many people face a real crisis when they reach retirement, for they feel that they're being put out to pasture—that they aren't needed any more and that their lives are really over. Loneliness and hopelessness are experienced by anyone who feels that there is little to look forward to or that he or she has no vital place in society, and such feelings are particularly common among older adults.

The loneliness of the later years can be accentuated by the losses that come with age. There can be some loss of sight, hearing, memory, and strength. Older people may lose their jobs, hobbies, friends, and loved ones. A particularly difficult loss is the loss of a spouse with whom one has been close for many years. In the face of such losses, a person may ultimately ask what reason remains for living. It may be no coincidence that many old people die soon after their spouses die or shortly after their retirement. However, the pangs of aloneness or the feelings that life is futile reflect a drastic loss of meaning rather than an essential part of growing old. Viktor Frankl has written about the "will to meaning" as a key determinant of a person's desire to live. He noted that many of the inmates in a Nazi concentration camp kept themselves alive by looking forward to the prospect of being released and reunited with their families. Many of those who lost hope simply gave up and died, regardless of their age.

At least until recently, our society has compounded the elderly person's loss of meaning by grossly neglecting the aged population. The number of institutions and convalescent homes in which old people are often left to vegetate testifies to this neglect. It's hard to imagine a more lonely existence than the one many of these people are compelled to suffer.

Despite this societal neglect, those who specialize in the study of aging often make the point that, if we have led rich lives in early adulthood, we have a good chance of finding richness in our later years. Certainly, if we have learned to find direction from within ourselves, we will be better equipped to deal with the changes aging brings. A few years ago, my wife and I had the good fortune to meet an exceptional man, Dr. Ewald Schnitzer, who retired from the University of California at Los Angeles in 1973 and moved to Idyllwild—a place that he considers his last and happiest home. For me, he provides an outstanding model of the way I hope I face my own old age.

Schnitzer lives alone by preference and continues to find excitement and meaning in his life in art, philosophy, music, history, hiking, writing, and traveling. He believes that his entire life has prepared him well for his later years. He has learned to be content when he is alone, he finds pleasure in the company of animals and nature, and he enjoys many memories of his rich experiences. I respect the way in which he can live fully now, without dreading the future. This spirit of being fully alive is well expressed in his book *Looking In:* "It would be painful should frailty prevent me from climbing mountains. Yet, when that time comes, I hope I find serenity in wandering through valleys, looking at the realm of distant summits not with ambition but with loving memories (Schnitzer, 1977, p. 88).[2]

Schnitzer is an example of someone who can accept the fact of his aging yet recognize that each stage of life brings its unique challenges and potentialities for creating a meaningful existence. This is how he expresses this thought:

[2]This and all other quotations from this source from *Looking In*, by E. W. Schnitzer. Copyright 1977. Reprinted by permission.

I am writing this as I stand on the threshold of old age. Like everybody at this stage I have to face the fact of my bodily decline. I am saying this with a tinge of sadness but without a trace of despair. For it has always seemed to me that each age has its own possibilities and challenges, and I have often taken heart from this remark of Roger Fry's: "It is a wonderful thing to recognize the advanced age of a person less by the infirmity of his body than by the maturity of his soul" [p. 87].

I'd like to conclude this discussion of the later years—and, in a sense, this entire chapter on loneliness and solitude—by returning to the example of Anne Morrow Lindbergh. In her later years, her lifelong courage in facing aloneness enabled her to find new and rich meaning in her life. I was extremely impressed with this woman when I first read her book *Gift from the Sea*, but my respect increased when I read the "Afterword" in the book's 20th-anniversary edition. There, she looks back at the time when she originally wrote the book and notes that she was then deeply involved in family life. Since that time, her children have left and established their own lives. She describes how a most uncomfortable stage followed her middle years—one that she hadn't anticipated when she wrote the book. She writes that she went from the "oyster-bed" stage of taking care of a family to the "abandoned-shell" stage of later life. This is how she describes the essence of the "abandoned-shell" stage:

> Plenty of solitude, and a sudden panic at how to fill it, characterized this period. With me, it was not a question of simply filling up the space or the time. I had many activities and even a well-established vocation to pursue. But when a mother is left, the lone hub of a wheel, with no other lives revolving around her, she faces a total reorientation. It takes time to re-find the center of gravity [Lindbergh, 1975, p. 134].

In this stage, she did make choices to come to terms with herself and create a new role for herself. She points out that all the exploration she did earlier in life paid off when she reached the "abandoned-shell" stage. Here again, earlier choices affect current ones.

Before her husband, Charles, died in 1974, Anne had looked forward to retiring with him on the Hawaiian island of Maui. His death changed her life abruptly but did not bring it to an end. Its continuity was preserved in part by the presence of her five children and twelve grandchildren; moreover, she continued to involve herself in her own writing and in the preparation of her husband's papers for publication. Here is a fine example of a woman who has encountered her share of loneliness and learned to renew herself by actively choosing a positive stance toward life.

Time Out for Personal Reflection

Complete the following sentences by writing down the first response that comes to mind.

1. *The most lonely time in my life was when* _____

   _____

2. *I usually deal with my loneliness by* _____

3. *I escape from loneliness by* _____

4. *If I were to be left and abandoned by all those who love me,* ____

   _____

5. *One value I see in experiencing loneliness is* _____

   _____

6. *My greatest fear of loneliness is* _____

7. *I have felt lonely in a crowd when* _____

   _____

8. *When I'm with a person who is lonely,* _____

   _____

9. *For me, being with others* _____

   _____

10. *I feel most lonely when* _____

11. *The thought of living alone the rest of my life* _____

   _____

Chapter Summary

In this chapter, I've suggested that experiencing loneliness is part of being human. We can grow from such experience if we understand it and use it to renew our sense of ourselves. Moreover, we don't have to remain victimized by early decisions that we made as a result of past loneliness. Some key points are:

1. Ultimately, we all are alone.
2. We can choose to face our aloneness and deal with it creatively, or we can choose to try to escape from it.
3. Most of us have experienced loneliness during our childhood and adolescent years, and these experiences can have a significant influence on our present attitudes, behavior, and relationships.
4. Times of solitude can give us an invaluable opportunity to gain perspective on the direction and meaning of our lives.
5. We have some choice concerning whether we will feel lonely or whether we will feel in touch with others. We can design our activities so that we reject others before they can reject us, or we can risk making contact with them.

List some other points from this chapter that were significant for you and that you would like to remember.

_____

_____

_____

_____

_____

Activities and Exercises

1. Allocate some time each day in which to be alone and reflect on anything you wish. Note down in your journal the thoughts and feelings that occur to you during your time alone.
2. If you have feelings of loneliness when you think about a certain person who has been or is now significant to you, write a letter to that person expressing all the things you're feeling (you don't have to mail the letter). For instance, tell that person how you miss him or her or write about your sadness, your resentment, or your desire for more closeness.

3. Imagine that you are the person you've written your letter to, and write a reply to yourself. What do you imagine that person would say to you if he or she received your letter? What do you fear (and what do you wish) he or she would say?

4. If you sometimes feel lonely and left out, you might try some specific experiments for a week or so. For example, if you feel isolated in most of your classes, why not make it a point to get to class early and initiate contact with a fellow student? If you feel anxious about taking such a step, try doing it in fantasy. What are your fears? What is the worst thing you can imagine might happen? Record your impressions in your journal. If you decide to try reaching out to other people, record what the experience is like for you in your journal.

5. Think about the person who means the most to you. Now let yourself imagine that this person decides to leave you. Imagine what that would be like for you—what you might feel, say, and do. How do you think his or her leaving would affect you?

6. Recall some periods of loneliness in your life. Select important situations in which you experienced loneliness, and spend some time recalling the details of each situation and reflecting on the meaning each of these experiences has had for you. Now you might do two things:

   a. Write down your reflections in your journal. How do you think your past experiences of loneliness affect you now?

   b. Select a friend or a person you'd like to trust more, and share this experience of loneliness.

7. Many people rarely make time exclusively for themselves. If you'd like to have time to yourself but just haven't gotten around to arranging it, consider going to a place you haven't been to before or to the beach, desert, or mountains. Reserve a weekend just for yourself; if this seems too much, then spend a day completely alone. The important thing is to remove yourself from your everyday routine and just be with yourself without external distractions.

8. Try spending a day or part of a day in a place where you can observe and experience lonely people. You might spend some time near a busy downtown intersection, in a park where old people congregate, or in a large shopping center. Try to pay attention to expressions of loneliness, alienation, and isolation. How do people seem to be dealing with their loneliness? Later, you might discuss your observations in class.

9 Imagine yourself living in a typical rest home—without any of your possessions, cut off from your family and friends, and unable to do the things you now do. Reflect on what this experience would be like for you; then write down some of your reactions in your journal.

10. Read a book or two on meditation and finding centeredness within yourself. Try doing some of the exercises you come across in these books.

Suggested Readings

Josephson, E., & Josephson, M. (Eds.). *Man Alone: Alienation in Modern Society.* New York: Dell, 1962. This is a book of articles dealing with the theme that the contemporary person—alienated from nature, self, and others—finds it difficult to achieve a sense of identity and relatedness.

Lindbergh, A. *Gift from the Sea.* New York: Pantheon, 1955, 1975. Although this book is over 25 years old, it is still timely for both women and men as a catalyst for thinking about the need for solitude. It is a deep, simply written, and poetic book. The recent edition contains an afterword about the author's life during the ensuing 20 years.

Moustakas, C. *Loneliness.* Englewood Cliffs, N.J.: Prentice-Hall (Spectrum), 1961. In this classic book the central message is that loneliness is an experience that enables us to realize a deeper meaning in our lives.

Moustakas, C. *Loneliness and Love.* Englewood Cliffs, N.J.: Prentice-Hall (Spectrum), 1972. This insightful book offers a unique approach to the positive dimensions of loneliness and emphasizes individuality, personal honesty, communication, and love in relation to oneself.

Moustakas, C. *The Touch of Loneliness.* Englewood Cliffs, N.J.: Prentice-Hall (Spectrum), 1975. This book contains many letters by the author and by people who have written accounts of their own loneliness.

Moustakas, C. *Turning Points.* Englewood Cliffs, N.J.: Prentice-Hall (Spectrum), 1977. In this book, Moustakas deals with the uncertainty associated with the various transitions in our lives. Its theme is that, by choosing to face these turning points, we can find strength within ourselves and reaffirm our existence.

Schnitzer, E. *Looking In.* Idyllwild, Calif.: Strawberry Valley Press, 1977. This is an inspirational book of essays on such topics as living creatively with solitude and finding meaning in life through travels and encounters with nature.

Sheehy, G. *Passages: Predictable Crises of Adult Life.* New York: Bantam, 1976. A number of cases described by Sheehy illustrate the loneliness many people experience as they make the passage from one life stage to the next. Some excellent cases depict the challenge of facing loneliness and aloneness and dealing with them creatively.

Stevens, J. *Awareness: Exploring, Experimenting, and Experiencing.* Moab, Utah: Real People Press, 1971. This book discusses how we can deepen and expand our awareness. It contains many exercises and experiments that you can do by yourself or with another person.

Yalom, I. D. *Existential Psychotherapy.* New York: Basic Books, 1980. Chapters 8 and 9 deal with the concept of existential isolation and the implications of our basic aloneness for the practice of psychotherapy. These chapters give a clear picture of the loneliness of being one's own parent.

Death and Loss

Prechapter Self-Inventory

For each statement, indicate the response that most closely identifies your beliefs and attitudes. Use this code: 5 = I *strongly agree* with this statement; 4 = I *agree* in most respects; 3 = I am *undecided*; 2 = I *disagree* in most respects; 1 = I *strongly disagree*.

_____ 1. If I'm afraid of dying, then to some degree I'm afraid of living.

_____ 2. I have some irrational fears concerning death.

_____ 3. The fact that I will die makes me take the present moment seriously.

_____ 4. Our culture tends to deny or avoid the reality of death.

_____ 5. When I think about dying, I feel that I'm ultimately alone in life.

_____ 6. If I had a terminal illness, I'd want to know how much time I had left to live, so that I could decide how to spend it.

_____ 7. Because of the possibility of losing those I love, I don't allow myself to get too close to others.

_____ 8. It's best to avoid discussing death and dying with a person who is in danger of death.

_____ 9. I can't really live a meaningful life unless I think about and accept the fact of my eventual death.

_____ 10. Believing in an afterlife is a way of denying the finality of death.

_____ 11. If I live with dignity, I'll be able to die with dignity.

_____ 12. Just as many parents are reluctant to educate their children about sex, many parents are reluctant to educate their children about death.

_____ 13. It's best to take a nonchalant attitude toward death, since thinking seriously about it only makes us morbid.

_____ 14. One of my greatest fears of death is the fear of the unknown.

_____ 15. I've had experiences of loss in my life that in some ways were like the experience of dying.

_____ 16. In a way, the experience of a divorce or separation can be like the experience of dying.

_____ 17. There are some ways in which I'm not really alive emotionally.

_____ 18. I'm not especially afraid of dying.

_____ 19. It's important to allow ourselves to fully mourn the deaths of loved ones and other losses.

_____ 20. I fear the deaths of those I love more than I do my own.

Introduction

In this chapter, I encourage you to look at your attitudes and beliefs about your own death, the deaths of those you love, and other forms of significant loss Although the topic of this chapter might seem to be morbid or depressing, I strongly believe that an honest understanding and acceptance of death and loss can be the groundwork of a rich and meaningful life. If we fully accept that we have only a limited time in which to live, we can make choices that will make the most of the time we have.

I also ask you to consider the notion of death in a broader perspective and to raise such questions as: What parts of me aren't as alive as they might be? In what emotional ways am I dead or dying? What will I do with my awareness of the ways in which I'm not fully alive? Finally, I discuss the importance of fully experiencing our grief when we suffer serious losses.

This discussion of death and loss has an important connection with the themes of the preceding chapter on loneliness and solitude. When we emotionally accept the reality of our eventual death, we experience our ultimate aloneness. I believe that this awareness of our mortality and aloneness helps us to realize that our actions do count, that we do have choices concerning how we live our lives, and that we must accept the final responsibility for how well we are living.

This chapter is also a bridge to the next chapter, in which I discuss meaning and values. The awareness of death is a catalyst of the human search for meaning in life. Our knowledge that we will die can encourage us to take a careful and honest look at how we are living now. With a realistic awareness of death, we can ask ourselves whether we're living by values that create a meaningful existence; if not, we have the time and opportunity to change our way of living.

Our Fears of Death

Although a realistic fear of death seems to be a healthy and inevitable part of living, it's possible to become so obsessed with the fear of our own death or of the deaths of those we love that we can't really enjoy living. We may be afraid of really getting involved with life, of allowing ourselves to care for others, or of building hopes for the future. On the other hand, we may numb ourselves to the reality of death by telling ourselves there's no point in thinking about it—"When it comes, it comes." Neither of these attitudes permits us to realistically confront death and its meaning.

Often, a fear of death goes hand in hand with a fear of life. If we're excessively fearful of death, we'll probably be fearful of investing ourselves in life as well, since nothing we cherish is permanent. By the same token, if we involve ourselves in the present moment as fully as possible, it's unlikely that we'll be obsessed with the thought of life's end.

In *Overcoming the Fear of Death*, Gordon (1972) writes about our refusal to face death because of our fears of it. He contends that we tend to view death as a remote possibility and that we unconsciously repress our fears as well as consciously try to forget about death. The following statement from his book has much meaning for me:

> Most of us are afraid to contemplate our own ending; and when anything reminds us that we too shall die, we flee and turn our thoughts to happier matters. The thought of our finitude and ephemerality is so frightening that we run away from this basic fact of existence, consciously and unconsciously, and proceed through life as though we shall endure forever [p. 13].

There are many aspects of death that we may be fearful of, some of which include leaving behind those we love, losing ourselves, encountering the unknown, coping with the humiliation and indignity of a painful or long dying, losing time in which we could be doing the things we most want to finish, and growing distant in the memories of others. For many people, it's not so much death itself as it is the experience of dying that arouses fears. Here, too, it is well to ask what our fears are really about and to confront them honestly, as Schnitzer (1977) does in *Looking In:*

> Death is feared because it seems to condemn us to utter loneliness and to the loss of identity. But consciousness also vanishes, and what is there to be feared when it is totally gone? "To fear death means pretending to know what we don't know," Plato once said. What we are afraid of is not death but dying, the phase that confronts us with the loss of our world and its familiar beings—the only home we know. And that indeed must be painful. There may be agony, both physical and mental. At that last stage we will be much in need of braveness [p. 89].

In his powerful book, *Facing Death*, Kavanaugh (1972) describes the fears of a woman who was dying of cancer. She related that the fears she was actually experiencing were not nearly so terrible as the ones she had expected to feel and that any attempt to escape her fears was more

painful than the fears themselves. She found that those friends who were
not busy running from their own fears were the people who could be the
most help and comfort to her as she neared death.

If we can honestly confront our fears of death, we have a chance to
work on changing the quality of our lives and to make real changes in

our relationships with others and with ourselves. I agree with Gordon (1972) when he says that, if we could live with the idea that this very moment might be our last, "we would find that many problems and conflicts would evanesce, and life would be simplified and become more satisfying (p. 17)."

At this point, you might pause to reflect on your own fears of death and dying. What expectations seem to arouse the greatest fears in you? Do your fears concern death itself or the experience of dying? In what ways do you think your fears might be affecting how you choose to live now? Were you close to someone who died? If so, how did the experience of that person's death affect your feelings about death and dying?

If you consider yourself relatively young, you might ask: "Why should this topic interest me? I've got lots of time left, so why think about morbid subjects?" I've found that even the very young can be at least temporarily shocked into the realization that they could die at any time. This happens when a classmate dies from an automobile accident, drowning, suicide, cancer, or some act of violence. While I am obviously not suggesting that you should morbidly focus on your death, I am encouraging you to think of how you deal with your fears of it and to consider what death means to you in terms of *living fully* now.

Death and the Meaning of Life

I accept the existentialist view that the acceptance of death is vitally related to the discovery of meaning and purpose in life. One of our distinguishing characteristics as human beings is our ability to grasp the concept of the future and thus the inevitability of death. Our ability to do so gives meaning to our existence, for it makes our every act and moment count.

In his book *Is There an Answer to Death?* Koestenbaum (1976) develops the idea that our awareness of death enables us to have a plan of life. It compels us to see our lives in totality and to seek real and ultimate answers. As Koestenbaum writes: "Many people think of death as unreal, as just beyond the horizon, as something they should postpone thinking about—in fact, as an event that is not to be mentioned. As a result, they are incapable of experiencing their lives as a whole, of forming any total life plan" (p. 32).

The awareness of death is also related to our ability to form distinctive personal identities. By accepting our mortality, we enable ourselves to define the quality of life we want; as Koestenbaum says, our anticipation of death reveals to us who we are. This anticipation is both an intellec-

tual awareness and an experiential understanding. It puts us in touch with our hopes and our anxieties and gives direction to our lives.

The meaning of our lives, then, depends on the fact that we are finite beings. What we do with our lives counts. We can choose to become all that we are capable of becoming and make a conscious decision to fully affirm life, or we can passively let life slip by us. We can settle for letting events happen to us, or we can actively choose and create the kind of life we want. If we had forever to actualize our potentials, there would be no urgency about doing so. Our time is invaluable precisely because it is limited. Consequently, without living in constant fear of death, it is well for us to dwell on the unique importance of the present moment, for it is all we really have.

Time Out for Personal Reflection

1. *What fears do you experience when you think about your own death? Check any of the following statements that apply to you:*

_____   *I worry about what will happen to me after death.*
_____   *I'm anxious about the way I will die.*
_____   *I wonder whether I'll die with dignity.*
_____   *I fear the physical pain of dying.*
_____   *I worry most about my loved ones who will be left behind.*

_____   *I'm afraid that I won't be able to accomplish all that I want to accomplish before I die.*
_____   *I worry about my lack of control over how and when I will die.*
_____   *I fear ceasing to exist.*
_____   *I worry about being forgotten.*
_____   *I worry about all the things I'll miss after I die.*

List any other fears you have about death or dying.

_____

_____

_____

_____

2. *How well do you think you're living your life? List some specific things you aren't doing now that you'd like to be doing. List some things you think you'd be likely to do if you knew that you had only a short time to live.*

_____

_____

_____

_____

_____

3. *In many of my courses, I've asked students to write a brief description of what they might do if they knew they had only 24 hours left to live. If you're willing to, write down what occurs to you when you think about this possibility.*

_____

_____

_____

_____

_____

4. *In what way does the fact that you will die give meaning to your life now?*

_____

_____

_____

_____

5. *For many people, it is not so much death itself as it is the experience of dying that arouses fears. Are you more anxious about dying than about death itself? If so, what is it about dying that you're most fearful of?*

_____

_____

_____

_____

6. *Are there ways in which you avoid facing the inevitability of your own death or the deaths of those you love? If so, in what ways do you try to deny this reality?*

_____

_____

_____

_____

_____

7. *In what ways do you think your fears about death and dying might be affecting the choices you make now?*

_____

_____

_____

_____

8. *What have you learned from these exercises?*

_____

_____

_____

_____

Suicide: An Ultimate Choice or an Ultimate Cop-out?

Suicide is one of the leading causes of death in the United States, and it is on the increase. Kalish (1981) writes that adolescent suicide, in particular, is rapidly increasing. The rate for those between 15 and 24 years of age is three times higher than it was two decades ago.

In looking up the leading causes of death for a person my age, I found the following rank order: heart disease, stroke, cancer of the lung, cancer of the large intestine and rectum, bronchitis and emphysema, pneumonia, cancer of the prostate, cirrhosis, diseases of the arteries, suicide, motor-vehicle accidents, cancer of the stomach, cancer of the bladder, and leukemia. I am aware that many of these causes of death are related to choice. People may be engaging in some form of slow suicide by a chronic lack of exercise or by a variety of other ways of abusing their bodies. So, the actual rate of suicide could be viewed as higher than is reported if we considered the multitude of ways in which we actually shorten our lives. Furthermore, many people live in a "half-dead" state of depression, without joy and with many regrets. How alive are these people?

I strongly believe that people who attempt suicide simply do not want to go on in such deadening patterns, or they see life as unbearable. If they feel that they do not have any options, that the chances of change are slim, then they may decide that being dead is better than engaging in a futile struggle to find meaning when none exists.

Is suicide an ultimate choice or an ultimate cop-out? This question is a complex one, and I don't pretend to have an easy answer. I do see suicide as an ultimate choice in one respect; as I've mentioned, there are many ways that we can kill ourselves, whether by neglect or by certain acts. What seems more critical to me is that we make conscious choices about how fully we are willing to live, realizing that we must pay a price for being alive. At the same time, for some people ending their lives does seem like a cop-out—the result of not being willing to struggle or being too quick to decide to give up without exploring other possibilities. In thinking about how you would answer this question, ask yourself under what circumstances you think suicide is a choice, as opposed to simply giving up. Consider the following questions as a way of taking a position on this matter.

1. *What does your personal experience reveal?*   At times you may have felt a deep sense of hopelessness, and you may have questioned whether it was worth it to continue living. Have you ever felt really suicidal? If so, what was going on in your life that contributed to your desire to end it?

What factor or factors kept you from following through with taking your life? Would this act have been an authentic choice, or would it have been an act motivated by the feeling that you had no choices?

2. What hidden meanings does suicide have? Taking one's life is such a powerful act that we must look to some of its underlying messages and symbolic meanings:

- A cry for help: "I cried out, but nobody heard me!"
- A form of self-punishment: "I don't deserve to live."
- An act of hostility: "I'll get even with you; see what you made me do."
- An attempt to be noticed: "Maybe now people will talk about me and feel sorry for the way they treated me."
- A relief from hopelessness: "I see no way out of the despair I feel. Ending my life will be better than hating to wake up each morning."
- An end to pain: "I suffer extreme physical pain, which will not end. Suicide will put an end to this nightmare."

3. Have you known anyone who committed suicide? Typically, people who have been close to a suicide experience a range of feelings—including guilt, anger, and fear—that often are unexpressed. "Maybe if I had been more sensitive and caring," they might feel, "this terrible thing would not have happened. I wonder whether I did everything I could have done to prevent this?" If they were to put their anger into words, they might say, "I am angry with you for shutting me out, and for leaving me. Why didn't you let me know how desperate you were?" And they may feel fear: "If this happened to him, then maybe I am capable of doing the same thing."

Have you known a person who decided that suicide was better than continuing to live? If so, what were your reactions?

4. Can suicide be an act of mercy? There have been victims of painful and terminal illnesses who decided *when* and *how* to end their lives. Rather than waste away with cancer and endure extreme pain, some people have actually called their families together and then taken some form of poison. What are your thoughts about a person's choice of ending his or her life when it is certain that there is no chance for recovery?

These are simply a few issues on the important topic of suicide as a choice. See if you can come up with some other questions that will help you formulate your own opinions on the meanings of suicide, as well as alternatives to this final act.

Freedom in Dying

The process of dying involves a gradual diminishing of the choices available to us. Even in dying, however, we still have choices concerning how we handle what is happening to us.

The following account deals with my reactions to the dying of Jim Morelock, a student and close friend of mine. I don't know of anyone who showed better than Jim did how we remain free to choose our attitude toward life and toward life's ending. (I am repeating the account as it appeared in this book's first edition. Many readers have commented to me about how touched they were as they read about Jim's life and his death, and in this way he seems to have lived on in one important respect.)

Jim is 25 years old. He is full of life—witty, bright, honest, and actively questioning. He had just graduated from college as a Human Services major and seemed to have a bright future when his illness was discovered.

About a year and a half ago, Jim developed a growth on his forehead and underwent surgery to have it removed. At that time, his doctors believed that the growth was a rare disorder that was not malignant. Later, more tumors erupted, and more surgery followed. Several months ago, Jim found out that the tumors had spread throughout his body and that, even with cobalt treatment, he would have a short life. Since that time, Jim has steadily grown weaker and has been able to do less and less; yet he has shown remarkable courage in the way he has faced this loss and his dying.

Some time ago, Jim came to Idyllwild, California, and took part in the weekend seminar I had with the reviewers of this book. On this chapter, he commented that, although we may not have a choice concerning the losses we suffer in dying, we do retain the ability to choose our attitude toward our death and the way we relate to it.

Jim has taught me a lot during these past few months about this enduring capacity for choice, even in extreme circumstances. Jim has made many critical choices since being told of his illness. He chose to continue taking a course at the university, because he liked the contact with the people there. He worked hard at a boat dock to support himself, until he could no longer manage the physical exertion. He decided to undergo cobalt treatment, even though he knew that it most likely would not result in his cure, because he hoped that it would reduce his pain. It did not, and Jim has suffered much agony during the past few months. He decided not to undergo chemotherapy, primarily because he didn't want to prolong his life if he couldn't really live fully. He made a choice to accept God in his life, which gave him a sense of peace and serenity. Before he became bedridden, he decided to go to Hawaii and enjoy his time in first-class style.

Jim has always had an aversion to hospitals—to most institutions, for that matter—so he chose to remain at home, in more personal surroundings. As long as he was able, he read widely and continued to write in his journal about his thoughts and feelings on living and dying. With his friends, he played his guitar and sang songs that he had written. He maintained an active interest in life and in the things around him, without denying the fact that he was dying.

More than anyone I have known or heard about, Jim has taken care of unfinished business. He made it a point to gather his family and tell them his wishes, he made contact with all his friends and said everything he wanted to say to them, and he asked Marianne to deliver the eulogy at his funeral services. He clearly stated his desire for cremation; he wants to burn those tumors and then have his ashes scattered over the sea—a wish that reflects his love of freedom and movement.

Jim has very little freedom and movement now, for he can do little except lie in his bed and wait for his death to come. To this day he is choosing to die with dignity, and, although his body is deteriorating, his spirit is still very much alive. He retains his mental sharpness, his ability to say a lot in a very few words, and his sense of humor. He has allowed himself to grieve over his losses. As he puts it, "I'd sure like to hang around to enjoy all those people that love me!" Realizing that this isn't possible, Jim is saying goodbye to all those who are close to him.

Throughout this ordeal, Jim's mother has been truly exceptional. When she told me how remarkable Jim has been in complaining so rarely despite his constant pain, I reminded her that I'd never heard her complain during her months on duty. I have been continually amazed by her strength and courage, and I have admired her willingness to honor Jim's wishes and accept his beliefs, even though at times they have differed from her own. She has demonstrated her care without smothering Jim or depriving him of his free spirit and independence. Her acceptance of Jim's dying and her willingness to be fully present to him have given him the opportunity to express openly whatever he feels. Jim has been able to grieve and mourn, because she has not cut off this process.

This experience has taught me much about dying and about living. Through Jim, I have learned that I don't have to do that much for a person who is dying other than to be with him or her by being myself. So often I have felt a sense of helplessness, of not knowing what to say or how much to say, of not knowing what to ask or not to ask, of feeling stuck for words. Jim's imminent death seems such a loss, and it's very difficult for me to accept it. Gradually, however, I have learned not to be so concerned about what to say or to refrain from saying. In fact, in my last visit I said very little, but I feel that we made significant contact with each other. I've also learned to share with Jim the sadness I feel, but there is simply no easy way to say goodbye to a friend.

Jim was a group leader in several of my personal-growth courses, and I can recall some of the things he confronted others with and what he said to them. Now he is showing me that his style of dying will be no different from his style of living. By his example and by his words, Jim has been a catalyst for me to think about the things I say and do and to evaluate my own life.

Time Out for Personal Reflection

1. *If you were close to someone during his or her dying, how did the experience affect your feelings about your life and about your own dying?*

2. *How would you like to be able to respond if a person who is close to you were dying?*

3. *If you were dying, what would you most want from the people who are closest to you?*

The Stages of Dying

Death and dying have become topics of widespread discussion among psychologists, psychiatrists, physicians, sociologists, ministers, and researchers. Whereas these topics were once taboo for many people, they are now the focus of seminars, courses, and workshops. A number of recent books, some of which are described in the "Suggested Readings" section at the end of the chapter, give evidence of this growing interest.

Dr. Elisabeth Kübler-Ross is a pioneer in the contemporary study of death and dying. In her widely read books *On Death and Dying* and *Death: The Final Stage of Growth*, she treats the psychological and sociological aspects of death and the experience of dying. Thanks to her efforts, many people have become aware of the almost universal need the dying have to talk about their impending deaths and to complete their business with the important people in their lives. She has shown how ignorance of the dying process and of the needs of dying people— as well as the fears of those around them—can rob the dying of the opportunity to fully experience their feelings and arrive at a resolution of them.

A greater understanding of dying can help us to come to an acceptance of death, as well as to be more helpful and present to those who are dying. For this reason, I'd like to describe the five stages of dying that Kübler-Ross (1969, 1975) has delineated, based on her research with terminally ill cancer patients. She emphasizes that these are not neat and compartmentalized stages that every person passes through in an orderly fashion. At times a person may experience a combination of these stages, perhaps skip one or more stages, or go back to an earlier stage he or she has already experienced. In general, however, Kübler-Ross found this sequence: denial, anger, bargaining, depression, and acceptance.

To make this discussion of the stages of dying more concrete, let me give the example of Ann, a 30-year-old woman dying of cancer. She was married and the mother of three children in elementary school. Before she discovered that she had terminal cancer, she felt that she had much to live for, and she enjoyed life.

The Stage of Denial

Ann's first reaction to being told that she had only about a year to live was shock. At first she refused to believe that the diagnosis was correct, and even after obtaining several other medical opinions, she still refused to accept that she was dying. In other words, her initial reaction was one of *denial.*

However, even though Ann was attempting to deny the full impact of reality, it would have been a mistake to assume that she didn't want to talk about her feelings. Her husband also denied her illness and was unwilling to talk to her about it. He felt that talking bluntly might only make her more depressed and lead her to lose all hope. He failed to recognize how important it would have been to Ann to feel that she *could* bring up the subject if she wished. On some level, Ann knew that she could not talk about her death with her husband.

During the stage of denial, the attitudes of a dying person's family and friends are critical. If these people cannot face the fact of their loved one's dying, they cannot help him or her move toward an acceptance of death. Their own fear will blind them to signs that the dying person wants to talk about his or her death and needs support. In the case of Ann, it would not necessarily have been a wise idea to force her to talk, but she could have been greatly helped if those around her had been available and sensitive to her when *she* stopped denying her death and showed a need to be listened to.

The Stage of Anger

As Ann began to accept that her time was limited by an incurable disease, her denial was replaced by anger. Over and over she wondered why *she*—who had so much to live for—had to be afflicted with this dreadful disease. Her anger mounted as she thought of her children and realized that she would not be able to see them grow and develop. During her frequent visits to the hospital for cobalt treatment, she directed some of her anger toward doctors "who didn't seem to know what they were doing," toward the "impersonal" nurses, and toward the red tape she had to endure.

During the stage of anger, it's important that others recognize the need of dying people to express their anger, whether they direct it toward their doctors, the hospital staff, their friends, their children, or God. If this displaced anger is taken personally, any meaningful dialogue with the dying will be cut off. Moreover, people like Ann have every reason to be enraged over having to suffer in this way when they have so much to live for. Rather than withdrawing support or taking offense, the people who surround a dying person can help most by allowing the person to fully express the pent-up rage inside. In this way, they help the person to ultimately come to terms with his or her death.

The Stage of Bargaining

Kübler-Ross (1969) sums up the essence of the bargaining stage as follows: "If God has decided to take us from this earth and he did not respond to any angry pleas, he may be more favorable if I ask nicely" (p. 72). Basically, the stage of bargaining is an attempt to postpone the inevitable end.

Ann's ambitions at this stage were to finish her college studies and graduate with her bachelor's degree, which she was close to obtaining. She also hoped to see her oldest daughter begin junior high school in a little over a year. During this time, she tried any type of treatment that offered some hope of extending her life.

The Stage of Depression

Eventually Ann's bargaining time ran out. No possibility of remission of her cancer remained, and she could no longer deny the inevitability of her death. Having been subjected to cobalt treatment, chemotherapy, and a series of operations, she was becoming weaker and thinner, and she was able to do less and less. Her primary feelings became a great sense of loss and a fear of the unknown. She wondered about who would take care of her children and about her husband's future. She felt guilty because she demanded so much attention and time and because the treatment of her illness was depleting the family income. She felt depressed over losing her hair and her beauty.

It would not have been helpful at this stage to try to cheer Ann up or to deny her real situation. Just as it had been important to allow her to fully vent her anger, it was important now to let her talk about her feelings and to make her final plans. Dying people are about to lose everyone they love, and only the freedom to grieve over these losses will enable them to find some peace and serenity in a final acceptance of death.

The Stage of Acceptance

Kübler-Ross found that, if patients have had enough time and support to work through the previous stages, most of them reach a stage at which they are neither depressed nor angry. Because they have expressed their anger and mourned the impending loss of those they love, they are able to become more accepting of their death. Kübler-Ross (1969) comments: "Acceptance should not be mistaken for a happy stage. It is almost a void of feelings. It is as if the pain has gone, the struggle is over, and

there comes a time for "the final rest before the long journey," as one patient phrased it" (p. 100).

Of course, some people never achieve an acceptance of their death, and some have no desire to. Ann, for example, never truly reached a stage of acceptance. Her final attitude was more one of surrender, a realization that it was futile to fight any longer. Although she still felt unready to die, she did want an end to her suffering. It may be that if those close to her had been more open to her and accepting of her feelings, she would have been able to work through more of her anger and depression.

The Significance of Kübler-Ross's Stages

I want to reemphasize that Kübler-Ross's description of the dying process is not meant to be rigid and should not be interpreted as a natural progression that is expected in most cases. Just as people are unique in the way they live, they are unique in the way they die; it is a mistake to use these stages as the standard by which to judge whether a dying person's behavior is normal or right. The value of the stages is that they describe and summarize in a general way what many patients experience and therefore add to our understanding of dying.

Kalish (1981) comments that many doctors and nurses regard the stage progression as something that everyone will naturally follow. Patients who do not make it to the acceptance stage are sometimes viewed as failures. For example, some nurses get angry at patients who take steps "backwards" by going from depression to anger, or they question patients about why they have "stayed so long in the anger stage." Kalish emphasizes that people die in a variety of ways and have a variety of feelings during this process: hope, anger, depression, fear, envy, relief, and anticipation. Those who are dying move back and forth from mood to mood. Therefore, these stages should not be used as a method of categorizing, and thus dehumanizing, the dying; they are best used as a frame of reference for helping them.

An Application of the Stages of Dying to Separation and Other Losses

The five stages of dying described by Kübler-Ross seem to have an application to divorce, separation, and other losses—experiences that bear some similarity to dying. To illustrate, I'll discuss a divorce in terms of the five stages. Of course, you can broaden this concept and see whether it applies to separation from your parents, your children, or even from an old value system or way of being. Although not all people who divorce go through the stages in the same way, I've found that many people do experience similar questions and struggles.

The Stage of Denial

Many people who are divorcing go through a process of denial and self-deception. They may try to convince themselves that the state of their marriage isn't all that bad, that nobody is perfect, and that things would be worse if they did separate. Even after the decision is made to divorce, they may feel a sense of disbelief that this could actually be happening to them. If it was the other person who initiated the divorce, the remaining partner might ask: "Where did things go wrong? Why is she (he) doing this to me? I really don't believe this is happening to me!"

The Stage of Anger

Once people accept the reality that they are divorcing, they frequently experience anger and rage. They may say "Why did this have to happen? I gave a lot, and now I'm being deserted. I feel as if I've been used and then thrown away." Many people feel cheated and angry over the apparent injustice of what is happening to them. Just as it is very important for dying people to express any anger they feel over dying, it's also important for people who are going through the grief associated with a divorce or other loss to express any anger they feel. If they keep their anger bottled up inside, it is likely to be turned against themselves and may take the form of depression—a kind of self-punishment.

The Stage of Bargaining

Sometimes people hope that a separation will give them the distance they need to reevaluate things and that they will soon get back together again. Although separations sometimes work this way, often it is futile to wish that matters can be worked out. Nevertheless, during the bargaining stage, one or both partners may try to make concessions and compromises that they hope will make a reconciliation possible.

The Stage of Depression

In the aftermath of a decision to divorce, a sense of hopelessness may set in. As the partners realize that a reconciliation isn't likely, they may begin to dwell on the emptiness and loss they feel. They may find it very difficult to let go of the future they had envisioned together. They may spend time wondering what their lives would have been like if they had made their relationship work. It isn't uncommon for people who divorce to turn their anger away from their spouses and toward themselves. Thus, they may experience much self-blame and self-doubt. They may say to themselves: "Maybe I didn't give our relationship a fair chance. What could I have done differently? I wonder where I went wrong?"

Depression can also be the result of the recognition that a real loss has been sustained. It is vitally important that people fully experience and express the grief they feel over their loss. Too often people deceive themselves into believing that they are finished with their sadness long before they have given vent to their grief. Unresolved grief tends to be carried around within a person, blocking the expression of many other feelings. For instance, if grief isn't worked through, it may be extremely difficult for a person to form new relationships, because in some ways he or she is still holding on to the past relationship.

The Stage of Acceptance

If people allow themselves to mourn their losses, eventually the process of grief work usually leads to a stage of acceptance. In the case of divorce, once the two persons have finished their grieving, new possibilities begin to open up. They can begin to accept that they must make a life for themselves without the other person and that they cannot cling to resentments that will keep them from beginning to establish a new life. Although sadness may persist, there can be an acceptance that what has occurred is done with and that brooding won't change things. They can learn from their experience and apply that learning to future events.

In summary, these stages are experienced in different ways by each person who faces a significant loss. People do not pass through these stages in neat fashion, and not all people experience all the stages in working through their losses. Some, for example, express very little anger; others might not go through a bargaining stage. Nevertheless, the value of a model such as this one is that it provides some understanding of how we can learn to cope with the various types of losses in our lives. Whatever the loss may be, and whatever stage of grieving we may be experiencing, it seems to be crucial that we freely express our feelings. Otherwise, we may not be able to achieve acceptance.

For me, the meaning of acceptance is well expressed in the prayer of Alcoholics Anonymous, and I'd like to close this section by quoting it here:

> God, grant me serenity to accept the things I cannot change, courage to change the things I can change, and wisdom to know the difference.

Time Out for Personal Reflection

1. *If you have suffered a serious loss in your life, to what extent did your experience correspond to the five stages of dying described by Kübler-Ross? In what ways was it different?*

_____

_____

_____

_____

_____

_____

2. *To what extent do you think you've accepted the major losses and transitions in your life? Do you sometimes find yourself returning to stages you've already experienced in regard to them, such as anger or bargaining? Do you have some feelings about these losses that you've never really allowed yourself to express?*

_____

_____

_____

_____

_____

Being "Dead" in Psychological and Social Ways

In talking about death in my university courses, I've found it valuable to broaden the conception of death and dying to include being "dead" in a variety of psychological and social ways. What is dead or dying in us may be something we want to resurrect, or it may be something that *should* die in order to make way for new growth.

Sometimes growth requires that we be willing to let go of old and familiar ways of being, and we might need to mourn their loss before we can really move on. You may have experienced a letting go of the security of living with your parents, for example, in exchange for testing your independence by living alone and supporting yourself. In the process, you may have lost something that was valuable to you, even if it was incompatible with your further development and growth.

I'd like to focus now on some ways in which we commonly allow parts of ourselves to die that we might want to bring back into our lives. I hope that the following questions will help you to decide whether you're living as fully as you'd like to be.

Can You Be Spontaneous and Playful?

Is the "child" part of you living, or have you buried it away inside? Can you be playful, fun, curious, explorative, spontaneous, inappropriate, silly? As adults, we sometimes begin to take ourselves too seriously and lose the ability to laugh at ourselves. If you find that you're typically realistic and objective to the point that it's difficult for you to be playful or light, you might ask what inner messages block your ability to let go. Are you inhibited by a fear of being wrong? Are you afraid of being called silly or of meeting with others' disapproval? If you want to, you can begin to challenge the messages that say: "Don't!" "You should!" "You shouldn't!" You can experiment with new behavior and run the risk of seeming silly or of "not acting your age." Then *you* can decide whether you like your new behavior and want to be like a child more often. Whatever your decision is, at least it will be your own instead of a command from your past.

Are You Alive to Your Feelings?

We can deaden ourselves to most of our feelings—the joyful ones as well as the painful ones. We can decide that feeling involves the risk of pain and that it's best to *think* our way through life. In choosing to cut off feelings of depression or sadness, we will most likely cut off feelings of joy. Closing ourselves to our lows usually seems to mean closing ourselves to our highs as well.

In my work with people, I sometimes find it difficult to help them even to recognize their flat emotional state, so insulated have they made themselves. To begin assessing how alive you are emotionally, you might ask yourself such questions as the following:

- Do I let myself feel my sadness over a loss?
- Do I try very hard to cheer people up when they're sad or depressed, instead of allowing them to experience their feelings?
- Do I let myself cry if I feel like crying?

- Do I ever feel ecstasy?
- Do I let myself feel close to another person?
- Are there some feelings that I particularly suppress? Do I hide my feelings of insecurity, fear, dependence, tenderness, anger, boredom?

Are You Caught Up in Deadening Roles?

Our roles and functions can eventually trap us. Instead of fulfilling certain roles while maintaining a separate sense of identity, we may get lost in our roles and in the patterns of thought, feeling, and behavior that go with them. As a result, we may neglect important parts of ourselves and thus limit our options of feeling and experiencing. Moreover, we may feel lost when we're unable to play a certain role. Thus, a supervisor may not know how to behave when he or she isn't in a superior position to others, an instructor may be at loose ends when he or she doesn't have students to teach, or a parent may find life empty when the children have grown.

Do you feel caught in certain roles? Do you depend on being able to identify with those roles in order to feel alive and valuable? Are you able to renew yourself by finding innovative ways of being and thinking? At this time in your life, you might find that you're so caught up in the student role that you have little time or energy left for other parts of your life. When our roles begin to deaden us, we can ask whether we've taken on a function or identity that others have defined, instead of listening to our own inner promptings.

Are Your Relationships Alive?

Our relationships with the significant people in our lives have a way of becoming stale and deadening. It's easy to get stuck in habitual and routine ways of being with another person and to lose any sense of surprise and spontaneity. This kind of staleness is particularly common in long-term relationships such as marriage, but it can afflict our other relationships as well. As you look at the significant relationships in your life, think about how alive both you and the other person in each relationship feel with each other. Do you give each other enough space to grow? Does the relationship energize you, or does it sap you of life? Are you settling into a comfortable, undemanding relationship? If you recognize that you aren't getting what you want in your friendships or intimate relationships, you can ask what *you* can do to revitalize them. You can also consider what specific things you'd like to ask of the other person. Simply asking more from your relationships can do a lot to bring new life into them.

Are You Alive Intellectually?

Children typically display much curiosity about life, yet somehow they often lose this interest in figuring out problems as they grow older. By the time we reach adulthood, we can easily become caught up in our activities, while devoting little time to considering *why* we're doing them and whether we even *want* to be doing them. It's also easy to allow our intellectual potential to shrivel up, either by limiting our exposure to the environment or by failing to follow our curiosity.

How might this apply to you as a student? Have you given up on asking any real and substantive questions that you'd like to explore? Have you settled for merely going to classes and collecting the units you need to obtain a degree? Are you indifferent to learning? Are you open to learning new things?

Are You Alive to Your Senses and Your Body?

Our bodies express to a large degree how alive we are. They show signs of our vitality or reveal our tiredness with life. Since our bodies don't lie, we can use them as an indication of the degree to which we're affirming life. As you look at your body, you can ask: Do I like what I see? Am I taking good care of myself physically, or am I indifferent to my own bodily well-being? What does my facial expression communicate?

We can also become deadened to the input from our senses. We may become oblivious to fragrances or eat foods without tasting or savoring them. We may never stop to notice the details of our surroundings. On the other hand, taking time to be alive to our senses can help us feel renewed and interested in life. You might ask yourself: What sensations have particularly struck me today? What have I experienced and observed? What sensory surprises have enlivened me?

Time Out for Personal Reflection

1. *How alive do you feel psychologically and socially? Check any of the following statements that apply to you.*

_____   *I feel alive and energetic most of the time.*
_____   *My body expresses aliveness and vitality.*
_____   *I feel intellectually curious and alive.*
_____   *I have significant friendships that are a source of nourishment for me.*
_____   *I can play and have fun.*
_____   *I allow myself to feel a wide range of emotions.*

———————   *I'm keenly aware of the things I see, smell, taste, and touch.*
———————   *I feel free to express who I am; I'm not trapped by my roles.*

2. *When do you feel most alive?*

_____

_____

3. *When do you feel least alive?*

_____

_____

4. *What specific things would you most like to change about your life so that you could feel more alive? What can you do to make these changes?*

_____

_____

_____

_____

_____

_____

Taking Stock: How Well Are You Living Life?

It seems tragic to me that some people never really take the time to evaluate how well they are living life. Imagine for a moment that you're one of those people who get caught up in the routine of daily existence and never assess the quality of their living. Now assume that you are told that you have only a limited time to live. You begin to look at what you've missed and how you wish things had been different; you begin to experience regrets over the opportunities that you let slip by; you review the significant turning points in your life. You may wish now that you had paused to take stock at many points in your life, instead of waiting until it was too late.

Writing Your Own Eulogy

One way to take stock of your life is to imagine your own death, including the details of the funeral and the things people might say about you. As an extension of this exercise, you might try actually writing down your

own eulogy or obituary. This can be a powerful way of summing up how you see your life and how you'd like it to be different. In fact, I suggest that you try writing three eulogies for yourself. First, write your *"actual"* eulogy—the one you would give at your own funeral, if that were possible. Second, write the eulogy that you *fear*—one that expresses some of the negative things someone could say of you. Third, write the eulogy that you would *hope* for—one that expresses the most positive aspects of your life so far. After you've written your three eulogies, seal them in an envelope and put them away for a year or so. Then do the exercise again, and compare the two sets of eulogies to see what changes have occurred in your view of your life.

This experience is not meant to be morbid; rather, it is a tool you can use in exploring the meaning of death and in creating a more meaningful life. For me, the exercise of writing my own eulogies was not an easy one. I found it difficult to separate my realistic view of myself from my hoped-for and feared assessments. At times when I was writing what I *feared* could be said about me, I wondered how much of what I was writing was actually true of me. I had much the same feeling as I wrote my hoped-for version—that some of what I wrote is true of me now. And no doubt my "actual" eulogy incorporated some of my hopes and fears as well as a truly objective assessment of my life. Nevertheless, the experience of writing my eulogies helped me to consider how fully I'm living life. It also challenged me to do something concrete about changing those aspects of my life that were reflected in the "feared" eulogy. For instance, in writing this eulogy I became aware of the great difficulty I have in living for the present moment. I tend to hurry about and put unnecessary pressure on myself, instead of allowing myself to be an experiencing, feeling, reflective human being. Of course, what you learn from writing your eulogies will be unique to you, but I believe that this exercise can help you see yourself and your life in a clearer perspective and challenge you to live more fully *now*.

Postscript: Taking Time

Before he died, Jim Morelock gave me a poster showing a man walking in the forest with two small girls. At the top of the poster were the words "TAKE TIME." Jim knew me well enough to know how I tend to get caught up in so many activities that I sometimes forget to simply take the time to really experience and enjoy the simple things in life. As I write this, I'm also remembering what one student wrote to me as we were writing what we hoped and wished for each person in the class. On one of my slips of paper was written "I hope you will take the time to smell a rose." In another class, one student gave each person an epitaph—what he thought could be written on that person's tombstone. Mine read "Here lies Jerry Corey—a man who all his life tried to do too many things at once." I promised myself that I'd make a poster with those words on it and place it on my office wall as a reminder for those times when I would begin to hurry and forget to take time to enjoy life. I think many of us could use reminders like these frequently—especially since it took me almost a semester to get around to putting that poster up! So I'd like to close this chapter with this simple message: *Take time.*

I wrote the preceding paragraph for the first edition of this book. Now, five years later, am I taking time to do fewer things at once and to enjoy life? In all honesty, I have to admit that I'm still a slow learner in this respect! Marianne and I were recently vacationing on the beach in Cancun, Mexico, and she asked me if the poster that Jim gave me had made any difference. My immediate response was "Sure, I'm taking time right now." "You could fool me," she replied. "It looks like you're working now!" She observed that we were sitting on the beach with *I Never Knew*

I Had a Choice in hand and talking about what to revise. Even though I was doing what I wanted at that moment, I realized how difficult I find it to *really* take time. So this time I'd like to close the chapter with another simple message: Even if something is difficult, and even if you learn slowly, don't give up!

Chapter Summary

In this chapter, I've encouraged you to devote some time to reflecting on your eventual death, because I'm convinced that doing so can lead you to examine the quality and direction of your life and help you to find your own meaning in living. I've suggested that the acceptance of death is closely related to the acceptance of life. Recognizing and accepting the fact of death gives us the impetus to search for our own answers to questions such as: What is the meaning of my life? What do I most want from life? How can I create the life I want to live? In addition, I've encouraged you to assess how much you are fully alive right now.

Some of the key ideas presented in this chapter are listed below. As a way of stimulating your own reflections, you might think about each statement and decide how much you agree or disagree with it.

1. Many of us fear death, largely because of the uncertainty that surrounds it.
2. Life has meaning because we are finite beings; thus, death gives life meaning.
3. If we're afraid to die, we may be afraid to live.
4. Our culture makes it easy for us to deny the reality of death.
5. There are many ways of being "dead" psychologically, socially, and intellectually. By recognizing ways in which we're not fully alive, we can make decisions that will lead to richer living.
6. The way in which we view death has much to do with the way in which we view life.

Now list some other ideas from this chapter that you want to remember.

_____

_____

_____

_____

_____

Activities and Exercises

1. For a period of at least a week, take a few minutes each day to reflect on when you feel alive and when you feel "dead." Do you notice any trends in your observations? What can you do to feel more alive?

2. If you knew you were going to die within a short time, in what ways would you live your life differently? What might you give up? What might you be doing that you're not doing or experiencing now?

3. Imagine yourself on your deathbed. Write down whom you want to be there, what you want them to say to you, and what you want to say to them. Then write down your reactions to this experience.

4. For about a week, write down specific things you see, read, or hear relating to the denial or avoidance of death in our culture.

5. Let yourself reflect on how the death of those you love might affect you. Consider each person separately, and try to imagine how your life today would be different if that person were not in it. In your journal, you might respond to such questions as: Do I now have the relationships with my loved ones that I want to have? What's missing? What changes do I most want to make in my relationships?

6. Consider making some time alone in which to write three eulogies for yourself: one that you think *actually* sums up your life, one that you *fear* could be written about you, and one that you *hope* could be written about you. Write the eulogies as if you had died today; then seal them in an envelope, and do the exercise again in the future—say, in about a year. At that time, you can compare your eulogies to see in what respects your assessment of your life and your hopes and fears have changed.

7. After you've written your three eulogies, you might write down in your journal what the experience was like for you and what you learned from it. Are there any specific steps you'd like to take *now* in order to begin living more fully?

Suggested Readings

Friedman, M., & Rosenman, R. *Type A Behavior and Your Heart.* Greenwich, Conn.: Fawcett World, 1976. This is an excellent book that deals with personality types and behavior associated with death from coronary diseases—and, more broadly, with learning to take time to enjoy life. Guidelines are given on how to recognize Type A behavior and what you can do about it.

Gordon, D. *Overcoming the Fear of Death.* Baltimore: Penguin, 1972. This is a very useful book dealing with the fear of death, the ways we avoid facing this fear, some aspects of dying, and the meaning of death.

Kalish, R. A. *Death, Grief, and Caring Relationships.* Monterey, Calif.: Brooks/ Cole, 1981. The author, who has been professionally interested in the themes of death and dying for over 20 years, has written an excellent and comprehensive textbook on the various aspects of death, the process of dying, and the grief process. If you had to select just one book for further reading on this topic, this would be my recommendation.

Kavanaugh, R. *Facing Death.* New York: Nash, 1972; Penguin edition, 1974. Kavanaugh discusses some unrealistic fears and attitudes toward dying and shows that a growing awareness of what we hope to achieve in life can bring about an accepting attitude toward death. Other topics include cultural expectations concerning dying, coping with tragic death, funerals, life after death, and grief work.

Koestenbaum, P. *Is There an Answer to Death?* Englewood Cliffs, N.J.: Prentice-Hall (Spectrum), 1976. This book discusses how a positive confrontation with death can be a liberating experience, how it can help us develop our individual identity and give us the security we need to live our lives courageously, and how an acceptance of death can bring greater meaning to life.

Kopp, S. *If You Meet the Buddha on the Road, Kill Him!* New York: Bantam, 1976. This insightful book deals with the theme that no meaning we take from outside of ourselves is real. In a moving section, the author describes his own choice between living and dying.

Kübler-Ross, E. *On Death and Dying.* New York: Macmillan, 1969. A thoughtful treatment of attitudes toward death and dying, this book is based primarily on interviews with terminal cancer patients. The author is one of the pioneers in the contemporary study of death and dying.

Kübler-Ross, E. *Death: The Final Stage of Growth.* Englewood Cliffs, N.J.: Prentice-Hall (Spectrum), 1975. This excellent book discusses such questions as: Why is it so hard to die? Are death and growth related? How is death the final stage of growth? What is the significance of death?

Lund, D. *Eric.* New York: Dell, 1975. This touching book demonstrates how a person can live to the fullest even in the face of imminent death. Even though Eric finds out that he has leukemia, he continues to make life-oriented decisions, and he distinguishes himself in sports.

Marris, P. *Loss and Change.* Garden City, N.Y.: Doubleday, 1974. This book discusses what happens to us when we lose someone significant, when we divorce, and when we make changes in our daily lives. It includes a good section on the process of grief and mourning.

Marshall, V. W. *Last Chapters: A Sociology of Aging and Dying.* Monterey, Calif.: Brooks/Cole, 1980. Death is viewed from a sociological perspective, and the focus is on issues such as making sense of death and dying, aging as it relates to dying, and death's implications for life.

Moody, R. *Life after Life.* New York: Bantam, 1975. The author describes case histories that focus on the question of what it is like to die.

Pearson, L. (Ed.). *Death and Dying: Current Issues in the Treatment of the Dying Person.* Cleveland: Case Western Reserve Press, 1969. This is an excellent treatment of the situation of the dying patient. The topics discussed include psychological death, the care of the dying person, effects of a death on the family, awareness of dying, and psychotherapy and the dying patient.

Ruitenbeek, H. (Ed.). *Death: Interpretations.* New York: Delta, 1969. This is a thought-provoking collection of 21 articles on the topic of death and mourning.

Russell, O. R. *Freedom to Die: Moral and Legal Aspects of Euthanasia.* New York: Dell, 1975. The central issue addressed in this book is our right to die as we choose.

Schnitzer, E. *Looking In.* Idyllwild, Calif.: Strawberry Valley Press, 1977. In this book of essays, Schnitzer shares his personal thoughts about death and life, growing old, and ways of finding meaning in life. The author is a positive example of a person who remains vital and alive by experiencing many facets of life.

Shneidman, E. (Ed.). *Death: Current Perspectives.* Palo Alto, Calif.: Mayfield, 1976. This book is an excellent collection of selections dealing with cultural, societal, interpersonal, and personal perspectives on death.

Yalom, I. D. *Existential Psychotherapy.* New York: Basic Books, 1980. Chapters 2 through 5 contain excellent resources for an in-depth analysis of the relationship of death to meaning in life. Written from an existential viewpoint, these chapters treat the interrelationships among life, death, and anxiety. Also discussed are children's concept of death and the implications of death for the practice of psychotherapy.

Chapter Eleven

Meaning and Values: Putting Life in Perspective

Prechapter Self-Inventory

For each statement, indicate the response that most closely identifies your beliefs and attitudes. Use this code: 5 = I *strongly agree* with this statement; 4 = I *agree* in most respects; 3 = I am *undecided*; 2 = I *disagree* in most respects; 1 = I *strongly disagree*.

_____ 1. At this time in my life, I have a sense of meaning and purpose that gives me direction.

_____ 2. Most of my values are similar to those of my parents.

_____ 3. Without some form of religious belief, we cannot expect to find meaning in life.

_____ 4. Accepting our capacity for freedom of choice is an essential part of finding a sense of purpose in living.

_____ 5. I have challenged and questioned most of the values I now hold.

_____ 6. Religion is an important source of meaning for me.

_____ 7. I generally live by the values I hold.

_____ 8. We must each actively engage in a search for meaning in life, because it is not automatically bestowed on us.

_____ 9. My values and my views about life's meaning have undergone much change over the years.

_____ 10. We must be willing to look within ourselves to discover how to live.

_____ 11. The meaning of my life is based in large part on my ability to have a significant impact on others.

_____ 12. Many of the people I encounter seem to be without a clear purpose in living.

_____ 13. The meaning of life can only be understood in terms of the reality of death.

_____ 14. I generally feel clear about what I value.

_____ 15. I let others influence my values more than I'd like to admit.

_____ 16. I sometimes subject my values to challenge from others.

_____ 17. The problem of meaninglessness in living is one of the most pressing problems of our society.

_____ 18. I have a clear sense of who I am and what I want to become.

_____ 19. The expectations and demands of others make it difficult for me to retain a firm sense of my own identity.

_____ 20. "A grown-up can be no man's disciple" (Sheldon Kopp).

Introduction

In this chapter, I encourage you to look critically at the *why* of your existence, to clarify the sources of your values, and to reflect on questions such as these: In what direction am I moving in my life? What steps can

366

I take to make the changes in my life that I decide I want to make? What do I have to show for my years on this earth so far? Where have I been, where am I now, and where do I want to go?

Many who are fortunate enough to achieve power, fame, success, and material comfort nevertheless experience a sense of emptiness. Although they may not be able to articulate what it is that is lacking in their lives, they know that something is amiss. The astronomical number of pills and drugs produced to allay the symptoms of this "existential vacuum"—depression and anxiety—are evidences of our failure to find values that allow us to make sense out of our place in the world.

There are other signs of this need for a sense of meaning, including the popularity of many different religious groups and practices, the widespread interest in Eastern and other philosophies, the use of meditation, the number of self-help and inspirational books published each year, the experimentation with different life-styles, and even the college courses in personal adjustment! It seems fair to say that we are caught up in a crisis of meaning and values, and in this situation it's easy to look to some authoritative source for answers to our most deeply felt questions. As I have throughout this book, I want to suggest in this chapter that only the meaning and values we affirm from within ourselves, whatever form they may take, can guide us toward autonomy and freedom.

Time Out for Personal Reflection

1. *In the space below, list the things that you most like to do or the activities that have the most meaning for you.*

_____

_____

_____

_____

_____

2. *How often do you do or experience each of the things you've just listed?*

_____

_____

_____

_____

_____

3. *Does anything prevent you from doing the things you value as fre-quently as you'd like? If so, what?*

_____

_____

_____

_____

4. *What are some specific actions you can take to increase the amount of meaningful activity in your life?*

_____

_____

_____

_____

5. *Do you experience a deep sense of meaninglessness from time to time? How does it manifest itself? Check any of the following that apply to you.*

_____   *bordeom in work, school, or other aspects of life*
_____   *apathy; lack of interest in life*
_____   *depression; feeling down much of the time*
_____   *a vague sense of unease; feeling anxious*

Others:

_____

_____

_____

6. *If you often feel a sense of inner emptiness, what do you think are some of its causes? Check any of the following that apply to you.*

_____   *falling into ruts of conformity and routine*
_____   *giving up old values and having nothing to replace them with*
_____   *studying to learn facts or skills without being able to raise questions of meaning and value*

Others:

_____

_____

_____

7. *Are there ways in which you're now searching for meaning in your life? If so, what are they?*

_____

_____

_____

Our Search for Identity

I believe that the discovery of meaning and values is essentially related to our achievement of identity as persons. The quest for identity involves a commitment to give birth to ourselves by exploring the meaning of our uniqueness and humanness. A major problem for many people is that they have lost a sense of self, because they have directed their search for identity outside themselves. In their attempt to be liked and accepted by everyone, they have become finely tuned to what *others* expect of them but alienated from their *own* inner desires and feelings. As Rollo May (1973) observes, they are able to *respond* but not to *choose*. Indeed, May sees inner emptiness as the chief problem in contemporary society; too many of us, he says, have become "hollow people" who have very little understanding of who we are and what we feel. May cites one person's succinct description of the experience of "hollow people": "I'm just a collection of mirrors, reflecting what everyone expects of me" (p. 15).

Moustakas (1975) describes the same type of alienation from self that May talks about. For Moustakas, alienation is "the developing of a life outlined and determined by others, rather than a life based on one's own inner experience" (p. 31). If we become alienated from ourselves, we don't trust our own feelings but respond automatically to others as we think they want us to respond. As a consequence, Moustakas writes, we live in a world devoid of excitement, risk, and meaning.

In order to find out who we are, we may have to let parts of us die. We may need to shed old roles and identities that no longer give us vitality.

Doing so may require a period of mourning for our old selves. Most people who have struggled with shedding immature and dependent roles and assuming a more active stance toward life know that such rebirth isn't easy and that it may entail pain as well as joy.

Jourard (1971) makes a point that I find exciting. He maintains that we begin to cease living when meaning vanishes from life. Yet too often we are encouraged to believe that we have only *one* identity, *one* role, *one* way to be, and *one* purpose to fulfill in a lifetime. This way of thinking can be figuratively deadly, for when our one ground for being alive is outgrown or lost, we may begin to die psychologically instead of accepting the challenge of reinventing ourselves anew. In order to keep ourselves from dying spiritually, we need to allow ourselves to imagine new ways of being, to invent new goals to live for, to search for new and more fulfilling meanings, to acquire new identities, and to reinvent our relationships with others. In essence, we need to allow parts of us to die in order to experience the rebirth that is necessary for growth.

To me, then, achieving identity doesn't necessarily mean stubbornly clinging to a certain way of thinking or behaving. Instead, it may involve trusting ourselves enough to become open to new possibilities. Nor is an identity something we achieve for all time; rather, we need to be continually willing to reexamine our patterns and our priorities, our habits and our relationships. Above all, we need to develop the ability to listen to our inner selves and trust what we hear. To take just one example, I've known students for whom academic life has become stale and empty and who have chosen to leave it in response to their inner feelings. Some have opted to travel and live modestly for a time, taking in new cultures and even assimilating into them for a while. They may not be directly engaged in preparing for a career and, in that sense, "establishing" themselves, but I believe they are achieving their own identities by being open to new experiences and ways of being. For some of them, it may take real courage to resist the pressure to settle down in a career or "complete" their education.

Our search for identity involves asking three key existential questions, none of which has easy or definite answers: "Who am I?" "Where am I going?" "Why?"

The question "Who am I?" is never settled once and for all, for it can be answered differently at different times in our lives. We need to revise our lives, especially when old identities no longer seem to supply a meaning or give us direction. As we have seen, we must decide whether to let others tell us who we are or to take a stand and define ourselves.

"Where am I going?" This issue relates to our plans for a lifetime and

the means we expect to use in attaining our goals. Like the previous question, this one demands periodic review. Our life goals are not set once and for all. Again, do we show the courage it takes to decide for ourselves where we are going, or do we look for a guru to show us where to go?

Asking the question "Why" and searching for reasons are characteristics of being human. We face a rapidly changing world in which old values give way to new ones or to none at all. Part of shaping an identity implies that we are actively searching for meaning, trying to make sense of the world in which we find ourselves.

At this point, you might pause to assess how you experience your identity at this time in your life. The following "Time Out" may help you do so.

Time Out for Personal Reflection

1. *Who are you? Try completing the sentence "I am . . ." 20 different ways by quickly writing down the words or phrases that immediately occur to you. Use the spaces provided on the next page.*

I am:

_____   _____

_____   _____

_____   _____

_____   _____

_____   _____

_____   _____

_____   _____

_____   _____

2. *What does this list tell you about your view of yourself?*

_____

_____

_____

_____

3. *What are some of the things that you value most in life?*

_____

_____

_____

_____

4. *Do you feel that you can identify in any way with the person who said "I'm just a collection of mirrors, reflecting what everyone expects of me"? In what ways?*

_____

_____

_____

_____

5. *Have you ever experienced an "identity crisis"? If so, what led up to it? What was the nature of your struggle? How did you deal with it?*

_____

_____

_____

_____

_____

_____

Our Quest for Meaning and Purpose

Humans are the only creatures we know of who can reflect on their existence and, based on this capacity for self-awareness, exercise individual choice in defining their lives. With this freedom, however, come responsibility and a degree of anxiety. If we truly accept that the meaning of our lives is largely the product of our own choosing and the emptiness of our lives the result of our failure to choose, our anxiety is increased. To avoid this anxiety, we may refuse to examine the values that govern our daily behavior or to accept that we are, to a large degree, what we have chosen to become. Instead, we may make other people or outside institutions responsible for the direction of our lives. I believe that we pay a steep price for thus choosing a sense of security over our own freedom—the price of denying our basic humanness.

One obstacle in the way of finding meaning is that the world itself may appear meaningless. It's easy, when we look at the absurdity of the world in which we live, to give up the struggle or to seek some authoritative source of meaning. Yet creating our own meaning is, to me, precisely our challenge and task as humans.

Creating meaning in our lives isn't all a somber and serious business, however. We can also find meaning by allowing ourselves to play. It seems unfortunate to me that, as we "mature," so many of us lose the capacity we had as children to delight in the simple things in life. We busy ourselves in so many serious details that we really don't take the time to savor life or avail ourselves of its richness. Thus, we may work hard, maintaining all the while that we'll have time for fun when we retire. Then, when we do retire, we're bored and don't know what to do with ourselves. This kind of continued emphasis on the future can keep us from enjoying both our present and our future—when it, too, becomes present.

Religion and Meaning: A Personal View

Religious faith can be a powerful source of meaning and purpose. For many people, religion helps to make sense out of the universe and the mystery of our purpose in living. Like any potential source of meaning, however, religious faith seems most authentic and valuable to me when it enables us to become as fully human as possible. By this I mean that it assists us to get in touch with our own powers of thinking, feeling, deciding, willing, and acting. The questions I would put to my religion in order to determine whether it is a constructive force in my life are the following:

- Does my religion help me to integrate my experience and make sense of the world?
- Does my religious faith grow out of my own experience?
- Do my religious beliefs assist me to live life fully and to treat others with respect?
- Does my religion encourage me to exercise my freedom and to assume the responsibility for my own life?
- Are my religious beliefs helping me to become more of the person I'd like to become?
- Does my religion encourage me to question life and keep myself open to new learning?

At the present time, there appears to be a resurgence of interest in religion in our society. Increasing numbers of people seem to be deciding that some sort of religious faith is necessary if they are to find an order and purpose in life. At the same time, many others insist that religion only impedes the quest for meaning or that it is incompatible with contemporary beliefs in other areas of life. I know that I was convinced for a time that looking to some higher being for the source of meaning was incompatible with looking within ourselves for our own power, strength, and direction. I'm changing my thinking about this issue, and I've seen how religious faith has helped people endure great suffering. What seems essential to me is that our acceptance or rejection of religious faith come authentically from within ourselves and that we remain open to new experience and learning, whatever points of view we decide on.

It's perhaps worth emphasizing that a "religion" may take the form of a system of beliefs and values concerning the ultimate questions in life, rather than (or in addition to) membership in a church. People who belong to a church may or may not be "religious" in this sense, and the same is true of those who don't follow an organized religion or even profess belief in God. Some of those whom I think of as religious don't believe in the existence of God or else say they simply don't know whether any higher being or force exists. Others who might claim to be religious find no incompatibility in using religious belief as a reason to be cruel, inhumane, or neglectful of others. For these reasons, I don't believe that a profession of religious belief is, in itself, necessarily valuable or harmful. Like almost anything else in human life, religion (or irreligion) can be bent to worthwhile or base purposes.

In my own experience, I've found religion most valuable when it is a challenge to broaden my choices and potential, rather than a restrictive influence. I find it hard to accept what seems to be the fairly common use of religion as a way of remaining dependent on external guidance or authority. I might add that I didn't always think this way; until I was about 30, I tended to think of my religion as a package of ready-made answers for all the crises of life and was willing to let my church make many key decisions for me. I now think that I experienced too much anxiety in many areas of life to take full responsibility for my choices; it was easier to lean on my religion for my answers. Besides, my religious training had taught me that I should look to the authority of the church for ultimate answers in the areas of morality, value, and purpose. Like many people, I was encouraged to learn the "correct" answers and conform my thinking to them. Now, when I think of religion as a positive force, I think of it as being *freeing*, in the sense that it encourages and even commands me to trust myself, to discover the sources of strength and integrity within myself, and to assume responsibility for my own choices.

Although, as an adult, I've questioned and altered many of the religious teachings with which I was raised, I haven't discarded all my past moral and religious values. Many of them served a purpose earlier in my life and, with modification, are still meaningful for me. However, whether or not I continue to hold the beliefs and values I've been taught, it seems crucial to me that I be willing to subject them to scrutiny throughout my life. If they hold up under challenge, I can reincorporate them; by the same token, I can continue to examine the new beliefs and values I acquire.

Developing a Philosophy of Life

A philosophy of life is made up of the fundamental beliefs, attitudes, and values that govern a person's behavior. Many students I've taught, from high school to graduate school, have said that they hadn't really thought much about their philosophies of life. However, the fact that we've never explicitly defined the components of our philosophies of life doesn't mean that we are completely without them. All of us do operate on the basis of general assumptions about ourselves, others, and the world. Thus, the first step in actively developing a philosophy of life is to formulate a clearer picture of our present attitudes and beliefs.

We all have been developing implicit philosophies of life since we first began, as children, to wonder about life and death, love and hate, joy and fear, and the nature of the universe. We probably didn't need to be taught to be curious about such questions; raising them seems to be a natural part of human development. If we were fortunate, adults took the time to engage in dialogue with us, instead of discouraging us from asking questions and deadening some of our innate curiosity.

During the adolescent years, the process of questioning usually assumes new dimensions. Adolescents who have been allowed to question and think for themselves as children begin to get involved in a more advanced set of issues. Many of the adolescents I've encountered in my classes and workshops have at one time or another struggled with questions such as the following:

· Are the values that I've believed in for all these years the values I want to continue to live by?
· Where did I get my values? Are they still valid for me? Are there additional sources from which I can derive new values?
· Is there a God? What is the nature of the hereafter? What is my conception of a God? What does religion mean in my life? What kind of religion do I choose for myself? Does religion have any value for me?
· What do I base my ethical and moral decisions on? Peer-group standards? Parental standards? The normative values of my society?
· What explains the inhumanity I see in our world?
· What kind of future do I want? What can I do about actively creating this kind of future?

These are only a few of the questions that many adolescents think about and perhaps answer for themselves. However, I don't see a philosophy of life as something we arrive at once and for all during our adolescent years. The development of a philosophy of life continues as long as we live. As long as we remain curious and open to new learning, we can revise and rebuild our conceptions of the world. Life may have a particular meaning for us during adolescence, a new meaning during

LIFE MAY HAVE MANY DIFFERENT MEANINGS BETWEEN CHILDHOOD AND OLD AGE

adulthood, and still another meaning as we reach old age. Indeed, if we don't remain open to basic changes in our views of life, we may find it difficult to adjust to changed circumstances.

I'm thinking now of a 37-year-old man who is facing a real crisis of meaning in his life, largely because he has been trying to structure his world and experiences the way he did as an adolescent. He has many fixed beliefs about how life should be, and, since his current life seems chaotic by these standards, he is really struggling to find a reason to continue living. What he hasn't realized is that he cannot force his experiences today into the value system he held as an adolescent, for his life has changed since that time.

Keeping in mind that developing a philosophy of life is a continuing activity of examining and modifying the values we live by, you may find the following suggestions helpful as you go about formulating and reforming your own philosophy:

· Frequently create time to be alone in reflective thought.

· Consider what meaning the fact of your eventual death has for the present moment.
· Make use of significant contacts with others who are willing to challenge your beliefs and the degree to which you live by them.
· Adopt an accepting attitude toward those whose belief systems differ from yours, and develop a willingness to test your own beliefs.

In concluding this section, I'd like to list some of the values I hope my daughters, Heidi and Cindy, come to share. I find that thinking about what values I'd like to see them choose helps me to focus on the things that are most important to me. If you have children or expect to have children someday, you might pause to think about the values you would most like to pass on to them.

· I hope that my children will be willing to dare and that they won't always choose caution over risk.
· I hope they form sets of values that are their own, not carbon copies of their parents'.
· I hope they always like and respect themselves and feel good about their abilities and talents.
· I'd like them to be open and trusting rather than fearful or suspicious.
· I hope they will respect and care for others.
· I like the way they can have fun, and I hope they don't lose this ability as they grow older.
· I'd like them to be able to express what they feel, and I hope they'll always feel free to come to Marianne and me and share meaningful aspects of their lives.
· I'd like them to be in touch with the power they have, and I hope they refuse to surrender it.
· I'd like them to be independent and to have the courage to be different from others if they want to be.
· I appreciate their interest in a religion that they freely chose.
· I'd like them to be proud of who and what they are, yet humble.
· I hope they will respect the differences in others.
· I hope they will not compromise their values and principles for material possessions.

Time Out for Personal Reflection

1. What do you think of the statement that the meaning of your life is largely the product of your own choosing and that emptiness in your

life is the result of your failure to choose for yourself? How does this statement apply to your own experience?

---

2. *Sheldon Kopp (1972) contends that "A grown-up can be no man's disciple." Have you ever looked to some authority or guru to provide you with answers? What do you think of Kopp's contention?*

---

3. *Have there been occasions in your life when you've allowed other people or institutions to make key choices for you? If so, give a couple of examples.*

---

4. *What role, if any, has religion played in your life?*

---

5. *In your view, when is religion a constructive force in a person's life? A negative force?*

---

6. *If you were to create a new religion, what virtues and values would you include? What would be the vices and sins?*

_____

_____

_____

_____

_____

7. *In the past, what have been some of the principal sources of meaning in your life?*

_____

_____

_____

_____

8. *At this time, what are some of the principal sources of meaning and purpose in your life?*

_____

_____

_____

_____

9. *What would you like to be able to say about the meaning in your life ten years from now? What do you hope will bring you meaning then?*

_____

_____

_____

_____

10. *What are some of the values you'd most like to see your children adopt?*

_____

_____

_____

11. *The following is a list of some of the things different people value. Rate the importance of each one for you, using a 5-point scale, with 1 meaning "extremely important" and 5 meaning "very unimportant."*

_____	companionship
_____	family life
_____	security
_____	being financially and materially successful
_____	enjoying leisure time
_____	work
_____	learning and getting an education
_____	appreciation of nature
_____	competing and winning
_____	loving others and being loved
_____	a relationship with God
_____	self-respect and pride
_____	being productive and achieving
_____	enjoying an intimate relationship
_____	having solitude and private time to reflect
_____	having a good time and being with others
_____	laughter and a sense of humor
_____	intelligence and a sense of curiosity
_____	opening up to new experiences
_____	risk taking and personal growth
_____	being approved of and liked by others
_____	being challenged and meeting challenges well
_____	courage
_____	compassion
_____	being of service to others

Now go back over your list, and circle the things you'd like to have more of in your life. You might think of what keeps you from having or doing the things that you value most.

Reviewing Some Dimensions of Meaning and Value in Your Life

There are many dimensions to a philosophy of life, and one of the best ways to clarify your own philosophy is to take a careful look at the specific things you value and find meaningful in your life now. In many ways, this entire book has dealt with the various sources of meaning in life, including learning, views about human nature, our autonomy as persons, the body, sexuality, loving and being loved, intimate relationships, work, being alone, and death and dying. At this point, I suggest that you review these areas in the light of these questions: What do I value? What values give meaning and substance to my life now? Do my actions reflect what I say I value?

Your Values and Learning

You've probably heard it said that learning is a lifelong enterprise. As you examine yourself as a learner, ask yourself whether you keep yourself open to new learning of all sorts—both in and out of school. You might consider what you've learned about yourself, about others, and about life during the past six months. You can look at what blocks your learning and think about your fears and resistances toward being open to learning. Are your beliefs and values fixed, or are they open to revision? Do you welcome new ideas as a way of expanding the meaning life has for you, or do new ideas threaten you?

Your View of Human Nature

How do you basically view human beings? Your assumptions about human nature can make a difference with respect to the choices you see yourself as having. If you think that we are determined by our past experiences, you may see yourself as a passive victim of forces that have shaped you and your life. You might dismiss values as being merely the products of conditioning and make little effort to create your own values. If, on the other hand, you believe that we are basically free to choose our stance toward life, even though we are affected by circumstances we haven't chosen, then you may actively seek to create your own basis of action.

Your Values and Your Autonomy

As you look at your own development from early childhood to the present, you can probably find some significant patterns in your choices of values. Some questions you might ask in looking at your own autonomy are: Where did I get my values? Are my values open for modification as I grow toward maturity? Do I insist that the world remain the same for me now as it was during an earlier period of my development? Have I challenged the values I live by and really made them my own, or have I looked to someone else to define what I should value?

The struggle for autonomy is well illustrated by the experience of Carl Rogers, whose theory of personality is based on the idea that we must each trust ourselves and rely on our subjective experience as our ultimate guide in forming our values and making our choices. It's interesting that Rogers's emphasis on the value of autonomy seems to have grown, in part, out of his own struggles to become independent from his parents. As a college student, he took the risk of writing a letter to his parents telling them that his views were changing from fundamentalist to liberal and that he was developing his own philosophy of life. Even though Rogers knew that his departure from the values of his parents would hurt them, he felt that such a move was necessary for his own intellectual and psychological freedom.

As you examine your own values, you might reflect on the value you place on your own autonomy. Is it important to you to feel that you are your own person? Are you satisfied with living by the expectations that others have for you? Do you want to become more independent, even though there are risks involved? Or do you prefer the security of being what others want you to be?

Your Values and Your Body

When you look at your body in the mirror, what does this reflection tell you about the degree to which you value that body? Your body presents an image, to both yourself and to others, of how you view yourself. Your ability to love others, to form nourishing sexual and emotional relationships with others, to work well, to play with joy, and to fully savor each day depends a great deal on your physical health. At this time you might think again about how well you are taking care of yourself physically, both through proper diet and regular physical exercise. Do you really value your body and your health, or are you choosing to neglect or abuse your body?

Your Values and Your Sexuality

Earlier in this book, I encouraged you to look at your identity as a man or a woman and to ask whether there are ways in which you're trapped by others' standards of appropriate sex-role behavior. If you looked at yourself in this way, perhaps you discovered that you've been restricting yourself to the narrow range of feelings and behavior prescribed by a male or female stereotype. Deciding what it means for *you* to be a man or a woman is an important part of deciding what kind of person you want to be.

Your sexuality can be an expression of your total self; it can enhance and vitalize you. However, sex can also be a meaningless act or a way of avoiding intimacy with others. Your values will have much to do with how you experience sex and how you choose to act as a sexual person.

It does seem evident to me that being a sexual partner implies valuing one's own sexuality. Thus, one important "value" question is how much you respect your sexuality. What importance do you place on developing your sexuality? Do fears, shame, or guilt keep you from experiencing your sexuality and sensuality in the way you'd like to experience them?

Love and Meaning

Freud defined the healthy person as one who can work well and love well. Like work, love can make living worthwhile, even during bleak times. We can find meaning in actively caring for others and helping them to make their lives better. Because of our love for others or their love for us, we may be enabled to continue living, even in conditions of extreme hardship. Thus, Frankl (1963) noted that, in the concentration camp, some of those who kept alive the images of those they loved and retained some measure of hope survived the ordeal, while many who lost any memories of love perished. From his experiences, Frankl concluded that "the salvation of man is through love and in love" (p. 59).

What place does love have in your life? How is your life different now because of those who love you or those whom you love? What meaning does love give to your life? What would your life be like if you didn't have love in it?

Your Values and Your Intimate Relationships

Do your friendships and other relationships contribute to the meaning in your life? Do you have friends with whom you can be completely yourself? Do they challenge or confront you concerning what you value and the degree to which you're living according to your beliefs? In these and many other ways, intimate relationships can be vitally related to our quest for meaning and values. I'm fond of Goethe's observation that, by taking people as they are, we make them worse, but by treating them as if they already were what they ought to be, we help make them better.

Your values have much to do with the relationships you choose. There are many ways of relating to another person, from a brief and casual encounter to a deep, long-term relationship. You may choose homosexual or heterosexual relationships, conventional marriage or your own variation of it, living with someone as an experiment, a group marriage, communal living, and so on. Whatever styles you choose, the important question is what values you find in them. What do your relationships bring to your life? Are you living in a certain life-style because parents, friends, or others expect you to, or have you selected a life-style that satisfies your own sense of values?

Your Values and Your Work

Work can be a major part of your quest for meaning, but it can also be a source of meaninglessness. Work can be an expression of yourself; it can be, as Gibran (1923) says, "love made visible" (p. 27). It can be a way for you to be productive and to find enjoyment in daily life. Through your work, you might be making a significant difference in the quality of your life or the lives of others, and this may give you real satisfaction. But work can also be devoid of any self-expressive value. It can be merely a means to survival and a drain on your energy. Instead of giving life value and meaning, it can actually be a destructive force that contributes to an early death, as Jess Lair (1976) describes in *I Ain't Much, Baby— But I'm All I've Got!* Lair relates that he was so caught up in succeeding in the business world that he had a heart attack. While he was recovering in his hospital bed, he looked at his life and saw that he had made many destructive choices and that his work was killing him. At that point he made a decision that he has stuck with since: "From this time on I am never again going to do something that I don't deeply believe in" (p. 11). I encourage you to ask yourself: Is my work life-giving? Does it bring meaning to my life? If not, what can I do about it? Is my most meaningful activity—my true work—something I do away from the job?

Your Values and Loneliness and Solitude

In *Shifting Gears*, the O'Neills (1975) suggest that many people fear loneliness so much that they will do almost anything to escape it:

> We are afraid to be alone or to feel loneliness because we do not depend on ourselves. We have become so accustomed to depending on others to give pleasure, to fulfill our needs and to give us direction that we are lost when alone. Fearing it, we avoid it, throwing ourselves into random movement, into *anything* that will prevent us from being alone. Fear of loneliness has become a national obsession [pp. 248–249].

What value do you place on the experience of solitude? Have you found meaning in loneliness or in being alone with yourself? Is avoiding loneliness of overriding importance for you? Is it important to you to take time to be with your own thoughts, to see what you really care about, and to discover the things that most give your life meaning?

Death and Meaning

In the preceding chapter, I stressed the idea that our awareness of death enables us to give meaning to our lives. The reality of our finiteness compels us to look at our priorities and to ask what we value most, what brings the most meaning to our lives. In this way, coming to terms with death can teach us how to really live. To run from death is to run from life, for as Gibran (1923) wrote, "Life and death are one, even as the river and the sea are one" (p. 71).

Time Out for Personal Reflection

Complete the following sentences by writing down the first responses that come to mind.

1. *My parents have influenced my values by* _____

   _____

2. *Life would hardly be worth living if it weren't for* _____

3. *One thing that I most want to say about my life at this point is*

   _____

4. *If I could change one thing about my life at this point, it would be*

   _____

5. *If I had to answer the question "Who am I?" in a sentence, I'd say:*

   _____

6. *What I like best about me is* _____

7. *I keep myself alive and vital by* _____

8. *I'm unique, in that* _____

9. *When I think of my future, I* _____

10. *I feel discouraged about life when* _____

11. *My friends have influenced my values by* _____

12. *My beliefs have been most influenced by* _____

13. *I feel most powerful when* _____

14. *If I don't change,* _____

15. *I feel good about myself when* _____

16. *To me, the essence of a meaningful life is* _____

17. *I suffer from a sense of meaninglessness when* _____

_____

Chapter Summary

Seeking meaning and purpose in life is an important part of being human. In this chapter, I've suggested that meaning is not automatically bestowed on us but instead is the result of our active thinking and choosing. I've encouraged you to recognize your own present values and to ask both how you acquired them and whether you can affirm them for yourself out of your own experience and reflection. This task of examining our values and purposes is, to me, one that lasts a lifetime.

The following are some of the key ideas in this chapter. I encourage you to think about each idea and to take your own position regarding it.

1. We need to have a sense of hope and a reason for living.
2. Many people who appear to have achieved success lead empty and unfulfilling lives.
3. When meaning is absent in our lives, we begin to die psychologically.
4. We create meaning by our own choices.
5. Only if we challenge our values and make them truly our own can they give us direction in living.
6. Developing a philosophy of life is a lifelong endeavor.

List some additional ideas from this chapter that you'd most like to remember:

_____

_____

_____

_____

Activities and Exercises

Writing Your Philosophy of Life

To integrate your thoughts and reflections on the topics raised in this chapter and throughout this book, I encourage you to develop, in writing, your philosophy of life. Your paper should represent a critical analysis of who you are now and of the factors that have been most influential in contributing to that person. You should also discuss the person you'd like to become; include your goals for the future and the means by which you think you'll be able to achieve them.

The following outline may be a helpful guide as you write your paper. Feel free to use or omit any part of the outline, and modify it in any way that will help you to write a paper that is personally significant. You might also consider adding poetry, excerpts from other writers, and pictures or works of art to supplement your writing, if they will contribute to the meaningfulness of your paper.

I. Who are you now? What influences have contributed to the person you are now?
   A. Influences during childhood
      1. Your relationship with your parents
      2. Your relationship with your siblings
      3. Important turning points
      4. Successes and failures
      5. Personal conflicts
      6. Family expectations
      7. Impact of school and early learning experiences
      8. Your relationships with friends
      9. Experiences of loneliness
      10. Other
   B. Influences during adolescence
      1. Impact of your family and your relationship with your parents
      2. School experiences
      3. Personal struggles
      4. Critical turning points
      5. Influence of your peer group
      6. Experiences of loneliness
      7. Successes and failures, and their impact on you
      8. Influential adults other than parents

      9. Your principal values

    10. Other

  C. Love and sex

      1. Your need for love

      2. Your fear of love

      3. The meaning of love for you

      4. Dating experiences and their effect on you

      5. Your view of sex roles

      6. Expectations of others and their influence on your sex role

      7. Attitudes toward the opposite sex

      8. Meaning of sexuality in your life

      9. Your values concerning love and sex

    10. Other

  D. Intimate relationships and family life

      1. The value you place on marriage

      2. How children fit in your life

      3. The meaning of intimacy for you

      4. The kind of intimate relationships you want

      5. Areas of struggle for you in relating to others

      6. Your views of marriage

      7. Your values concerning family life

      8. How social expectations have influenced your views

      9. Sex roles in intimate relationships

    10. Other

  E. Death and meaning

      1. Your view of an afterlife

      2. Religious views and your view of death

      3. The way death affects you

      4. Sources of meaning in your life

      5. The things you most value in your life

      6. Your struggles in finding meaning and purpose

      7. Religion and the meaning of life

      8. Critical turning points in finding meaning

      9. Influential people in your life

    10. Other

II. Who do you want to become?

  A. Summary of your present position

      1. How you see yourself now (strengths and weaknesses)

      2. How others perceive you now

      3. What makes you unique

   4. Your relationships with others
   5. Present struggles
  B. Your future plans for an occupation
   1. Nature of your work plans and their chances for success
   2. Kind of work that is meaningful to you
   3. How you chose or will choose your work
   4. What work means to you
   5. What you expect from work
  C. Your future with others
   1. The kind of relationships you want
   2. What you need to do to achieve the relationships you want
   3. Plans for marriage or an alternative
   4. Place of children in your future plans
  D. Future plans for yourself
   1. How you would like to be ten years from now
    a. What you need to do to achieve your goals
    b. What you can do now
   2. Your values for the future
   3. Your view of the good life
    a. Ways to achieve it
    b. How your view of the good life relates to all aspects of your life
   4. Choices you see as being open to you now
    a. Choices in work
    b. Choices in school
    c. Value choices
    d. Other areas of choice in your life

Suggested Readings

Deikman, A. *Personal Freedom*. New York: Bantam, 1976. This book is a guide to finding your way to the "real world." It offers a challenging view of reality and shows how we have been deceived and how we deceive ourselves in regard to reality.

Dyer, W. *Your Erroneous Zones*. New York: Avon, 1976. In this popular self-help book, Dyer describes ways of discovering pitfalls that lead to stale living and ways of taking charge of your life.

Fabry, J. *The Pursuit of Meaning*. Boston: Beacon Press, 1969. This book, which is based on Viktor Frankl's logotherapy, treats such topics as meaning in life, values, freedom, religion, and traditions.

Frankl, V. *Man's Search for Meaning*. New York: Washington Square Press, 1963; Pocket Books, 1975. In describing his experiences in a concentration camp, Frankl shows how it is possible to find meaning in life through suffering. His thesis is that we all have a need to discover meaning.

Frankl, V. *The Doctor and the Soul*. New York: Bantam, 1965. This book goes into more detail on how to find meaning in death, suffering, work, and love.

Frankl, V. *The Will to Meaning: Foundations and Applications of Logotherapy*. New York: New American Library, 1969. This book sets forth the basic assumptions underlying logotherapy, which include the freedom of the will and the drive to find meaning. Frankl also describes in depth the existential vacuum of meaning that many people experience.

Gale, R. *Who Are You? The Psychology of Being Yourself*. Englewood Cliffs, N.J.: Prentice-Hall (Spectrum), 1974. This is a very readable account of a humanistic perspective of human nature and personal identity. There are good chapters on love, meaning, self-actualization, validating your identity, and becoming an authentic person.

Gibran, K. *The Prophet*. New York: Knopf, 1923. A famous book of poetic essays on such topics as religion, death, friendship, self-knowledge, joy and sorrow, and prayer.

Jourard, S. *The Transparent Self* (Rev. ed.). New York: Van Nostrand Reinhold, 1971. This book has a very worthwhile chapter on "the invitation to die."

Kalish, R. A., & Collier, K. W. *Exploring Human Values: Psychological and Philosophical Considerations*. Monterey, Calif.: Brooks/Cole, 1981. Topics include the nature of meaning, freedom and determinism, knowing as a way of valuing, humanistic psychology and personal growth, and mental health and human values. This is a personal book that focuses on personal and social values from the psychological and the philosophical viewpoints.

Koestenbaum, P. *Managing Anxiety: The Power of Knowing Who You Are*. Englewood Cliffs, N.J.: Prentice-Hall (Spectrum), 1974. This useful book deals with pain, consciousness, meaninglessness, death, guilt, and other existential themes.

Kopp, S. *If You Meet the Buddha on the Road, Kill Him!* New York: Bantam, 1972. The message of this powerful book is that no meaning that comes from outside ourselves is real. The book deals with the theme of finding meaning in life by accepting freedom and responsibility.

Lair, J. *I Ain't Much, Baby—But I'm All I've Got!* New York: Fawcett World, 1976. This popular self-help book deals with a range of topics, including an appraisal of the meaning of life.

Maslow, A. *Toward a Psychology of Being* (2nd ed.). New York: Van Nostrand, 1968. This book contains some excellent material on creative values, personal growth, and self-actualization.

May, R. *Man's Search for Himself*. New York: Dell (Delta), 1973. This is a powerful and provocative work that addresses the issues of rediscovering selfhood, freedom and inner strength, becoming a person, meaning and emptiness, and the unique dimensions of being human.

Moustakas, C. *Finding Yourself, Finding Others.* Englewood Cliffs, N.J.: Prentice-Hall (Spectrum), 1975. A book of brief commentaries on topics such as remaining alive as a person, the path of alienation, the search for self, and valuing one's self.

O'Neill, N., & O'Neill, G. *Shifting Gears.* New York: Avon, 1975. This book deals largely with finding values in a changing society. It can inspire reflection on topics such as formulating a philosophy of life in a world of crisis, changing values, and renewal of self.

Perls, F. *Gestalt Therapy Verbatim.* Lafayette, Calif.: Real People Press, 1969. Much of the material in this book deals with autonomy, identity, and the accepting of responsibility for our own lives.

Powell, J. *Why Am I Afraid to Tell You Who I Am?* Niles, Ill.: Argus Communications, 1969. An easy-to-read and popular book of insights concerning self-awareness, personal growth, and the meaning of life. Powell discusses the human condition, interpersonal relationships, dealing with emotions, and methods of ego defense.

Rogers, C. *On Becoming a Person.* Boston: Houghton Mifflin (Sentry), 1961. In this excellent book, Rogers develops the theme that we each have a natural urge to become a "fully functioning person."

Yalom, I. D. *Existential Psychotherapy.* New York: Basic Books, 1980. Chapters 6 and 7 deal with freedom and responsibility as crucial factors in creating meaning in one's life. Chapters 10 and 11 consider the problem of finding meaning in life and the implications of meaninglessness for psychotherapy. These chapters contain rich clinical material and interesting case examples.

Chapter Twelve

A Consumer's Guide to Resources for Continued Personal Growth

For each statement, indicate the response that most closely identifies your beliefs and attitudes. Use this code: 5 = I *strongly agree* with this statement; 4 = I *agree* in most respects; 3 = I am *undecided*; 2 = I *disagree* in most respects; 1 = I *strongly disagree*.

_____ 1. There is a social stigma attached to going to a counselor or psychotherapist.

_____ 2. Counseling is aimed at producing drastic changes in a person's character and life-style.

_____ 3. Although counseling is an effective way of treating people with emotional problems, it has little to offer people who aren't experiencing some sort of crisis.

_____ 4. Most people experience crises at various times in their lives.

_____ 5. Personal growth requires a willingness to tolerate uncertainty.

_____ 6. Most people who seek counseling or therapy are experiencing some kind of crisis.

_____ 7. Once people achieve insight into their problems, they usually change their behavior.

_____ 8. The experience of pain is an inevitable part of personal growth.

_____ 9. My friends would think that something was wrong with me if I went to a counselor or therapist.

_____ 10. I've experienced personal growth through involvement in intimate relationships.

_____ 11. I want to seek out ways in which I can grow as a person by using my own resources.

_____ 12. Encounter groups and therapy groups are suitable for everyone.

_____ 13. It's important to shop around carefully before selecting a personal counselor or group leader.

_____ 14. The basic goal of counseling and psychotherapy is to teach people how to understand and resolve their own problems.

_____ 15. Counseling is essentially a form of advice giving.

_____ 16. Reading good books is one way to grow as a person.

_____ 17. Personal growth is a continuing process rather than something that essentially ends when we reach adulthood.

_____ 18. I would be interested in some type of group experience as an avenue to personal growth.

_____ 19. I'd be willing to get involved in some type of individual counseling if I felt the need to do so.

_____ 20. Even as adults, if we're not growing, we're stagnating.

Introduction

Now that you're completing this book and your course, you may want to consider ways of continuing your personal learning. In this final chapter, I describe some ways of expanding your self-awareness, beginning with steps you can take for yourself. I also present a "consumer's guide" to continued personal growth through individual and group counseling. Although counseling is often very helpful in times of crisis, I'll be emphasizing the use of counseling as a way of expanding our awareness of ourselves and of others. In other words, I encourage you to think of professional assistance as a resource you can use in increasing your self-understanding and thus your range of choices, rather than as a place to turn only when you feel overwhelmed by problems in living.

Choosing Experiences for Personal Growth

You can deliberately choose experiences for yourself that will enhance your growth as a person. Perhaps you remember reading a book or viewing a film that had a profound impact on you and really seemed to put things in perspective. Certainly, reading books that deal with significant issues in your life can be a growth experience in itself, as well as an encouragement to try new things.

Often, we make all sorts of resolutions about what we'd like to be doing in our lives or about experiences we want to share with others, and then we fail to carry them out. Is this true of you? Are there activities you value yet rarely get around to doing? Perhaps you tell yourself that you prize making new friendships; yet you find that you do very little to actually initiate any contacts. Or perhaps you derive satisfaction from growing vegetables or puttering in your garden and yet find many reasons to neglect this activity. You might tell yourself that you'd love to take a day or two just to be alone and yet never get around to arranging it. When you stop to think about it, aren't there choices you could be making right now that would make your life a richer one? How would you really like to be spending your time? What changes are you willing to make today, this week, this month, this year?

In addition to activities that you enjoy but don't engage in as often as you'd like, there are undoubtedly many new things you might consider trying out as ways of adding meaning to your life and developing your potentials. You might consider making a contract with yourself to start now on a definite plan of action, instead of putting it off until next week

or next year. Some of the ways in which many people choose to challenge themselves to grow include the following:

- finding hobbies that develop new sides of themselves
- going to plays, concerts, and museums
- taking courses in pottery making, wine tasting, guitar playing, and innumerable other special interests
- getting involved in exciting work projects or actively pursuing forms of work that will lead to the development of hidden talents
- spending time alone to reflect on the quality of their lives
- initiating contacts with others and perhaps developing an intimate relationship
- enrolling in continuing-education courses or earning a degree primarily for the satisfaction of learning
- doing volunteer work and helping to make others' lives better
- experiencing the mountains, the desert, and the ocean—by hiking, sailing, and so on
- becoming involved in religious activities
- traveling to new places, especially to experience different cultures
- keeping a journal

Any list of ways of growing is only a sample, of course; the avenues to personal growth are as various as the people who choose them. What I want to suggest is that growth can occur in small ways and that there are many things that you can do on your own (or with friends or family) to continue your personal development. Perhaps the greatest hindrance to our growth as persons is our failure to allow ourselves to imagine all the possibilities that are open to us.

Time Out for Personal Reflection

1. *Check any of the following activities involving professional resources that you think you might like to pursue in the near future as a way of continuing your personal development.*

_____   *attend a personal-growth group*
_____   *take another psychology course*
_____   *become involved in some kind of personal counseling*
_____   *seek family counseling*
_____   *seek marital or relationship counseling*
_____   *take a class in Eastern philosophies*
_____   *learn to practice yoga*
_____   *attend an assertiveness-training workshop*
_____   *join a consciousness-raising group*
_____   *get involved in some type of self-control program (for example, to lose weight or stop smoking)*
_____   *attend a massage workshop*
_____   *learn relaxation exercises*

2. *List any other activities involving professional resources that you might want to pursue in the near future.*

_____

_____

_____

_____

_____

3. *What are some of the reasons that you haven't previously done the things you've listed? Check any of the following responses that fit you.*

_____   *I haven't known about some of the available resources.*
_____   *I haven't been able to afford some of the activities I've listed.*
_____   *I'm afraid of failing.*
_____   *I'm hesitant about trying new things.*
_____   *I haven't had the time.*

List any other reasons that apply to you.

_____

_____

_____

4. *What are some things you'd like to do more often, or begin doing, that would not demand the use of professional resources? Check any of the following that fit you.*

_____   *play more often*
_____   *spend more time alone*
_____   *exercise more frequently*
_____   *do more reading*
_____   *keep a detailed daily journal*
_____   *attend church more often*
_____   *be more open in my intimate relationships*
_____   *take better care of my body*
_____   *increase my enjoyment of sex and sensuality*
_____   *do things for other people*
_____   *cultivate more hobbies*

5. *List any other things that you'd like to do, either by yourself or with others:*

_____

_____

_____

_____

_____

6. *What are some of the reasons that you haven't done the things you've listed more often?*

_____

_____

_____

7. *Review your responses so far, and then write down some specific things you're willing to do for yourself or others within the next month.*

_____

_____

_____

_____

_____

Individual and Group Counseling as Avenues to Personal Growth

So far in this chapter, I've encouraged you to think of things that you can do on your own to further your personal growth. In addition, there are professional resources we can utilize to increase our understanding of ourselves and others. A counselor or psychotherapist can provide a unique relationship by means of which we can gain insight into our early decisions and learn to make new choices for more effective living. The rest of the chapter describes a range of professional resources that you might consider using.

Counseling and Psychotherapy

What are counseling and psychotherapy? How are they alike? How are they different? I use the term *counseling* to refer to the process whereby people are given an opportunity to explore personal concerns with a trained professional. Frequently, this exploration leads to an increased awareness of their possibilities for choice. Generally speaking, counseling is short term, focuses on problems, and helps people remove blocks to their personal growth and to discover their inner resources. Unlike counseling, *psychotherapy* frequently focuses on unconscious processes and is much more concerned with changes in personality structure. Rather than being aimed merely at the resolution of particular problems, psychotherapy generally is geared toward the development of an intensive self-understanding of the inner dynamics that give rise to these problems.

I want to emphasize that counseling and psychotherapy don't have to be thought of in terms of a medical model, according to which clients are patients who need to be cured of mental illnesses. It's true that psychotherapy is one process used with people who function ineffec-

tively or who have become overwhelmed by stresses and conflicts. However, individual counseling and therapy, as well as group methods, have much to offer those who simply want to increase their self-awareness and more fully develop their personalities. The remainder of this chapter discusses counseling approaches primarily in terms of their value as resources for personal growth.

The Experience of Individual and Group Counseling

The counseling experience is difficult to describe in general, since it varies with the personalities of clients and counselors, the styles and orientations of counselors, and the particular relationships that are established between clients and their counselors. The following general remarks may give you some idea of what the experience of counseling is like; however, you should keep in mind that counseling is a highly subjective and personal experience.

Most clients enter counseling with definite expectations, although these will be different for each client. Some expect relief from disabling symptoms. Some are searching for an answer to their conflicts from the counselor; others hope that the counselor will help them find their own answers. In addition to their hopes or expectations, most clients have some fears about what counseling will be like or about what they might discover about themselves. During the initial stages one of the best ways for a client to establish a trusting relationship with the counselor is to talk about these expectations and fears. Rapport is a prerequisite of any real progress.

As counseling progresses, clients usually begin to express feelings and thoughts that they formerly kept out of awareness. They become able to talk about themselves in deeply personal ways and to trust that their feelings are being accepted. Because of the care and acceptance they receive from the counselor, they are increasingly able to accept themselves. They feel less need to be defensive, and they move in the direction of being open to all the facets of themselves. This openness enables them to achieve a clarity about themselves that they did not have before.

It isn't unusual for clients to feel worse before they feel better, however. As people open up to another human being (and to themselves), they become more vulnerable and exposed. As they shed the defenses that have been shielding them from threat, they experience some anxiety before they develop new resources with which to replace these defenses. Some people may say: "Sometimes I wonder whether it was wise to begin counseling, because I *feel* my sadness and fear more now than I ever did before. Maybe I should have stayed less aware and more comfortable." Fortunately, if they have the courage to stay with the counseling process for a time, they generally discover resources within themselves that they can draw on in making changes.

The expression of feelings, the reliving of past experiences, and the discussion of current struggles are all a part of counseling, but they are not the whole story. As clients express themselves, they begin to see connections between their past and their present, they come to see their own role in creating their own unhappiness or dissatisfaction, and they generally gain new insight into themselves. For most counselors, this achievement of self-awareness is not the end of counseling but merely the beginning. The crucial issue is what clients choose to do with the awareness they acquire. For this reason, most approaches emphasize that it's very important for clients to work on actively changing their behavior outside of the counseling sessions in ways that accord with their new insights. As they make specific changes in their behavior, they generally feel more in control of their own lives. When a client and counselor decide to discontinue their sessions together, the client takes an important step toward greater autonomy. Ideally, by the time clients come to the end of the counseling process, they have acquired some of the tools they need to continue their own growth and to challenge themselves. They aren't "finished products," any more than anyone else, but they have become able to make clearer, more authentic choices.

This general description of psychological counseling is applicable to both individual and group counseling. Although these two broad types of counseling have much in common, each has its unique features and strengths.

Individual counseling provides an opportunity for an in-depth involvement between clients and counselors. The one-to-one relationship can provide the continuity and trust that enable clients to explore highly personal material. Further, it can give them the opportunity to relive past and present conflicts with the significant individuals in their lives. Through the counseling relationship, clients can come to understand how their other relationships affect them.

In therapeutic groups, the one-to-one relationship is not the primary focus. Generally, a group is a microcosm of society. Group members, in relating to one another, can begin to appreciate how others perceive them. They can use the group situation to try out new behavior among people who are responsive and accepting. Through this process of experimentation, they can make decisions about what changes they want to make in their everyday behavior. Groups also give people the chance to learn interpersonal skills. The members open themselves to certain risks; they confront others and are confronted by others; they give and receive support; and they have an opportunity to get a clearer picture of themselves.

Time Out for Personal Reflection

In the next section, I discuss the values and limitations of counseling, some cautions and risks associated with it, and a few common misconceptions about it. This discussion may help you decide whether some type of counseling would be useful to you. Before going on, however, pause a moment to focus on your own present beliefs and attitudes about counseling.

Mark each of the following statements with a T or an F to indicate whether you think the statement is true or false.

_____   1. Counselors generally decide on the goals a client should have.
_____   2. Therapeutic groups are artificial and unreal.
_____   3. Only people who are psychologically disturbed seek individual or group counseling.
_____   4. It's wise to begin counseling when someone close to you recommends it.
_____   5. Counseling can be an effective way of resolving crises.
_____   6. If I become involved in counseling, the counselor or group leader will be able to tell me what I do wrong and how I can correct a situation.
_____   7. Pursuing either individual or group counseling would be an indication that there was something wrong with me.
_____   8. If I seek out counseling, things may get worse before they get better.
_____   9. It's acceptable for a client to disagree with a counselor.
_____   10. If I join a counseling group, I can expect to like some members more than others.
_____   11. It can be useful to talk about feelings and problems.
_____   12. Counseling is really a form of brainwashing.
_____   13. Most people experience some fear and anxiety when beginning individual or group counseling.
_____   14. If I'm honest and disclose my true feelings, the counselor or group leader will provide me with answers to my problems.
_____   15. Counseling may disrupt a person's life.
_____   16. By participating in a counseling group, I would come to realize that I'm not alone in my struggles.
_____   17. Going to a counselor or group can be a way of remaining dependent.
_____   18. Counseling involves risks.
_____   19. Only counselors can really help people change.
_____   20. Counseling can teach people that they are responsible for their own problems.

Basic Issues in Individual and Group Counseling

Values of Individual and Group Counseling

Although they are surely not the only means of growing, individual and group counseling can help you come to a greater awareness of yourself and lead to greater self-development. The following are some of the values I see in them:

1. Counseling provides a learning situation in which we can openly explore our style of relating with others.
2. Counselors can offer support and encourage us to experiment with new behaviors.
3. Through counseling, we can hear how others see us, and we can use this reaction to better understand the impact we have on others.
4. Through counseling we can realize that we're not alone in our struggles and thus come to feel less isolated.
5. Counseling can help us gain insight into the nature of our problems, and it can help us in our decision making by teaching us to look within ourselves for our own answers.
6. Counseling can show us new sides of ourselves. We can discover things about ourselves that disturb us, yet at the same time we can discover latent strengths that we have denied.

Limitations of Individual and Group Counseling

Although counseling can have the values I've mentioned, there are also some common limitations.

1. Counseling isn't appropriate for everybody at all times. Individuals should decide for themselves whether they want counseling and whether the time is right for them to pursue it. Some people may feel ready for a relationship with an individual therapist but not for a group experience. Others, while not feeling a need for individual counseling, may want to become involved in a short-term personal-growth group. If you consider counseling, it's important that *you* be the one who decides whether you should become involved in it and what type is right for you.
2. Individuals can use counseling to remain dependent on others for direction. They may look to the expectations and values of the counselor or of the members of a group for guidance, instead of deciding on their own expectations of themselves.
3. Some people become addicted to a group or to their weekly counseling sessions and make the counseling process an end in itself rather than a means to change.
4. Some people use counseling sessions as a forum for venting their misery, in the hope that they will be rewarded for being "open." Although there is a value to expressing our woes, it seems to me that it's important to work on actually changing our situations and that too many people get stuck in the mere expression of problems.

5. Neither individual nor group counseling is a cure-all. A person who looks to the professional for all the answers to his or her problems will be disappointed.

Risks in Individual and Group Counseling

When considering counseling, you should be aware of some of the hazards involved and of what you can do to protect yourself from them. The following are a few important guidelines.

1. Keep in mind that either individual or group counseling may lead to a disruption in your life-style. For example, you might have a style of asking for very little for yourself and so tolerate a mediocre marriage. As a result of counseling, you may begin an intense process of searching and questioning that leads to drastic changes in your values and behavior. Of course, these changes may be constructive and lead to a revitalization of your personal life, but the process may also involve crisis and turmoil. Your spouse, for instance, may not welcome or be ready for changes, and this can create a difficulty for you.

2. Be aware of your rights as a client. You can choose whether to enter into individual counseling or try a group. You have the right to disagree with or question the therapist or group leader, as well as the right to terminate your counseling. If you don't feel satisfied with a therapist, you can select another one. Realistically, in some situations (such as in a community mental-health center), you may not have options presented to you. You may be assigned to a group because groups enable a therapist to see more than one client at a time. However, various resources are usually available in a community, and you should keep in mind that you don't have to be a passive agent in your counseling.

3. There is a risk that you will be turned off to counseling because of a single negative experience with a counselor. Consequently, it's important to recognize that counselors don't all function in the same way and that personality differences among counselors are also significant. Thus, you may have a very positive experience with another counselor even if you're unhappy with your first one.

4. It's important not to quit counseling prematurely. There is a danger of opening up vulnerable areas and then terminating counseling before they are really dealt with. In addition, you should realize that counseling may lead to some changes that affect the people you're close to. For example, you might decide to risk more and to tell a person that you'd like to have his or her support—and then discover that, instead of sup-

porting you, the other person fights your changes. As a result, you may become discouraged and undo the work you began in your counseling. Ideally, you and your counselor will agree on when the time comes to discontinue your sessions together.

5. Keep in mind that you are the one who should decide on the goals of your counseling. Some groups fall into the trap of imposing the values of the group on its members. Of course, the imposition of the counselor's values is a real danger in individual counseling also. Remember that counseling is a tool to help you clarify your own issues and provide you with resources for making choices; it's not a way of having your decisions made for you.

Misconceptions Concerning Individual and Group Counseling

Some common myths and misconceptions may lead you to conclude that the disadvantages of counseling far outweigh the advantages. For this reason, I want to comment briefly on some of these misconceptions.

1. *Counseling is a form of brainwashing.* On the contrary: counseling should assist you to look within yourself for your own answers to present and future problems in your life. Counseling is not synonymous with advice giving; nor does it involve the indoctrination of a "correct" philosophy of life.

2. *Only sick people seek individual or group counseling.* Although some forms of counseling are specifically aimed at helping people in crises or assisting people who are psychologically disturbed, many people utilize individual and group counseling to come to a fuller recognition of their potential and to remove blocks to personal growth.

3. *People in counseling become more unhappy, because their problems come to the surface.* There is some truth in this statement. Conflict *can* arise if you face painful truths about yourself, but it's important to realize that this increased awareness can lead to decisive steps toward change. Once you accept that you contribute to your own unhappiness or dissatisfaction, you have the choice of doing something to change your life.

4. *Counseling leaves a person defenseless.* People frequently express the fear that counseling will only rob them of defenses and that they won't have the resources to cope successfully without them. In fact, many people learn through counseling that rigid defenses aren't always necessary and that they can decide to shed unnecessary defenses that seal them off from others.

DOCTOR, THERE'S A MAN IN A PLAIN BROWN ENVELOPE TO SEE YOU.

5. *Fear of counseling isn't normal.* On the contrary: most people who enter individual counseling or join a group do experience some anxiety. The important thing is how we deal with the fears we experience as we confront ourselves.

6. *Counselors will make you dependent on them, and they will keep you coming to them for longer than is necessary.* Both the client and the counselor should be involved in determining the length of the counseling program. If you have any doubts, you should bring them up and discuss them.

7. *Counseling provides an instant cure.* It is not uncommon, when people begin to experience immediate relief (mainly because someone is listening to them), for them to have the illusion that "all is well." They may quit prematurely after the first or second session, believing that they have effectively dealt with the problem that brought them to the counselor. It is important to realize that counselors are not magicians and that people change only through difficult and sustained work.

8. *An effective counselor has resolved all of his or her own struggles and problems.* It is a myth that counselors are problem-free people. What is important is that they face and deal with their problems in a constructive way. Counselors who have major unresolved problems that they are not recognizing or working on will encounter difficulty in effectively working with others.

9. *Counseling is useful for those who seek it primarily to help others.* You can directly change only yourself. Thus, if a man seeks counseling so that he can "help" his wife or change her, he is bound to experience frustration. However, he could deal in counseling with his own reactions toward her and toward his marriage.

10. *Marriage counseling is a last resort before a divorce.* There is a danger in deciding on a divorce before entering marriage counseling and then using participation as evidence of a serious attempt to make the marriage work. Marital counseling can be useful in helping couples take an honest look at their relationship without blaming each other. Through this process they can make decisions about what they want to change, and surely one option is separating or divorcing. However, both parties should enter counseling with a sincere interest in exploring whether they want to remain together.

Some Consumer Guidelines for Selecting a Counselor or a Group

With the range of professional services available, the consumer is sometimes at a loss in making a decision and knowing what to look for. Although there are no assurances that the group or counselor you pick will be the right one for you, the following suggestions may be helpful in making your selection.

1. It's generally unwise to initiate private counseling or to join a group simply because someone else thinks you should. Instead, decide for yourself whether you want to be a client of a particular kind of group or of a particular counselor.

2. Try to check with others who know the counselor or group leader before you make your decision. Although some reports may be biased (either positively or negatively), information from people who have worked with a counselor or group leader can be valuable.

3. Before you begin, interview the counselor or group leader. For example, suppose that you're considering joining a group. Many group leaders will want a private session with a prospective member to deter-

mine the person's readiness for the group. By the same token, you have a right to know about the personal and professional qualifications of the leader. If the group leader resists such a request, you should probably avoid this person's group. If you do speak with the leader, try to decide the degree to which he or she inspires trust in you.

4. Learn to be an intelligent consumer of psychological services. After all, if you were interested in buying a car or a house, you would probably shop around and make some comparisons. Since the selection of a therapist that you will want to trust with intimate aspects of yourself is a crucial decision, devote the necessary time to looking for the service and the person that will best fit your needs. In making your selection, you might consider some of the following questions:

- What are the responsibilities of the therapist and of the client?
- What are the expectations of the therapist or group leader?
- What are some of the psychological risks involved in participating in this type of counseling?
- What are the desired outcomes, and what measures are taken to achieve them? What techniques does the therapist use?
- What are the fees? Will insurance cover a portion of them?
- What background, training, and experience does the therapist have?
- What is his or her specialty? What degrees and licenses does he or she possess?

As you consider the selection of a counselor, keep in mind that this is a highly personal decision. Consequently, even though you want to select a qualified person, one of the most important aspects of your decision is your degree of trust in that person.

5. If you have any reservations about your own readiness to enter individual counseling or to participate in a group, I suggest discussing them with the counselor or group leader before making a commitment. For example, you may have some anxiety concerning your readiness for counseling, you may wonder whether a group is really what you need, or you may have fears about participating. Any of these matters could be productively explored in a precounseling interview.

6. Be very cautious about responding to advertisements or to brochures and pamphlets circulated in the mail. Referrals from agencies, from professionals, and most of all from clients who have worked with a counselor can more appropriately guide you in your selection.

7. Check with your college or university counseling center to find out what professional services they offer. These counseling services are gen-

erally offered free to students and are designed especially for the needs of college students of all ages.

8. Look into the continuing-education or extension programs and summer sessions of the community colleges and other colleges and universities in your area. Increasingly, departments of psychology, education, and counseling are offering many types of experiential courses, personal-growth groups, weekend workshops, and special-interest programs. For instance, most college-extension programs offer several types of workshops or groups, such as groups for the divorced, assertiveness-training groups, groups for professionals, couples' workshops, and consciousness-raising groups for both men and women.

9. Check out the resources for individual counseling, marriage and family counseling, and groups available at community mental-health centers. Many local agencies provide counseling services on an ability-to-pay basis.

Counseling for Crisis Resolution

This discussion of individual and group counseling has focused primarily on the use of these resources as aids in personal growth. However, the same guidelines apply if you find yourself in some type of crisis at any time in your life. For example, a divorce can precipitate a crisis in an entire family, or an adolescent son or daughter who gets heavily involved in drugs can cause a crisis that involves every person in the family. You may experience a crisis if you fail to get a promotion or if you lose a job. Many people experience a mid-life crisis when they begin to realize that many of their dreams and hopes will not be fulfilled. Loss of a loved one through death or separation can also lead to a crisis. In short, there are many sources of minor or major disruptions in our lives, and at times you may want to seek some form of counseling to help you get through a crisis more effectively than you would by coping with the problems yourself.

Deciding Whether You Need Professional Services

Often people are unclear about whether they need or want to get involved in psychological counseling. How can you know whether you have a need for psychological services? This is an extremely difficult question to answer in general, but I'll give as examples some reasons that clients typically seek professional assistance. *Some* people initiate personal therapy because:

- They are facing a situational crisis in which they feel their subjective world (or some part of it) is collapsing.
- They have been unable to get free from a prolonged period of depression, anxiety, or guilt.
- They find that their work is no longer meaningful and that they want to explore other options.
- They are hurting over a situation and want help in understanding how to deal with their hurt.
- They find their marriage intolerable and want to resolve their conflicts by discovering more constructive ways of living together.
- They feel a deadness and lack of meaning in their lives.
- They have certain symptoms that interfere with their functioning, such as being overweight, frequently getting sick, having exaggerated fears, and so forth.

No set of guidelines concerning whether you need counseling or psychotherapy can be complete, of course, because so much depends on how much you want for yourself. Some people are satisfied as long as they are relatively comfortable. Some seek therapy only when they are in emotional turmoil; as soon as they begin to feel less emotionally upset, or as soon as the crisis passes, they terminate their counseling. Some people hope that a counselor will take away all their problems. Others who feel they have grown stale want to do something to get out of a rut they're in. Thus, the decision to seek professional help depends greatly on whether you want what you have now or want to risk doing whatever is necessary to make greater progress in your life.

You may be hesitant to initiate personal therapy because you feel that there is a stigma attached to being in therapy. Many people feel that it is a sign of weakness or inadequacy to need help from others, and they believe that they should be able to resolve any crisis by themselves. However, it takes courage to recognize things about yourself that you want to change and then to follow through by actually doing something to change. This may involve trusting a therapist to challenge you and assist in your learning, and doing so is hardly a confession of weakness.

Where to Go for Professional Assistance

If you decide that you want to use professional resources, where can you go for help, and how can you find out what resources are available? In most communities, there are mental-health centers and free clinics that offer a variety of services. These agencies can also give you leads on where to go for assistance with particular problems. You can check with friends to see whether any of them have been involved in counseling and, if so, what their impression of the counselor was. The university or college counseling center is another place to look. If you're enrolled in the college, the services may be free or available on an ability-to-pay basis. If you aren't enrolled, the center can probably give you a list of professionals in private practice or in community clinics. Ministers and physicians can also refer you to counseling professionals.

You should also have some understanding of the different types of mental-health professional. Each type has its own strengths, but they all have much in common. Members of the helping professions generally try to minimize or eliminate the environmental conditions that may be causing and maintaining behavioral problems. They all are concerned with developing therapeutic (growth-producing) relationships with clients, and many of them use similar techniques.

In practice, the lines between the various professionals and professional services are not always clearly drawn, and there may be considerable overlap in functions. With this in mind, let's look at the various personnel who offer these human services.

Members of the Helping Professions

Clinical psychologists.   Clinical psychologists have Ph.D.s in psychology and have had two years of supervised clinical practice (internship). They deal with psychological testing, psychotherapy, and research. Clinical psychologists are usually trained in both individual and group therapy; in most states, they must also possess a license to engage in private practice.

Counseling psychologists.   Counseling psychologists hold a doctoral degree, either a Ph.D. or an Ed.D., from a counseling program at a university. They have had essentially the same kind of training as clinical psychologists, although their internships are with clients who have problems related to educational, vocational, and personal/social matters. Counseling psychologists often work in college counseling centers or for community mental-health agencies. They might also have a private practice in which they perform individual and group counseling or therapy, in which case they must be licensed by the state.

Educational psychologists and school psychologists.   Educational and school psychologists specialize in learning, problems in learning, and testing and evaluation. Some school psychologists, who usually hold a master's degree, do some counseling with parents, families, or children, but they are more likely to do testing and make referrals to other professionals if treatment is indicated.

Psychiatrists.   Psychiatrists are trained doctors (M.D.s) who have had specialized training in psychiatry in mental hospitals or clinics. In addition to practicing verbal therapy, psychiatrists can prescribe medication and may use various drugs in conjunction with therapy. Psychiatrists often perform the same services as clinical psychologists, except that they tend to specialize in cases of more severe disturbances or of psychosomatic disorders, such as high blood pressure, migraine headaches, respiratory problems, skin disorders, and so on. Many psychiatrists are oriented toward the psychoanalytic approach to therapy originated by Freud.

Psychoanalysts.   Psychoanalysts are usually psychiatrists who have had extensive training in the theory and practice of intensive psychotherapy founded by Freud. Although psychiatrists may also make use of psychoanalytic techniques, psychoanalysts base their treatment procedure on the lengthy process of analysis described in Chapter 2.

Behavior therapists.   Behavior therapists are psychologists who specialize in behavior modification—that is, in the use of learning principles in eliminating maladaptive behavior and shaping more effective behaviors. Behavior therapy was also described in Chapter 2.

Psychiatric social workers.   Psychiatric social workers have master's degrees in social work and have had supervised internships in psychiatric settings. They may work in clinics, in private practice as psychotherapists, or in social-service agencies. Their training makes them especially qualified to work with families of clients in treatment, with social and cultural realities that cause personal stress, with community groups, and with individuals.

Psychiatric nurses.   Psychiatric nurses have had specialized education and training in work with emotionally disturbed patients. They often work in conjunction with psychiatrists; they may also practice individual and group therapy with supervision or work with families.

Marriage and family therapists.   These counselors hold master's or doctoral degrees in a behavioral-science field (usually counseling or psychology) or in marriage, family, and child counseling. They specialize in problems in relationships and often help couples with their sexual conflicts.

Paraprofessionals.   In addition to the professionals who work in the mental-health field, there are increasing numbers of paraprofessionals who perform many of the same psychological services. Paraprofessionals usually have A.A. degrees in human services from a community college or B.A. degrees in human services from a college or university. There are also paraprofessionals who are serving internships as part of their master's degree programs; these people work under supervision and have an opportunity to meet with their supervisors and other interns. Many paraprofessionals are both talented and qualified for the work they do with clients—a fact that may not be appreciated by clients who are disappointed when they have their first session with an intern or a paraprofessional. Sometimes clients ask to see the "real doctor" or have reservations about trusting a person who has not had advanced professional training. You should know that much more than training goes into the making of a sensitive and helpful counselor, and many paraprofessionals have had life experiences that are most advantageous to them in their work with clients.

Evaluating Members of the Helping Professions

To maximize your chances of benefiting from any form of psychological services, you should apply some of the guidelines given in this chapter and realize that you must ask questions if you're to become an intelligent consumer of these services. Some questions to consider are: Do I feel a need for professional help? Am I willing to invest the necessary energy, time, and money? Am I prepared to develop a set of goals that I want to achieve through counseling? What do I hope to get from the process? Once you've decided that you want professional help and determined what you want from the counselor, you can consider the range of professionals to see who might best meet your needs.

In evaluating different counselors, a crucial issue is how to determine their competence. Degrees and licenses ensure a minimum level of competence, but there are qualitative differences among those who hold these credentials. Moreover, many qualified persons who work in institutions such as schools and churches are not required to have licenses yet may be very effective counselors. Ultimately, after you have consulted others and considered a counselor's qualifications, you still need to trust your own feelings and judgment concerning whether to work with a particular person.

Chapter Summary

In this chapter, I've emphasized that counseling is one resource we can turn to in expanding our awareness and discovering possibilities for change. Thus, counseling and psychotherapy should not be viewed merely as methods of treating people who have emotional and behavioral disorders.

There are any number of reasons why people who might benefit from counseling never make use of it: they don't recognize their need for professional help; they are frightened of getting involved; they accept certain misconceptions; they don't know where to look for professional assistance; or they think they should be able to deal with their difficulties without help from others.

When people do decide to become involved in a counseling experience, they should be aware that it is a highly personal process and that many factors influence the results achieved. For counseling or therapy to be helpful, clients must be motivated to change and willing to become actively involved. Counseling is not something that is done *to* clients or *for* them; rather, they are partners with their therapists in a joint undertaking. For this reason, clients should select their counselors wisely, for the client/counselor relationship is of central importance in determining the outcomes of therapy.

There is a very wide range of therapeutic styles and theoretical approaches. However, most members of the helping professions develop their own styles and use methods drawn from various approaches. More important than theoretical orientation is what kind of person a counselor is; hence, prospective clients need to pay attention to how much trust they feel in the person and should avoid selecting a counselor merely on the basis of what "school" he or she belongs to. Moreover, no therapeutic approach has a monopoly on truth or value; each has something valuable to offer. Some approaches may work well for certain people and yet be inappropriate for others.

Although I've presented a great deal of information about counseling in this chapter, my primary purpose has been to encourage you to consider ways of realizing your potential more fully, whether with professional assistance or on your own. Now that you have completed this book and this course, the hard work of making significant changes in your thinking, feeling, and behaving can begin. You can decide for yourself whether to take the time to decide on your priorities and begin to do for yourself and others some of the things you want to do. You can assume control of your life by choosing your direction instead of waiting for good things to happen to you. Once you fully recognize that you *do* have a choice, you have a gift that no one can take from you.

Activities and Exercises

1. Consider asking some friends, acquaintances, or fellow students to respond to the statements in this chapter's "Self-Inventory" or "Time Outs." What are their views of counseling and therapy?
2. If you've had any contact with professionals in the mental-health field, describe what your experience was like. Based on this experience, would you recommend psychological assistance to a friend?
3. List the criteria *you* would most look for in selecting a therapist for individual counseling. Would your list include fees? Degrees and credentials? Type of specialization? Recommendations from those who have worked with the professional? Your own impressions? The theoretical approach used? The techniques used?
4. List any factors that might keep you from seeking some form of counseling even if you felt a need and desire to do so. For example, would the possible reactions of your family or friends keep you from getting involved in counseling?
5. Look in your telephone directory under the listings "Psychologists" and "Marriage and Family Therapists." What types of counselors or agencies are available in your area?
6. If you know people who have been involved in either individual or group counseling, ask them to talk with you about the experience. How did they feel when they first began? What is it like to be in counseling? What do they think they've derived from the experience?
7. Describe what you would want from group or individual counseling. What conflicts and problems would you want to gain a fuller understanding of? What decisions would you want to make?
8. Check with the counseling center at your college or university (or at a local mental-health clinic) to find out what psychological services

are available. Is crisis counseling available? Is long-term individual counseling available? How about other services, such as counseling groups, personal-growth groups, vocational counseling, psychological and vocational testing, family counseling, marriage counseling, groups for couples, assertiveness training, and relaxation training? Once you've looked into the available resources, you might consider whether you'd want to take advantage of any of these services at some time.

Suggested Readings

Corey, G. *Theory and Practice of Group Counseling*. Monterey, Calif.: Brooks/Cole, 1981. This text presents an overview of the various types of groups, the stages in the evolution of groups, and some basic issues in group membership and leadership. Eleven basic theoretical approaches to group work are given, using common chapter organization to highlight similarities and differences. There is an accompanying *Student's Manual* designed to apply the concepts and techniques to group practice.

Corey, G. *Case Approach to Counseling and Psychotherapy*. Monterey, Calif.: Brooks/Cole, 1982. How counseling actually works as it is applied to various approaches is the subject of this book. Reader involvement is encouraged, for there are exercises dealing with each of the 24 cases presented.

Corey, G. *Theory and Practice of Counseling and Psychotherapy* (2nd ed.). Monterey, Calif.: Brooks/Cole, 1982. This text presents a survey of the major concepts and practices of the contemporary systems of counseling and therapy. It includes discussions of the ethics of counseling and of applying the concepts of the book to the personal growth of the reader. There is an accompanying *Student's Manual* designed to make theory come alive through practical application.

Corey, G., & Corey, M. *Groups: Process and Practice* (2nd ed.). Monterey, Calif.: Brooks/Cole, 1982. Part I deals with the basics of group process, including the practical matters for maintaining groups at each stage of development. Part II gives practical guidelines for designing specific groups for children, for adolescents, for college students, for couples, for the elderly, and for residential personal-growth workshops.

Corey, G., Corey, M., & Callanan, P. *Professional and Ethical Issues in Counseling and Psychotherapy*. Monterey, Calif.: Brooks/Cole, 1979. Designed for readers who wish to get involved in exploring ethical issues in counseling practice, this book contains many problem situations, cases, examples, and open-ended questions.

Corey, G., Corey, M., Callanan, P., & Russell, J. M. *Group Techniques*. Monterey, Calif.: Brooks/Cole, 1982. This book is designed to help readers learn about how groups function, with a special emphasis for those who are interested in a rationale for creating and using techniques for all the stages of group development.

Dass, R. *Journey of Awakening: A Meditator's Guidebook.* New York: Bantam, 1978. The book has many resources for those who wish to learn more about ways of meditation, as well as some guidelines for developing regular practices in meditation.

Produska, B. *You Can Cope: Be the Person You Want to Be through Self-Therapy.* Englewood Cliffs, N.J.: Prentice-Hall (Spectrum), 1976. The author provides a brief description of several contemporary approaches to psychotherapy and then shows how some of these concepts can be used as pathways to self-discovery.

Rainwater, J. *You're in Charge! A Guide to Becoming Your Own Therapist.* Los Angeles: Guild of Tutors Press, 1979. The author has written a very informative book on ways to achieve self-understanding, including journal writing, autobiography, working with dreams, meditation, being in charge of one's physical health and one's death, and learning how to choose for oneself. The many exercises make this an excellent self-help book.

Shapiro, D. *Precision Nirvana.* Englewood Cliffs, N.J.: Prentice-Hall (Spectrum), 1978. The author has done a fine job of combining concepts from Eastern and Western approaches to help readers cope with personal problems and find a method to make changes.

Postscript

The writing of this book has been a source of excitement, joy, and pain. It was a difficult and challenging book to write, because it provided a stimulus for me (as well as for Marianne and our daughters) to look at the choices we make and to examine the quality of our lives. The personal challenge that I continue to face through my writing, teaching, consulting, and practice as a psychologist is: To what degree am I attempting to live by the values that I espouse? What choices do I make each day, and what do these choices say about what I really value in life?

In the courses I teach, I can converse with my students and get their reactions to what I say. But in a book the conversation is decidedly one-way. Nevertheless, Marianne and I would very much like to know how you are affected by *I Never Knew I Had a Choice*, and we hope that, if you want to, you'll write and tell us your impressions and reactions. We'd be very interested in finding out how you'd like to see this book changed, as well as knowing the topics that affected you the most (and the least). At the end of the book is a form for your convenience, which you could send to us in care of Brooks/Cole Publishing Company, Monterey, California 93940.

I*ndex*

To the owner of this book:

We hope that you have been significantly influenced by reading *I Never Knew I Had a Choice* (second edition). We'd like to know as much about your experiences with this book as possible. Your comments can help us improve the book for future readers.

School: _____ Instructor's name: _____

1. What I like *most* about this book is: _____
   _____
   _____

2. What I like *least* about this book is: _____
   _____
   _____

3. How much personal value did you find in the "Time Out for Personal Reflection" sections? _____
   _____
   _____

4. Of how much interest and value were the end-of-the-chapter "Activities and Exercises"? _____
   _____
   _____

5. Specific topics in the book you thought were most relevant and important: _____
   _____

6. Specific suggestions for improving the book: _____
   _____
   _____
   _____

7. Some ways I used this book in class: _____
   _____

8. Some ways I used this book out of class: _____
   _____

9. The name of the course in which you used this book: _____
   _____

10. In the space below—or in a separate letter, if you care to write one— please let us know what other comments about the book you'd like to make. We welcome your suggestions!

Optional:

Your name: _____ Date: _____

May Brooks/Cole quote you, either in promotion for *I Never Knew I Had a Choice* or in future publishing ventures?

Yes _____   No _____

Sincerely,

Gerald Corey

Fold Here

NO POSTAGE
NECESSARY
IF MAILED
IN THE
UNITED STATES

BUSINESS REPLY MAIL

FIRST CLASS   PERMIT NO. 84   MONTEREY, CALIF.

POSTAGE WILL BE PAID BY ADDRESSEE

Gerald Corey
Marianne Schneider Corey
Brooks/Cole Publishing Company
Monterey, California 93940